Social Work and Criminal Law
in Scotland

George Moore, M.A., M.Litt., was for many years responsible for the whole range of probation and after-care services within an English probation service. In 1971 he became an Adviser on Offender Services with the Social Work Services Group in the Scottish Office, where his work involved the development of offender services in Scotland in the years following the implementation of the *1968 Social Work (Scotland) Act.* Subsequently, as Senior Lecturer in Social Work at Jordanhill College of Education, he continued to work for the improvement of services in this field. His publications (in addition to the first and second editions of *Social Work and Criminal Law in Scotland*) include *The Practice of Social Inquiry* (Aberdeen University Press, 1984) and *A Guide to the Children's Hearing System* (Green and Son, 1988).

Bill Whyte M.A. (Hons), Dip.S.W., C.Q.S.W. lectures in Social Work at the University of Edinburgh and is Programme Director of Advanced Social Work Studies in Criminal Justice Social Work at the Universities of Edinburgh and Stirling. Prior to this he was a local authority social worker and social work manager. His research has included government-financed studies on Criminal Justice Social Work, Children's Hearings, Youth Homelessness and Mental Health Officers.

Moore and Wood's

SOCIAL WORK AND
CRIMINAL LAW IN SCOTLAND

George Moore and Bill Whyte

Third Edition

MERCAT PRESS
EDINBURGH

First published 1981
Second edition published 1992
This third edition published 1998 by Mercat Press
© George Moore and Bill Whyte

ISBN 1873644 833

Set in Times New Roman at Mercat Press
Printed and bound in Finland by WSOY

'Ought it not to be said that the most likely means of preventing crimes are to preserve uncorrupted that large and unfortunate description of persons who are born in misery and differ from us in nothing but the accidents of rank and fortune and are entitled to our utmost care and protection?'

SAMUEL ROMIILLY (1757-1818)

'We have made considerable efforts to discover what sort of person the offender is and why he has broken the law, and we rack our brains to find out what to do with him.'

HERMAN MANNHEIM
Criminal Justice and Social Reconstruction, 1946

Contents

Acknowledgements

We are indebted to numerous people for their assistance in the preparation of this edition: to Sheriff M. Gimble and Sheriff K. McIver for their assistance in updating Chapter 2; to Sheriff R. Scott who prepared the draft of Chapter 2 for the previous edition; to John Waterhouse, SWSI, for reading an early draft of the manuscript and offering much useful advice; to Malcolm Schaffer, Reporter Manager, SCRA, for his assistance with Chapter 6; and to Detective Superintendent John McGowan of Lothian and Borders Police. Many social work professionals read parts of the typescript and provided valuable help; in particular, we would like to thank Ron Lancashire, Donald Dickie and Suzanne Wallace of the City of Edinburgh Council, Robert Fyffe of the City of Glasgow Council court section, Ed Finlayson of the State Hospital, Carstairs, Jo Knox and Janice McGhee of the University of Edinburgh.

We are grateful to the Stationery Office for permission to quote from government documents and reports.

Any omissions and errors are our responsibility.

GEORGE MOORE and BILL WHYTE

Notes

Throughout the text we refer to both the person in trouble with the law and to the social worker as 'he'. The intention is to make reading easier and no implication about the gender of either party is intended. We appreciate that many social workers are women and that women get in trouble with the law.

When dealing with fines and financial penalties, we refer to 'levels' on the standard scale rather than actual amounts of money, as this is subject to change from time to time.

As we go to press major changes in policy, practice and legislation are taking place in Scotland. Many provisions within the Crime and Punishment (Scotland) Act, 1997 are recently implemented and many new provisions are proposed under the Crime and Disorder Bill, 1998, which we have assumed will be enacted in 1998.

Introduction

This third edition has been prepared against a backdrop of rapid and intense change in criminal justice social work. The first Labour government for eighteen years was elected in May 1997, and is as committed as previous administrations to review, change and develop the Criminal Justice System. It will be some time before it is clear if it will bring a distinctive policy direction. In the meantime this edition deals with the raft of legislative and policy initiatives introduced in recent years, many of which have still to be fully implemented.

These include revised *National Objectives and Standards for Social Work Services in the Criminal Justice System,* particularly on Throughcare and Supervised Attendance; the *Criminal Procedures (Scotland) Act,* 1995, consolidating previous legislative change; the *Children (Scotland) Act,* 1995 which deals with service delivery to the Children's Hearings System, and the associated guidance, particularly on home supervision of children and young people; the *Crime and Punishment (Scotland) Act,* 1997 (whose main proposal, the replacement of the early release system introduced by the *Prisoners and Criminal Proceedings (Scotland) Act,* 1993, have not yet been implemented by the incoming administration) and the introduction of Restriction of Liberty Orders including electronic tagging; the *Sex Offenders' Act,* 1997 and *Commitment to Protect* (SWSI, 1997), the associated review of supervision and monitoring of sex offenders in the community, and its implications for local authorities in registering and exchanging information on certain sex offenders; and the implementation of *Crime and Disorder Act,* 1998, which makes provision for introducing a Sex Offender Order, an Anti-Social Behaviour Order, a Drug Treatment and Testing Order, and extended post-release supervision.

All of these are set in the context of local government reform under the *Local Government (Scotland) Act,* 1994, which has resulted in the development of specialist criminal justice social work services in unitary authority departments (some of which are now jointly housing and social work sections or departments under a non-social work manager), and in the context of proposals for the establishment of a Scottish Parliament by the millennium, which will have responsibility both for policy and legislation in criminal justice matters and may provide the platform for further radical change in policy and practice.

The strategy of establishing *National Objectives and Standards for Social Work Services in the Criminal Justice System* (NOS) and the provision of 100% central funding for social work services to the criminal justice system is now well established and some of the rather controversial issues which occupied attention in the previous edition have been subjected to the test of practice experience and have been set in a better formulated national policy. The pace of change in the service has been dramatic.

A review and revision of National Objectives and Standards has been undertaken; Probation and Community Service were reviewed and re-issued in 1996; new NOS on Throughcare were re-issued 1997; and NOS for Supervised Attendance are due in 1998. Those relating to social enquiry reports for the courts (SERs) are currently under review. Seven evaluative studies on the implementation of National Objectives and Standards were published in 1998 as part of the first two phases of a social research programme. They cover the early arrangements, the national and local context, advice to courts and the Parole Board, Probation and Throughcare, and highlight significant progress and changing models of practice (*Social Work in Criminal Justice*, Vols 1-7, 1998). Specialist post-graduate training has been established in the Universities of Edinburgh and Stirling and a national development centre for criminal justice social work is promised.

The Social Work Services Inspectorate (SWSI) have been engaged in a continuing programme of inspections. The first report of the SWSI, issued in 1994, provided an optimistic 'progress report' on how social work was dealing with the demands of NOS, bringing to an end the tag of 'two wasted decades', which summarised developments in the 1970s and 1980s. Subsequent reports such as *Realistic and Rigorous* (SWSI, 1996) on community service, and *Helping the Court Decide* (SWSI, 1996) on social enquiry reports, document significant progress, while identifying the need for considerable improvement. Positive and forward looking as the Inspectorate and evaluation reports are, it is clearly not time for either management or practitioners in social work to assume that the attainments are sufficient or that the objectives have been achieved.

The impact of policy and financial investment, which has seen the budget for 100% centrally funded criminal justice services rise from around £10 million in 1989 to nearly £35.4 million in 1998/99, has still to show significant effects in reducing the number of fine-defaulters, petty offenders and young offenders in the prison population. Despite falls in many areas of reported crime and steady increases in non-custodial disposals, there has been no corresponding decline in prison numbers since 1989. A Review of Criminal Justice Social Work Services (SWSG, 1997) instigated by the incoming Labour government indicated that between 1989 and 1995 increases in probation by 61% and community services orders by 33% were accompanied by an 18% drop in the use of fines and a 19% increase in custody. Paterson and Tombs (1998) report that the use of custody rose from 11% of all sheriff court disposals in 1991 to 15% in 1994. However they offer a glimmer of optimism since in the same period the proportion of short sentences of up to three months fell from 61% to 53% of disposals.

Nonetheless the crisis of the prison population continues. Scotland, with a prison population of 110 per 100,000, ranked third highest against eighteen major Western European Counties in 1995—even higher than England and Wales with 99 per 100,000 (Prison Reform Trust, 1997). There is, and will continue to be, an ever-demanding call on knowledge, ingenuity and initiative to meet the challenge of criminality. There is an urgency, in the face of political challenge, to provide practice evidence which demonstrates that the strategy of providing and funding social work represents 'best value' and an effective approach to crime in the community.

Chapter 1

New Frameworks in Perspective

Looking back; a new approach; the situation in Scotland; policy, legislation and practice

Looking back

The reference point for the first edition (1981) was an agenda that had been set in the 1960s, and which had found expression in the *Social Work (Scotland) Act*, 1968. The inspiration was described as the 'Kilbrandon Philosophy' (*Children and Young Persons (Scotland)*, 1964; cmnd 2306). It produced a distinctively Scottish pattern in social work provision. Central was the concern to see children in trouble removed from the jurisdiction of the criminal courts that were then dealing with them. The change achieved was radical—a punishment system was replaced by a welfare system in the form of the Children's Hearing System, as legislated for in Part III of the *Social Work (Scotland) Act*, 1968 (now Chapters 2 and 3 of the *Children (Scotland) Act*, 1995).

Changes to other social work services—probation and after-care work, welfare services for groups other than children—were made somewhat on the back of this fundamental one but nonetheless within the policy framework set by it. There was pride in a unique arrangement whereby the Scottish Probation Service was abolished and the full range of social work services were grouped together in one all-purpose local authority department, and the principle of 'promoting social welfare' written into legislation (s.12 of the 1968 Act). There was less certainty among agencies in the criminal justice system as to the appropriateness of the new arrangements in dealing with offenders. The model of practice within the policy envisaged the 'matching field staff' as specialists (not generalists) whose location within local authorities would allow them, in addition to delivering their own specialism, to work collaboratively with other professionals and to co-ordinate service provision across and between authorities and other sectors of provision—a model that has still to fulfil its potential. Social work with adult offenders was widely perceived as having suffered as a result of the new arrangements, in which general practice social workers lacked some of the most elementary knowledge, information and skills required for practice in this field.

The Kilbrandon report remains the policy framework for service provision. It was re-issued in 1995 with the introduction of the *Children (Scotland) Act*, 1995, which replaced those sections of the 1968 Act dealing with the Children's Hearings system. The brief summary which follows cannot be other than an encouragement to serious students of social work policy, law and practice to master the original texts in order to appreciate the development of policy and practice in this field.

Three germinal reports, each in its own way, set the scene for much of what was to follow. The Ingleby report of 1960 'found no difficulty in advising that local authority services should have greater freedom to offer aid and assistance to children in trouble or in danger of becoming delinquent. The difficult aspect of the inquiry proved to be an insoluble problem for the committee, and it failed to find a satisfactory solution to the vexing question of how to deal with the crime/punishment **and** welfare aspects of the child offender within the ambit of the juvenile court system' (Moore 1989: 3).

Scotland presented a different scenario. Arguably the Kilbrandon report was the best and most coherent report of the post-war period. Almost all of its recommendations found expression in the subsequent White Paper, *Social Work in the Community*, 1966 (cmnd 3065) and in the *Social Work (Scotland) Act*,1968. Two major matters which failed to find government approval were, firstly, that the sheriff should be cast in a primary role within the hearings system—this debate re-emerged in the 1990s and the *Children (Scotland) Act*, 1995 reintroduced aspects of this concept by giving sheriffs powers to make disposals on appeals—and secondly, that the main agency spearheading the new arrangements should be a 'social education department' within local authority education departments; instead social work departments were created. It is again of interest to note that single social work departments are being replaced in many unitary authorities by sections which integrate social work with other provision such as housing.

It is open to debate that had Ingleby found a 'solution' to the crime versus welfare problem within the English court system, Kilbrandon might well have been inclined in directions other than the one chosen. Indeed it has been suggested (Cowperthwaite, 1988) that the committee was determined to find an alternative Scottish solution to juvenile courts which were viewed as an English solution to the problem.

The integration of the Scottish Probation Service within the Social Work Department as a result of Kilbrandon made an organisational leap which set Scotland on a path of what can justly be called 'welfarism' in the criminal justice field, which was to have long-lasting effects on practice ideologies and on academic teaching in Scotland. Bottoms' comment (1974: 342) probably reaches the heart of the matter, '…it is possible that the very thoroughness of the Kilbrandon report was itself a silencer, as people were unable to think of more convincing replacements for the previous heterogeneity'. Indeed, the same may well be said for government in its acceptance of the report.

A third report, the Seebohm Report (1968) advocated the creation of unified local authority social service departments in England and Wales. This reflected a growing mood among social workers in favour of a single professional organisation in place of the multiplicity of existing organisations. This reorganisation, in turn, led to the formation of the British Association of Social Workers (BASW). England failed to follow Scotland in incorporating the probation service into the unified social service departments. Many of these basic structures have again been under review.

The recent agenda

Central to the agenda for criminal justice social work in Scotland is the wider UK context where the emphasis in the 1990s has been much more on punishment than on social work. This represents a major challenge to social work practitioners. The place of welfare in justice, or functions of advising and assisting that were at the core of probation work since its inception, have been downplayed in England and Wales. Developments across the border have seen the removal of the requirement for a social work qualification for probation officers following the recommendations of the Dews report (1995).

The 1980s saw government policy emphasise a just deserts approach to law and order. The focus of interest shifted from offender rehabilitation towards compensation for victims, the protection and well-being of society, and to a renewed emphasis on deterrent sentencing. By the end of that decade the criminal statistics were showing that these policies had not managed even to contain crime at its former levels. Alongside this, Britain's prisons had erupted. From Peterhead to Pentonville, from Strangeways to Shotts, prisoners appeared on rooftops, showering staff, police and press with roof tiles, waving banners and destroying the prison real estate. Prisoners nearly achieved what prison reformers had failed to do for decades—the closure of prisons.

Policy started to change. Attention turned to fighting crime in the community rather than through the criminal justice system. Neighbourhood Watch schemes and closed circuit television were encouraged and flourished. Even so, the crime figures continued their inexorable rise upwards. Attention turned, in England and Wales, to the probation service—the community arm of the criminal justice system. The 'success' rate for probation—by which was meant largely that the order was completed with the probationer still being at liberty—was claimed to be of the order of 55% to 65%. Against this, the 'success' rates of Borstal, Youth Custody and Detention Centre Training had increasingly become derisory. Probation satisfied two important criteria—it was considered effective, and it was relatively cheap to administer.

HARBINGERS OF THE NEW APPROACH

The agenda was set partly by the Home Office in England and Wales. The English debate set a backcloth against which Scottish National Objectives and Standards for social work (NOS) were developed, and the subsequent distinguishing features of Scottish policy and legislation to which local authorities are required to adhere.

The White Paper *Crime, Justice and Protecting the Public* (1990, cmnd 965) set the scene. It was the basis for the *Criminal Justice Act*, 1991. Its main concern was to see the creation of 'a cohesive legislative framework for sentencing, with the severity of the punishment matching the seriousness of the crime, and a sharper distinction in the way courts dealt with violent and non-violent crimes' (p.i).

It proposed:

- new powers for courts to impose longer sentences for violent and sexual offences—reducing the maximum sentences for theft and property offences other than those against people's homes;
- requiring courts to consider a report before imposing custodial sentences, encouraging fines and compensation orders;
- altering prison remission and parole arrangements;
- supervision after prison sentences of 12 months and above;
- national standards for probation and parole supervision;
- the combination of probation with compensation, fines, and community service (the latter combination not being available in England and Wales);
- a new 'curfew' order.

The underlying thinking behind the proposals was that punishment should be seen as being 'just and suitable' according to the seriousness of the offence (just deserts). It indicated that 'sentencing principles and sentencing practice are matters of legitimate concern to Government', suggesting 'that those who commit very serious crimes, particularly crimes of violence, should receive long custodial sentences'. Many other (less serious) crimes 'can be punished in the community, with greater emphasis on bringing home to the criminal the consequences of his actions, compensation to the victim and reparation to the community' (para. 2.1 p. 5).

The 1991 Act implemented a new approach to community disposals. It challenged the concept of alternatives to custody, and posed the idea of 'other ways of punishing'. It saw the scope for a range of community-based sanctions which would, to a greater or lesser extent, impinge on the liberty of the offender. It notes 'these orders intrude on normal freedom and the court should be satisfied that such is justified'. It changed the legal status of probation in England to that of a sentence, and removed the requirement for the offender's consent. *Strengthening Punishment in the Community* (Home Office, 1995, Cm 2780) proposed a new framework and the introduction of an integrated community sentence. This shift in emphasis was continued by the *Crime and Sentencing Act,* 1997 which removed the need of the court in England and Wales to require the consent of the offender for probation and community service (except when imposing a condition of mental health, drug or alcohol treatment). The aim was to ensure that the more restrictive and usually more expensive community disposals were reserved for more serious offenders, such as persistent thieves and non-domestic property offenders. The Green Paper *Supervision and Punishment in the Community* (1990, cmnd 966) developed further the organisational implications of this approach.

Twin-track policy

While these policy papers are ostensibly addressing an English situation, the key concepts and ideas such as 'just deserts', and the concept of a 'twin-track' strategy for targeting offenders, which distinguishes between responses to violent and non-violent offenders, with a strong emphasis on the young offender, were reflected in Scottish policy. They were contained in a policy statement set out by Malcolm Rifkind (then Secretary of State for Scotland) in November 1988 when he gave the Kenneth Younger Memorial Lecture to the Howard League for Penal Reform. This policy statement acknowledged, in effect, that prison does not work if re-integration is the intended outcome and that consequently it should be 'used sparingly':

> There will always be those who commit serious or violent crimes and who pose a threat to society which requires them to be confined for significant periods. Nevertheless there are many good reasons for wishing to ensure that, as a society, we *use prisons as sparingly as possible*. While the use of imprisonment may be inescapable when dealing with *violent offenders* and those who commit *the most serious crimes*, we must question to what extent *short sentences* of imprisonment and periods of custody for fine-default are appropriate means of dealing with offenders. Prisons are expensive both to build and to run and do not provide the ideal environment in which to *teach* an offender how to live a normal and law-abiding life, to work at a job or to maintain a family. If offenders can remain in the community under suitable conditions, they should be able to maintain their family ties, opportunities for work or training and they may be better placed to make some reparation for their offence' (emphasis added) (Rifkind, 1989, p.85).

This thinking, with its emphasis on increased use of community supervision, particularly for the non-violent and for young offenders, and its emphasis on meaningful throughcare services for those who do experience custody, underscores the practices required by NOS which were subsequently introduced in 1991. This policy statement is contained in the introduction to the revised document published in 1996.

The emerging policy climate raised the question as to whether generic social work training could sufficiently equip people to operate as social workers within the criminal justice system in Scotland. This had been a live issue in Scotland since 1968, and funding was made available in 1993 to Edinburgh and Stirling Universities to establish programmes of advanced specialist training in social work in the criminal justice system. Local government reorganisation saw the development of specialist sections within social work in almost all authorities, most with their own specialist senior operational manager.

Promoting value for money

The report *The Probation Service: Providing Value for Money* (Audit Commission, 1990) was influential on both sides of the border. It undertook a wide-ranging review of probation practice in England, drawing on examples of schemes well beyond one-to-one supervision. There had been shifts in probation practice in England and Wales during the 1980s in response both to the assessment of need (ACOP, 1989a), and in response to policy pressures from government. There had been marked increases by Crown Courts in the use of probation and community service,

particularly for young offenders (ACOP, 1989b). The report, however, drew attention to the dangers of over-simplistic evaluations of 'success'. The effects of probation intervention on re-offending appeared small and difficult to detect. Research
began to suggest that probation services were ineffective in influencing sentencers,
in the sense that increases in social inquiry reports had had little effect on reducing
the numbers going to custody. Increases in community-based orders seemed to
indicate that many people were being drawn inappropriately into social work measures to their detriment (McMahon, 1990).

The Audit Commission report recommended that the Probation Service (criminal justice social work) take 'centre stage' in the provision of community-based
disposals for key target groups, particularly medium to serious non-violent offenders and young adult offenders. The emphasis was on the need to take on more
serious offenders and more 'problematic' people, who would otherwise be sent to
prison. The report recognised the importance of moving away from the notion of
the individual practitioner towards a new emphasis on managed programmes promoted by research, and boldly suggested that **half the young offender age group
currently in custody could be supervised in the community**. The emphasis within
research on the use of cognitive-behavioural and social education techniques reflects many of the aspirations of the Kilbrandon approach in Scotland which had
never been systematically developed within the criminal justice services.

The strategy proposed by the Audit Commission is consistent with the policy
directive issued in Scotland and involves targeting the middle range of those at risk
of custody as the best means of providing value for money—particularly given the
relative costs of the various disposals. Current estimates are that prison costs on
average £12,800 for a six-month place; the average probation order costs £1,400
(SWSG, 1997).

The Commission's report described six areas in which progress could be made
in delivering value for money:

- demonstrating effectiveness;
- spreading good practice;
- developing management systems;
- clarifying lines of accountability;
- developing skills in a multi-disciplinary service;
- working with other agencies.

Partnership in Dealing with Offenders in the Community (1990), known as the
'peppermint' paper, was the final paper in the series issued in England and Wales,
and was a consultation document. Its central theme was the role of the independent
sector in the strategy to deal with more offenders in the community, underlining
the point that the statutory sector is only one party in the scheme of things, and that
there was a role for profit-making organisations (the 'private sector') in the provision of services, both custodial and non-custodial, in the criminal justice system.
The paper sets out possible divisions of roles and tasks and suggests that the prime
focus of the statutory sector should be on the most serious cases, and the task of

'confronting offenders with their offending', which it suggests the statutory sector alone has the necessary skills to perform.

This 'peppermint' paper has to be seen in the context of the contemporary debate on how state social services and the independent sector might work together in providing for various client groups within the community. The Griffiths Report *Community Care*, which led to the subsequent legislation, proposed a model of working together centred around the idea of contracts and service-level agreements and on purchaser/provider relationships. It is interesting and important to note that this Home Office paper is less committed to such a model in the field of criminal justice and suggests that the bulk of provision involving public protection should be provided by the statutory sector. The emphasis on 'value for money' is now expressed in Labour's 'best value' strategy, and remains equally insistent, whatever model or configuration of services is to be used.

No similar policy statements concerning the role of the independent sector were made in Scotland. However paras 117-131 of the 'General Issues' section of NOS (1996) contain very similar sentiments in their outline of the role of the independent sector, emphasising partnership arrangements, innovation and community involvement.

Local Authorities should *concentrate on the direct provision of services* which entail statutory supervision of offenders including *the development of innovative approaches* to this task; and require the *skill of professionally qualified social work staff*.

The independent sector should seek to initiate and develop specialist services which *complement* those provided by the local authority; provide services necessary to fill gaps in existing provision;...develop innovatory projects to meet identified needs (paras 123-125).

It is rather ironic that most intensive probation projects which should deal with high-risk offenders, and many innovative approaches for more serious offenders, are provided within the independent sector in Scotland; a situation that must change if the statutory services are to demonstrate that they represent 'best value' in the field of community safety.

THE SITUATION IN SCOTLAND

In contrast to the flood of papers and reports from London, with the exception of Rifkind's paper (1989), much of the philosophical and policy debate in Scotland was muted, with only the end result—*National Objectives and Standards for Social Work Services in the Criminal Justice System*, given a high profile. There were many similar concerns, not least the prison riots and the number of deaths of young people in custody, in Scotland earlier in the 1980s. The Scottish Prison Service (SPS) was changing and a series of discussion papers on social work in prison were produced, in particular *Continuity through Co-operation* (SWSG, 1990), which updated an earlier document *A Shared Enterprise* (SWSG, 1979) (see Chapters 10 and 11).

In Scotland there had been limited developments in the use of probation, although use of community service had increased over this period. More generally, however, the concerns of those engaged in the criminal justice field remained the poor level of social work provision by local authorities as against all the indices of Scotland's high levels of use of imprisonment; the lack of definition as to what should constitute the core of such services; and the reluctance of local authorities to accept a proposed shift of funding for community service schemes when the initial five year development phase was completed.

In the mid-1980s a Joint Review Group on Services to Offenders involving the Scottish Office and the Convention of Scottish Local Authorities (COSLA) was undertaken. There is no publicly documented account of these developments. While local authorities claimed that there was a significant shortfall in the funding to Scottish social work departments for providing services, it is possible that the lack of any convincing evidence about the number and seriousness of cases taken on was so damning as to render publication unduly embarrassing to all parties. Some new initiative had to be found. Despite COSLA opposition to specific funding, it came in the form of proposals for 100% Scottish Office funding of core criminal justice social work services which were to be provided by local authorities. This was enacted in the *Law Reform (Miscellaneous Provisions) (Scotland) Act,* 1990, and took effect from April 1991.

While this initiative marks a formal partnership arrangement between central and local government, to some extent the local authority became an agent of central government for the purpose of providing 100% centrally funded services in criminal justice held accountable through strategic planning mechanisms, fiscal accountancy, and inspection of targeting and service standards.

The local authority is responsible for meeting NOS by providing criminal justice social work services under sections 12 and 27 of the *Social Work (Scotland) Act,* 1968. Section 12 makes provision for the local authority to promote social welfare, by making available 'advice, guidance and assistance...as may be appropriate for their area'. The recognition that criminal justice social work contributes to the promotion of the community's social welfare through the reduction of individual offending has been one of the radical shifts in emphasis in recent years. Section 27 sets out the obligations of local authorities towards the criminal justice system. The practice philosophy, which brings together an emphasis on the social responsibility of the offender and on the community's well-being and safety, is underscored by the legislation and provides a uniquely Scottish framework for this type of provision. In principle it allows for the best of both worlds, a national service identity integrated and delivered locally, adapted and supplemented according to local priorities as a form of partnership provision. This partnership, in effect, recognises the importance of a balance between justice as a national concern and tackling crime effectively, which must be a concern of local communities.

There have been no published assessments of need, nor audit of the scale of the task required to shift from custody to the use of community-based disposals as a basis for calculating the funding necessary to accomplish the required objectives.

This planning vacuum which has existed will, hopefully, improve as authorities move from annual financial bids based on guess-work, to three-year strategic plans, which will require more accurate data on projected service provision.

The direction of officially stated government policy is clear. Parts of the NOS have the flavour of precise, directive instruction and procedures. The need for government to provide such detailed direction, focusing as much on process as outcomes, reflects not only the strength of its intentions, but also the deficiencies of previous practice and the lack of attention given to criminal justice services over the previous two decades. One of the most significant areas of deficiency in Scotland was the apparent reluctance of many social workers and their authorities to take on more serious offenders, particularly for probation supervision. Scottish probation orders ran at about half the rate of England.

Scotland led the world in providing a unique, integrated service. Yet the 'promotion of welfare' and the *Social Work (Scotland) Act*, 1968 seemed to lead to practices of recommending probation only where the social worker could identify a social need for the individual offender that could be met, whether or not it was related to the offence or to the well-being or safety of the community. Offending behaviour in itself seemed not to be regarded as a legitimate or primary reason for intervention (Whyte *et al*, 1995). This may have some bearing on the fact that although probation and community service orders rose significantly in the early 1990s, they had limited impact on the custody figures.

Changes emanating from the *Law Reform (Miscellaneous Provision)(Scotland) Act*, 1990 have had some, but still too limited, impact on the use of probation for medium to serious non-violent offenders, who continue to represent a significant proportion of those sent to custody. Social workers, with some exceptions, were perceived by courts as being 'hot' on support and personal welfare, but less enthusiastic about the use of supervision as a mechanism of social control which was more humane and effective than imprisonment (Ford, 1992). These attitudes are changing rapidly.

The present government claims its intention is to be 'tough on crime and tough on the causes of crime'. Social control is an important part of that policy. The challenge to social work is to demonstrate that effective authority can be combined with helping services, if there is to be any significant shift away from the use of custodial sentences. It will take a great deal of effort and rigour on the part of social work to convince judges that the purpose, focus and effect of the services in the 1990s has changed sufficiently to justify operating a twin-track approach suggested by Scottish policy.

The new framework should not obscure that fact that good practice was developing in pockets across Scotland, though far from consistently. Many initiatives ran into the sand of an under-enthused generalist workforce, coping with a seemingly unending stream of new referrals, with a view of probation work as low priority compared to their child care responsibilities. While recent signs are positive, it remains to be seen whether the development of 'dedicated' and specialist criminal justice social work management can create an organisational culture that will promote and sustain corporate, long term, consistent and effective provision.

National Objectives and Standards

NOS are the outcome of much shared work between Social Work, COSLA representatives, academics and civil servants. They provide detailed minimum benchmark standards for social work services. However it is within the objectives, rather than the benchmark standards and the process, that the direction and intent are provided. The statement of objectives set out in paragraph 13 in the 'General Issues' section applies across the board and these are identified as:

13.1   to enable a *reduction in* the incidence of *custody*, whether on remand, at sentence, or in default of financial penalty, where it is used for lack of a suitable, available community-based social work disposal;

13.2   to promote and enhance the *range* and *quality* of *community-based social work disposals* available to the courts and ensure that they are managed and supervised in such a manner that they *have the confidence of courts*, the *police*, and the *public* at large;

13.3   to ensure that social work disposals are provided to the courts or other agencies in such a way that *the full range of disposals is available when required* so that the most appropriate one can be used, particularly with the *persistent offender*;

13.4   to give *priority* to the development of community-based social work disposals and other services to *young adult offenders*;

13.5   to promote the *development of schemes* to enable the courts to grant *bail* in an increased number of cases;

13.6   to provide and facilitate services for prisoners, and their families, to help them *prepare for release from custody*, and to assist them to resettle in the community;

13.7   to help offenders *tackle their offending behaviour*, to assist them to live socially responsible lives within the law, whenever appropriate, through the involvement and support of their families, friends, and other resources in their community;

13.8   to *assist the families* of offenders where family life suffers as a consequence of offending behaviour;

13.9   to promote, provide, and facilitate the development of *schemes for diverting accused persons from prosecution* to social work in those cases where there is sufficient evidence to prosecute but it is not deemed necessary to do so in the public interest;

13.10 to promote and assist the development of *services to the victims of crime*;

13.11 to promote and assist action *to reduce and prevent crime*.

The key services which are directly funded, in full or on a pilot basis, include

- Community Service by Offenders both s.229 and s.238 orders;
- Diversion from Prosecution Schemes including reports for the Procurators Fiscal and Children's Hearings under s.27 of the 1968 Act amended by s.32 of the 1997 Act;
- Parole and early release services and supervision;
- Probation—Standard Orders, Orders with conditions, Intensive Probation Programmes (IPP);

- Social Enquiry Reports including supplementary and pre-trial and services in Courts;
- Social Work in Prison—funded by Scottish Prison Service (SPS) and managed and delivered by local authority social work;
- Supported Accommodation and Bail services—including residential establishments when provided in relation to above services;
- Supervision and Treatment Orders;
- Supervised Attendance Orders;
- Throughcare including Parole, Non-Parole, short sentence licences and Supervised Release Orders;
- Voluntary Assistance.

Other services are provided by local authorities under the 1968 Act and funded by different mechanisms including means/fines enquiry, bail services, aspects of court social work, victim services, domestic violence services, family work, crime prevention and community safety work.

The NOS contain objectives of direction and intent rather than specific targets or qualitative outcome measures. They rely on professional interpretation within the local context. A major challenge to authorities is to translate these broad objectives into local service objectives that are 'SMART'—specific, measurable, achievable, relevant and time-limited. These kinds of service objectives are required for various aspects of the service if local authorities are to generate and promote evidence of their effectiveness. More collaborative approaches to providing and developing services are likely to be required by smaller unitary authorities if they are to provide a comprehensive range of services.

National Objectives and Standards have introduced a high level of social and administrative direction and control from the centre with the primary emphasis on performance and outcome. As para 15 of Part 1 'General Issues' puts it, 'The Secretary of State can only pay grant if he is satisfied with the standard of service and the arrangements made to provide it. The...standards are therefore intended to ensure that local authorities make appropriate arrangements for the service. They will also be used by the Secretary of State in judging the extent to which the arrangements made by individual authorities meet his objectives'. Arguably, the reduced size of individual authorities under local government re-organisation has created structures which are, in themselves, more amenable to such influence and control compared to what formerly existed.

Inspection reports (SWSI, 1994; 1996) indicate that the local authorities, both before and after local government re-organisation, have found it easier to meet quantitative and process indicators rather than qualitative outcomes. The serious demand for head-counts on the number of orders, contact hours, numbers of SERs, breaches etc., in itself does not indicate an effective service. The **qualities** associated with good social work intervention need to be harnessed to techniques of effectiveness if the social worker is to operate as an effective professional and not simply be reduced to a bureaucrat. There are risks that the management culture in local authorities will neglect such concepts in the push towards so-called efficiency by 'spreading the butter thinly'; where quantitative measurement rather than the quality of service, geared to the acquisition of knowledge, social and problem solving skills intended to change anti-social attitudes and criminal activity is what is sought and valued. The trading standards definition of quality is 'fit for purpose'.

If the need to address the requirements of legislation and government policy is to be met and advanced this cannot be done on the basis of previous models of practice. The service needs not simply to change but to be transformed. Managers need to be familiar, up-to-date and committed to new ways of working in criminal justice social work that are research-led. A worrying aspect of UK practice has been the perceived absence of the integration of academic interest in developing models of social work, of professional practice which circumvents 'social work by numbers'. The proposal for a national centre for criminal justice social work could signal an end to this weakness.

The purposes of NOS are to secure crime control, personal change and re-integration. Narrow conformity to the associated guidance and the expressed thinking of the draftsmen is not, nor can it be, the sole target. It has to be clearly understood that coherent professional practice has the capacity to document and to influence inspectorial thinking in the shorter term and policy making in the longer term.

The early evidence from evaluations indicates that the service is moving in the right direction. There is evidence of greater focus on offending and on the key target groups, particularly young adult offenders at risk of custody (Paterson and Tombs, 1998). However outcome data suggests a great deal of progress has still to be made. Adequate information systems, both nationally and locally, are required to identify demand (targets) and evaluate response (resource usage). The absence of a National Core Data system suggests that the service is still to some degree operating in the dark. McAra (1998:8) notes that while implementation of some elements of policy was subject to careful planning, there has been no coherent implementation plan for the national core data system. This is essential if the tension between costs and quality is to be addressed.

It is difficult for any commentator not to conclude that if NOS had not been established and the funding dedicated or earmarked in some way, this service would have remained in the doldrums of the previous twenty years. The risk of withdrawing this national service from its local base is always a possibility. Failure to deliver the service effectively with specially trained staff within local authorities would be a lost opportunity.

POLICY, LEGISLATION AND PRACTICE

It is axiomatic that legislation cannot be enacted in a vacuum. There has to be a policy which informs the legislative programme. From this, as in any field of practice activity, operations conform to the letter and to the spirit of the enactment. Such at any rate is the baseline—if a somewhat simplistic one.

Scotland finds itself in many ways in a unique position compared to other UK countries and indeed compared to many western countries, where the emphasis on punishment and punitive intervention seems greater than the emphasis on control, change and help, despite the wealth of experience and research to indicate that punitive strategies alone have limited impact on offenders' behaviour. Scotland is possibly the only country in world with its 'probation-type' services integrated with mainstream social services, where the key responsibilities for delivering service to the criminal justice system (under section 27 of the *Social Work (Scotland) Act,* 1968) lies with agencies who have a duty (under section 12 of the same Act), first and foremost, to promote well-being within the community.

Scottish policy in this area has been and remains distinctly Scottish. There is ample evidence of a refusal simply to follow former Home Secretary, Michael Howard's 'line', when he abandoned a twin-track approach for the rhetoric of **'prison works'**. Lord Fraser, then the Minister of Home Affairs (including Social Work) in Scotland until 1994, is to be applauded for his low-key but deliberate reinforcement of the role of social work in criminal justice in that political climate. He continued to emphasise the importance of community disposals, particularly for non-violent and young offenders, aimed at assisting the individual to change rather than simply providing sterile punishments; he argued for the provision of alternatives to custody and better throughcare for those who do receive custody. In his Kenneth Younger Memorial Lecture in February 1993 he re-quoted sections of Rifkind's policy statement of 1988 (referred to above) and firmly stated 'This remains our policy', a clear message, should anyone have doubted it, that whatever may have occurred in England and Wales between 1990 and 1993, the policy in Scotland remained consistent with the 1988 statement and had found expression in NOS and in subsequent legislation. In his address to the Association of Directors of Social Work in December 1994 he said:

> Government clearly has a number of objectives for the criminal justice system as a whole. The prevention of crime, the protection of the public and assisting victims are clearly over-riding aims. Social work services in the criminal justice system have a vitally important role to play in pursuing these.

He further identified the key objectives for social work as:

- the increasing replacement of prison sentences which are not necessary for public protection with effective community disposals;
- significantly reducing the use of imprisonment for fine default; and
- a special concentration of services for the young offender.

Broadly the Labour Administration has endorsed these objectives.

Policy conflict

It is said that a week is long time in politics. The criminal justice debate in Scotland was re-opened following a re-shuffle of Scottish Office ministers in 1995. The new Secretary of State for Scotland, Michael Forsyth, placed greater emphasis on tougher sentences, on punishment in the community and on custody consistent with the Westminster approach. A **'prison works'** policy seemed to replace the 'twin-track' strategy overnight. In practice the indications were that a dual policy was in operation—a twin-track approach in some circumstances and a 'prison works' approach in others. This change in emphasis seemed to promote a policy of '**protective detention**' for persistent as well as for serious offenders, insofar as the minister continued to stress that prison protects the public by keeping offenders out of the community.

For the first time the judiciary became involved publicly in the policy debate and the retiring Lord President, Lord Hope, in the 1995 Kenneth Younger Memorial Lecture, publicly attacked the minister for undermining the tradition of Scottish justice by introducing an 'English' approach with more emphasis on punishment than on justice.

The consultative document *Making the Punishment Fit the Crime* (1995), which resulted in the *Criminal Justice (Scotland) Act,* 1995 and the subsequent White Paper *Crime and Punishment* (Cm 3302), which resulted in the *Crime and Punishment (Scotland) Act,* 1997, contained conflicting policy statements. The importance of effective community disposals and of preventive intervention for offenders who do not present serious risk to the public was stressed:

> There remains an important place in the criminal justice armoury for non-custodial disposals. These are appropriate where the offence does not require a period of custody…to protect the public…or deter. **Custody should not be used for the want of a suitable community-based disposal** and is particularly inappropriate for fine default (39% of all receptions in 1995 down 3%). (para 9.1)

> The public are fully entitled to expect that where a community disposal is made…it is properly supervised and imposes significant **demands** upon the offender. As with a custodial penalty, non-custodial disposals must be intended to provide a rigorous response to the offence and to discourage or prevent further offending. (para 9.2)

Few formal changes were proposed for social work disposals *per se*, although those that were reflected a shift in emphasis to tougher and more punitive community-based disposals in addition to proposals to change the parole and early release system. Despite these proposed changes, much of the legislative framework, only recently established, remained intact and continued to support the role of social work in criminal justice.

Business as usual?

At the time of writing, the incoming Labour government's concern is once again to end the rising numbers of prisoners and costs of prison, while, at the same time, being seen to maintain the previous administration's 'tough' line on crime. The new climate has allowed Lord Bingham, the Lord Chief Justice, to express his concerns about the outcome of previous policy and to offer a warning to judges. He said at a Police Foundation meeting (10.7.97)

> In the public mind, I think that custody is generally seen as the only truly retributive or punitive sentence. Anyone who commits a crime of any seriousness and is not sentenced to custody is generally perceived to have got away with it. This is

very unfortunate, because of the inherent drawbacks of imprisonment…because the efficacy of imprisonment is in many cases open to question; because the cost of imprisoning offenders is very high, and invariably absorbs resources which would otherwise be available for schools, hospitals and other facilities of more obvious benefit to the public than prisons; and because the prison system is already bursting at the seams…Given the temper of our society in the last five years I do not find it surprising that the prison population should have increased by fifty per cent, reflecting the more ready resort to custody by sentencers and an increase in the length of sentences imposed. The tenor of political rhetoric has strongly favoured the imposition of severe sentences…Against this background judges have, understandably, sought to avoid the unwelcome experience of passing sentences which the Attorney General has sought leave to refer to the Court of Appeal as unduly lenient. So we have the extraordinary paradox, that judges and magistrates have been roundly criticised for over-lenient sentencing during a period when they have been sending more defendants to prisons for longer periods that at any time in the last forty years…Judges…should take care not to be blown hither and thither by every wind of political or penal fashion.

While the policy climate, as distinct from the sentencing patterns previously noted, is again sympathetic to community disposals, quite properly it will be no less demanding of effective, efficient and credible provision. The main challenge for the new government will be to steer public and political debate on crime away from an obsession with the use of custody towards prevention and the use of community disposals and diversion.

The Labour administration has re-emphasised the distinctiveness of Scots law, criminal justice policy and the central role for social work within it. It has reiterated a twin-track policy, with its emphasis on 'using prisons sparingly'. This has been accompanied by an emphasis on prison as a 'last resort', only for those who present significant risk to the community, and an emphasis on the importance of credible and effective community disposals. The administration has recognised that a range of hostel accommodation is required for vulnerable offenders as an alternative to custody, and Scotland's first 24-hour supervised hostel, with places for 16 offenders, opened in Dundee in 1998. A series of new community-based orders is proposed in the *Crime and Disorder Act*, 1998 to supplement those introduced by the 1997 Act, including restriction orders and remote restriction (electronic tagging).

Sam Galbraith, the Social Work Minister (16 May, 1997), re-stated the twin-track policy in Scotland, and confirmed the place of social work within it.

Making our communities safer will be a central aim of our policies on law and order. Social work departments have an important contribution to make to this objective…Community safety will always demand a custodial sentence for those *serious offenders* who pose a *threat to the public*. However, prisons are expensive. They are not the best environment in which to *teach* an offender to live a normal law-abiding life…to maintain a family. If offenders can serve their sentence in the community with…supervision and carrying out useful work and without posing a risk, there are clear advantages. Our basic *aim of community safety* and a long-term reduction in offending will…often be best addressed through one of the non-custodial options which social work provides...We are committed to reducing crime and tackling its underlying causes. This must include working with those who have already committed offences to ensure they confront their behaviour and lead law-abiding lives. It will also include an imaginative approach to tackling crime at its roots throughout our society. We will have *a particular focus on young people* to prevent them getting involved in criminal activity in the first place and helping those who are already into that way of life give it up. Clearly social workers have a crucial role to play here...I believe there is a need to understand more about what works best in meeting our aims and then applying this *to achieve greater effectiveness.* Here you social work have a leading role to play in applying...best practice to achieve the most effective outcome to meet agreed goals.

While the policy climate is again sympathetic to community disposals, the configuration of services may still be subject to review. It may be coincidental and practical but the division of responsibilities between the Minister for Social Work, now excluding criminal justice social work, and the Minister of Home Affairs, which includes prisons and criminal justice social work, reflects a possible future alternative structure proposed by Labour in 1994, should criminal justice social work be seen as unable to demonstrate effectiveness and the value of its location within the local authority structure. In practice some re-configuration or partnership arrangements will be necessary to avoid the duplication of Scottish Office, SPS and voluntary agencies having to negotiate with 32 separate local authorities. Strategic planning is not assisted by these arrangements.

A *Review of Criminal Justice Social Work Services* (SWSG, 1997) was produced by the Labour administration with a view to informing a more detailed consultation paper in 1998. It stressed the importance of community-based disposals as a means of reducing unnecessary custody. The main policy aims of criminal justice social work given were:

- to provide community-based programmes which maintain public safety;
- to enable offenders to address their offending behaviour and live within the law;
- to reduce the unnecessary use of custody by increasing the availability and improving the quality of community-based court disposals;
- to target use on those most at risk of custody, especially young adult repeat offenders.

Henry McLeish, the Minister of Home Affairs, issued a number of statements as part of the service review (27 November, 1997).

I want to offer a wider range of tough options that extends the scope of choice for sentencers...My main objective remains the promotion of public safety. But cramming jails with repeat offenders at great cost to the public purse is not necessarily the answer. We must aim to make more, and better, use of non-custodial sentences, confronting offenders with their behaviour and encouraging a law-abiding lifestyle. That is the tough approach.

He identified four key elements in the policy which reflect a twin-track approach:

- Offenders who commit *serious crimes* face the real prospect of prison sentences;
- There are many offenders who, if they are *not a danger to the community* could be considered for community-based disposals;
- Non-custodial disposals provide an opportunity to *tackle offending behaviour* and for offenders to *give something back to their community*. Dealing with crime is about punishment and deterrence, and community-based disposals meet both these criteria;
- We should ensure the availability of a fully comprehensive and widely available *range of effective non-custodial disposals*, confronting offenders with their behaviour and encouraging a law-abiding lifestyle.

Recent evaluative studies provide evidence of rapid and positive change suggesting a growing credibility in community disposals. Throughcare services remains an area in need of urgent development. Following the publication of evaluative studies (Scottish Office, 1998) the Minister said:

National Objectives and Standards have been found to make a substantial contribution to strengthening, and increasing the availability of, community-based disposals. There is consistent evidence that courts have greater confidence in the quality and efficiency of social work services, through reports to the courts and programmes made available for offenders in the community. This is reflected in an increased use of probation and a reduction in the number of offenders serving short prison terms...Organisationally this has involved the development of specialist criminal justice social work services based on a responsibility model of practice. The responsibility model, with its focus on offending, has required the development of new social work expertise in risk assessment to assist with the targeting of organisational resources and to indicate their potential to impact on criminal behaviour. Much of this development has taken place, although full implementation of the policy will take longer as it requires fundamental changes within professional social work culture, so the responsibility model comes to be widely understood and accepted as good practice. (McLeish, 20.2.'98)

The social inclusion agenda, driven by the European anti-poverty strategies and ignored by the previous government, now sets a context for integrating community well-being and criminal justice services. It is important that politicians do not separate out the individual 'responsibility' component from the component of community well-being, which as well as recognising the importance of community safety also implies efforts on behalf of the community towards the social inclusion of offenders.

It remains to be seen if this bold policy will be sustained in its current organisation framework by the Labour administration or by the Scottish Parliament, as a Scottish solution for a Scottish situation. A Labour party consultative document (*Protection and Justice*, 1994) recommended, in passing, that social work services to the criminal justice system in Scotland should be part of a Department of Criminal Justice based in a Scottish administration along with prison services. These issues will come to the fore when the Scottish Parliament is established, where justice is likely to be a central concern of this institution.

There is a greater, and justifiable, political support for criminal justice social work than ever before in Scotland. This window of opportunity for social work agencies demands the demonstration (with some urgency) that the significant body of research on effective intervention can be translated, with some consistency, into effective social work services that have an impact on custody and on reducing offending in Scotland.

Chapter 2

Towards Effective Management and Practice

Effective supervision; understanding criminal behaviour; safer communities and social work values; managing services for offenders; practice issues towards the millennium.

EFFECTIVE SUPERVISION

Social Work Supervision—Towards Effective Policy and Practice, the supplement to National Objectives and Standards (NOS) was added to the document after its initial publication. In addition to reinforcing the policy framework outlined in Chapter 1, this promotes the importance of effective performance and outcome measures. It identifies a set of operational principles derived from research on effective intervention which are summarised under the following headings:

- Identifying and managing risk of re-offending and risk of custody;
- Focusing on offending behaviour;
- Tackling behaviour associated with offending;
- Addressing underlying problems;
- Re-integrating offenders within the community;
- Using authority positively;
- Ensuring diversity of practice.

Essentially, these concepts have to be seen as integrative in approach and cannot be reduced simply to a check-list of benchmark standards. It remains a challenge for practitioners to demonstrate how best to meet the objectives set; to identify the linkages between offending, social circumstances and the individual characteristics of the offenders; and to calculate the effectiveness of the methods of intervention being employed.

Research findings have brought a renewed optimism to policy and practice that community-based approaches can be effective (McGuire, 1995). No-one has ever been able to show that punishment (inflicting pain as a means of achieving change) reforms or leads to lasting positive change in individuals subjected to it, nor that other people are deterred by the example of its infliction. While research reinforces that no single approach will be universally effective, it demonstrates that the most effective forms of intervention conform to five broad principles.

- **Risk Principle**: services should involve minimum intrusiveness. Maximum levels of intervention should be reserved for those assessed as showing high-risk offending behaviour. Low-risk offending behaviour requires lower levels of intervention with grades in between. Indiscriminate targeting is counterproductive.

- **Criminogenic (Need) Principle**: the best predictors of success are with offenders assessed (either by criminal history or standardised measure) as being at medium to high risk of recidivism and where programmes focus on crime-related or crime-producing (criminogenic) factors. Intervention should focus specifically on intermediate targets which contribute to the risk problem and offending. **The most promising intermediate targets** include changing anti-social attitudes, habitual patterns of thoughts and feelings that support criminality, personal control issues and peer associations; developing social skills; promoting familial support etc.—in other words intervention should be appropriately offence-focused.

- **Responsivity Principle**: the selection of styles and models of service that are capable of influencing these intermediate targets. Programmes of intervention should be matched to the way people change and learn; this also requires matching staff skills to client need. The most successful programmes are, generally, **but not exclusively**, directed by behavioural or social learning principles and include a cognitive component which focuses on challenging attitudes, values and beliefs that support anti-social behaviour; on skill acquisition through modelling, rehearsal, role playing, resource provision and detailed guidance and explanation. In other words people are helped to learn, not just talked to.

- **Community-based Principle:** the evidence for the effectiveness of community-based intervention is much stronger than that for residential or institutionally-based intervention, whose effects tend to 'wash out' on return to the community.

- **Programme Integrity Principle:** the type and method of intervention is important. Structured and focused approaches are more effective than less structured and unfocused ones. The most effective programmes have clear and stated aims and objectives; the methods are appropriate to achieve the objectives; are carried out by staff who are trained and skilled in the particular method; are adequately resourced and managed; the programme initiators are involved in all the management phases of the programme; and the programme is subjected to some form of ongoing evaluation—in other words there is effective management and planning to ensure that what is intended is actually done (see Andrews *et al*, 1990; McGuire, 1995).

Andrews *et al* suggest that research provides evidence about what seems not to work i.e. those forms of intervention associated with poor or negative outcomes. The research suggests that inappropriate service involves:

- service delivery to lower-risk cases and/or mismatching the intervention to the crime-related needs or learning styles of the offender;
- non-directive relationships and/or unstructured psycho-dynamic counselling,
- all milieu and group approaches with an emphasis on within-group communication, without a clear plan for gaining control over pro-criminal modelling and reinforcement,
- non-directive or poorly targeted academic and vocational approaches, and 'scared straight' programmes. (Andrews *et al*, 1990: 379)

These findings are supported by recent reviews of social work effectiveness in Britain. Sheldon (1994:226), while emphasising that counselling approaches in other fields of social work have produced positive gains, acknowledges

that without undue pessimism...rarely do we see offenders exposed to a therapeutic programme giving up criminal behaviour in large numbers in comparison with their control counterparts and maintaining these gains at two year follow up (p.226).

Counselling methods seem to have a more positive effect when they are part of a 'multi-modal' (combined methods) approach. Russell (1990) suggests that in so far as evaluations of casework have been more encouraging, it is because more structured approaches, such as task-centred or behaviourally-based methods, have been adopted within it.

There is a clear warning to those social workers (and sheriffs) who think a sympathetic discussion will equip offenders with the knowledge, skill and opportunities to change their attitudes and ultimately their offending. Given the complexities of many offenders' problems, and in particular, the well-established association between offending and the misuse of drugs and alcohol, effective supervision requires individualised programmes which draw on a variety of methods of intervention. This is likely to require the collaboration of a number of professionals and will draw on a range of activities, services and resources from social work and other agencies. McIvor and Barry (1998) note that most probation supervision, in practice, seems to be carried out by the supervisor alone on a one-to-one basis.

The NOS supplement emphasises the policy intention of re-integrative and restorative justice or social inclusion, rather than more punishment-focused rhetoric, and offers a more positive and more wide-ranging view of the role of social work. The supplement identifies the components of that role diagramatically in the form of an NOS Triangle, with services focused on offending behaviour at its apex, supplemented by a continuum of locally-based services, specialist offence-related services through to mainstream provision. Within any strategy of social inclusion, it is important that issues of poverty and social disadvantage associated with offending are addressed.

Offence-led social work

The diagram in the NOS supplement emphasises the nature of offence-led intervention and that offending is the primary legitimacy for statutory intervention. While offending behaviour is the primary, it is unlikely to be the exclusive, focus of intervention. The Audit Commission (1990) suggested that social work's contribution should be geared to changing behaviour by

- assisting individuals to focus on the underlying causes of offending behaviour and the risks of further offending;
- adopting methods needed to contain and reduce offending behaviour.

Offence-led intervention must be viewed, not as a labelling process, but as an ethical approach to social work intervention; one which minimises discrimination caused by 'net widening'. The only legitimacy for intervening in the life of the individual within the criminal justice process (in most cases a relatively involuntary relationship) is the individual's offending behaviour. Those individuals appropriately targeted within the criminal justice process are likely to need a range of help to address many aspects of their lives in addition to offending itself. If individuals have social needs which require to be met but are not crime-related or crime-producing, or if the offence is not sufficiently serious to fall within the criteria of the 'twin-track' approach, services should be offered, as far as possible, through voluntary provision under section 12 of the 1968 Act (local authority's duty to promote welfare) or through diversionary mechanisms. **No-one should be drawn into criminal justice processes in order to receive social work help**.

Scottish legislation still requires the offender to agree to the imposition of a probation order and of a community service order, emphasising the importance of social responsibility. While it may be fanciful to suggest 'free choice' on behalf of the offender, there is a significant ethical difference between coercion and informed choice within restricted options, in which the offender understands clearly the implications of agreement and his responsiblities within it. It is essential that the offender is well informed and understands the undertaking given to the court and the consequences of non-compliance. This sets the culture within which all social work services should operate and is a scene-setter for supervision and guidance.

Victim-focused social work

In legal systems based on common law, such as Scots Law (where the state prosecutes), victims have no special status since the state prosecutes, except in rare instances. Victims of crime often lack information (e.g. on disposal), consideration and direct involvement in the criminal justice process, except as witnesses. It can seem as if the conflict between victim and offender is no longer their property and their interests are not articulated (Moody and McKay, 1995). The cause of victims' rights has been taken up since the 1980s. The Justice Charter for Scotland (1991) recognised that victims of crime often need help and support and that criminal justice processes must be more sensitive to victims' needs. This now forms a major platform in political policy to such an extent that commentators are suggesting political manipulation of the victim agenda may result in a polarisation of victims and offenders. This, in turn, it is suggested, can be used to feed and perpetuate the demand for more retributive and punitive criminal justice responses to 'please' victims and appease public concern. Despite the rhetoric, constructive practices of conflict resolution would seem to be foreign to an adversarial system which sees offending, not as a human action, but rather as a legal one.

The issue of victims has been given a greater profile in criminal justice social work's responsibility for and contribution to **public protection and safer communities** by policy statements on victims (ADSW,1996). Statutory social work is seen to work not so much *with* victims as *on their behalf. Helping the Court Decide* (SWSI, 1996) concludes that 'practitioners should have more information relating to the current offence and its impact on any victim where available' (para. 4.26). In the USA, Victim Impact Statements provide opportunities for victims or others affected by crimes to express their views in writing. Understanding the impact of an offence on a (visible or invisible) victim is central to a social worker's understanding of the nature and seriousness of the offence as well as the offender's motivation and culpability. It should form a central part of any assessment and intervention programme under supervision. However we do not believe that the social worker responsible for an SER should be responsible, in any way, for generating victim impact statements.

UNDERSTANDING CRIMINAL BEHAVIOUR

To be effective, social workers and their managers must have a critical and sophisticated understanding of crime both in theory and in practice. Local data on the nature of crime committed, local crime rates and patterns are essential for planning and developing service. In the past criminology has often been seen as too theoretical and as having little significance for service planning and delivery. It is important for social workers to examine this legacy and the continuing controversies in criminology and crime control: the idea of criminality as a reflection of basic human nature; the apparently inexorable rise of crime in modern society; the image of crime as a product of the urban way of life; the relationship between crime and unemployment and/or social inequality; the role of the family and the problem of youth and juvenile delinquency.

Commentators such as Wilson and Hernstein (1985:253) have usefully pointed up the value of **marginal gains** from carefully monitored intervention as opposed to throwing money at the problem:

> If we grant that it is possible to try to improve the criminal justice system without apologising for the fact that those efforts do not attack the root causes of crime, the next thing to remember is that we are seeking, at best, marginal improvements that can only be discovered through patient trial and error accompanied by hard-headed and objective evaluations. Above all we can try to learn more about what works and, in the process, abandon our ideological preconceptions about what ought to work.

Theorists have also attempted to provide a synthesis of competing ideas (Young, 1994) which addresses the victim, the offender, and social reaction issues as part of understanding criminal behaviour in a community context, placing an emphasis on interaction between police and other agencies of social control, the public, the offender and the victim. These four definitional elements of crime are sometimes referred to as the 'square of crime'. The relationship of the four elements of the 'square' varies with differing types of crime. The proponents argue that to understand the nature of crime requires an examination of

- background causes of crime
- the moral context of opting for criminal behaviour
- the situation of committing crime
- detection of crime
- response to the offender
- response to the victim

and knowledge of its component parts :

- the form of crime,
- the social context,
- the shape,
- direction through time, and
- its enactment in space.

This paradigm provides the beginning of both theoretical and empirical support for a community approach to crime reduction in which local authority services, particularly criminal justice social work, can make a significant contribution to community safety.

TOWARDS A SAFER COMMUNITY—SOCIAL WORK VALUES

The Association of Directors of Social Work policy statement *Towards a Safer Community* (ADSW, 1996) is a clear attempt to emphasise that the objective of service provision is not to provide 'offender services' but to provide services which contribute to community welfare and safety in the belief that social work can make a significant contribution by assisting the offender in personal change.

In a paper to SWSG (1991) Felim O'Leary, the then Senior Advisor, drew attention to the question of fundamental values and principles underlying the detail of NOS and to social work's contribution as not merely 'helping the offender' in some vague personal welfare-oriented way. Principles directing practice should be directly offence-focused, such as reducing the frequency and severity of offending behaviour, and enhancing individual responsibiltiy. Others should include:

- social work intervention must not exceed what is necessary in the interests of justice and fairness (thus accepting that offenders have rights in this context);
- responding to offenders as members of families and communities with frequently complex personal and social problems, not all of which are directly related to their offending behaviour;
- the interests of victims and of the wider community, as well as those of the offender, are legitimately included within the focus of social work;
- offenders should be involved as much as possible in any decisions which affect them;
- social work should address conflicts between individual offenders and the community with the objective of effecting reconciliation wherever possible.

This last is the most radical. In one sense, it could be construed simply as a reference to schemes for reparation and mediation (see Chapter 8); at a more fundamental level, it predicts that the familiar association of ideas, crime—punishment, might more productively be replaced by the association of ideas, offence—reconciliation—re-integration (Wood, 1991). The concept of 'making amends' and providing services which allow offenders to 'make good' to 'give something back', where practical, do not yet feature strongly in Scottish practice. McIvor and Barry (1998) suggest poorly targeted work remains very welfare-oriented rather than focusing on offending behaviour.

While the context of social work in the criminal justice system is different in Scotland from elsewhere in the UK, the practice is based around similar ideological frameworks. These frameworks contain competing and conflicting demands on the role of social workers, particularly in relation to issues of care and control and on the role social work plays in community sanctions.

NOS continue to emphasise that assisting offenders to change their behaviour by social work help is an effective way of protecting the public. One of the challenges facing social work following local government re-organisation is to demonstrate that the organisational structures and their operation are appropriate to deliver efficient and effective services, and to promote the kinds of provision that can help offenders change their offending behaviour and their success in contributing to protection of the public and making communities safer.

MANAGING SERVICES FOR OFFENDERS

The management of social work services in Scotland is now coloured with the language of commerce and business of which the approach to criminal justice social work is but part. The 'welfare consensus' of the past is no more. Changing also is the pattern of local generic management which may have viewed offenders, or criminal justice social work, as relatively low-priority and one of a number of responsibilities to be undertaken from competing resources. The immensity of the task of changing patterns of thought and management practices that were first adopted in the crisis of having to fit criminal justice work into the priorities of all-purpose departments, is now being addressed. Child care and protection still dominates the priorities of local authorities, particularly in authorities where fieldworkers carry responsibility for more than one specialism, and where there are no senior managers with specialist expertise in the field of criminal justice. However the development of a tier of dedicated specialist managers in criminal justice gives scope for optimism that the service will find its proper place within integrated community-based social work provision, providing financial resources allow for the cost of such a staffing structure in each authority.

An important first step in developing the strategic and corporate approach now required involves social work clearly defining its role and purpose, particularly in terms of its 'client', 'customer' or 'user' base. In the past social work operated on the assumption that there were two clients, the individual person in trouble and an agency, such as a court. In practice there are numerous 'customers', each with differing requirements for information, resources etc. The term 'offender service' has almost disappeared. It puts the individual offender at the centre of the system, instead of seeing him/her as but one element of the service provision. There is equally a danger in putting the court at the centre of the system as 'customer', in that the essential work with the individual in trouble could be lost in the effort to meet the growing demand of the various service 'users'. Increasingly, however, the system needs to be seen as providing for, and involving, not just the person in trouble and the agencies dealing with him, but as also involving other 'stakeholders' in criminal justice, the court, the prosecutor, the victim, other professionals, politicians and significant others in the local and wider community.

The view that the court, and others, are 'customers' or 'users' of an offered social work service is now readily recognised (Statham, 1990). The primary purpose of the service is its contribution to community well-being and safety. While this is no longer controversial in social work, many, including the public, politicians and other 'players' in the criminal justice system, have still to be convinced that helping offenders change their behaviour is an effective, and, in the long term, an efficient way of protecting victims and of contributing to community safety.

Managing change

The pace and demand for change in the service is extraordinary. Each local authority is required to produce strategic plans based on the nationally-set objectives and standards, as part of the funding mechanism. Commercial business practice has focused on 'downsized' management structures, in effect getting rid of layers of middle management. Evidence suggests that public sector provision is moving in the same direction. There are indications that meeting NOS has been judged by some managers under pressure as requiring mainly quantitative and process measures only. Early inspections following the introduction of NOS indicated that while quantitative measures of delivering NOS were being achieved, the quality of service provided to the offender varied greatly and the use of effective methods of intervention promoted by the NOS supplement were still the exception rather than the norm. 'The best may have been good, the average was not'; the issue of consistency of provision is a major challenge. Recent evaluations (Paterson and Tombs, 1998) give a more optimistic picture but one where many fundamental changes have still to take place. There is a very real urgency now, some years into the 'strategy', for local authorities to demonstrate that they have created agencies which can apply the lessons of research to local circumstances and provide evidence of the effectiveness of the services on offer, within the resource base available.

The policy framework and NOS provide a crucial starting point for the kinds of data generation, priority-setting and forecasting of service demand required to plan the quality of provision. General professional management has taken its toll in Scotland in this respect. There have been limited opportunities for experienced and senior people to work exclusively in developing and managing criminal justice social work services.

A further development that requires consideration with some urgency is a financial reward structure which will encourage senior practitioners to remain in practice rather than having to look to management posts for more money or recognised status. Bureaucratic line management structures of local authorities have not been successful, to date, in providing experienced practitioners with the authority and status, professional and structural, to deal with high-status practitioners in other criminal justice agencies, such as lawyers, judges, prison governors, etc. on an equal footing of status and regard, or with opportunities to contribute their expertise to strategic planning within their own organisation. Non-practising managers, who view themselves as having greater expertise than those delivering the service, are unlikely to create the professional culture of learning essential to risk taking in this field.

PRACTICE ISSUES TOWARDS THE MILLENIUM

Central to working in this rapidly changing environment are the issues of preserving, enhancing and developing professional practice. The concept of a professional worker capable of operating with limited direct supervisory control and clearly delegated responsibility for action and decision making was never well established in Scottish practice. Indeed, one of the major criticisms presented to the Kilbrandon Committee (1964) was that Probation was a 'minor' local authority service, lacking the ethos and individuality of the English Probation Service. The establishments of the social work departments within regional authorities in 1975 heavily imbued with bureaucratic structures, did little to improve the situation. The relationship between social work and the courts never achieved a sense of mutual respect (Aitken-Smith, 1981). The introduction of NOS, whatever their other merits, will not, in itself, promote the professional image of social work with the judiciary or others. This is having to be won in day-to-day practice.

In England it became very clear that the Home Office had negative views about the value of social work in criminal justice and 'alternative' training proposals were developed. In Scotland, though facing a similar political climate, formal policy continues to stress community disposals and the value of social work intervention, particularly for non-violent offenders .

The Central Council for Training and Education in Social Work (CCETSW, 1992; 1997) created a framework for post-qualifying training which recognises that social workers with responsibility for people at risk require further specialist training (a Post-Qualifying Award) and that even these specialists need the support of social work staff with more specific professional expertise (the Advanced Award) to act as consultants and champions of quality services. Such a structure is essential in criminal justice social work to promote the role of practitioner as a high-status one within agencies. It is to be hoped that the demise of CCETSW will result in the establishment of a professional social work body in Scotland whose primary concern will be professional standards rather than organisational ones.

It remains to be seen if the Labour administration will continue to promote these uniquely Scottish policy developments. The relationship between the Scottish Parliament and local authorities will be a significant determinant in any future configuration of services. Undoubtedly economies of scale have been lost through local government reorganisation. Some authorities have chosen to provide services in new joint departments such as social work and housing. It remains to be seen whether 32 local authorities can operate independently within a strategic framework. Many may need to operate in consortia or partnerships between authorities and the voluntary sector to ensure expertise across the range of demand.

The shifts in policy and service design place much greater responsibilities on social work for providing credible community-based disposals for those who do not represent a significant threat to public safety—a group which represents the majority of people dealt with by summary courts; and for post-prison supervision of others, some of whom present a significant risk to the community on their return. If government is serious in its intent to reduce the custody figures, then radical steps are required to curtail the summary courts' use of custody for persistent but often minor offenders, such as limiting the prison beds available, or qualifying the powers of these courts by suspending custodial sentences until community options have been tried. The passing of the *Prisoners and Criminal Proceedings (Scotland) Act*, 1993 renewed the emphasis on throughcare services. Revised NOS (1996, 1997) were produced which place social work in the central role of supervising and assisting the reintegration of many 'high-risk' offenders on their return to the community (see *Commitment to Protect*, 1997). Estimates are that only about 6% of expenditure goes on throughcare; much more needs to be spent and delivered in this area of provision.

The success of community-based disposals will have a direct impact on the requirements of throughcare. Sentencers must have confidence that to put an offender on a community-based order such as probation is, *in itself*, a sufficient guarantee that certain things will happen. The emphasis on public safety and public protection requires a new partnership between local authorities, the Scottish Prison Service, the Parole Board, the police and the community.

Social work services in the criminal justice system in Scotland are at the beginning of a steep learning curve now that there is optimistic evidence of the possibility of real influence on offending behaviour. The exact scope and limitations of that influence are not fully understood and practice and evaluation methods need further development and refinement (Roberts, 1993). It is crucial that the organisation and management of the service is supportive of effective practice.

Organisational style and structure

Organisational structures need to promote a sense of joint purpose and mutual accountability, one which is open and receptive to outside influences; community resources are needed for offenders; courts need to understand social work's responsibilities within the policy framework and have confidence in the services on offer, as do other criminal justice agencies; other professions and the academic world should be tapped as a source of knowledge and expertise.

The services as 'products' must be presented and promoted properly to the outside world and 'marketed' appropriately to the different users and to the public. Clear accounts of service provision are needed with mechanisms for addressing non-delivery. Courts must be discouraged from indiscriminate use of scarce resources for offenders and should be influenced by explicit criteria and by data on service outcomes. The service requires a confident and knowledgeable workforce. In small, unitary local authorities, if staff are to have access to specialist expertise and consultancy, the organisation has to be managed and structured in ways which support this. Pooled and shared resources are required. Staff training and development should stem from explicit service priorities. Every member of staff must regard it as their shared responsibility to promote good public understanding of the work of the service. The interests of the press and media must be actively responded to and proactively sought. Special attention needs to be given to minority groups who are often subject to systematic discrimination.

A culture of learning

At this stage of service development in criminal justice social work, it is important that new organisations adopt a *culture of learning* about effectiveness, described by Raynor and Vanstone (1994) as a *culture of curiosity*—a culture in which managers and practitioners alike are interested in whether or not their work with people has the intended effect. A consumer focus is important and a wide repertoire of measures is required to deliver a full service. These need to have clear aims and objectives with identified outcomes that can be measured to some acceptable degree. Experience needs to be shared within and across authorities as a means of establishing an *information community*. A major challenge will be creating practice and programme integrity in which provision is planned and sufficiently consistent over time to allow some measure of effectiveness.

Chapter 3

Prosecution and the Criminal Courts in Scotland

Legislature in Scotland; system of prosecution; the courts; bail; legal aid; police powers

LEGISLATURE IN SCOTLAND

The United Kingdom Parliament is the legislature in which, traditionally, most laws are passed. The Parliament of the United Kingdom comprises the Sovereign, the House of Lords, and the House of Commons. In this it reflects the traditions of the English Parliament rather than the Scots. Traditionally the United Kingdom constitution was considered to display parliamentary **supremacy** or **sovereignty**, namely that there are no legal boundaries to parliament's legislative power. Such supremacy as a constitutional principle is unusual in modern states as nearly all others have a written constitution which, among other things, limits the powers of the legislature. However membership of the European Community has required Acts of Parliament to be subordinate to Community legislation. This compromise of UK supremacy is a source of much political debate.

Within the House of Commons there exists a Scottish Grand Committee, comprising of all Scottish MPs and ten others, which may take certain business, including some legislative stages of Scottish Bills. There are, additionally, two Scottish Standing Committees which can take certain other legislative stages. In 1992 the Scottish Select Committee was resurrected after many years in abeyance to examine the work of the departments of state in a relatively impartial way. Legislation to re-establish a Scottish Parliament with devolved powers has allowed the capacity for Scottish legislation on devolved matters to be passed independently of other countries in the United Kingdom.

The Scottish Parliament

The Scottish Parliament is the body to which the Scottish Executive, headed by a First Minister, will be accountable. It will operate in a way that is similar to the United Kingdom government. It will be the forum for scrutinising much of Scotland's domestic legislation and will be able to exercise its law-making powers in all areas which are not specifically reserved to Westminster. The White Paper *Scotland's Parliament* (Cm 3658) identified the main devolved powers as relating to:

- the law and home affairs;
- local government;
- social work, education and training;
- health, housing and the environment;
- economic development;
- agriculture, fisheries and forestry, transport, sports and the arts.

The Parliament will consist of one house; there was no perceived need for an Upper House to revise legislation. It will sit for fixed-term periods of four years or less, if two thirds of the members so vote, and will be composed of 129 members, known as Members of the Scottish Parliament (MSPs). Of this number, 73 will be elected under the 'first past the post system', one for each of the existing Westminster constituencies plus one extra for Orkney and Shetland. The remaining 56 MSPs will be elected by means of a party list system. The White Paper does not detail how the Parliament will operate, rather it is proposed that it will make standing orders to govern its own operation. It is expected that the Parliament will adopt modern methods of working, for example, enhanced use of committees to scrutinise legislation and the Scottish Executive; and, the use of electronic voting systems to speed decision making. The Scottish Executive's First Minister will be able to appoint ministers and allocate portfolios. The law officers will be the Lord Advocate and the Solicitor General, since the areas for which they are currently responsible will be devolved to the Parliament.

Sovereignty will continue to rest ultimately with the Westminster Parliament. Reserved powers are retained by Westminster and defined in law as including foreign policy, defence and national security, macro-economic policy; employment and social security; and transport regulation. It remains to be seen if a satisfactory mechanism can be found to enable any potential disputes which may arise between the two parliaments to be resolved without recourse to Westminster legislating on behalf of Scotland.

The mechanism proposed is to operate on three levels: firstly pre-legislative scrutiny to ensure the legislation is within the Scottish Parliament's powers; secondly a period of 'quarantine' after a bill is passed, before receiving Royal Assent, to enable the UK government to satisfy itself that it is within the powers of the Scottish Parliament: disputes will be dealt with by a Judicial Committee of the Privy Council composed of at least five Lords of Appeal in Ordinary. Strangely there is no requirement for a Scottish judge to be a member. Finally there will be a mechanism for resolving any subsequent disputes in relation to secondary legislation and Acts of the Scottish Parliament after Assent, again by a judicial committee. It is expected that there will be liaison machinery between the two parliaments, including links between Scottish and Whitehall departments; between the Scottish Executive Secretary and the Cabinet office; and between Scottish and UK ministers (Haggerty, 1997).

THE SYSTEM OF PROSECUTION

The Lord Advocate is responsible for the prosecution system in Scotland. He is assisted by the Solicitor General, and a number of Advocates Depute. These law officers are known collectively as Crown Counsel. The administrative base of the system is the Crown Office in Edinburgh. The Lord Advocate and the Solicitor General are both political appointments, and are members of the government.

The local officers of the Lord Advocate across Scotland are the procurators fiscal. The office is an old one: originally the fiscal was an officer responsible for all monies and financial matters connected with the Sheriff Courts. The role extended with the passage of time and, influenced to an extent by Scottish links with the continent, has become that of a public prosecutor. Traditionally, in Scotland, the prosecutor had no formal interest in sentence, in so far as he did not ask the court for a particular type of sentence, or a prison sentence in a given range of length. However in recent years provisions have been introduced for the prosecutor, under certain circumstances, to appeal against what he may consider an unduly lenient sentence (see sections 108 and 175 of the CP Act, 1995 and s23 of the 1997 Act). Recent years have also seen new debates about prosecution policy in Scotland, as procurators fiscal have experimented with alternatives to prosecution, such as social work diversion, and reparation and mediation schemes, which afford alternative ways of responding to crime other than prosecution before a criminal court.

It is to the procurators fiscal that the police report alleged crimes. In Scotland, as in many other countries, the true extent of law-breaking is unknown. Much is unknown, unrecorded, unpunished. Criminologists debate the extent of the 'dark figure' that does not come to public attention. A host of social mores and norms dictate what behaviour is regarded as worth—whether morally or practically— reporting to the authorities. Even then, attitudes and values within the police service may dictate different levels of response; for example, the police have changed previous attitudes to domestic violence, following political pressure and 'zero tolerance' campaigns in the direction of treating it as a much more serious crime. So various social pressures, the mores and culture of the police service, just as much as the content of the law itself, will determine what, at the end of the day, is reported to the public prosecutor.

Since the nineteenth century the whole system of prosecution in Scotland has been under central control. Private prosecution is all but unknown, though it is technically possible in the High Court. The very rarity of this practice serves to underline the basic norm that the system of prosecution is a public one through the Lord Advocate and the procurators fiscal. The word **crime** is used to refer to breaches of **common law**, for example, theft, fraud and assault. Common law is a body of non-statute law which has been developed over the centuries. It is more prevalent in Scotland than it is in England and Wales; for example, theft is a common law offence in Scotland, but in England and Wales is an offence against the *Theft Act*, 1968, a specific statute defining thefts of various kinds.

Some statutes are specific to Scotland, and have the designation *(Scotland)* in the title, for example, the *Social Work (Scotland) Act*, 1968. Sometimes a Scottish Act may be very similar to, and follow hard on the heels of, a comparable English Act, for example the *Mental Health (Scotland) Act*, 1984, following the *Mental Health Act*, 1983. Some statutes are particular to England, and may have no directly corresponding Scottish Act, for example, the *Powers of Criminal Courts Act*, 1973. Other Acts may cover the whole of the United Kingdom, for example, *Rehabilitation of Offenders Act*, 1974. Yet again, some matters may originate with United Kingdom legislation, but follow different developments in Scotland, for example, the *Criminal Justice Act*, 1967 introduced Suspended Sentences of Imprisonment into England and Wales, but the relevant sections did not, and do not, apply to Scotland.

The word **offence** refers to breaches of particular statutes—for example, section 103 (1) (b) of the *Road Traffic Act*, 1988 identifies driving whilst disqualified as an offence. It is important to note that particular examples of otherwise common law crimes may have been made the subject of a special statute. Such a statute may give a court greater powers than would have been available at common law. For example, theft of mail is governed by *Post Office Acts*, and assaults on police officers by the *Police (Scotland) Act* 1967.

There are two methods for the prosecution of crime, once a procurator fiscal has decided that there is a *prima facie* case, and that the circumstances justify the mounting of a prosecution. These methods are known as **solemn procedure**, and **summary procedure.** In some instances the law may govern which of these methods of procedure shall be used. Otherwise the choice lies with the prosecuting authorities, and their discretion can be considerable. Especially it should be noted that many commonplace crimes and offences can be prosecuted by either method. Social workers should always ask themselves not just what the charge is, but by which method of procedure it is being prosecuted. In each instance the procurator fiscal exercises discretion according to the intrinsic circumstances surrounding the charge, and with regard to broader considerations of the public interest.

THE COURTS

There are **two methods** of procedure for the prosecution of crime, but there are **three levels** of criminal courts. Consequently a recognition of the type of procedure being used by each is crucial to an understanding of the overall system. A detailed description of the two methods of prosecution is given below: here we outline the three levels of courts. One factor in the prosecution's choice of which method to use will be the sentencing powers available to a particular court:

- the High Court hears cases only on solemn procedure;
- the Sheriff Court can hear cases using both methods;
- the District Court hears cases only on summary procedure.

One consequence of these arrangements is that the Sheriff Court, hearing cases using both methods of procedure, deals with the bulk of criminal matters in

Scotland. When the Sheriff Court is dealing with cases on solemn procedure, its sentencing powers are restricted to a maximum custodial sentence of three years imprisonment. However, if the court considers that a longer sentence is required, it can send the case on ('remit for disposal') to the High Court for disposal to be decided there.

When the Sheriff Court is hearing cases on **summary** procedure, its sentencing powers are generally restricted to a maximum custodial sentence of six months, and to a 'level 5' fine (see Chapter 7 regarding levels of fines). However, it should be noted that the Sheriff Court hearing cases on summary procedure cannot send the case on anywhere else with a view to a more substantial sentence. It cannot, as it were, turn itself into a court dealing with the matter on solemn procedure and impose a more substantial penalty. This is one illustration of the powers of the prosecuting authorities in determining the choice of prosecution method.

The District Court, hearing cases only on **summary** procedure, has maximum powers of 60 days imprisonment, and fines not exceeding 'level 4'. The District Court cannot send cases on to a higher court with a view to a more substantial penalty. The Glasgow Stipendiary Magistrate Court has the same powers as a summary sheriff court.

The judges of the High Court are also judges of the Court of Session, the supreme civil court in Scotland. Sheriffs also deal with a whole range of civil or other matters which fall outside the scope of this book. One implication of this, however, is that the judges in these courts do not specialise in criminal matters, but are, as it were, 'generic' judges. Also, in any court building the people present may not necessarily be present in connection with criminal cases.

The High Court of Justiciary

The High Court of Justiciary is the supreme court in criminal matters. It is a trial court for major crimes and an appeal court for all crime in Scotland. It consists of the Lord Justice General, the Lord Justice Clerk, and a number of Lords Commissioner of Justiciary (Judges). When dealing with a trial a High Court Judge usually sits alone. In appeals, the High Court sits usually with a bench of three judges, although a bench of five or more can be convened to review precedents which are doubted.

The High Court deals only with the most serious cases. It has exclusive jurisdiction in cases of murder, rape and treason. Those offences which cause deep public concern (for example, bank robberies, serious assaults) will almost always be tried in this court. Also, where the prosecuting authorities consider that the likely sentence will be greater than the maximum a Sheriff Court can impose, they will arrange for the High Court to hear the case. The High Court will also deal with those cases that have been begun in the Sheriff Court but remitted from that court for disposal.

The pronouncements of High Court Judges when passing sentence concerning the relative seriousness or prevalence of certain types of offence influence the practice of lower courts. Traditionally the Lord Justice Clerk has been regarded as having a role within the High Court bench in relation to general aspects of sentencing. The High Court also has powers to pass **Acts of Adjournal**, to regulate the workings of lower courts. The format of a Probation Order, for example, is specified by an Act of Adjournal.

The High Court hears all criminal **appeals**. It hears appeals against **conviction** (on the grounds that there have been procedural flaws or miscarriage of justice) and appeals against **sentence**. It can happen that appeals may be in respect of more than one aspect—in other words against conviction and sentence. The High Court also deals with bail appeals—a dispute concerning the detention of a person in custody prior to trial by a lower court.

The *Criminal Justice (Scotland) Act,* 1995 introduced significant changes to the quorum of the High Court, distinguishing between appeals against conviction and appeals against sentence. For any appeal under solemn procedure the quorum is three judges except for appeals against sentence alone where the quorum is two. Similarly in summary appeals the quorum is three except for appeals against sentence, absolute discharge, admonition or court orders such as probation, community service or deferred sentence, where the quorum is two judges. Only one judge sits for other matters such as granting leave to appeal, applications for leave to appeal, extending the time within which intention to appeal may be given, and bail appeals. These provisions are included in Parts VIII and XI of the *Criminal Procedure (Scotland) Act,* 1995. The High Court is empowered under ss.118(7) and 189(7) of the *CP Act,* 1995, in considering appeals, to set **sentencing guidelines** which other courts, in sentencing, 'shall have regard to' (s.197).

Two further facts are worthy of note. First, sentences can be *increased* by the High Court dealing with appeals; and, second, there is no appeal from the High Court when dealing with criminal appeals. When sitting as an appeal court, the High Court sits in Edinburgh. As a trials court, the High Court of Justiciary sits in Edinburgh or at any number of locations across Scotland, but mainly in the major cities and towns.

The Sheriff Court

The Sheriff Court deals with the bulk of criminal prosecutions. It hears cases both on solemn procedure and on summary procedure. In the course of their investigations, social workers should always ascertain from anyone telling them that a case is in the Sheriff Court which kind of procedure is being used.

Scotland is divided into six Sheriffdoms, each with a Sheriff Principal and a varying number of Sheriffs. Each Sheriffdom is further divided into a number of Sheriff Court Districts, to which, for the most part, individual Sheriffs will be allotted. The boundaries of a Sheriff Court will not necessarily be coterminous with those of District Courts and Local Authorities. Sheriffs are appointed by the Crown from among the legal profession, and enjoy considerable independence under the law. The Sheriff Principal may appoint a number of honorary Sheriffs, who have the same power as a Sheriff, and who exercise jurisdiction in the absence of other Sheriffs. In criminal matters (but not in civil ones) the powers of a Sheriff Principal are the same as any of the other Sheriffs.

1. Solemn Procedure

The sentencing powers of the Sheriff Court in solemn procedure cases include:

i)   custodial sentences of up to and including three years: the court has to obtain any reports required by legislation before certain categories of people can be sentenced to imprisonment (Chapter 5);

ii)   remit to the High Court for disposal, if a disposal longer than three years is considered appropriate;

iii)   unlimited fines;

iv)   community service order, provided that the necessary reports have been obtained and considered (Chapter 9);

v)   probation order, provided any necessary reports have been obtained; such an order may include extra requirements (Chapter 8), non-harassment orders, and restriction of liberty orders, drug treatment and testing orders when implemented (Chapter 7);

vi)   supervised release orders on custodial sentences between twelve months and four years (Chapter 11); and extended post-release supervision, when implemented;

vii)   supervision and treatment order, provided that any necessary reports have been obtained (Chapter 12);

viii)   supervised attendance order—a disposal introduced by the *Law Reform (Miscellaneous Provisions) (Scotland) Act*, 1990 in connection with fines enforcement (Chapter 7);

ix)   caution (unlimited amount) (Chapter 7);

x)   compensation order (unlimited amount); such an order can be combined with some other penalties (Chapter 7);

xi)   hospital or guardianship order, provided the necessary pre-conditions are met and reports have been obtained and information is available (Chapter 12);

xii)   detention (of children) under section 205 of the *Criminal Procedure (Scotland) Act*, 1995, for up to two years OR remit of case to the High Court for disposal if a longer sentence is considered appropriate (Chapter 10);

xiii)   remit to Children's Hearing for disposal, in any case involving a child (Chapter 6);

xiv)   admonition (Chapter 7);

xv)   absolute discharge (Chapter 7);

xvi)   deferring of sentence (Chapter 7);

2. Summary Procedure

The sentencing powers of the Sheriff Court in summary cases include:

i)   custodial sentence of not more than three months;

ii)   custodial sentence of not more than six months, **providing** the person is convicted of a second or subsequent offence inferring dishonest appropriation of money (which includes theft), or attempt thereat, or a second or subsequent offence inferring personal violence;

iii)   custodial sentences in terms of statutory provisions. These can be up to 12 months;

iv) custodial sentences cannot be passed on certain categories of person without the court obtaining and considering various reports (Chapter 5);

v) fines up to and including 'level 5';

vi) community service order, provided that various reports and information have been obtained (Chapter 9);

vii) probation order, provided that any necessary reports have been obtained (Chapter 8), non-harassment orders and restriction of liberty orders, drug treatment and testing orders when implemented (Chapter 7);

viii) supervised release orders on custodial sentences between twelve months and four years (Chapter 11); and extended post-release supervision, when implemented;

ix) supervision and treatment order, provided that any necessary reports have been obtained (Chapter 12);

x) supervised attendance order—a disposal introduced by the *Law Reform (Miscellaneous Provisions) (Scotland) Act*, 1990 in connection with fines enforcement (Chapter 7);

xi) caution, up to a maximum equivalent to a 'level 5' fine;

xii) compensation order, up to a maximum equivalent to a 'level 5' fine; such an order can be made in addition to some other penalties (Chapter 7);

xiii) hospital or guardianship order, provided the necessary preconditions are met and any necessary reports and information have been obtained (Chapter 12);

xiv) residential accommodation for children under section 44 of the *Criminal Procedure (Scotland) Act*, 1995 (Chapter 10);

xv) remit to a Children's Hearing for disposal, in a case involving a child (Chapter 6);

xvi) admonition (Chapter 7);

xvii) absolute discharge (Chapter 7);

xviii)deferring of sentence (Chapter 7).

Section 13 of the *Crime and Punishment (Scotland) Act,* 1997 made provision to increase the custodial powers of the sheriff court at solemn procedure from three to five years and at summary procedure from three months to six months and six months to twelve months, respectively. These provisions have not yet been implemented.

The District Court

District Courts are local courts dealing with minor crime and offences which a statute has declared competent to it. They came into being on 16 May 1975, following the enactment of the *District Courts (Scotland) Act*, 1975. The District Court serves an area defined as a District by the *Local Government (Scotland) Act*, 1975. There are 56 such Districts in Scotland, and each has its own District Court, except one Island area where there would have been insufficient business. The District Courts replaced a variety of courts of summary jurisdiction (Burgh Courts, Justice of the Peace Courts) that previously existed, and they reflect an amalgam of different aspects of their predecessors. The District Court only hears cases on summary procedure. It has no powers to send a case on to a higher court with a view to a sentence being passed that is greater than its own maximum powers. In Glasgow there is a District Court presided over by a full-time Stipendiary Magistrate. The jurisdiction and powers of this court are equivalent to those of the Sheriff Court hearing cases on summary procedure. Otherwise, the sentencing powers of the District Court include:

i)   custodial sentence of not more than 60 days, provided that any necessary reports have been obtained (Chapter 5);

ii)   community service order, only if a scheme has been made available to the court, and this is rare;

iii) probation order, provided that any necessary reports have been obtained (see Chapter 8); 'level 4' fine (Chapter 7);

iv)   Supervised Attendance Order—a disposal introduced by the *Law Reform (Miscellaneous Provisions) (Scotland) Act*, 1990 in connection with fines enforcement (Chapter 7);

v)   caution, up to a maximum equivalent to a 'level 4' fine (see Chapter 6);

vi)   compensation order, up to a maximum equivalent to a 'level 4' fine (see Chapter 6);

vii) admonition (Chapter 7);

viii) absolute discharge (Chapter 7);

ix)   deferring of sentence (Chapter 7).

The following disposals are NOT available to the District Court—Hospital and Guardianship Orders, and **any disposal relating to children** (Chapter 6).

Whilst the maximum penalties at common law open to the District Court are of the order of magnitude indicated, many of the statutory offences with which they deal may carry much lower maximum penalties. Appeal is possible against conviction and/or sentence, to the High Court of Justiciary, both to the person convicted or to the prosecutor.

The District Court also deals with a whole range of 'social nuisance' offences, the precise details of which are set out in a variety of local bye-laws, which differ in each town or locality. These may include practices such as loitering, begging and vagrancy, as well as regulatory matters such as bus lanes, car parking and so on.

The criminal jurisdiction of the District Courts was relatively restricted when they were first introduced—for example only dealing with first offenders, or cases involving small amounts of money. However, section 7 of the *Criminal Justice (Scotland) Act*, 1980 lifted many of these restrictions. As all summary cases are also competent in sheriff courts, this adds to the discretion and flexibility of procurators fiscal in determining in which court to prosecute cases in the light, among other things, of the limits to the District Court's sentencing powers. One intention of the change was to shift some of the criminal workload away from the Sheriff Courts to the District Courts. By 1991 the District Courts dealt with almost half of all criminal proceedings in Scotland. In 1995 they dealt with 28% of all young people proceeded against in Scottish courts.

The judges in the District Court are known as Justices or Magistrates, and are addressed in court as 'Your Honour'. It is competent for a justice or magistrate to sit alone in a District Court, but the preference is for a multiple bench. They are lay people who receive some training for the post, and are not qualified lawyers or judges. The Secretary of State has powers to order a period of training for justices, but his role in their selection is a complex and finely balanced one. Each local authority will have a Justices Committee, which regulates the running of the court. The importance to the lay justice in the District Court of relying on a legally qualified Clerk is crucial. The clerk of the court and the staff are employees of the local authority, whereas staff in the Sheriff and High Courts are civil servants.

The District Court is entitled to the full range of services which local authorities are obliged to provide under section 27 of the *Social Work (Scotland) Act*, 1968. These include the attendance of officers of the authority at the court as required (see Chapter 4). District Courts make relatively little use of social work and yet have significant custodial powers.

It is rather paradoxical in the context of a policy of 'using prisons sparingly' (see Chapter 1) that while the District Courts do not have the power to disqualify from driving except in terms of penalty points (*Road Traffic Offenders Act,* 1988 section 35 as amended by the *Road Traffic Act* 1991) they do have the power of custody. It is clearly government's intention as highlighted by Henry McLeish, the Minister of Home Affairs, in a speech to the District Court Association (28.2.1998) that 'custody should rarely be in prospect for cases proceeded against in the District Court'. One may ask why they have the power at all. In reality fines are the most common disposal in District Courts. However given Scotland's high levels of custody for fine default, this is an area where social work should be more proactive. The Minister indicated justices should be 'particularly interested in the development of Supervised Attendance Orders'. It is to be hoped that such social work services will be readily available to and used by these courts in the future.

THE METHODS OF PROCEDURE

Solemn procedure

The indictment
No case can go forward on solemn procedure without the authority and approval of Crown Counsel based at the Crown Office in Edinburgh. They also decide whether the case will be heard in the Sheriff Court or in the High Court.

The charge(s) in any case on solemn procedure will be contained in a document known as an *indictment*. The indictment is a full written statement of the charge(s) that the person will have to face at the trial in any case on solemn procedure. The indictment proceeds in the name of the Lord Advocate, being authorised and initiated by him.

The part of the indictment which contains the charge(s) is known as the *libel*. The indictment will also include a list both of the material evidence, known as the *productions* in the case of documentary evidence, and the *labels* in the case of non-documentary evidence. It will include a list of the names and addresses of prosecution witnesses. At a trial the prosecution cannot make use of any person not so listed, except in very special circumstances. The copy served on the accused will have attached to it a full schedule of his previous convictions, if applicable.

The prosecution of a case on solemn procedure in the Sheriff Court will usually be undertaken by the procurator fiscal, although the Lord Advocate or one of the Advocates Depute may prosecute. In the High Court, the prosecution is normally undertaken by one of the Advocates Depute, although occasionally the Solicitor General or the Lord Advocate appears in person to prosecute.

The petition

Because the use of solemn procedure requires the approval and authority of the Crown Office, the procurator fiscal has to report the case to the Crown Office before the indictment can be prepared and issued. Thus a series of preliminary stages occur during which the case is investigated by the fiscal, and the person is *committed for trial* with a view to prosecution on solemn procedure. Where police or other evidence suggests there is a *prima facie* case for prosecution by solemn procedure—whether because of the intrinsic nature or seriousness of the offence; because of the person's previous record; or because of his or her involvement with other people; or for whatever reason—the procurator fiscal first charges the person *on petition*. At this stage the charge(s) are laid by the fiscal on the petition, and a series of inquiries and investigations instigated by the fiscal follow. At this petition stage the matter is not dealt with in open court at the Sheriff Court, as this is not the stage of actual trial. During this part of the procedure the person appears before the Sheriff Court, even if it is known that eventually the actual trial will be before the High Court or the Crown may petition for a warrant to arrest the accused. The trial, whether in Sheriff or High Court, will be heard in open court.

Judicial examination

The process of judicial examination is often a part of petition procedure and, as with all petition procedure, has been subjected to significant changes in recent years. The judicial examination is held in private, outwith the presence of any co-accused or their agents. Before the *Criminal Justice (Scotland) Act* 1980, the stage of judicial examination was largely a formality. Its origins can be found in the *Criminal Procedure (Scotland) Act* 1887 and after the passing of the *Criminal Evidence Act*, 1898, the practice of making 'no plea; no declaration' became almost universal. This stage was used to commit the person for trial or for further examination, with the major point at issue being whether or not he was remanded in custody or was released on bail in the meantime. The *Criminal Justice (Scotland) Act*, 1980 revived the earlier practice of judicial examination. The changes were made as a result of recommendations in the second report of the Thomson Committee on Criminal Procedure (1975).

The changes made are now incorporated and further amended in the *Criminal Procedure (Scotland) Act*, 1995, ss.35-39 which governs this stage of the proceedings. The intention of judicial examination is to make the accused state his defence at the earliest stage in proceedings and to make it more difficult to concoct a defence while awaiting trial. While it remains competent for an accused to 'emit a declaration' at any time before the service of the indictment, it is now a rare event.

The accused has the right to a private interview with his solicitor prior to judicial examination or court appearance (s.17(5)) and, while there is no requirement that this should have taken place, in effect, section 35(2) places the court under an obligation to ensure that access has been offered by allowing for a 48-hour delay to the examination and a further 24 hours for any subsequent examination. A previously prepared statement can be declared by the accused provided that the words used are truly his own. **No-one, not even his agent, is allowed to edit the declaration**. No oath is taken by the accused and he cannot be cross examined (Shiels and Bradley, 1996: 48).

The provisions give the procurator fiscal the right to question an accused person, arguably at any time until the trial commences, 'insofar as such questioning is directed towards eliciting any admission, denial, explanation, justification or comment which the accused may have...' (s.36 (1)) as regards 'matters averred in the charge' (s.36(2)). This is subject to certain safeguards. The prosecutor's questioning is restricted to eliciting whether or not the accused will advance any sort of defence or to any extra-judicial confession or admission (to or in the hearing of a police officer), providing that the accused has received a written record of any statement (s.36(3)). The provision at s.36(2) is drafted more broadly than previous legislation and so, as well as generally understood defences of self-defence, alibi, incrimination and consent, it could be argued that temporary insanity, certain forms of automatism, lawful authority or coercion could each equally constitute a defence (Shiels and Bradley, 1996: 50). A number of important procedural points are made about the form of such questions (subsections 2-11).

The procedure for conducting a judicial examination is laid out in s.36 of the CP Act, 1995 and ss.37 and 38 specify the form of the record of proceedings. Additional provisions are found in the *Act of Adjournal (Criminal Procedure Rules) 1996*. In summary these allow direct questioning of the accused; require the Crown to make reasonable inquiry into any defence tendered by an accused; and oblige the sheriff, by way of warning, to inform the accused; for example, if the accused answers any question in such a way as to disclose an ostensible defence, the sheriff has a duty to warn him or her that the prosecutor will investigate that defence.

The role of the defence solicitor is somewhat circumscribed, in so far as he may only consult the accused when advice is sought and only with the permission of the sheriff can he ask the accused a question to clarify some ambiguity in his response or to give the accused an opportunity to answer a question previously refused (s.36(7)). The latter is particularly significant since the introduction, by s.32 of the *Criminal Justice (Scotland) Act,* 1995, of the right of the prosecutor to comment on the accused's failure to give evidence. **In effect the accused can now be asked questions which are directly aimed to achieve his self-incrimination and his refusal to answer can be used against him**. The prosecutor has a limited obligation under s.36(10) to examine any defence disclosed. During the committee stage of the Bill, the Lord Advocate indicated that if the procurator fiscal discovered evidence at this stage which might assist the accused, then it would be the Crown's duty to make the fact known to the defence (*Hansard*, HL. Vol. 560, col. 369 in Shiels and Bradley, 1996:51).

Committal for trial

Either at the first appearance on petition for examination, or after a period allowed for further examination, the accused person will be committed for trial. Thereafter the procurator fiscal will carry on with his investigation of the case and will see witnesses and take their 'precognitions' (statements) as necessary, and will then submit a report to the Crown Office.

If the Crown Office accepts on the basis of this that a trial should proceed, an indictment will be prepared and served on the person, showing at which court and on what date he must appear for trial. Alternatively the Crown Office may instruct the fiscal to proceed with the case on summary procedure, for which no further authority is required. Social workers may see on court lists the designation 'petition reduced to summary' which indicates that a case started life, as it were, on petition with a view to the use of solemn procedure, but that the Crown Office instructed that it should proceed only by way of summary procedure. A further possible outcome is that the Crown Office instructs that no proceedings of any kind should be taken. In this event the person is informed and, if he had been detained in custody, is immediately liberated.

The Criminal Justice (Scotland) Act, 1980 changed the earlier system of setting two diets (dates) for the hearing of any case which did proceed on solemn procedure. The indictment then contained notice of one diet, until 1995 when a further change was made. Mandatory first diets for sheriff and jury cases were introduced by s.13 of the *Criminal Justice (Scotland) Act*, 1995 and are incorporated within the *Criminal Procedure (Scotland) Act*, 1995. Separate provision is made for preliminary diets in High Court cases. Mandatory first diets must be held 'not less than 15 clear days after the service of the indictment and not less than 10 clear days before the trial diet' (s.66(6)). The purpose of this first diet is for the court to 'ascertain whether the case is likely to proceed to trial on the date assigned' (s.71). The provision of s.71 has two objectives; first, to minimise the likelihood of adjournments and cancellation of trials, and second, to restrict the length and expense of trials. The court may postpone the trial and fix a further first diet or adjourn the first diet.

The defence can, if they wish to pursue various legal matters such as the competency or relevancy of matters set out in the indictment, give written notice that a diet is required in order to deal with these. This is known as a 'preliminary diet'. Unlike first diets in sheriff and jury cases, preliminary diets now apply only to the High Court and are not compulsory. A preliminary diet must be held to consider any issue of competency or relevancy but any other reason is at the discretion of the court. At such a diet the court can both postpone the trial (full hearing of all the issues) for up to 21 days and deduct that period from computation of any statutory time-limit. At the end of the preliminary diet the accused person must appear and will be required to indicate the intended plea at that trial. Section 74 regulates appeal procedures both from first diets in the sheriff court and preliminary diets in the High Court.

The position of an accused person committed to trial on solemn procedure is protected by an important provision known colloquially as the '110 day rule'. This rule is regarded as a notable feature of the Scottish legal system to prevent unduly long periods of custodial detention between committal for trial and the actual hearing of the case. The position is set out in section 65 of the *Criminal Procedure (Scotland) Act,* 1995. The current position, introduced by the 1980 Act, is that no accused person shall be tried on **indictment** unless the trial commences **within 12 months** of his or her first appearance on petition and 'failing such commencement within that period, the accused shall be discharged forthwith and thereafter *he shall be for ever free from all question or process for that offence'* (s.65(1)) (as amended—see below).

Because of the wide and unrestricted declaration in section 65(1), it was held in *Gardner v Lees* that the 12-month period applied to cases reduced to summary procedure and that such summary trials had to be concluded within 12 months (Mulholland, 1996). However section 73 of *Criminal Procedure and Investigations Act,* 1996 removed the effect of *Gardner v Lees* on 4 July 1996. Section 73 amended section 65 (1) of the *CP Act*, 1995 by substituting for the words 'shall be discharged forthwith and thereafter he shall be forever free from all question or process for that offence' with

a) shall be discharged forthwith from any indictment as respects the offence; and
b) shall not at any time be proceeded against on indictment as respects the offence

The effect of the amendment is to remove the operation of the 12-month period from cases reduced to summary procedure without affecting the principle for those on indictment.

The relevance of the provision applies to people who have been released on bail at the stages of examination and committal—it ensures some protection for them as well as for those detained in custody. The section does not apply if the person fails to appear for trial and a warrant has to be issued as a result. However the section goes on to state that a person who has been detained at the stage of committal may not be detained for more than:

- 80 days, unless within that period the indictment is served on him, which failing he shall be liberated forthwith; or

- 110 days, unless the trial of the case is commenced within that period, which failing he shall be liberated forthwith and thereafter he shall be for ever free from all question or process for that offence. (s.65(4))

There are various miscellaneous provisions for these periods to be extended in certain circumstances.

Shortened procedure
If a person intends to plead 'guilty' to a charge on solemn procedure, there is provision whereby the hearing of the case can be hastened. This has existed for

some time in Scots law. The provision is currently set out in section 76 of the CP Act, 1995. An accused person may 'intimate in writing' to the Crown Agent an intention to plead guilty to the offence charged in the petition, and a desire to have the case disposed of at once. Thereafter the person is served with an indictment which lacks any list of witnesses or productions. The indictment will show at which court, Sheriff or High, the case will be heard. If in the event the person pleads not guilty, or guilty to parts of the charge such that the fiscal finds the plea unacceptable, then the diet is 'deserted pro loco et tempore' (put off for the time being). The person still remains committed for trial, and the longer procedure will be (re-)initiated. Social workers may, at times, be in a position to advise people of the availability of this procedure. Equally it means that there will be occasions when social enquiry reports may legitimately be written pre-trial, in the full knowledge that the person intends to plead guilty. (See Chapter 5 below).

The trial
A trial in a case on solemn procedure in which the person pleads not guilty will be heard by a Sheriff or a High Court Judge (as the case may be) sitting with a jury. In Scotland a jury consists of 15 persons. The jury's task is to decide questions of fact. The Judge or Sheriff directs the trial and rules on any questions of law. A jury may return a simple majority verdict. It may return one of three verdicts: guilty, not guilty, or not proven. Only the first (guilty) allows the court to proceed to sentence or disposal. It is further open to a jury to find the person guilty of a lesser or alternative charge; or to find the person guilty of only one or more of the total number of charges that may have been included in an indictment.

It can be noted that **in Scotland an accused person has no *right* to a jury trial**: the trial will only involve a jury if the case is heard on solemn procedure, and the person pleads 'Not Guilty'. Also in cases on solemn procedure, even after a guilty verdict, the court can only proceed to sentence if the prosecutor 'moves' for it to do so. As noted earlier, unlike practices in some continental countries, traditionally in Scotland, the prosecutor had no formal interest in sentence. However in recent years, provisions have been introduced for the Lord Advocate and the prosecutor in Scotland, under certain circumstances, to appeal against what he may consider an unduly lenient sentence (see sections 108 and 175 of the CP Act, 1995 and s.23 of the 1997 Act). Traditionally there has been no formal tariff for sentences in the criminal courts in Scotland and the selection of the appropriate sentence or disposal has been clearly a matter for the individual discretion of the judge. These more recent provisions invite the High Court of Justiciary to express an opinion, and in effect to provide a check on sentencing practice (see ss.118(7), 189(7) and 197 of the CP Act, 1995).

Summary procedure
Cases on summary procedure may be heard in either the Sheriff Court or the District Court. There are restrictions on the types and/or severity of cases which can be heard in the District Courts, reflecting their generally lower maximum penalties.

The Lord Advocate may from time to time issue instructions to procurators fiscal about the general distribution of cases as between the two different levels of court. Otherwise, unless a specific statute determines the choice, the discretion lies with the procurator fiscal. Cases can be brought by the procurator fiscal on summary procedure without reference to the specific authority of the Lord Advocate or of the Crown Office.

In general there are no preliminary proceedings in cases on summary procedure comparable with the stages of examination and committal in cases on solemn procedure. However, cases which may have started out with a view to prosecution by the solemn procedure method can be 'reduced to summary', and thus may have been through some preliminary proceedings.

The charge(s) in any case on summary procedure is/are contained in a document known as a **complaint**. A complaint normally proceeds in the name of the local procurator fiscal, not in the name of the Lord Advocate. However section 138 also allows other authorised prosecutors (for example, local education authorities) to initiate proceedings by a complaint. The principal complaint must be signed by the prosecutor.

Where applicable, the complaint should contain any previous convictions to be founded upon by the prosecutor in the event of a conviction. **Previous convictions should not normally be made known to the court until a conviction is recorded either after a plea of guilty from the person, or after a trial which has resulted in conviction**. There are, however, two accepted exceptions to this general rule, namely, where proof of conviction is essential to the proof of the charge (e.g. driving while disqualified) and when the accused has represented himself to be of good character. Social workers may find it useful to establish that the person has a copy of all the relevant documents and understands their content and significance.

If the person has pled guilty by letter, rather than an appearance at court, it is assumed that they accept that the contents of the schedule are true and do apply. However, the person can indicate any objection or error in the schedule as part of the letter pleading guilty. If the person appears in person in court, then they are specifically asked by the court whether these do indeed apply, and there is an opportunity to indicate any disagreement as to the contents, and to resolve the matter. Again, social workers may find that it helps both the person and the court if these matters are raised beforehand and resolution attempted.

A person who is detained in custody after arrest, and who is to be charged on summary procedure will appear before the court on the 'next lawful day'. It should be noted that the police may, after arrest, release the person on his giving an undertaking to appear in court at a certain time on a certain day. Otherwise the person will be **cited** (ordered by letter) to appear at court by the fiscal, and the citation will show the date (diet) of the hearing.

At the first hearing a plea is usually taken. One exception can be that either the prosecution or the defence 'move' the court to **continue without plea**, for some specific reason, which then has to be given, and the issue is decided by the court then and there. If the plea is guilty, no trial of the evidence is needed, and the prosecutor gives such account as is felt necessary to fill out the details of the charge(s). There is no need to 'move' for sentence in cases on summary procedure. After hearing any mitigation by the accused person, or (more usually) by a defence agent, the court is in a position to proceed to sentence or disposal. It is only after guilt has been admitted or proved that any social enquiry report can be considered (see Chapter 4 below).

If an accused person pleads not guilty, or if the plea of guilty as tendered (for example to a lesser or alternative charge) is not acceptable to the prosecution, then a further diet is almost invariably required for a trial to take place. The trial diet will usually be proceeded by an **intermediate diet** (s.148), about two or three months before the trial, for the purposes of establishing the position of the prosecution and the accused and ascertaining whether or not the case is really likely to proceed to trial. This is intended to save court time. It had become practice that where it was evident at the intermediate diet that the trial was un-likely to go ahead, the court, if it felt that the case should continue, could post-pone the trial to a new diet and , if appropriate, fix a further intermediate diet (Shield and Bradley 1996:162).

However it seems there were limitations to this process. In the case of Mackay v. Ruxton (1998 J.C.51) it was held that the requirement of section 148(1) of the CP Act, 1995, as modified by an order under subsection 7, that an intermediate diet should be fixed when the case is adjourned for trial **applied only to the period between the first diet and the trial diet to which the case is adjourned.** 'It is not in dispute that the clear implication of that decision is that section 148(1) does not authorise the fixing of an 'intermediate diet' after the trial diet is adjourned.' Gov-ernment rushed through the *Criminal Procedure (Intermediate Diets)(Scotland) Act*, 1998, with almost immediate effect, to amend the legislation and restore the established practice. 'No-one wanted to see trials being abandoned or convictions quashed on a legal technicality...the Act will restore the validity of decisions taken at intermediate diets which have been taking place...ever since the procedure was first introduced in 1981' (Scottish Home Affairs Minister, 8.4.'98).

Summary trials are not time-barred in the same way as those on solemn proce-dure (see above). The immediate question for the court is on what terms the person will be released, or not, in the meantime. In the event of a not guilty plea in cases on summary procedure, there is no trial involving a jury. The person cannot re-quest a hearing in a higher court in order to obtain a jury hearing. These cases are determined by a sheriff or justice (in District Courts) sitting without a jury—the decision on legal matters and on establishing facts is theirs alone, though lay jus-tices can rely on the advice of a legally qualified clerk. The same verdicts—guilty, not guilty and not proven—are available. Only if the verdict is guilty does the question of disposal arise.

Specimen documentation

A number of documents are in common use in court settings. Some of these, such as lists of previous convictions libelled by the procurator fiscal, will be sent directly to social workers if they are necessary for tasks that social workers are required to perform; others will not. Social workers may be in touch with many people who receive such forms and who will not necessarily be familiar with their significance. Explanation and information can be a real help, and there may be opportunity to help the person avoid falling foul of the law through ignorance or apathy (for example, by reducing the risk that warrants may be taken out for their arrest as a consequence of not attending court when required). Equally the social worker's broader task of functioning within the criminal justice system is assisted, and the worker's credibility with other professionals in the system is enhanced, if a working knowledge of the documents is obtained and displayed in action. The following specimen documentation is provided below:

a) petition
b) indictment
c) complaint (common law example)
d) complaint (statutory offence example)

a) Petition

UNTO THE HONOURABLE THE SHERIFF OF THE LOTHIAN AND BORDERS, EDINBURGH

1 December 1998

The petition of GEORGE SMITH
Procurator Fiscal of Court of BLACKTOWN for the Public Interest:
HUMBLY SHEWETH
That from information received by the Petitioner, it appears, and he accordingly charges, that STEVEN JAMES, (born 30.10.60), 49, Philip Street, Blacktown—at present in custody—you did on 30th November, 1998, in the premises at 50 Jericho Lane, Blacktown, assault Michael Redpath, hit him on the head with a broken glass whereby he sustained multiple lacerations, jump on him, kick him, and repeatedly hit him about the head and body with your fists, all to his severe injury.

Signed . . . .
Procurator Fiscal Depute

In order, therefore, that the said accused may be dealt with according to Law,
May it please your Lordship to grant Warrant to Officers of Law to search for and apprehend the said Accused
STEVEN JAMES
and meantime, if necessary, to detain him in a police station, house, or other convenient place and to bring him for examination respecting the premises: and thereafter grant Warrant to imprison him within the prison of EDINBURGH therein to be detained until liberated in due course of law: Further, to grant Warrant to search the person, repositories, and domicile of the said Accused, and the house or premises in which he may be found, and to secure, for the purpose of precognition and evidence, all writs, evidence, and articles found therein tending to establish guilt or participation in the crime aforesaid, and for that purpose to make patent all shut and lockfast places; and also to grant Warrant to cite Witnesses for precognition, and to

make production for the purposes foresaid of such writs, evidents, and articles pertinent to the case as are in their possession: to grant the Warrant of Concurrence necessary for enforcing that of your Lordship within their respective territories; or to do further or otherwise as your Lordship may seem meet.

According to Justice, &c
Procurator Fiscal Depute.

b) Indictment

BY AUTHORITY OF HER MAJESTY'S ADVOCATE

Signed . . . .
Procurator Fiscal

STEVEN JAMES, (born 30.10.60), prisoner in the prison of Edinburgh, you are indicted at the instance of the Right Honourable . . . . , Her Majesty's Advocate, and the Charge against you is that you did on 30th November, 1998, in the premises at 50, Jericho Lane, Blacktown, assault Michael Redpath, hit him on the head with a broken glass whereby he sustained multiple lacerations, jump on him, kick him, and repeatedly hit him about the head and body with your fists, all to his severe injury.

List of Productions

1. Glass
2. Photographs of injury to Michael Redpath

List of Witnesses

1. Michael Redpath, 50, Jericho Lane, Blacktown
2. Philip Redpath, 50, Jericho Lane, Blacktown
3. Wendy Redpath, 50, Jericho Lane, Blacktown
4. Dr James North, M.B. St James Hospital, Blacktown
5. Police Constable A 93, Ronald MacDuff
6. Police Constable A 32, David Campbell

Schedule of previous convictions

STEVEN JAMES, take notice that in the event of your being committed under the indictment to which this notice is attached, it is intended to place before the Court the undernoted previous conviction applying to you.

Date	Place of Trial	Court	Offence	Sentence
18.12.95	Blacktown	District	Theft	Fined

c) Complaint

i) common law crime example

Under the *Criminal Procedure (Scotland) Act* 1995

In the Sheriff Court of Seatown

The COMPLAINT of the PROCURATOR FISCAL against

Joe Smith   Date of Birth: 14.10.60

The charge against you is that

on 5th August, 1998, at the premises in Hillhall St., Seatown occupied by F.W. Beans and Co you did steal £10 of money

Signed . . . .
Procurator Fiscal Depute

Diet

Apprehension and Search

(date) The Court grants Warrant to apprehend the said Accused and grants warrant to search the person, dwelling house, and repositories of said Accused and any place where they may be found and to take possession of the property mentioned or referred to in the Complaint and all articles and documents likely to afford evidence of guilt or of guilty participation.

Signed ....
Sheriff

ii) statutory offence example

Under the *Criminal Procedure (Scotland) Act, 1995*

In the Sheriff Court of Seatown

The COMPLAINT of the PROCURATOR FISCAL against

Joe Smith, Date of Birth: 14.10.60

The charge against you is that

on 17th September, 1998, on a road, other public place, namely Blank Square, Whiteville, you did, drive a motor vehicle, namely Ford Escort ABC 123 after consuming so much alcohol that the proportion of it in your breath was 100 micrograms of alcohol in 100 millilitres of breath which exceeded the prescribed limit namely 35 micro-grams of alcohol in 100 millilitres of breath

Contrary to the Road Traffic Act, 1988, s 5(1)(a).

Signed ....
Procurator Fiscal Depute

Diet

5 November, 1998. The Court assigns 18 December 1998, at 10.00 a.m. within the Sheriff Court House, Seatown, as a Diet in this case.

Signed ....
Clerk of Court

Notes:

i)   in both types of complaint there is likely to be a schedule of previous convictions if such applied; and

ii) in the second type (statutory offence) there would also be a notice of penalty (see text above) showing what the maximum penalties specific to section 5(1)(a) of the Road Traffic Act, 1988, were.

PROSECUTION AUTHORITIES

The prosecuting authorities are not only responsible for decisions about whether and how to prosecute, but they also have to arrange, in co-operation with the clerks of the various courts, for the ordering of court business and the preparation of court lists. The prosecutor is termed the 'master of the instance' and is in charge of the presentation of any case, up to and including the point at which guilt or otherwise is determined. During the progress of a case, he may have to decide matters such as: whether a plea of guilty to a reduced charge is acceptable; whether to ask that a person is remanded in custody, and whether to appeal against the granting of bail if such is the court's decision; how much information about the person's individual circumstances to give; whether to apply for forfeiture of items such as weapons and/or drugs that may have been involved in a case; whether to take issue with any comments in a social enquiry report which appear to contradict evidence in his possession; and so on.

Solemn procedure

People who are charged on petition, that is, with a view to prosecution on solemn procedure, first appear before the sheriff either in Chambers, or in closed court. Members of the public are not present; neither are social workers, unless present in loco parentis of a child, in respect of whom the local authority has parental responsibilities under the *Children (Scotland) Act,* 1995. Court duty social workers, or social workers supervising the person on probation, community service, or a prison licence are not usually present at this stage of proceedings on solemn procedure. The press can only report that a person appeared on petition, and what the outcome was. In the case of a child, they must not publish any information which may lead to the identification of the child, except under circumstances outlined in s.47(3) of the CP Act, 1995.

At this first appearance for examination, two outcomes are possible:

a) the prosecutor may ask the court to 'commit for further examination', and may make a motion as to whether the committal should be in custody. If a person is to be detained in custody for further examination, the maximum period of that detention is eight days. The fiscal does have the right to bring the person back to court before the eight days have expired and in practice usually does so seven days later. The period of eight days can only be used once. This short period allows for a preliminary report to be submitted to the Crown Office or for further enquiries. At the subsequent hearing, after this committal for further examination, the fiscal must either move for 'full committal', or reduce the matter to a summary complaint and proceed accordingly, OR,

b) the prosecutor may ask the court to 'fully commit' the person for trial, and may make a motion as to whether that committal should be in custody. One implication of a motion to fully commit is that the fiscal considers the investigations are sufficiently far advanced as to provide sufficient 'prima facie' evidence to justify the use of solemn procedure; and that the prior authority of Crown Counsel may already have been sought for the use of this procedure. The restrictions noted above on the period within which any trial must begin are calculated from the moment of full committal.

A person who is released on bail for further examination does not necessarily have to make a further appearance for full committal, and the Crown Office can simply go straight ahead with the preparation of an indictment to proceed on solemn procedure, OR instruct the fiscal to prepare and serve a summary complaint.

One further possible outcome after either committal for trial, or for further examination, is that the decision is not to proceed with the case at all, by either method. In this event, the person is liberated from custody, or released from the obligations of bail, as the case may be. There are various permutations about the respective rights of the accused person and of the prosecutor to appeal decisions made by the court about bail in these early stages of solemn procedure.

a) At the stage of committal for further examination, the accused person may apply for bail. If the court refuses bail, the person cannot appeal against that refusal. If the court grants bail, the prosecutor can appeal against that decision, and the person remains in custody until the appeal can be dealt with by a High Court Judge sitting in chambers. In view of the short time period involved (maximum eight days) many people do not apply for bail at this stage.

b) At the stage of full committal, irrespective of what may have happened at any previous stage of examination, the person may apply for bail. If the court refuses bail at this stage, the person can now appeal against that decision, and have the matter determined by a High Court Judge sitting in chambers. The prosecutor still has the right, at the stage of full committal, to appeal against a decision of the Sheriff to grant bail, and, again, the person remains in custody if the prosecutor does so appeal. However, if the High Court decides the matter in favour of giving the person bail, the prosecutor cannot appeal against that decision.

All these appearances at the preliminary stages of solemn procedure take place in private.

Summary procedure

The cases of people charged on summary procedure can start life in a number of ways:

a) the person may be kept in custody after arrest, and appear in court on the next lawful day, the police having decided not to use the procedure of allowing release on a written undertaking; or

b) the person may have been in custody for up to 8 days, having originally been charged on petition with a view to prosecution on solemn procedure, but with that person having been reviewed; or

c) the person may have been arrested by the police and released on a written undertaking by him to appear on a particular date—in this event he is responsible for making his own way to court, and he will there be served with the complaint;

d) the person might not have been arrested but told that the facts would be reported with a view to prosecution, and have subsequently received a citation requiring attendance to answer a charge(s); or

e) the citation might have allowed that the person need not necessarily attend the court, but use the option of writing a letter in the first instance indicating his response to the charge(s). In this situation, if the court decides that attendance in person is necessary, it will need to continue the case in order to allow for this to happen, and the person will be sent a letter ordaining (ordering) him to appear. It can be noted, for example, that a person is only very exceptionally disqualified from driving in his absence.

A person who fails to attend, having been cited or ordained so to do, renders himself liable to a warrant for his arrest as a result. There is also the danger that the failure will be regarded as contempt of court, and attract additional penalty as a result.

The court hearing

Once the court is assembled, the cases are 'called' at the instance of the prosecutor, usually by the Clerk of Court, or a bar officer, or by a police officer assigned to court duties. Calling simply involves naming the person whose case is to be heard, and if necessary shouting his name around the court precincts. In cases on solemn procedure, the calling is usually prefaced with 'Her Majesty's Advocate against…', but in cases on summary procedure the name alone is used.

Once the person is before the court, the clerk identifies him and ascertains that he is the person whose name has been called. Following identification, a solicitor or agent may indicate that he appears on behalf of the person. If the accused is not represented, he is asked if he has received a copy of the complaint and understands the charge(s). In cases on solemn procedure the plea is likely to be known in advance, in view of the facility (under section 76 of the CP Act, 1995) for those wishing to plead guilty to have the case hastened, and the court business will have been arranged accordingly.

In cases on summary procedure it cannot usually be known in advance what the plea will be, unless the person has written in and then been required to attend. If the plea is not guilty, it is usually necessary to fix another date for a full hearing of the evidence and the issues, and the only matter to be resolved is whether the person will be in custody or at liberty in the interim. In cases where the plea is guilty, further hearings only become necessary if the court's decision in regard to sentence requires it—for example, because reports are needed prior to sentence, or because the decision is to defer sentence for a specific purpose. At the conclusion of the hearing of any case, the Clerk of Court will confirm the court's decision by re-announcing the decision, and ensuring that the accused has heard and understood what was said.

Three other miscellaneous matters can usefully be mentioned under the heading of proceedings in court.

1. **The possibility of having offences 'taken into consideration'** (often colloquially referred to as 't.i.c.'), along with a main or substantive charge, which is available in England and Wales, **is not accepted in Scotland**. Any offences admitted, if they are substantiated and corroborated, have to be separately charged. One consequence of this, particularly for young offenders recently discharged from the children's hearings system, can be an involvement in a series of different cases, in respect of different charges, each of which has a life of its own, with hearings overlapping. Those who are familiar with the workings of the courts can use this complexity to their advantage. Others who are less mature can become even more confused, missing important hearings with attendant risks of breaching bail, and being arrested on warrant as a result.

2. One motion open to a prosecutor is to ask the court to 'continue without plea'. Such a continuation cannot exceed 3 weeks duration. The continuation may

involve the accused either being in custody or at liberty, in accordance with the ordinary procedures for making that decision. A motion of this kind can reflect matters such as: further inquiries into the charge being necessary; other cases pending; or even the need to inquire into his fitness to enter a plea to the charge, with consequent need for medical assessment. On occasion a similar motion can be made by the defence. Whoever makes the motion, the request can be resisted, and the court may need to determine the issue before the case can proceed further.

3. A further motion open to a prosecutor is to apply for a case to be 'deserted'. Cases may either be deserted 'pro loco et tempore' (for the time being); or deserted 'simpliciter'. In the first instance the charge(s) can be reinstated in future proceedings: in the second they cannot.

BAIL

A great many cases cannot be dealt within their entirety at one hearing, particularly at their first 'calling'. The main procedure used to ensure a person's appearance at subsequent hearings or diets is release on bail, unless the person is to be detained in custody. Other than the system of bail, the only way that a person could retain their liberty between hearings was the system of **ordaining** them to appear; a limitation of this system was that if the person did not appear when ordained to, the maximum penalty that could be exacted of them for this failure—and that after the event—was £10. The system of ordaining to appear is still in existence alongside the provisions for bail.

The system of bail is set out in the *Bail Etc. (Scotland) Act,* 1980 as amended by the *Criminal Justice (Scotland) Act*, 1995 and now consolidated in the *Criminal Procedure (Scotland) Act,* 1995. Before the 1980 Act the system of bail required that the person was kept in custody until a sum of money was lodged with the court. The 1980 Act removed the need to lodge money as a standard condition.

The purpose of 1980 Act was to minimise the number of people held in custody for first court appearance, for trial or for sentence. However between 1981 and 1985 annual figures for remand receptions rose by over 40% in Scotland. During this period Lord Wheatley set out principles (sometime known as the Wheatley guidelines) for interpreting bail legislation which identified exceptions to the presumption in favour of bail. A downward trend in remand receptions began. From around 1985 until 1992 when figures started to rise again. Scottish Office research indicated that with regard to the Wheatley guidelines there 'is presently a gap in understanding about bail between the High Court and those in the lower courts and a lack of communication about the reason for High Court decisions is contributing to this' (Paterson and Whittaker, 1994: xxxii).

In 1992, fuelled by findings of police research in England and Wales, which argued that the figures reflected significant levels of bail abuse and that the English *Bail Act* (1976) as amended, had fallen into disrepute, considerable press attention was given to the threat posed to the public by those released on bail. The Scottish Office research indicated that the operation of bail is a 'subject about which there is much speculation and little systematic information'. It concluded that 'the problem of a high level of recorded offending while on bail, which is sometime taken to be an indication of the court's failure to remand those who are involved in serious repeat offending, has been found in this study to be a consequence of the way in which bail is used in a locality'(p. xii); in other words more a function of the police use of the system than an indicator of bail abuse.

The *Bail Etc. (Scotland) Act* 1980 legislates the procedure for bail. Unlike the 1976 Act in England and Wales, it does not seek to define any 'right' to bail, or the circumstances in which detention in custody is justified. Previous legislation had provided that all crimes except murder and treason were bailable, in principle. Section 26 of the CP Act, 1995 (derived from s.3 of the *Criminal Justice (Scotland) Act,* 1995) extended the list of circumstances which are not bailable. Bail must be refused in cases of attempted murder, culpable homicide, rape or attempted rape, if the accused already has a conviction for murder, manslaughter or one of the four above-mentioned crimes (Shiels and Bradley, 1996: 42). Conviction for this purpose includes not guilty by reason of insanity and conviction resulting in a probation order, or discharge absolutely or conditionally.

Appeals
Decisions about bail can be appealed against, both by the person charged and also by the prosecutor. Section 31 allows the prosecutor to apply to the court to reconsider a decision to grant bail. Application must be made on the basis of information relevant to the decision to grant bail which was not available to the court when the decision was taken. Bail appeals are dealt with by the High Court, usually by a Judge sitting in chambers to hear them. Section 112(3) contains an '**exceptional circumstances rule**' which allows the High Court to admit an appellant to bail pending determination of an appeal, providing the appellant has shown 'cause'. This is subject to the limitation set out in section 26 (Shiels and Bradley, 1996:134).

Standard conditions
Section 24(5) of the CP Act, 1995 contains the standard conditions which are to be imposed: 'that the accused

a) appears at the appointed time at every diet relating to the offence with which he is charged of which he is given due notice;
b) does not commit an offence while on bail;
c) does not interfere with witnesses or otherwise obstruct the course of justice whether in relation to himself or any other person; and
d) makes himself available for the purpose of enabling enquiries or a report to be made to assist the court in dealing with him for the offence with which he is charged.'

The *Criminal Procedure (Scotland) Act,* 1995 also specifically provides for the imposition of other necessary conditions to ensure that the standard conditions are observed and that 'the accused makes himself available for the purpose of participating in an identification parade or of enabling any print, impression or sample to be taken from him' (s.24(4)(b)). The Act neither limits nor lists the range of conditions which can be imposed in pursuit of these objectives. A condition of residence in a bail or other hostel, if one exists, or a place is available, would be entirely competent within the provisions of the Act.

Money Conditions

Although the main objective of the 1980 Act was to replace the system of 'money bail' as the normal one, s.24(6) of the CP Act, 1995 maintains a provision 'that the accused or a cautioner on his behalf deposits a sum of money in court, but only where the court or, as the case may be, the Lord Advocate is satisfied that the imposition of such condition is appropriate to the special circumstances of the case'. Section 29 of the CP Act, 1995 specifies the circumstances in which any money deposited can be ordered to be forfeited. Normally compliance with all the conditions of bail enables the person who deposited the money to reclaim it at the end of the proceedings. If the person fails to appear the prosecutor may move that the money be forfeited, but the court may, 'if it is satisfied that it is reasonable to do so in all the circumstances' (s.29(2)), direct that the money forfeited be refunded. The court's decision is final and is not subject to review.

If the person fails to observe any of the conditions of bail, the money can only be forfeited on the motion of the prosecutor where the person is convicted of the specific offence of breach of bail. For example, a person who turns up for trial but does not make himself available for reports can only lose his (or strictly his cautioner's) money if he is prosecuted for the specific offence of not making himself available. In the event of a prosecution for breach of bail, the cautioner can still recover the money if

a) the charge is not proceeded with; or
b) the person is acquitted of the charge; or
c) on the accused's conviction of the offence, the court has determined not to order forfeiture of the sum deposited (s.29(4)).

Procedures

The *Criminal Procedure (Scotland) Act,* 1995 requires that the person is given a copy of the bail order, which shows all the conditions, and any others that have been added. The order also shows an address, known as the 'proper domicile of citation', which is the address at which any documents relating to the case can be served on the person. If there is a change of address whilst on bail, application has to be made to the court in writing for the 'domicile of citation' shown on the bail order to be changed. Failure to do so can result in the person becoming liable to penalties for breach of bail.

Breach

An important principle established by the *Bail Etc. (Scotland) Act,* 1980 was that failure to appear on the due date after being released, or failure to comply with any of the conditions of bail, constitutes a criminal offence. Where the accused, in failing to comply with any condition, has committed a further offence, known as a 'subsequent offence', providing the offence is libelled in the indictment or specified in the compliant, the court will 'have regard' to the fact that it was committed while on bail and the number of bail orders to which the accused was subject and any previous convictions. The penalties for breach of bail can be added to whatever is imposed for the original offence, even if the total penalty exceeds the powers normally available to the court. Where the maximum penalty for a subsequent offence is specified by law, it can be increased

a) where it is a fine, by the amount for the time being equivalent to level 3 on the standard scale; and
b) where it is a period of imprisonment
   (i) as respects a conviction in the High Court or the Sheriff Court, by 6 months; and
   (ii) as respects a conviction in the District Court, by 60 days. (s.27(5))

In cases on solemn procedure, where the accused fails to appear, the maximum penalties are:

a) unlimited fine; and
b) imprisonment for a period not exceeding 2 years.

Section 28 goes on to add breach of bail to the list of those offences for which a person can be arrested without warrant, if the police officer considers that the person is 'likely to break any condition imposed on his bail'. Where a person is arrested for this reason, he has to be brought where practicable before the court to which the application for bail was first made. In this event the powers of the court are to:

- recall the order granting bail (thus sending the person to custody); or
- release the accused under the original order granting bail; or
- vary the order granting bail by imposing extra or alternative conditions.

However, the person has the same rights of appeal against the decision as against the original order of the court granting bail.

Reports
The CP Act, 1995 also makes specific provision about the release of people for both social enquiry and medical reports. The Act allows a person to appeal against being remanded in custody for reports, a possibility that was not previously available. One very practical implication of this for social workers is that they may receive information that a person has been remanded in custody for reports, but the person may have been able to appeal successfully against the custodial aspect of the remand in the meantime, without the social worker knowing about the appeal. Checking that the person is actually in a particular prison before setting off is a sensible precaution.

In view of the fact that breach of bail is a criminal offence, failure to 'make oneself available' for reports can result in prosecution. Social work administrative arrangements need to be able to generate the required standard of evidence (for example, maintenance of correspondence, and records of office visits by receptionists) necessary as a basis for any subsequent prosecution. The law treats breach of bail seriously, and strengthens the social worker's power and authority in seeking the availability of people for reports that the courts have ordered.

Young offenders, especially those between 16 and 18, many of whom may have had recent involvement in the children's hearing system, may be particularly at risk of breaching bail, since they are often involved in a series of offences leading to separate appearances, and are at risk of early custody. It is important for social workers to be vigilant about local police practices, where bail breaches may be seen as an effective way of getting difficult young people off the streets, whether or not the seriousness of the offences merit it. The importance of making good bail advice available to the offender, where this is possible, cannot be over stressed.

Bail information and support

A major non-legal change in the bail system in recent years has been the introduction of Bail Information Schemes. The idea of an independent agency offering courts verified information about defendants being considered for bail originated in New York in 1960. The system was adapted for use in a Home Office experiment in co-operation with Inner London Probation Service in 1975. Many studies noted the need for support facilities, including supervision and hostel accommodation, especially for young offenders (Williams, 1992:23).

The concept re-emerged in the late 1980s and pilot schemes were initiated in Scotland. NOS note that in 1995 the Scottish Office commissioned two local authorities to participate in an extended pilot project to develop bail information and supervision services. These seek to provide additional verified information to procurators fiscal on the circumstances of accused persons where bail is initially opposed. The intention of the scheme is that where relevant information can be verified, it may allay the specific concerns of fiscals or the court and result in the release of the accused on bail; and where the accused is granted bail and attends court as required, the likelihood that they will receive a non-custodial sentence **may be** increased. Similarly the offer of bail supervision in certain cases may enable the court to release the offender on bail. The practice of bail supervision is relatively recent in Scotland. The provision of such services is not without its dilemmas and reports on the evaluation of these schemes are awaited with interest.

Bail applications

The *Bail Etc. (Scotland) Act,* 1980 lifted the previous requirement on criminal courts to sit on a Saturday. It also gave Sheriffs Principal the power to determine court holidays, up to a maximum of 10 days, in the various districts of the sheriffdom, with a residual power for the business of criminal courts to be conducted on any day if necessary. The main practical implication of the provision is its effect on what the 'next lawful day' may be—for example, where a person is arrested on a Friday afternoon after court has risen, and on a bank holiday weekend.

Examples

Joe Campbell is arrested on a Friday afternoon for stealing a motor car. It is a bank holiday weekend, and there is no court due to sit until the following Tuesday. If the police feel unable to liberate him, he will be detained in custody until Tuesday morning, without any opportunity to appeal, or recompense if the court subsequently liberates him on the Tuesday. Alternatively, the police may liberate him on a written undertaking to appear at the Sheriff Court on the following Tuesday. If, on the Tuesday, the procurator fiscal decides not to proceed with the case, Campbell will be: liberated from custody if he had been detained; or freed from the effects of the written undertaking. However, if he is freed on a written undertaking on the Friday, but fails to appear at court on the Tuesday morning, the procurator fiscal will obtain a warrant for his arrest on a charge of breach of his written undertaking to appear. Later that Tuesday afternoon, the police succeed in arresting Campbell, and hold him in custody to appear before the Sheriff Court on the Wednesday morning. If he is found guilty of both the theft of the motor car, and of the breach of the undertaking, the court could eventually sentence him to 6 months in custody for the theft, and 3 months custody consecutively for breaching the undertaking, even though the total sentence thus effected (9 months custody) is in excess of the powers normally available to the Sheriff Court hearing cases on summary procedure.

John MacLean, who is arrested along with Campbell, is 17 years old, but technically a 'child' by virtue of being under the supervision of the Children's Hearing. The police release him on the Friday evening on a written undertaking signed by both MacLean and his father to attend court the following Tuesday. If MacLean fails to appear, both he and his father become liable to the penalties for breaching the undertaking, in addition to whatever penalty is imposed on MacLean for his part in the offence.

Angus Ferguson, who is arrested along with Campbell and MacLean, is charged with causing death by reckless driving, and a number of other traffic offences. (He drove the stolen car, and killed a pedestrian, when a number of police officers tried to stop his progress.) It is accepted that Campbell and MacLean only participated in the original theft, and had no idea of Ferguson's future actions. Ferguson is detained in custody until the following Tuesday morning, and appears before the Sheriff in private on petition, with a view to prosecution by solemn procedure. The procurator fiscal opposes bail, but the sheriff grants it with three extra conditions: that he resides in a bail hostel; and that he lodges £100 with the court; and that a cautioner on his behalf also lodges caution of £100 with the court.

Both Ferguson and the cautioner lodge the money, but 24 hours later he absconds from the bail hostel. Some weeks later, Ferguson is arrested by the police and brought before the sheriff. In the meantime the case has been reported to the Crown Office, and an indictment has been prepared charging him with the offences and requiring him to appear at the High Court. The sheriff recalls the bail order and he is detained in prison. However, he is successful in appealing against this, and a High Court Judge hearing the matter in chambers allows him out on bail on the original terms, until the hearing of the trial in the High Court. He duly turns up at the High Court and pleads guilty to all charges. Ferguson can now be sentenced by the High Court (the necessary reports having been obtained) as follows:

- sentence for the substantive offence (the death);
- up to 5 years custody, which could be served consecutively, for the breach of bail, i.e. absconding from the bail hostel;
- forfeiture of both his own £100, and that of his cautioner.

Even supposing he had pled not guilty to the main charge, and had been acquitted of it, he could still be dealt with for the breach of bail, assuming that charge had been added to the indictment.

LEGAL AID IN CRIMINAL CASES

The provision of legal aid and assistance in criminal cases is now widely accepted, and viewed as something of a normal right. Although a system of free legal aid for the poor can be traced back to the 15th century, the basis of present provision is the *Legal Aid (Scotland) Act,* 1986.

The provision of legal aid derives from the principle that, in cases where in the interest of justice, legal representation should be provided, and the accused is too poor to afford it, it should be provided from public funds. This is shown, for example, by sections 23(1) and 24(1) of the 1986 Act: 'legal aid in criminal proceedings shall be available to an accused person where the court is satisfied, after consideration of the accused person's financial circumstances, that the expenses of the case cannot be met without undue hardship to him or his dependants'. It is important to note that legal aid is not necessarily a matter of absolute entitlement and the court has significant discretion. Criminal legal aid is available for advice and assistance, under certain circumstances, and for prosecutions brought in the district, sheriff and high courts including appeals from all courts. A duty solicitor can also represent people appearing at identification parades.

Legal aid is initially available automatically to all those who find themselves in custody on a criminal charge and who are not otherwise represented. At every district and sheriff court a duty solicitor (on a rota) is available to advise and represent people held in custody at their first appearance in court. It is not always appreciated by accused persons that this representation does not automatically extend to the rest of the case, whatever the outcome. If an accused person pleads guilty at the first hearing to one or more charges, the duty solicitor will make a statement in mitigation, and would also attend again in the event of the case being continued—for example, for a social enquiry report. There is no other provision for legal aid in these circumstances. However, if the plea is one of not guilty to one or more charges, the accused person needs to make a specific and separate application for legal aid if he wishes it during the rest of the case, even if he is held in custody until the next hearing. Also, those who are released after apprehension and then are cited to appear need to make an application for legal aid if they wish to be represented.

In cases taken under solemn procedure the granting of legal aid is a matter for the court. The court must be satisfied after consideration of financial circumstances that the expenses of the case cannot be met without undue hardship to the accused or dependants. It is also for the court to decide to grant legal aid where a person who has not previously been sentenced to imprisonment or detention has been convicted in summary proceedings and the court is considering a sentence of imprisonment or detention.

In all other summary cases legal aid may be available through the Scottish Legal Aid Board (SLAB) or assistance by way of representation (ABWOR). The clerk of court or the duty solicitor should be able to provide applications forms, which must be submitted within 14 days of the first court appearance.

Most people served with a summary complaint are not in custody. Legal advice and assistance may be available from a solicitor depending on financial circumstances. If the intention is to plead not guilty to some or all of the charges, at first appearance, an application to SLAB can be made **after** the plea. Criminal legal aid, if granted, will not cover the initial appearance although arrangements can be made for a written plea using advice and assistance.

Assistance by way of representation (ABWOR) allows a solicitor, in certain circumstances, to represent a person not in custody who intends to plead guilty or having made a not guilty plea, now intends to change the plea. Apart from guilty pleas ABWOR may also be available for some other criminal matters, subject to financial eligibility.

It should be noted that section 35 of the 1986 Act makes it an offence for any person seeking or receiving legal aid or advice and assistance to knowingly make a false statement or representation. A person found guilty of this offence will be liable, on summary conviction, to a fine not exceeding level 4 on the standard scale or to imprisonment for a term not exceeding 60 days, or both.

Criminal legal aid is NOT available in respect of the children's hearing system. It is possible to obtain legal advice and assistance about any children's hearing matter, and to qualify for legal aid in regard to that advice or assistance, but it is not possible to obtain legal aid to be legally represented at a children's hearing. However, in the event of a ground of referral being referred to a court for proof or in the case of any appeal, legal aid may be granted

Consideration of legal aid also varies according to the type of procedure being used i.e. solemn or summary. In summary cases both main considerations namely, can the person afford it and is representation necessary in the interests of justice, apply, and the court has to consider both. However, in cases on solemn procedure, the only question relates to the person's financial circumstances. Where an application to SLAB is refused there is a right to ask for the decision to be reviewed. If the court refuses legal aid, there is no appeal against that refusal.

Legal aid is also available in criminal cases in the event of an accused person wishing to appeal against conviction. As always, the usual financial considerations apply, but in this instance the Scottish Legal Aid Board has to be satisfied that there are substantial grounds for the appeal, and that the granting of legal aid is reasonable.

The theme of finance is clearly a recurring one. *The Legal Aid and Assistance (Financial Considerations) Regulations* govern this issue, and set out the criteria. The regulations made under the 1986 Act stipulate two basic criteria:

- persons whose disposable income does not exceed a stated amount (and that would be one of the matters for discussion with a solicitor), or
- persons in receipt, either directly or indirectly, of DSS benefits or family income supplement, and
- in either case, having limited disposable capital, as defined by the Regulations.

Where legal aid has been granted, the person concerned is regarded as eligible in connection with most subsequent proceedings arising from the case, including guidance as to the advisability of an appeal. The potential demands on the scheme are thus considerable, and thus the issue of how the interests of justice are defined is crucial to practice. Whereas the financial criteria are regularly updated and are publicly available, the interests of justice criterion is much more complex and a good deal less tangible.

The *Crime and Punishment (Scotland) Act,* 1997 has provision under sections 49-54 for radical changes to the legal aid system to ensure more efficient use and accountability of the public funds involved. It proposes a register for solicitors providing criminal legal aid subject to supervision by SLAB and a new code of practice. More radically, it proposes powers for the Board to employ and/or contract specific solicitors to offer criminal legal aid. Two pilot projects are underway in Glasgow and Edinburgh to evaluate the benefits of an American-style **Public Defender scheme.**

At present if legal aid is granted, the person may nominate a solicitor of his choice to represent him, and may indicate such a nomination on the application. The duty solicitor scheme, however, is run on a rota basis. Social workers may frequently be in contact either with duty solicitors at the early stages of a case, or subsequently with individual solicitors at stages such as the consideration of a social enquiry report. In that solicitors very clearly have an advocacy role in relation to any person that they may represent, their concerns will converge with that part of a social worker's duty which involves the giving of advice and assistance of benefit to the person. The social worker also has duties to the court, and to society at large, and good practice involves consideration being given to the matter of confidentiality in respect of information that the worker may subsequently impart to the court.

POLICE POWERS

Legal safeguards

The importance of social workers understanding police procedures and the legal basis of police powers, together with the statutory limitations imposed, should be self-evident. This is a complex area since historically police have had wide ranging powers under common law. Over the years these have increasingly been defined within statute, partly for clarification and partly for reasons of accountability. Situations can arise for social workers which 'test' their understanding of police powers; for example, people allege that they have not been treated 'fairly', or allege to the social worker in the process of an SER that they have been ill-treated by interviewing police officers, and variations on this theme. These statements or allegations cannot simply be ignored, nor, equally, should these statements be regarded simply as factual. Without some knowledge of the procedures the social worker is poorly placed either to assist the accused, or to act responsibly as an agent of the administration of justice.

The right to silence

The privilege against self-incrimination is an old one and almost universally recognised in Western legal systems (the most famous example being the Fifth Amendment to the U.S. Constitution). Generally it has become almost axiomatic that in a criminal case any defender has a right to silence beyond entering a plea to the stated charge. At one time silence was enforced. There was an assumption that by silence the accused was indicating that he had nothing to prove and that the onus of proof lay with the prosecution. As the system developed procedural rules were established. The codification of cautions at the point of arrest and charge became necessary and eventually found expression in the familiar 'you are going to be asked questions about (description of crime). You are not bound to answer but if you do your answers will be noted and may be used in evidence. Do you understand?'

In this there are many grey areas, as *Greeawald* (1974: 247) commented 'in both England and the United States most observers believe that there are substantial failures by the police to comply with rules protecting silence...Suspects may be invited, in rather strong terms "to help the police with their enquiries"...the police may invent damaging admissions...or obtain actual confession by using impermissible methods that are later denied in court...'. The *Criminal Justice and Public Order Act,* 1994 in England intended to provide judges with a mechanism, whereby they could comment on the weight of evidence as opposed to the statements of the accused.

Historically, matters in Scotland have been handled somewhat differently. 'Scots law on this matter has proceeded not so much on any fundamental constitutional or philosophic basis, such as the privilege against self-incrimination, as on a conception of fairness and a determination by the courts to control police activity in the interests of fairness' (Thomson Committee, 1975, para. 7.02). In Scotland the right to silence has always been considered 'a sacred and inviolable principle...zealously protected by the common law, even in the face of apparently contradictory statutory provision. At common law there is no duty to answer police questions' (Ewing and Finnie, 1988:123). However legislation in the 1990s has attempted to introduce significant changes into the organisation and operation of police practice paralleling changes south of the Border.

The police in Scotland are a civilian service, currently organised on a geographical and regional basis under joint local police committees representing the constituent local authorities, e.g. Highlands and Islands are one force, as are the authorities within Lothian and Borders area. The *Police (Scotland) Act* 1967 regulates the governance of the police under a tripartite arrangement involving the Secretary of State, local police committees and the Chief Constable. The 1967 model created a relationship which, though fraught with tensions, emphasised local accountability and professional independence.

Far-reaching changes were introduced, with little public discussion, to the organisation of the police in Scotland via the *Police and Magistrates' Courts Act*, 1994. While the bulk of the Act deals with England and Wales, it has all the worst features of such legislation, introducing significant changes to Scotland in the absence of a transparent consultation and policy process. Part II (ss.47-65), most of which came into force on 1 January, 1995 (*Police and Magistrate's Court Act 1994 (Commencement No 4 and Transitional Provisions) (Scotland) Order 1994 (SI 1994/3075)*), contains various amendments and additions to the *Police (Scotland) Act* 1967 which continues to regulate the constitutional position of the police in Scotland. The provisions display a move towards greater involvement of central government in the operation of the police and a move towards establishing national objectives and standard indicators. These changes emerged from two key policy documents—the Sheehy inquiry in *Police Responsibilities and Rewards* (Cm 2280), which included Scotland, and the White Paper on *Police Reform* (Cm 2281), which did not.

Chief Constables have operational power over manpower, but not resources. The police authority's role has been reduced, in particular with regard to police policy. It has been suggested that the resulting changes create a peculiar hybrid of the previous Scottish and current English models, shifting the balance of accountability, while reinforcing many of the tensions and uncertainties of the 1967 model (for a detailed discussion see Walker, 1995).

In many ways these changes may only be the beginning. A Scottish Parliament 'will want to look again at the number of police forces and...start a period of consultation and information gathering, to put the (Scottish) Parliament in a position, early in its life to consider whether the present eight forces are the correct basis for the new decade.'(Secretary of State for Scotland, 22.4.'98). It is likely that the number of forces will be reduced to three or four and open up the debate of central versus local control over the police. However the Secretary of State indicated that 'a national police force is not on my agenda. I would certainly not dissent from the (Police) Federation's view that the police should be locally based, locally accountable and politically independent.'

The statutory powers of the police to arrest and detain people without a warrant are set out in the *Criminal Procedure (Scotland) Act*, 1995. Technically the investigation of crime is a function of the procurator fiscal assisted by the police. It is not the task of the police, per se, in carrying out an investigation, to obtain a confession, and the decision to prosecute rests with the procurator fiscal, who may decide to proceed, and then arrange for the necessary documents to be served on the person at home; alternatively he may feel that the circumstances justify the obtaining of a warrant for the person's arrest. In some situations, as an investigation into a crime or offence proceeds, the police may reach a position at which application for a warrant to arrest is apparently justified, and will do so, before reporting the case in full to the fiscal. A warrant is a written authority issued by a judge of any court, or a justice of the peace, typically authorising the apprehension and arrest of a named person, or the search of specified premises. The basis for the granting of a warrant, depending on the circumstances, may be information placed before the judge or justice by the procurator fiscal, usually in the form of a complaint or petition, or sworn information by a police officer, customs officer, social worker or other person.

As matters now stand, while all citizens may have a moral duty to assist the police, subject to certain statutory requirements, the police have no power to compel anyone to give a statement. Equally under common law, police may question whomsoever they wish without administering a caution, without cause to suspect them of an offence, and while no-one has an obligation to assist them, any statements made are admissible as evidence including declining to answer. However if the person is a potential suspect there are three main stages, not all of which need necessarily be followed

- **voluntary interview**: the interviewee is under no legal obligation to remain with the police.
- **detention**: the person can be detained for up to 6 hours under sections 14 and 15 of the CP Act, 1995; normally they have the right to inform a solicitor, relative or friend;
- **arrest or charge**: the person is cautioned and charged and then released or detained; if detained they will be brought to court the next day it sits; they have a right to have a lawyer and someone else notified (subject to certain qualifications).

If an arrest is to be effected the accused must be cautioned. The effect of caution, when the suspect is cautioned but not charged, is to warn the suspect that he is going to be asked questions but is under no obligation to answer.

Against this background, the *Criminal Procedure (Scotland) Act*, 1995, section 13, gives a general power to police officers, when they have 'reasonable cause' for believing that either an offence has occurred or is in the course of commission, to demand information, either from the person suspected of the offence or from a potential witnesses. Subsection 1 may require:

a) that person, if the constable finds him at that place or at any place where the constable is entitled to be, to give his name and address, and may ask him for an explanation of the circumstances which have given rise to the constable's suspicion;
b) any other person whom the constable finds at that place or at any place where the constable is entitled to be and who the constable believes has information relating to the offence, to give his name and address.

No definition of reasonable cause is provided by the legislation. The police power has been interpreted fairly loosely so that Lord Wheatley (Dryburgh v. Galt, 1981 SCCR 27) noted

> the fact that the information on which the police officer formed his suspicion turns out to be ill-founded does not in itself necessarily establish that the police officer's suspicion was unfounded. The circumstances known to the police officer at the time he formed the suspicion constitute the criterion, not the facts as subsequently ascertained (Shiels and Bradley, 1996:24).

The CP Act, 1995 is clear that these powers can only be exercised 'at any place where the constable is entitled to be'. While this too remains undefined, the legitimacy of the police officer's presence will impinge on his right to exercise these powers.

Failure on the part of suspects to provide particulars or to remain while the officer verifies name and address and takes a note of any explanation proffered constitutes an offence which can attract arrest without warrant. No time limit is stipulated for completion of initial inquiries under section 13, other than that verification must be capable of completion 'quickly'. The police officer 'may use reasonable force to ensure that the person...remains' (13(4)). The meaning of 'remains' is vague since the section avoids the term detain as defined by s.295. As far as potential witnesses are concerned, the police officer must give a general explanation of the alleged offence being investigated and state that the witness is believed to possess information relevant to the investigation. Failure to provide personal particulars in these circumstances constitutes an offence subject to arrest without a warrant. However no force can be employed to cause a witness to remain at the scene.

Any decision to arrest without a warrant is a sensitive issue. In addition to the circumstances discussed above, a police officer has the power to arrest without a warrant any person committing an offence under Schedule 1 of the CP Act, 1995 i.e. an offence against children under the age of 17 (see Chapters 6 and 11).

Detention during investigation is defined at section 14 and regulates the practice of removing persons to and detaining them at police stations for the purpose of questioning in relation to specific allegations prior to charge. The provisions were introduced by the *Criminal Justice (Scotland) Act*, 1980 following recommendations of the Thomson Committee and bring some clarity and flexibility to a previously grey area of voluntary attendance. A fixed six-hour period of detention was introduced along with a statutory form of caution distinct from the common law caution. Section 14(1) gives a general power to detain a suspect to facilitate investigations into the offence and to establish whether criminal proceedings should be instigated against that person. The intention is to allow time for further enquiry by police where there are reasonable grounds for suspecting that the person has committed or is committing an offence but there is insufficient evidence immediately available to charge him. In other words detention should not be a reason for delaying arrest and charge if sufficient evidence has been gathered. Once the police officer considers that there is sufficient evidence the suspect should be cautioned and the charge preferred without delay. While detention should be terminated when there is sufficient evidence or six hours have passed, the legislation does not require that arrest must follow. As a safeguard only one period of detention is permitted on the same or related grounds (14(3)).

It should be noted that these provisions only relate to offences punishable by imprisonment on conviction. In theory this should mean serious offences. However, in practice, most offences can result in imprisonment, leaving the section fairly loosely cast. The detention may be at 'a police station or...other premises'. Detention cannot be used as a preventive measure to inquire into an offence that has yet to occur. Subsection (2) requires that detention shall be terminated when sufficient evidence is gathered and not more than six hours after it began, or (if earlier)

a) when the person is arrested; or
b) when he is detained in pursuance of any other enactment; or
c) when there are no longer such grounds as are mentioned in the said subsection (1).

Subsection (b) is a recent addition to the provisions of the 1980 Act. It re-enacts provisions contained in s.129 of the *Criminal Justice and Public Order Act, 1994* in England and Wales and represents a significant alteration to the old six-hour rule in that detention may only be a prelude to other statutory detention (e.g. in cases of drug smuggling, terrorism). Subject to subsection (b) the status of the suspect at the end of the six-hour period must change to that of a prisoner or a citizen allowed to go free (Shiels and Bradley, 1996: 28).

As a safeguard against oppressive use of detention, subsection (3) prevents the repeated use of this power in regard to the same offence, but it is still possible in relation to that offence for the police to obtain a written warrant, if subsequent events call for such action.

At the time of detention the suspect must be informed of the suspicion, of the general nature of the offence and the reason for detention. The following must be recorded

- the place where detention begins and the station or premises to which the person is taken
- any other place to which he is taken;
- the general nature of the suspected offence;
- the time detention begins and arrival at the place of detention;
- the time when he is informed of his rights to inform a solicitor or another person named by him;
- where such a request is made, a note that it was complied with;
- time of release.

The police may put questions in relation to the suspected offence and exercise the powers of search available on arrest, using 'reasonable force' if required. The suspect is under no obligation to answer.

The Act creates a specific offence of failing to remain with the constable without reasonable excuse, or failing to give a name and address without reasonable excuse. The maximum penalty for this offence is a fine not exceeding level 3 on the standard scale for the suspect, and a fine not exceeding level 2 on the standard scale for any other person believed to have information, who fails to provide name and address. It gives a specific power to arrest, without a warrant, someone suspected of committing these 'newly created' offences. Important procedural matters regarding the rights of the individual are in-built, so that a person has a right to refuse to answer any question, other than to give his name and address. He also has the right to have someone (including a solicitor, as allowed for in the CP Act, 1995) 'reasonably named by him' informed of his detention and the place where he is being held.

There are added powers for the police to search suspected persons for offensive weapons; obstruction or concealment of such a weapon itself constitutes a separate offence, carrying a maximum penalty not exceeding level 4 on the standard scale. This whole area of search is complex and is covered by a number of different statutes such as the *Misuse of Drugs Act*, 1971, and the *Criminal Law (Consolidation) (Scotland) Act,* 1995.

Any admissible evidence must be made voluntarily, in the sense that it has not been obtained by any unfair means and without any regard to promise or threat while the suspect is with the police.

After a caution and charge only voluntary statements which are offered not in response to police questioning are admissible. Police can be expected, however, to ask questions after a charge regarding the whereabouts of stolen property, of a missing child etc. The suspect will be told that he has the right to consult a solicitor: notices to this effect ought to be clearly on display.

If police notes, which may be referred to in court, contain any statement, comment, or confession by the suspect, the accused will be given the chance to read the text and to append his signature. He can refuse to sign, and any statement made and recorded can be retracted. The dating and timing of notes is intended to ensure correctness and to allay allegations that the notes were made at dates or time other than as stated by the arresting officer. Most interviews involving voluntary statements, detainees under section 14 and those who have been arrested should now be tape recorded. Video cameras are used in interview rooms in Lothian and Borders under certain circumstances, but are not common elsewhere in Scotland. Interviewing officers are well aware that anything in the interview which could be construed as being overbearing or threatening could render the evidence inadmissible. In the presence of the interviewee, the tape should be removed from the machine and a copy sealed, thus rendering it tamper proof. In practice transcriptions of the tapes will only be made when a decision to prosecute has been taken. There are some obvious circumstances when recording is not possible, for example, where exchanges take place between a suspect and the police at the scene or in the vehicle transporting him to the police station; where the interviews are not held at a police station and no equipment is available; and of a more mundane nature, when the equipment fails.

Once an arrest has been made and a charge laid, all the related material in the case is open to inspection and scrutiny by the defence, so that by the time the case reaches a court the defence has (or should have) an intimate knowledge of the prosecution case. Thus a range of legal safeguards have been established to protect the innocent and to ensure a fair and understandable process from the moment of arrest to the point when the accused faces the court and the prosecution opens its case against him.

Some specific social work considerations

Normally social workers will not be involved at any stage of these police procedures. It is important for them to be conversant with the general run of police enquiries and the suspect's rights and obligations under the law as it now stands. Complaints or concerns, from whatever quarter, can only be dealt with if the worker is familiar with local police practices. However there are a number of areas where social work may be directly or indirectly involved.

Where a suspect or a witness is a 'vulnerable' person, for example, a child in care or a person who is mentally disordered (as defined by the *Mental Health (Scotland) Act*, 1984 which includes mental handicap or learning disability) the police are obliged to conduct interviews in the presence of an **appropriate adult**, namely someone appointed who is completely independent of the police and the interviewee and who has a sound understanding of and experience or training in dealing with mentally disordered people (see Appropriate Adult Schemes in Chapter 12). The responsibility of such a role is not to interfere with the proper attempts of the interviewing officers to arrive at the truth, but to see that matters, which may appear to be beyond the understanding or comprehension of the suspect, are put in a perspective which is clear to him. One example of this might be simply to serve to ensure that the person has the services of a solicitor at this stage, and beyond, if necessary; another might well be simply to see that he was in a sufficiently calm and receptive frame of mind to serve his own best interests.

Cross-border issues

Much attention has been given to the removal of internal borders within the European Union (EU) and its consequences for policing in the last decade. Nine EU states have entered accords which provide a framework for policing a continent without land barriers. The UK and France have reached a detailed agreement to deal with policing and jurisdictional issues raised by the opening of the channel tunnel. It is rather paradoxical, therefore, that until 1994 little attention had been given to the consequences for police powers and the investigation of crime, given the existence of distinct legal systems in Scotland and England. A joint Scottish Office and Home Office Consultation Paper pointed out in 1993 that the powers of the police applied only in the country in which they were based. It also acknowledged that, in practice, informal co-operation of questionable legality operated to ensure fleeing offenders were, in fact, apprehended.

The *Criminal Justice and Public Order Act*, 1994 set out a statutory framework for cross-border policing. Section 137 allows officers from either side to arrest a suspect without warrant in the other jurisdiction, subject to certain conditions. For a Scottish police officer, it must appear to him that it would have been lawful to exercise the power had the suspect been in Scotland. The Act does not appear to require that the officer should be correct in his judgement on this; good faith will, it seems, be enough (Brown, 1994). It may be interesting to note that this is not so for the English officer, where the suspected offence must actually be an arrestable offence, an expression with precise meaning under the *Police and Criminal Evidence Act*, 1984 (PACE). Scottish officers are also be able to exercise their power of detention in England subject to the same condition (detention before arrest is unknown in English law). The police officer must then take the suspect either to the nearest convenient police station in Scotland or to one in the sheriffdom where the offence is being investigated.

Section 136, in a similar way, allows for cross-border execution of warrants. Here the basis for arrest is much clearer since the officer is executing an order of the court. As above the suspect must be taken to a police station, or in the case of Scottish warrants taken when a person on bail from petition fails to appear for trial, to the appropriate prison. The legislation also gives powers of arrest to officers in the 'other' jurisdiction equivalent to the powers for any officer in that jurisdiction.

Liberation by police

The *Criminal Procedure (Scotland) Act,* 1995 (s.22) gives the officer in charge of a police station discretion to release an arrested person charged with an offence, which may be tried summarily, on the basis of a written undertaking that they will appear at court when told to do so; or to detain him until appearance at the court the next lawful day. Any refusal to liberate an arrested person 'shall not subject the officer to any claim whatsoever'(s.22(3))—in a word, there is no right to liberation by the police. There is also power for the police to release people without such an undertaking, with the implication that the person is believed likely to attend court in response to any subsequent ordinary citation. Whilst release on a written undertaking cannot include additional conditions other than to appear, its effects are entirely akin to those of a full bail order, not least in that the person is liable to almost identical penalties as for breach of bail if he fails to appear after giving a written undertaking.

The CP Act, 1995 also empowers the police to release children who may have been arrested on the basis of a written undertaking given by the parent or guardian, or by the child him/her self. The maximum penalty for any breach of such an undertaking is a fine not exceeding level 3 on the standard scale, which would presumably fall on the parent or guardian. Of particular note for social workers is that the very fact of being under supervision can become the grounds for a refusal of bail in the event of arrest for a further offence. It is important that this fact is known by people under supervision, although prosecutors still have an area of discretion. Social workers need to establish the practices that normally operate in their area in this respect.

Designated places for drunken offenders

Criminal Justice (Scotland) Act, 1980, introduced a power, at section 5, now contained in section 16 of the CP Act, 1995, for dealing with people who are drunk:

> Where a constable has power to arrest a person without a warrant for any offence
> and the constable has reasonable grounds for suspecting that person is drunk, the
> constable may, if he thinks fit, take him to any place designated by the Secretary of
> State as a place suitable for the care of drunken person.

People cannot be detained in such places against their will, and remain liable to be charged and dealt with for the offence involved. Conveyance to a designated place is without prejudice to any further proceedings arising from arrest. It is worth noting that the offence need not be one of drunkenness, only that the offender offended while apparently drunk.

There were some limited initiatives in Scotland in the late 1970s involving taking drunken offenders to be 'dried out' in hospital settings, rather than to police cells at a time when it was estimated that drunkenness offences accounted for 23% of receptions in Scottish prisons. The expense was not necessarily less than detention within the criminal justice system, and, of themselves, the shelters, or designated places, could not solve the problems of alcohol abuse experienced by those whose behaviour also involved their coming to the attention of agencies in the criminal justice system. Since the implementation of the 1980 Act only two designated place have been established in Scotland.

The use of designated places is not intended only for people whose offence is plain drunkenness, but is conceived in much wider terms. Wilkins (1998) indicates that the designated place in Aberdeen has a wide range of usages including 'one offs'—young people where drinking gets out of control; homeless people who have recently arrived in the city; people where a crisis has triggered a drinking episode; and the habitually drunken offender.

An important focus of concern is the habitually drunken offender, where vulnerability is as much a concern as offending or drunkenness itself. The *Civic Government (Scotland) Act*, 1982 (s.50(1) recognised this combination: 'Any person who, while not in the care or protection of a suitable person is, in a public place, drunk and incapable of taking care of himself shall be guilty of an offence'. There are three elements to the offence

- being so intoxicated as to be incapable
- being in a public place whilst in this state
- being outwith the care or protection of a suitable person.

There is clear inference that the offender is vulnerable by virtue of being drunk. The most common profile of the habitually drunken offender is of a persistent street drinker, white, unemployed, male, thirty-five or older, who is probably homeless and sleeping rough or living in temporary accommodation. He may be alcohol dependent, certainly often drunk and may be misusing drugs. He may be suffering from a psychiatric disorder, poor physical health and is at risk of arrest for public drunkenness, shop theft, begging or public order offences (Mental Health Foundation, 1996). Habitully drunken offenders are not confined to men.

It is very disappointing that an imaginative and flexible provision of legislation has not been matched by equal imagination in the development of services to assist people whose offending and alcohol abuse are related.

Chapter 4

Social Work and the Criminal Courts

Services to courts; services at court

The *Social Work (Scotland) Act*, 1968 (s.27(3)(b)) requires each local authority to make 'arrangements for the attendance of officers of the local authority at court' and for 'co-operation…with the courts' (s.27(3)(c)). This chapter outlines the services which authorities have a duty to provide. It sets out the tasks and functions which social workers undertake at court and considers some day-to-day practicalities which need agreement with the courts.

Any social worker attending or operating within the court in the exercise of their responsibilities under National Objectives and Standards (NOS) has a two-fold task. Part of the task involves assisting the court and providing a social work service to it, and part of the task involves assisting people in trouble who appear before the court, providing a service to them and their families or others involved with them. There are at times unavoidable tensions, difficulties, and dilemmas in this duality. Nonetheless the two elements in the social worker's task in court are inseparable. Many of the larger authorities have specialist court-based social workers. This core social work role comes under the 100% central funding arrangement and is subject to NOS, which locate the authority embodied in the various tasks.

NOS identify a range of tasks associated with the provision of information and advice to the courts and with services for offenders and their families, victims and witnesses which require to be undertaken by court-based social work staff. These include

- dealing with requests for reports and speaking to them when required;
- monitoring the quality and standard of reports;
- providing oral and stand down reports for the court;
- interviewing offenders following a request for a report by the court;
- interviewing offenders/accused following a custodial sentence or remand;
- interviewing offenders following a decision by the court to make a disposal involving social work;
- providing support to victims or vulnerable people such as witnesses who appear before the courts
- representing the local authority in the court setting and liaising with other professional groups;
- seeking to divert people suffering with mental health problems, who may be a risk to themselves in custodial remand, to appropriate care including bail accommodation under s.200 of the *Criminal Procedure (Scotland) Act*, 1995.

SERVICES TO THE COURT

Presenting Social Enquiry and Other Reports

Local authorities have a statutory duty to provide services to the court, 'making available to any court such social background reports and other reports relating to persons appearing before the court which the court may require for the disposal of a case' (section 27(1)(a) of the *Social Work (Scotland) Act,* 1968). Courts, in turn, are empowered to adjourn a case where a person has been convicted or the court has found that he has committed an offence for the 'purpose of enabling enquiries to be made or of determining the most suitable method of dealing with a case' (section 201 of the *Criminal Procedure (Scotland) Act,* 1995). Reports are prepared by a qualified social worker, who is an officer of the local authority (see Chapter 5).

The intention of the legislation is to ensure that as far as possible no-one is given a custodial sentence (or indeed any disposal by the court) without providing the court with professional assistance as required. Sentencers interviewed in *Helping the Court Decide* (SWSI, 1996), the Social Work Inspectorate report on social enquiry reports (SERs), emphasised that the purpose of these reports is to inform sentencing decisions by providing information about the offender and his or her circumstances. It makes clear that information in this context should include 'not just factual information but also

- **analysis,** for example analysing a possible association between offending and substance misuse;
- **comment**, for example, commenting on the implications of an identified health problem for disposal; and
- **advice on disposal**, for example, advising on the feasibility of different disposals especially those involving social work services.' (para. 3.2)

In busy courts, the court-based social work staff may be full time; in less busy courts they will be part time or attached staff. The local authority is responsible for making arrangements for court-based staff to pass requests to the relevant social work area, normally within a day of receipt. Reports are normally prepared by field social workers who are specialists in criminal justice social work.

'Ideally the officer who prepared the (social enquiry) report should be available... 'directly to the court to offer their professional opinion as required', asserted the Morison Committee (1962). This remains equally the ideal today. The author's presence is likely to be essential if the defence wish to cross-examine him on information contained in the report, which they have every right to do; the prosecutor has a right to comment on any statement in a report which may conflict with information in his possession and the presence of the author may be required if this becomes a significant matter requiring clarification; equally the sheriff may take the initiative and require the author's presence in order to put questions or to request further information or to ask for more assistance and advice.

In practice there are few occasions when the SER author will appear in court. NOS recognise that 'it is neither practical nor necessary for authors of reports to be present on every occasion'. Such requests are normally dealt with by court-based social workers. 'It is therefore necessary (for court-based social workers) to liaise with SER writers at short notice and to have a good understanding of the work of the social work department and other relevant agencies' (NOS, SER section).

The reality is that a social worker who is a known figure at court can provide a valuable service to the court and to people appearing at it more effectively than a social worker who makes only occasional appearances. Key to the effectiveness of court-based social work is the nature and quality of liaison, particularly with field social workers who fulfil their authorities' responsibilities by providing assessments and undertake community-based supervision on behalf of the court. It is equally important that court-based social workers have good links with children's panels and with other professionals such as mental health personnel, for example, mental health officers and psychiatrists, since they, the court-based staff, are in the best position, possibly more than anyone else, to be able to identify vulnerable offenders and high levels of anxiety or stress or other mental health signs which may indicate risk in people appearing before the courts. NOS emphasise the importance of court-based social workers' contribution to

- liaison with sheriffs and justices with regard to-day-to day issues of mutual concern, providing them with information on provision and new initiatives;
- liaison with sheriff and district clerks, particularly to ensure that arrangements for dealing with breaches of community social work disposals, and with procurators fiscal, solicitors, the police and other agencies operating in the court.

There are a number of ways in which social work staff assist the court in sentencing on a day-to-day basis by providing information and advice. These include

- oral reports;
- stand down reports;
- reports following accelerated pleas;
- pre-trial reports;
- supplementary reports;
- other reports such as means/fine enquiry reports.

The presence of a suitably experienced and qualified court-based social worker provides the opportunity to enhance the presentation of submitted reports, for example, by speaking to them, by being able to clear up possible misinterpretations, by adding updated information that may have come to light since the reports were prepared, or by providing on-the-spot assessment or information gathering which both assists the court's decision making and can aid speedy disposal. They equally are in a position to clarify for the court or others the nature and implications of any structured programmes that may be proposed and, should be equipped with written material from agencies on these matters and with any outcome data that exists.

Guidance requires the local authority to have agreed arrangements with the Clerk of Court for sending requests for reports to the court-based social work staff usually within a day of the request, for transferring orders etc. It is important to note that any report is the court's property, and is only distributed by the court at the relevant point in the proceedings. In any High Court case, for example, in which a report has been ordered pre-trial, the report will only be available after conviction or a finding of guilt and the report will be destroyed if the subject is acquitted, or the verdict is not proven.

In more typical instances where a report has been prepared after a finding of guilt, or after a conviction, copies will be available to all the relevant parties before the hearing for the contents to be read and considered carefully. In practice all the copies will go to the court in the first instance. It is then up to procurator fiscal, agent, and anyone else who is entitled to a copy to make arrangements with the court to obtain that copy.

Where a person appearing before the court is not represented, the court-based social worker can assist them in meeting the duty solicitor and ensure they have seen a copy of any report and understand its implications, if this is not already the case. Where they do have a solicitor, then it is the latter's responsibility to ensure that the copy is obtained from the court clerk and is discussed with his client.

Presenting other information

Social work can also assist the court, solicitors, procurators fiscal, police etc. by providing more general information including information about social work resources and other services. The availability of welfare benefits, accommodation, employment, local service and so on, may be helpful in the determination of sentence in some instances, whether or not a report may have been obtained. Authorities have been slow to produce attractive and accessible information to promote available services for the range of 'users' who may benefit from it in the court setting.

Equally it may fall to court-based social work to have to clarify the absence or non-availability of various services and facilities; examples may include the admissions policy of a particular hostel and its occupancy levels or the priority of allocation to a particular programme or the absence of such a programme. The situation may be a sensitive one, since often those services and facilities are ones for which the authority is responsible. Nonetheless up-to-date information on services may be of importance to effective disposal or even to the liberty of a person and may be of wider public interest with the possibility of being reported by the press.

The public's understanding of social work provision to the criminal justice system remains limited, and media interest, particularly local press interest, which extends to much of the business of the courts, seldom extends to the successful completion or outcome of community disposals; or to comments on the value of its content, or on the limitations of available services and resources. Much could be done by local authorities to promote examples of good service provision, and court-based social workers could play an important part in any strategy for disseminating information.

Stand down interviews

Occasionally the court-based social worker may be asked to undertake or may suggest that they undertake an interview while a case is adjourned or 'stood down' for that purpose so that they can report to the court orally or in writing later in the day. Such interviews are usually associated with the need for specific information and advice to assist decision making. For example if there is doubt about the person's plea when they are not legally represented, a social worker may be asked to help ensure that the accused understands the situation sufficiently; alternatively the social worker when interviewing in the court cell may have elicited information of concern to the court, not verifiable in the circumstances or examined in detail because of the pressure of time, or may express concern about the vulnerability or mental health of an accused.

More typically, information may be required to assist the court in considering issues of bail or remand. A sheriff may be considering whether to continue the case for a full written social enquiry report and a short interview may either elicit sufficient information to enable the case to proceed to disposal straight away, or confirm that there are matters which require the greater length and depth of investigation that a full report will supply. In such circumstances it is the task of the court-based social worker to respond to the request for specific information; to make clear when they consider a full SER or a medical report is necessary and to assist in any investigation and arrangements that may allow for bail.

The results of any stand-down interview are normally communicated to the court orally and will be recorded where the outcome involves social work action. This kind of brief oral report needs to be distinguished from 'oral' reports where a social worker who knows the individual well but has been unable to provide a written report will present their assessment orally to the court. Unless the subject is currently under supervision or licence they must consent to the information being given. This practice appears, fortunately, now to be a rarity. NOS emphasis that oral reports of any sort are not sufficient where the offender is at risk of custody. However requests for full reports in Scotland are escalating at such a rate that many authorities find they are putting more resources into enquiry than they are into intervention. Not all requests require or receive in-depth investigation. The future may see more need to provide briefer on-the-spot reports as a filter to requests for full assessments reports.

In this context court-based social workers have a valuable contribution to make in maintaining and improving the standard of reports and advice to the courts. Many court-based units carry out formal monitoring exercises of SERs and other reports drawing management attention to the strength and weaknesses of current practice and provision. This role is particularly crucial in monitoring and providing consultancy for the preparation of reports for breach cases. Many criminal justice social workers will require some specialist assistance in framing the grounds for a breach to satisfy the legal requirements of the court, as well as detailing accurately the nature of the original offence, when it occurred, and the details of the order. Court-based social workers can play an important role in training for their criminal justice colleagues in the field.

SERVICES AT COURT

There are real opportunities for court-based social workers to offer assistance to those people appearing before the court and to those dealt with by the court, in what for many, may be a crisis situation. Stress, anxiety and uncertainty can manifest itself in many different forms of behaviour, some of which may disadvantage the accused in the court setting. Court systems on the whole are not geared to dealing with emotions, and, if anything, the structure and formal adversarial processes are intended to subdue and control expressions of feeling. The adversarial culture of Scottish courts deliberately places power in the hands of the sheriff and professionals and many commentators suggest that various forms of discrimination can manifest themselves in this type of discretionary decision making (Hudson, 1987). Many of these aspects can be seen as, and can indeed be, constraints on social work activity in the court setting. Equally they constitute one of the reasons for a social work presence. A degree of professional security, confidence and credibility is required of court-based social workers in order to operate effectively. Not only is the situation different from the more typical setting of an office or home-based interview; it is a secondary setting involving other professionals and also is a distinctively public setting.

Any disposal or decision which results in a statutory social work activity (an SER request, probation, community service, supervised attendance etc.) will require the person to be seen immediately after the hearing and 'before they leave the court precincts' (NOS SER section) in order to establish that he or she understands the procedure or the basic requirements of the order to which he/she is now subject. The practicalities of contact with the field social worker can be raised and explained and any immediate queries or difficulties dealt with.

Interviews following requests for reports

It is noteworthy that *Helping the Court Decide* (SWSI, 1996), suggested that almost a third of offenders interviewed did not know or understand the purpose of a social enquiry report and very few thought it was concerned with addressing their offending (par 3.7) or their attitude towards their victim. Most offenders seemed not to receive or to absorb information about the purpose of the report from the sheriff or from the court social worker. Indeed only a third remembered having been seen by a court-based social worker at the time a report was requested. Less than half recollected having received a leaflet from social work outlining the purpose of the report in advance. If correct, this cannot be an acceptable state of affairs, particularly when NOS indicate that court-based social workers 'have responsibilities to interview all offenders whose cases are continued for an SER or other social work report'. NOS identify the tasks following a request for a report as

- making sure the offender has understood the court's decision and its implications;
- confirming the offender's address and availability for interview;

- giving the offender's details to the appropriate social work area; and
- giving the offender a leaflet which explains the nature and purpose of the report.

It is crucially important that offenders are given adequate information verbally, supplemented in writing, before leaving the court, and that a check is made that they really understand what has happened and what will follow.

Interviews following custodial remand or sentence

Any custodial disposal, remand or sentence, creates an immediate focus for social work involvement. This is so whether or not the disposal involves a period of post-prison supervision or licence or a Supervised Release Order (see Chapter 11) as part of the sentence. NOS emphasise that a custodial disposal 'may be distressing for the person' and that they 'may have no time to deal with practical matters which require attention'. The practice of automatically undertaking a 'post-sentence interview' is based on the essential principle that 'prison throughcare begins at the point of sentence'. NOS stress that the objectives of throughcare include 'to seek to limit and redress the damaging consequences of imprisonment on prisoners and their families, including dislocation from their family and community ties', and 'to assist families of prisoners cope and to deal with the practical and emotional consequences'.

This principle stresses the longer-term considerations as well as the very practical and mundane issues such as which prison the person will be sent to; and how family members can visit (see Chapters 10 and 11). NOS identify the key aims of the post-sentence interview as

- clarifying the decision of the court;
- establishing whether any practical problems need to be dealt with immediately;
- informing the offender of social work services available in the prison and how they can be used;
- making an assessment about whether the offender may constitute a risk to him/herself and notifying the prison authorities.

Particular care is required with vulnerable offenders including children, people with a learning disability (mental handicap) or a history of mental disorder, those with a history of self injury, single parents and those experiencing custody for the first time. The prison-based social work unit should receive information, as soon as is practicable, highlighting issues for follow up. If at all possible the court-based social worker should follow up the interview by informing family members of the court decision, particularly where custody was not anticipated, or by contacting the local social work service to follow up. NOS recognise that there may be difficulties in busy courts to interview every offender or accused remanded or sentenced to custody and identifies priorities as

- those under 16 not accompanied by a social worker;
- offenders/accused for whom custody may be particularly distressing;
- offenders receiving life sentences;

- offenders convicted of offences against children;
- single parents;
- offenders/accused facing the first experience of custody;
- offenders/accused who are HIV positive or who suffer from AIDS.

Interviews following a social work disposal

The most frequent situation in which court-based social workers should interview an offender is when the court orders a social work disposal. The role of the court-based social worker interviewing an offender given a disposal involving statutory social work is likely to include:
- allowing for and dealing with reactions and anxieties;
- checking the offender understands and explaining the reasons for social work involvement;
- explaining broadly the nature and methods of intervention that will follow;
- preparing the ground for the first appointment with the supervising social worker;
- discussing issues of confidentiality and the person's rights;
- fulfilling the necessary requirements of documentation and procedures;
- dealing with practical issues in the immediate situation.

Court-based social work assistance

Often simple services, like the provision of basic information about court procedure and personnel, can help to allay unnecessary anxieties. There are a range of other services that court-based social workers may be able to provide. Families and friends who attend courts are often equally stressed by the experience or the outcome of court proceedings. It is to be expected that professional social workers will respond sensitively and constructively by providing clear information and practical advice and may refer them on to appropriate agencies where they can find support and help.

The social work response to victims has often been underplayed in the past. Court-based social workers are well placed to provide victim witnesses appearing in court with information, support and advice, particularly with regard to available help through local victim support or domestic violence schemes.

For some people, offender or victim, the court experience will constitute a very real crisis and the court-based social worker is well placed and skilled to provide an immediate response, in kind or in cash, as well as able to facilitate referral to other agencies who deal, for example, with drug or alcohol problems, accommodation, or support. A particular priority identified by NOS is the provision of advice and assistance to court personnel in dealing with vulnerable people, particularly children or young people 'looked after' by the local authority (see Chapter 6) who attend court either as witnesses or as offenders. This now forms an important part of their role, particularly in busy courts.

Specialist High Court social workers will normally receive advanced copies of indictments and are able to identify potentially vulnerable witnesses, such as children, rape victims or people with learning difficulties and offer assistance prior to their appearance. More commonly social workers seek help for vulnerable people who are to be witnesses from their court-based colleagues, by way of a pre-court visit to show them around the courtroom and discuss the procedures as a way of allaying fears and anxieties. In some courts this function will be carried out by the fiscal's office, but there is growing recognition that the task is a sensitive one that benefits from the involvement of a professional social worker.

As we have noted there are a number of important roles that court-based social workers bring to prominence in the court setting. While it is essential to have expertise in law and social work practice, court-based social workers are an important source of advice and guidance, particularly for field workers and staff from voluntary agencies less familiar with the procedural and administrative aspects relevant to operating within the court.

Etiquette

Scottish courts are often criticised for 'trappings' such as dress, etiquette and language, which exclude the lay person and are considered anachronistic in most modern western democracies. Recently Lord Prosser, a senior High Court judge, has led a debate (rather than action) to modernise practices. In the meantime, tedious though it may seem, failure to observe etiquette can diminish both the credibility and effectiveness of a social worker. It was traditional to bow to the court if approaching the bar or when approaching to address the court, although in practice this can be dispensed with. The bow was intended to acknowledge the court as representative of the Crown as are the terms of address: High Court Judges are addressed as 'Your Lordship', 'My Lord' or 'My Lady'; Sheriffs are addressed as 'My Lord' or 'My Lady'; and Justices in the District Court, (including Stipendiary magistrates) are addressed as 'Your Honour'.

Access to cells

The police have responsibility for the security of people held in custody. Court-based social workers will have good liaison with the police and can assist colleagues in making arrangements for access to cells, if required, subject to normal means of identification.

Court lists

Social workers cannot operate in court effectively without information about the charges against those appearing there. At first glance this is obtained from court lists, and is supplemented by the prosecutor's account of the actual circumstances. The lists will also show the distribution of business between the various court rooms. A very important and practical task, in the absence of IT systems, is to identify those appearing on court lists who are already on a statutory order (or other social work supervision) since conviction will constitute an automatic breach. It will also be important for court social workers to note any previous or actual convictions which require an offender to register under the *Sex Offender Act*, 1997 and to notify both social work and police, as appropriate.

Court language and abbreviation

In Chapter 3 we incorporated samples of documents which are regularly used by courts. Copies of these are sent to social workers when they are required to prepare a report. There are also a number of abbreviations commonly used, either as notes written on these documents by court clerks, to indicate what decisions may have been taken as a case progresses, or in the everyday parlance of various personnel within the criminal justice system..

Abbreviations commonly found on court documents

CFE	Continued for further enquiry (this indicates the case started life on solemn procedure— see Chapter 3)
FC	Fully committed (this means that the person was committed for trial on solemn procedure)
T	Trial—followed by a date (indicates an original plea of Not Guilty)
G or NG	Guilty or Not Guilty (showing original plea)
SD Sentence	Deferred
PA Personal	Appearance (indicates that the individual may originally have pled by letter, but was required to appear in person at a subsequent date, for example, to be disqualified from driving, or because the offence was serious)
I/C	In Custody
B	On bail
OTA	Ordained to appear
CSER	Continued for a social enquiry report
CSO or CSR	Continued for a community service report
SSER	Supplementary report. The name of a solicitor is often also shown.

It is quite possible, from a series of such abbreviations that may appear on court documents, to trace the history of a person's appearances: for example

3.1.98 NG	T. 4.2.98 B.
4.2.98 CSER & 25.2.98 I/C	
25.2.98 SD	25.8.98 SSER
25.8.98 Fined £200	

This represents the case of someone who first appeared in early January, pled Not Guilty, and trial was fixed for 4 February, with bail allowed. The person must have either then pled guilty, or been found guilty, because he was then remanded in custody for three weeks for a social enquiry report. However, at the conclusion of that, sentence was deferred for 6 months, and a supplementary report ordered for that occasion. The final outcome, after that period of deferment, was a fine of £200. These notes made by clerks are for their convenience: the official record of what happened is in the court minutes.

Abbreviations for offences

The referral forms used by criminal justice social work for court work often show shorthand indications for the offences charged. The most common include:

Att	Attempt at a crime (e.g. att. theft)
w.i.	with intent
ass	assault
ass to s.i.	assault to severe injury
ass to s.i.	assault to severe injury
p.d., and d.o.l.	permanent disfigurement and danger of life
HB	housebreaking
OLP	opening lockfast place
THB	theft by housebreaking
TOLP	theft by opening lockfast place
attHBwi	attempt housebreaking with intent (to steal)
L&L	lewd and libidinous practices
BOP	breach of the peace
PCA 53	Prevention of Crime Act, 1953
Pol(S)A, 67	Police (Scotland) Act, 1967
C&YP 37	Children and Young Persons Act (of which s.12 refers to child neglect)
CPC(S)A	Prisoners and Criminal Prodeedings (Scotland) Act, 1993
CP(S)A	Criminal Procedure (Scotland) Act,1995
C(S)A	Children (Scotland) Act, 1995

The passage of legislation

We noted in Chapter 3 the important distinction between common law and statute law, the former being an unwritten body of law passed down over the centuries, and the latter being contained in Acts passed by Parliament. Assuming the Scottish Parliamentary structures reflect existing practices, there are a number of stages typically involved in the passage of legislation.

Consultation

Governments often issue various 'Papers' as methods of consultation. Legislation may also result from reports of various Committees or Inquiries, or be part of a political manifesto.

Green Papers are preliminary documents, setting out the government's provisional thinking and inviting comment; for example, the Green Paper, *Punishment in the Community*, 1988.

White Papers more typically set out specific intentions for legislation—for example the *Crime and Punishment (Scotland) Act*, 1997, was preceded by the White Paper of the same name.

Government reports and White Papers carry a **command number** to enable easy identification, and as a form of shorthand to denote a longer title of the full report or paper.

Passage through Parliament

Legislation is drafted in the form of a Bill for debate in Parliament, and the Queen's Speech at the commencement of each Parliament will describe the legislative programme for the coming session. Various amendments will be made during the passage through Parliament before an Act emerges in its final form. It then receives the Royal Assent. Practice began to change in the 1990s in recognition of the distinctiveness of Scottish legislation e.g. the first stages of the *Criminal Justice (Scotland), Act,* 1995 and *Children (Scotland) Act,* 1995 were dealt with by the Scottish Grand Committee in Edinburgh, which is Scottish MPs sitting in committee to consider Scottish Bills. When a Scottish Parliament is established most legislation relevant to criminal law will be dealt with there and it is likely to see the end of the practice of English legislation with Scottish inclusions.

Implementation
Even when an Act has received the Royal Assent, and is on the 'Statute Book', its implementation may be staged over a period of time. It is worth noting that some sections of Acts never actually become law for a variety of administrative or political reasons e.g. Part III, Chapter 1 of the *Crime and Punishment (Scotland) Act,* 1997 on Early Release has not been implemented, and section 4 of the same Act which proposed extensive changes to Supervised Release Orders will be repealed by the *Crime and Disorder Act,* 1998. This can apply to individual sections of an Act and can cause some embarrassment to the unwary.

Statutory Instruments are orders laid before Parliament which can serve a number of purposes:

• they may determine the implementation date of various sections of an Act;
• they may contain rules governing the way sections of an Act are implemented;
• they may define the meanings of certain parts of Acts.

Circulars may also be issued by various government departments, by way of clarifying sections of Acts, or advising on preferred methods of implementation, or the detailed operations of government departments which may have responsibilities under sections of Acts.

Amending legislation
Particular sections of legislation can be amended by later Acts. Often the later Act will 'rewrite', as it were, an original section of an Act. It is therefore important to remember that obtaining a copy of a particular Act (for example, an original version of the *Social Work (Scotland) Act,* 1968) does not necessarily mean that everything that is contained within it represents the current state of the law. Indeed section 32 of the original 1968 Act, which sets out the important matter of the grounds on which a child can be referred to a Children's Hearing, has been amended by sections of three subsequent Acts—the *Children Act,* 1975, the *Solvent Abuse (Scotland) Act,* 1983, and by the *Health and Social Services and Social Security Adjudications Act,* 1983. All of these have been consolidated and further amended by section 45 of the *Children (Scotland) Act,* 1995. Similarly the *Criminal Procedings (Scotland) Act,* 1995 which is the key piece of criminal legislation, is constantly being amended by subsequent legislation such as the *Crime and Punishment (Scotland) Act,* 1997.

Chapter 5

Reports for Criminal Courts

Legal context; administrative and procedural matters; issues of practice and opinion

LEGAL CONTEXT

The term social enquiry report (SER) is commonly used to describe reports prepared for criminal courts by Scottish local authority social work in fulfilling its duties under the *Social Work (Scotland) Act*, 1968. The term, social enquiry report, however, does not actually appear in Scots law. What the law does incorporate are some general powers enabling, and in some instances, obliging courts to obtain information under certain specified circumstances.

As so often in social work and criminal law, the law does not specify how this should be done; nor does it specify issues such as report content, or the factors which sentencers should take into account, or whether it is appropriate to extend advice to include recommendations for a particular disposal, which are central concerns in everyday practice. The law does not indicate whether or not it is appropriate for the authors of reports to comment on the suitability of offenders for probation, for example, but, strangely, is explicit on this point with regard to community service orders. While the law does not require reports to comment on the feasibility or appropriateness of a named community-based disposal (except community service), this, however, is inferred (SWSI, 1996:4). Nonetheless the law is clear that the information provided should assist the court to decide whether there are ways of dealing with the offender in the community which enable the court to avoid the use of detention or custody.

National Objectives and Standards for Social Work Services in the Criminal Justice System (NOS), deal with many of the points raised above and contain extensive guidance on reports. It is important to stress that SERs have no other purpose in law than to serve the needs of sentencers and are only one of a number of information sources available to the court when sentencing.

Some important principles and some specific obligations concerning reports were established by the *Criminal Justice (Scotland) Act*, 1949. Subsequent legislation has extended the range of circumstances in which a report must be obtained.

General power to order reports

A general power to order reports was established by section 26 of the 1949 Act.

This power is now located in the *Criminal Procedure (Scotland) Act*, 1995, section 201. This section describes the court's power to adjourn cases, and declares that this includes power:

> to adjourn the case for the purpose of enabling inquiries to be made or of determining the most suitable method of dealing with his case (s.201(1)).

The following should be noted:

- adjournment for the purpose of reports must follow a conviction or a finding of guilt, but precede sentence or disposal;
- no such adjournment may exceed a period of three weeks where the accused is remanded in custody; four weeks where the accused is remanded on bail or ordained to appear, or eight weeks on 'cause shown'; these arrangements allow for the fact that reports may be incomplete, or may show the need for further information (for example, medical assessment), but ensures that delays which are damaging to the individual and costly to the public purse are kept within reasonable bounds;
- the legislation suggests two purposes for such an adjournment: enabling inquiries (or further) to be made ; and assisting the court determine the most suitable method of dealing with the case;
- the purpose of assisting determines the most suitable disposal is very general, and does not constrain the court in any way. However it is important to note that some disposals available to the court are only competent when a report has been obtained.

A considerable number of authoritative decisions based on appeals emphasise the statutory distinction between adjourning a case before sentence and deferring sentence, and of operating within the legal time limits set (Shiels and Bradley, 1996:204).

The 1949 Act made it clear (at Schedule 3) that the undertaking of inquiries was a task for the then probation service. The wording of section 4 of that Schedule adds further interesting commentary on how the task was seen at the time; the duties of probation officers were to include:

> to inquire, in accordance with any directions of the court, into the circumstances or home surroundings of any person with a view to assisting the court in determining the most suitable method of dealing with the case.

Following the implementation of the *Social Work (Scotland) Act,* 1968 this duty became a function of the local authority, not individual officers, in terms of section 27 of the 1968 Act. The Act introduced the term 'social background report' into legislation (not social enquiry report), and defined the authority's responsibilities as including:

> making available to any court such social background reports and other reports relating to persons appearing before the court which the court may require for the disposal of the case.

Obligatory reports

The law requires that reports must be considered in respect of certain offenders, or in specific circumstances, before certain disposals can competently be ordered. There are two sets of circumstances in which a custodial sentence cannot be ordered unless the court has obtained a report. There are also circumstances in which certain non-custodial disposals cannot competently be ordered in the absence of a report. The court must always obtain a report when it is dealing with a child, i.e. a person under the age of 16 years or a young person aged 16-18 who is subject to a supervision requirement under the Children's Hearings system (s.42(8) of the CP Act, 1995). The court (except a district court) is required to obtain a report before disposal of any case involving a person specified in section 27(1)(b)(i) to (vi) of the 1968 Act as amended (section 203 of the CP Act, 1995) namely

- those under supervision by order of a court;
- those under supervision following release from prison or any other form of detention;
- those subject to a community service order or a probation order including a requirement of unpaid work;
- those subject to a supervised attendance order;
- those subject to a supervision and treatment order.

Custodial disposals

A persistent theme in the sections which define these circumstances is that the report's purpose is to help the court determine that '**no other method of dealing with him is appropriate**'. The law can be seen to underscore the policy principle of 'using prisons sparingly' and, that for some offenders in some situations, the use of custody should be a last resort; equally social workers in preparing reports for courts should include a focus on the potential of measures other than custody.

There are two sets of circumstances in which courts must obtain a report before ordering a custodial disposal: **young offenders** (that is, people aged 16 to 21)— ever since the 1949 Act, courts have been obliged to consider a report before sentencing any young offender to a period of detention. The obligation is now located in the *Criminal Procedure (Scotland) Act*, 1995, at section 207. This section states:

> the court shall not…impose detention on an offender unless it is of the opinion that *no other method of dealing with him is appropriate*; and the court shall state its reasons for that opinion…(and further)…to enable the court to form an opinion…it shall obtain from an officer of a local authority or otherwise *such information as it can* about the offender's circumstances; and it shall also take into account any information before it concerning the offender's character and physical and mental condition (s.207(3) and (4)).

The report is directed to help the court form a crucial opinion and the wording of the legislation underlines a number of important issues

- no minimum content for reports is specified, the only criterion being 'such information as it can obtain'
- **the person's circumstances and character** are factors that are germane to the issue of sentencing, not exclusively the offence;
- there is specific mention in this section of the physical and mental condition of the

young person when considering a possible custodial sentence. The Chiswick Report (1985) on Suicide Precautions at HM. Institution Glenochil drew attention to the vulnerability of some young people in custody, and the point was emphasised in circulars issued at the time, for example, SHHD 1/1986 (see Chapter 10);
* reports can be obtained 'from an officer of a local authority or otherwise'. The wording may simply maximise the flexibility open to the court; it may equally pave the way for reports to be prepared by agencies in the 'independent' sector, including agencies operating for profit, and is a recognition, in law at least, that the current role of the local authority could be subject to change. In any case the requirement is not fulfilled by the court obtaining information from the prosecution or defence.

The 'first time' rule

The *Criminal Justice (Scotland) Act*, 1980, sections 41 and 42, introduced a requirement on courts to consider a report before adults (that is offenders aged 21 and over) can be sent to prison for the first time. The requirement is that, **whatever the person's previous record**, a report shall be considered before an adult is sent to prison for the first time (section 204(2) of the CP Act, 1995):

A court shall not pass a sentence of imprisonment on a person of or over twenty-one years of age who has not been previously sentenced to imprisonment or detention by a court in any part of the United Kingdom unless the court considers that *no other method of dealing with him is appropriate*; and for the purpose of determining whether any other method of dealing with such a person is appropriate the court shall obtain (from an officer of the local authority or otherwise) such information as it can about the offender's circumstances, and it shall also take into account any information before it concerning the offender's character and physical and mental condition.

Imprisonment or detention may only be imposed if the court is of the opinion that 'no other method of dealing with the offender is appropriate' and in summary jurisdiction the reasons for this opinion must be stated and entered in the record of the proceedings. While loosely worded, the legislation places a strong emphasis on sentencers using prison as a last resort. In time it might be expected that SERs will provide important information for appeals based on the case that other appropriate methods for dealing with offenders were, in fact, available. However the appropriateness of other methods remains a matter of the court's judgement. It is worth noting that because of the definition of a sentence in section 307(1) no SER is required before imprisonment for contempt of court (see Forrest v. Wilson, 1994, S.L.T., 490).

Non-custodial disposals

There are circumstances in which the court may not impose certain non-custodial disposals without first obtaining a report and specific information. Prior to the *Criminal Justice (Scotland) Act* 1987, it was considered desirable that no probation order should be made without first obtaining a report (Nicholson, 1992). It became mandatory by amendments introduced by the 1987 Act (Schedule 1, para. 10). The CP Act, 1995 requires the court to obtain a report 'as to the circumstances and character of the offender' before making **any** probation order under s.228, and the court must be satisfied 'that suitable arrangements for the supervision of the offender can be made'. The court must also obtain a report 'about the offender and his circumstances' before making a supervised release order (s.209(2) or a community service order (s.238). Specific examples include:

- **Probation Orders with additional requirements**: in particular, requirements of residence; the court must 'consider the home surroundings of the offender' and the name of the place and the time period involved must be specified up to a maximum of twelve months (section 229).
- **Probation orders with a requirement of treatment for a mental condition:** the court must be satisfied that the arrangements for treatment 'have been made' (section 230).
- **Orders and requirements for unpaid work:** Courts may not make an order for unpaid work (a community service order) or a requirement for unpaid work within a probation order without considering a report about the offender and his circumstances, together with an assessment as to suitability for such work and that arrangements 'can be made'. These requirements are located at sections 229 and 238. It should be noted that in section 238 the report must be by an officer of the local authority; the provision does NOT include the words 'or otherwise' as in other sections to do with reports (see Chapter 7).
- **Children:** The law requires that courts consider reports in those cases where children are prosecuted before the courts instead of being referred to the Reporter to the Children's Hearings (see Chapter 6).

Rights of the offender

There is one all-embracing obligation concerning **every report** prepared to assist the court, and that is that a 'copy of the report **shall be given** by the clerk of the court to the offender or to his solicitor'. This obligation was first enacted by section 10 of the *Criminal Justice (Scotland) Act*, 1949. It is now located in the *Criminal Procedure (Scotland) Act,* 1995, s.203(3). The law states that this duty of giving a report to the person is one for the Clerk of Court, even if, in practice, the task is undertaken by a social worker. The appropriate authority and procedure is clear that this is not a private matter between the social worker and the person about whom the report is written. The law is silent as to the person's right to retain that copy after the hearing; it is likely that the term 'given', suggests a right to keep the copy. *Helping the Court Decide* (SWSI, 1996), indicates that 'offenders…should be able to retain a copy if they wish'.

Ordering reports

The sections of the law that empower the ordering of reports reflect a variety of purposes and principles. The purposes range from the most generalised 'enabling inquiries to be made', through to the more focused 'assisting the court's disposal of the case', to the most specific concerns with the character and physical and mental health of young people who may be facing custody. A whole series of terms—'home surroundings', 'such information as it can', 'social background report'—are used within the various sections of legislation to specify the scope of the enquiry.

Nicholson (1992:125) draws both report writer and sentencer to a useful list suggesting the circumstances in which obtaining reports is frequently desirable, whether or not there is a statutory requirement:

- cases involving children;
- cases involving young offenders where the offence is of at least moderate gravity;
- cases where the offence is one of violence, and in particular domestic violence, and offences where offender has a previous record of violence;
- cases where the offence is of at least moderate gravity and the offender either has no previous conviction or has been free of convictions for a substantial period;
- cases where the offence is of least moderate gravity and the offender is female;
- cases where the offender is presently, or has recently been, the subject of a probation or a community service order.

He suggests that psychiatric reports are desirable in:

- cases where the offence is of a sexual nature;
- some, but not all cases, where the offence is related to the misuse of drugs or alcohol;
- cases where the offender has a previous history of mental disorder;
- cases where the offence shows bizarre or unusual behaviour on the part of the offender;
- cases where the offender's behaviour in court is bizarre or unusual;
- some cases where the offence is one of violence, particularly where the offender has a previous record of similar offence.

One of the main problems for practice is that reports are simply ordered, typically without any indication of what may be in the court's mind. Courts do not even order reports in terms of a particular section of an Act, such that the report writer might have a clue as to whether the main concern is exploring alternatives to custody, or simply obtaining information about a person. Most sentencers seem reluctant, even if they have a specific purpose in ordering reports, to disclose what is initially in their mind, in case they raise false expectations in the mind of the offender, or appear to prejudice the decision they finally reach in the light of having the report.

In many a court, the pressure of business, and the sparse nature of the basic information that the court has about an offender, are such as to make the formulation of even a provisional idea about sentence somewhat restricted. The report is called for precisely to obtain information and to help form an opinion in the light of it.

ADMINISTRATIVE AND PROCEDURAL MATTERS

There are a number of administrative and procedural matters that report writers need to attend to as they seek to compile and prepare their reports.

Previous convictions

Reference to past criminality is an integral and necessary part of any report. Report writers need to know their authority for both obtaining and using information about the subject's past criminality in the preparation of the report. Normally, information about previous convictions is made available to the court by the prosecutor; this usually occurs either after an admission of guilt, or after conviction following a trial to determine guilt—but prior to disposal. It is therefore important for report writers to be familiar with the practices of local prosecutors in their use of previous convictions, as this is, often, the only source of information available to the court prior to disposal.

The Rehabilitation of Offenders Act, 1974, (see Chapter 13) does not apply to the practices of prosecutors in this matter. However, prosecutors have been encouraged to observe the spirit of this Act, and, therefore, use their discretion to select from the total picture of the person's past record. The effects of this practice can often be as follows:

- Appearances before a Children's Hearing are not normally shown, although the court must be informed if the person is currently subject to a supervision requirement, in terms of section 70 of the *Children (Scotland) Act*, 1995, because in this circumstance, the court may wish, or may be required, to obtain the advice of the Panel prior to disposal (see Chapter 6).
- Someone who appears as a first offender may not, in fact, have an 'unblemished' record.
- Often only like-convictions are quoted—particularly, for example, in cases of drunkenness, and some traffic offences.

Prosecutors may only quote convictions considered by them to be relevant, thus the general discretion allows scope for a variety of individual interpretations in the compilation of lists for court. Moreover, only convictions prior to the date of the offence's commission can be quoted. It can be that, while a person has been awaiting trial, for example, he may have acquired subsequent convictions. NOS provide detailed guidance for the provision of reports.

Obtaining information

The report writer needs to have access to full information about the extent and nature of the subject's past criminality. Report writers should have at least two main sources of information before they interview the offender; information contained in and included in the SER request; and information from social work records, including any previous SERs, where they exist. Information contained in or with the SER request sent by the clerk of the court should include

- a copy of the complaint or indictment;
- a note of whether there has been a finding of guilt;
- a copy of the list of previous offences presented to the court by the fiscal;
- a note of any relevant comments or remarks made by the bench in relation to the case;
- a note of whether any other reports were requested, e.g. medical or psychiatric;

- details about the offender;
- details about the court procedure, including when the report is due, next court appearance, court address etc., and the offender's status—ordained to appear/bailed/remanded.

In addition it should include a copy of the full list of previous convictions obtained from the Criminal Convictions Enquiry Unit (CCEU) in Stirling. In all areas, arrangements exist with the Scottish Criminal Records Office (SCRO) to obtain information from CCEU to supply social work with a full list of all the appearances made before both courts and children's hearings. The *Rehabilitation of Offenders Act*, 1974, does make it clear that the disclosure of information about a person's past record is illegal unless authorised. Circulars make it clear that in the view of the Secretary of State, the disclosure of convictions by the police to social workers for the purpose of social enquiry reports should not be regarded as contrary to the *Rehabilitation of Offenders Act*, 1974. The practice is seen as being under the heading of a disclosure to persons who have a lawful use for information about convictions. Two matters need careful attention in this context:

i) the disclosure is **only** authorised for the purposes of preparing social enquiry reports, and not for general information, or for any other function imposed by section 27 of the *Social Work (Scotland) Act*; 1968;

ii) the lists supplied by SCRO/CCEU (or local police) contain information over and above specific disposals, and because of this, the list needs editing before any of its contents appear in a social enquiry report.

The following should NOT appear in a social enquiry report:

- No Action (by Reporter to the Children Hearing)
- No Proceedings
- Desert Pro Loco et Tempore
- Desert Simpliciter
- Not guilty
- Not proven
- Continuations
- Deferments

Moreover any reference that may be necessary to appearances before a Children's Hearing should NOT describe them as previous 'convictions', rather as 'appearances'. Any use of this material should not be presented in such a way as to suggest a tariff approach to disposal. Additionally NOS place detailed **requirements** on report writers to obtain specific information for all offenders about any period of previous detention or custody, and about their physical and mental health. Report writers need to be familiar with the detailed arrangements in their areas for obtaining this information. These topics should be investigated for the purposes of a report, whatever the age of the person, but it is essential to obtain this information in the cases of young offenders. Guidance of this nature is contained in the relevant section of the NOS.

Using information

The report writer, then, has lawful use of this information and has authority to quote and/or refer to convictions that the prosecutor may not have listed. Whilst this authority exists, it is more important to underline the criteria for its use in practice:

- there is no statutory requirement on the social worker to provide a full list of convictions (i.e. as an end in itself);
- this can be done if considered relevant or necessary to the purpose of the report.

The function of a report writer in obtaining, and, in turn, relaying to the court, information about past criminality has a different focus from that of the prosecutor. Report writers are required to analyse and interpret, as far as is possible, the person's offending behaviour. To do this effectively social workers require an expertise in understanding the nature of crime as well as understanding those who commit it. It is no longer fanciful to think that, where appropriate, the person's current and past offending should be examined in the light of local patterns and trends of crime and set within local knowledge of factors which contribute to or sustain certain criminal behaviour, including factors relating to geography, time and social context.

SER authors therefore need to take an overview of the pattern of offending behaviour, its frequency and seriousness, not just what the prosecutor may have selected, and may, have to refer the court to matters that the prosecutor has NOT included in the list initially submitted to the court. One obvious example is the circumstance in which a prosecutor may not have quoted a conviction which resulted in social work supervision of some form, but it will clearly be essential for the report writer to comment on that supervision in the report. The use of the information should be determined by the purpose of the report. There can be no automatic practice that meets this criterion: it is a matter of professional judgement.

The report writer's task is not to provide a fuller list than that of the prosecutor—the dictum 'if it's known, put it in' which Curran and Chamber's (1982) study suggested was common practice in the distant past, is not helpful. To carry out the task of report writing adequately, particularly with the increasing emphasis on assessing the risk the offender may pose to the community, social workers need full information about the person's past criminality, about his response to any periods of supervision or to custody, and about his physical and mental health, particularly where this is relevant to the possibility of custodial disposal.

In practical terms, any information supplied in reports about past criminality which exceeds that initially provided by the fiscal, will need to be put to the person by the court, in the same way that the fiscal's list is, so that any contentious items can be challenged and/or checked.

Pre-trial reports

Normally reports are ordered, as we have seen, after an admission or a finding of guilt, under the terms of the various sections of legislation set out above. However, there are some circumstances in which reports are requested by courts in advance of a trial, or prior to an admission or a finding of guilt. There are also some circumstances in which reports can helpfully be prepared voluntarily in advance of a court hearing. The situation is a potentially complex one.

Requests by courts for pre-trial reports

The High Court may request a social enquiry report to be prepared for the date of the trial. It is normally the practice of the High Court to request reports pre-trial when any person under the age of 21, or anyone over 21 who has not previously been sentenced to custody, has been committed for trial at the High Court. This practice derives from the seriousness of the matters with which the High Court deals, the legislative requirements for reports in certain circumstances, and the expense involved in convening hearings of the High Court, particularly if it is sitting outwith Edinburgh or Glasgow. Faced with a request for a pre-trial report, the report writer has to consider the following issues:

Consent to pre-trial reports

The person must consent to the preparation and submission of a report pre-trial. He has the right to refuse preparation of a report at this stage. In order for him to exercise this right, the writer needs to explain in detail:

- the basis on which the report has been requested;
- the method of inquiry and the topics to be included;
- the role of the report in the administration of justice.

Given the complexity of these issues, particularly in the context of cases before the High Court, it is advisable that the approach to the person for consent is through his solicitor. Moreover if the person stipulates conditions surrounding the method and/or content of the report this should be treated as a refusal of consent and conveyed to the solicitor. It is not part of the social worker's function to be involved in any discussion about plea bargaining. NOS direct the social worker in cases of non-cooperation to write to the Clerk of the Justiciary indicating that consent has been refused (NOS SER section).

Plea

Establishing the intended plea is of paramount importance.

a) If the intended plea is one of not guilty, this does not prevent the preparation of a report, though it is often a valid reason for refusal of consent. If, however, consent is given, but the indication is that the plea will be one of not guilty, there are some **restrictions** on the content of the report. In these circumstances, the report cannot discuss anything to do with the charge(s), nor, by logical extension, can it include any discussion of disposal.

b) However, it may be known in advance that a guilty plea is to be tendered, for example, if the papers from the High Court indicate that the procedure under section 76 of the CP Act, 1995 (guilty pleas) is being used, and shows that the person has previously submitted a letter intimating a plea of guilt (see Chapter 3). In this circumstance, it is competent for the report to include coverage of the charge(s), and to venture into the question of disposal.

c) Occasionally, a person will indicate an intention to plead guilty to a lesser or alternative charge to the one shown on the indictment. In this situation the writer can simply say to the court 'I understand that (name of the subject) intends pleading not guilty to the charge as libelled', and proceed as if the overall plea was one of not guilty. There are dangers in assuming that the court might accept any lesser charge.

d) Even more rarely, the accused may indicate an intention to plead not guilty, but make what amounts to an open, full and voluntary admission to the report writer that he is in fact guilty. Here the writer is under obligation to tell him that the report will contain this information, with all its consequences, and then to write the report.

Voluntary submission of reports in advance of a hearing

A social worker may consider it helpful both to a person with whom she is in contact, and to a court before which the person is due to appear, to prepare a report in advance of a hearing. Typically this can be the case when the police or even someone under supervision tells the supervisor of a forthcoming appearance. It is in order for a worker to submit a report in advance of a hearing, or a letter indicating some knowledge of the person, provided the same requirements in relation to the issues of consent and intended plea discussed above are met. NOS provide a framework for the content of reports.

Submission of pre-trial reports to the court

Once prepared, a pre-trial report should be lodged with the Clerk of Court. The report should only be made available **by the clerk** once guilt is either admitted or proved in court. Any request for advance copies—for example, from the person or his solicitor—will be refused.

Limitation of pre-trial reports

The chief objection to the preparation of reports pre-trial is that, whatever the intended plea, the full circumstances of the charge(s) have not been disclosed in public by the prosecutor. Accordingly information relating to the offence, the matters of the person's attitude to the offence(s), and discussion of the question of disposal, are more than usually problematic. Writers can usefully include in any discussion of these matters in a pre-trial report an indication of the limited nature of the information available to them about the charge(s). While it has always been assumed that pre-trial reports can be of some assistance to the court, *Helping the Court Decide* (SWSI, 1996), indicated that High Court judges were lukewarm about the usefulness of these reports, and that they had limited value because they contain background information only and no meaningful information about the accused's offending behaviour. Practitioners equally saw little value in them because they could not deal with offending behaviour and appropriate disposals. They felt these reports were inefficient both because the information might not be used and because it was often out of date by the time a case was heard. Increasingly courts are requesting second reports, post-trial, or postponing requests for reports until after the verdict in cases going to trial. The

SWSI report concluded that the case for retaining pre-trial reports was not strong and recommended that 'the practice of requesting pre-trial reports in the High Court other than those covered by section 76 (guilty pleas)...should be discontinued' (p37).

Non-cooperation in the preparation of reports

Whilst offenders may not be in a position to prevent a court ordering or requiring a report in their case, they can create difficulties for the report writer by varying degrees or forms of non-cooperation with the preparation of the report. The only circumstance in which a person has the right to refuse the preparation of a report is that in which a report has been requested pre-trial. Most reports are ordered or required post-conviction, and there is nothing the subject can do to prevent the report being ordered. The court too may be an 'involuntary client', in that it may be compelled by law to consider it.

The ordering of a report is not a referral nor a request for a service that the authority has the liberty to debate with the referrer at an individual level. It is an order of a court. The writer has both authority and obligation to obtain the information necessary to the court's task of sentencing.

Local authorities are obliged by section 27 of the *Social Work (Scotland) Act*, 1968, to 'make available...such reports as the courts may require'. The courts may regard the wishes of the person on whom the report is to be written as of relatively minor account. NOS indicate that, before the first interview, local authority social work should provide the offender with a leaflet explaining the purpose of the SER, setting out the responsibilities of the writer and the responsibilities and rights of the offender, and explaining the limits of confidentiality. Writers may wish to underline both the obligations on the courts, and the approach they take, should the offender try to impose restrictions on the inquiry. Non-cooperation may be construed by the court as contempt, and extra penalties imposed.

Availability

The subject's availability to the report writer can be the first area in which any degree of non-cooperation manifests itself. If the subject is on bail (see Chapter 3), it is a specific condition of the bail order that he 'makes himself available for the purposes of any report'. The subject therefore runs the risk of being in breach of bail, and of the extra penalties that may bring. Third party information should be detailed and specific, including copy correspondence, if necessary, as it may become the basis of a prosecution for breach of bail. The report writer, therefore, goes about the preparation of the report in the knowledge that the quite specific authority of the bail order is the basis on which appointments can be made and visits required.

The position of someone remanded in custody is less specifically defined. Even so, the behaviour of someone who refuses to attend for interview even though detained in custody, or who attends but remains silent, could well be interpreted as contempt of court. It is not part of the social worker's job to persuade people to co-operate with reports, only to point out the potential consequences of non-cooperation.

Evasion and restriction

People can be unco-operative in manner, be evasive, or seek to restrict the scope of an inquiry to the extent that no report adequate to the court's purposes can be prepared. This is a matter for the professional judgement of the writer. The following points are worth noting:

i)   The court has the opportunity when ordering a report to explain its scope and purpose; the accused and/or his agent can make known any objections or difficulties at that stage.

ii)   Either in lieu of, but preferably in addition to this, the court-based social worker should, in a brief interview, explain the matter more fully and provide information in writing: any immediate problems can be noted and the social worker who has to write the report alerted to them.

iii) The report writer should, at the start of the inquiry, explain the purpose of the SER and setting out the responsibilities of the writer and the responsibilities and rights of the offender.

iv)   The first working contact should be with the named person directly, and should ensure the person understands the position indicated above.

v)   On meeting with a refusal to co-operate, or with a specific objection which appears to negate the value of any report that could be made, the report writer should satisfy himself that the position and the potential consequences of that refusal to co-operate is fully understood; in deciding whether the refusal or objection negates the value of any report, the writer should bear in mind that the court works under an obligation to obtain 'such information as it can'—the question is simply can an adequate report be prepared with the information available, or does the refusal/objection render any report meaningless?

vi)   If the person is represented, the matter should be disclosed to his representative.

vii) A report should be submitted, outlining the steps followed, and indicating the limitations of the information that was obtained.

viii) The court is then in a position to:

- proceed to disposal in the light of information available;
- rule on the difficulties and continue for a further period; and/or
- deal with the issue as a contempt of court.

ISSUES OF PRACTICE AND OPINION

There are many aspects of report writing which legislation does not define. The everyday concerns of social workers, 'what to put in?', and, typically, 'what shall I recommend?', cannot be treated by legal prescription. NOS provide detailed guidance on reports. In addition to basic factual data and a summary of current domestic and social circumstances and essential biographical details, NOS identify four main sections which must deal with:

- information relevant to offending;
- information relevant to sentence/disposal;
- review and conclusions;
- recommendations (NOS SER section).

Improving practice

Brown and Levy's evaluation (1998) and *Helping the Court Decide* (SWSI, 1996) provide the most recent data on SER practice. Both suggest that there have been considerable improvements in the quality of reports submitted to courts since the introduction of NOS but also that there is 'considerable room for improvement' (1996, p.i). Social workers undertaking reports are qualified and, in the main, specialists in criminal justice. Despite this change the SWSI report estimated that as much as 37% of reports were 'not very good', with only 8% rated as 'very good'; 55% were 'quite good' (p.34). Six out of ten reports were viewed as broadly having conformed with NOS.

The main strengths of reports lay in providing information about the offender relevant to understanding his or her offending and to sentencing. However the positives are heavily qualified in the report and in its conclusions 4 out of 10 fell short of NOS. The main weaknesses were lack of *analysis* (of the current offences and previous offending), of *assessment* (of risk factors and the offender's motivation to stop offending), and the limited *use of evidence* (failing to draw on information sources other than the offender to draw conclusions and to support any conclusions to be drawn (para 8.7). Sentencers suggested that the 'relevance of advice about the risk of re-offending, risk of harm to others and motivation to change would be improved if they could be clearer about the basis on which it was given'. NOS on SERs are currently under review in the light of the findings and a revised version is expected in 1998.

More recently, Brown and Levy (1998) found that although sheriffs were generally satisfied with the quality of reports, the reports did not always provide the key information which sheriffs sought, such as pattern of offending and risk of re-offending. Reports were viewed as descriptive rather than analytic and that there was scope for improvements.

While practice is changing rapidly there is a worrying similarity between recent findings and those of studies which pre-date NOS (Creamer and Williams, 1989). Whilst Curran and Chambers' much earlier study (1982) found that only 21% of reports carried a recommendation for probation, Creamer and Williams found that, in relation to 16-21 year olds, this had dropped to 10%—'our findings suggest that the chances of an offender having a social work recommendation for probation included in his social enquiry report are less than was the case some years ago', and conclude that when no recommendation is made within a report, **'the chances of receiving a custodial sentence are greater'** (p.79, emphasis added). **This is the group that government policy is most concerned to see kept out of prison** (see Chapter 1).

Ford's study (1992), which was the last largest-scale Scottish study before the introduction of NOS, confirmed and strengthened these earlier findings and the need for radical changes in practice. The sheriffs interviewed were clear about what they wanted from SERs:

- significant background information to illuminate the person;
- discussion of the offenders' attitude to the offence and the degree of motivation;
- suggestions about what can be done to help the offender and the resources available;
- realism (p.12-13).

Ford's findings are incorporated within the guidance and provide a broad but helpful framework for writing SERs which should address:

- social and domestic circumstances;
- factors relevant to the offence;
- factors relevant to disposal;
- review and conclusions

A small-scale study commissioned by The Scottish Office (Whyte *et al*. 1995) suggested that this framework was not in common usage and that far too many reports continued to demonstrate the lack of structure and clarity of purpose found by earlier research. *Helping the Court Decide* (SWSI, 1996) also suggested that few reports followed the sequence of headings set out in the NOS. A generalised approach in some social enquiry reports which owes little to research findings, government guidance, or even to the repeated comments from sentencers, still seems to hold good for too many reports. Most local authorities now undertake regular monitoring of SERs with a view to ensuring adequate standards in report writing.

The content of reports

In the 1960s, the subject of social enquiry reports was exhaustively discussed by the Streatfeild and the Morison Committees. These discussions still have some validity today. There was unanimous agreement that a central function of reports was to portray to the court the person in trouble before it as an individual human being, from a particular background with a unique biography, and facing a specific set of life circumstances. We noted earlier that legislation recognises the individuality of the offender and his social characteristics as factors that are germane to sentencing. Here social work values harmonise well with this feature of the criminal justice system. The emphasis on analysis and assessment of relationships, attitudes and factors which support and sustain criminal behaviour were seen as central ingredients of a social enquiry report. These remain central concerns today. *Helping the Court Decide* (SWSI, 1996) suggests that 'practitioners tended not to probe a great deal into the attitudes and views of offenders about the effects and consequences of their crimes for themselves and others including their victims' (para 4.25).

The main weakness of reports was in those aspects of report writing which required **analysis** (of current offence and previous offending), **assessment** (of risk and the offender's motivation to stop offending) and the use of **evidence** (drawing from information sources other than the offender, reaching conclusions and making the case for specific sentencing proposal) (SWSI, 1996, para 8.7).

NOS identify key areas for examination in interviews. These include:

- economic and material factors;
- the family;
- learning opportunities including educational skill attainments;
- social factors such as employment and lifestyle;
- physical and mental health, including addiction;
- offending behaviour.

There is authority here, then, for report writers to tell courts what they need to know, not simply what the court thinks it wants to hear. Social workers should provide *their* professional view on the nature of the criminality, and as indicated by NOS, 'provide information relevant to the understanding of offending behaviour and be prepared to comment of the subject's perceptions of their culpability, the seriousness of their offending behaviour and its impact on their victims'.

A long-standing criticism of social work reports has been the failure or reluctance of social workers to deal adequately with finance in reports. The offender's means should always be taken into account and clearly the best vehicle for so doing is the SER. Information should always be clear, verified so far as is possible, and comprehensive, identifying disposable income when inescapable commitments are met; for example the provisions of the *Child Support Act*, 1991 may have a bearing on the offender's ability to pay a fine.

The purpose of reports

Any discussion on the content of reports can only have meaning in the context of the central theme about report writing, namely the purpose of the report. What is to be included, what is deemed to be 'essential', or 'relevant' has to be decided by the report writer with reference to the court's purposes in having the report. The legislation incorporates a variety of reasons for the calling for reports, and it is rarely, if ever, obvious which of those purposes, and it may be more than one, may be in the court's mind. Nonetheless there is little disagreement about the basic purpose of a report:

The main purpose of a social enquiry report in law is to provide information about the offender and his or her circumstances to assist the court in determining the most suitable method of dealing with the case (SWSI, 1996, para 3.1).

The quotation underlines the following points:

a) the client or customer is the court—it is the court's needs that the document is intended to serve;

b) information is an essential ingredient in reports;

c) advice to the courts is the legitimate function of report writers.

Sentencing is not an easy task. Many sentencers will acknowledge, informally, that it is the hardest part of a judge's job. The purpose of the report is to aid that task. Often the weight of hard, socially relevant facts assembled in the report may indeed pose extra problems for the sentencer, in line with the conflicting responsibilities they have.

There is little written about how sentencers approach their task. Sentencers are not generally encouraged to discuss their role in public and often have to undertake it in considerable personal isolation. Nicholson (1992) provides a useful insight on how one sentencer, at least, views the different disposals, and generally goes about the task of sentencing.

It seems important to emphasise the point that report writers and sentencers alike need to be clear that social assessment may equally serve to re-inforce, as much as reduce, the restrictive elements in sentencing. Social work in the past has been perceived as only concerned about the welfare of the offender and not the interests of the victim or community. It is from this that some sheriffs have construed some social work reports as 'pleas in mitigation', and as encroaching on the defence agent's role. It is not the function of reports, or any advice provided to be solely, or necessarily even centrally, concerned with what is good for the subject. Both court and report writer have wider-ranging concerns.

Helping the Court Decide (SWSI, 1996) suggested that sentencers generally considered that social work advice, particularly on the feasibility of community disposals, would help them provided the advice was 'balanced, objective, realistic and recognised the court's wider responsibilities for sentencing' (para 3.2). There was still concern expressed that reports read at times as if they were written on behalf of the offender. The provision of a community disposals assumes that helping the offender change is an appropriate approach in which the social worker has dual responsibilities; firstly to assist the court and the community and secondly to assist the offender and his or her family. This should be reflected in reports.

Discussing the offence

The offence is central to the court's concern. It is the only legitimate reason for involvement with the subject. The SWSI report (1996) indicated that while most offenders thought the key purpose of reports was to supply background information about them, almost a third did not know what the purpose was and very few thought it was concerned with addressing their offending (para. 3.7). The report concludes that the main purpose of the SER is to provide information and advice to the court, in particular, by assessing

• the offender's attitude to the offences, motivation and capacity to change;

• the risk of future offending and harm to others;

• the feasibility of a community-based disposal even in more serious cases where custody is likely;

- the need for supervision on the offender's release from custody where this could contribute to reducing the risk to public safety (para 3.14).

NOS stress that '(reports should) be prepared to comment on the subject's perceptions of their culpability, (and) the seriousness of their offending behaviour...' and again 'consider the extent to which an offender's own views may be relevant to the court's assessment of culpability' (NOS SER section).

A key word here is **culpability**. It is not a concept that is developed in the NOS. Traditional positivist approaches to social science can over-emphasise a deterministic view of human nature—people as products, even passive victims, of their environment, upbringing, peer group, and social circumstances, which can be viewed as providing excuses rather than an explanation or understanding of criminal behaviour. This way of thinking contrasts very sharply with a classical view of individual responsibility and intentionality which are at the root of much legal and jurisprudential thinking. Most contemporary criminology recognises the interplay between the two (Young, 1994). If report writers are to assist the court's sentencing function, they need to find ways of enabling courts to consider and understand possible explanatory or associated factors in the offender's social circumstances, while at the same time offering interpretations that can be recognised within the ideological terms of reference of the courts.

Attention can be given , for example, to four components of culpability (Gross, 1979:74 *et seq.*).

Intentionality
All conduct proscribed by law is deemed to cause harm, of one sort or another. The harm resulting from recklessness calls down blame, but if the same harm is caused deliberately then even greater blame is attached to the act. Engels' dictum that 'anything that sets men in motion must go through their heads' was transposed by Bucholz as 'the cause of a (criminal act) is the individual himself to the extent that his action originated in his head' (1974:210). Thus shop breakers do not simply 'find themselves' inside lockfast premises; stationary cars, whatever the level of security used by owners, have to be entered and set in motion before an offence occurs; the sexual act following a plea to desist; the concealing of goods in a supermarket with the intention of avoiding payment—all these to some degree or another involve certain thought (cognitive) processes and choices. There is a growing expectation that assessment of motivation and attitudes by standardised measures or by individual professional judgement is an important task for social workers in conjunction with the social circumstances leading to the offence.

Harm to victims
'Harm is an untoward occurrence consisting in a violation of some interest of a person' (Gross, 1979:78/115). 'All provisions of the criminal law create criminal liability for conduct because that conduct is believed to bring about, or to threaten, some undesirable state of affairs' (ibid.). The court will have information such as a list of stolen property, or the basic injury sustained, and it is no part of social work's function to replicate that. Social work can, however, make a useful contribution based on

a knowledge of victimology. An obvious example is where a child has been a victim of abuse, where the authority's child protection strategy can add a helpful dimension to the court's assessment of the harm caused. Beyond that, there are indications, for example, that frail and older people can be affected by 'secondary harm'—not so much the sentimental value of items stolen that may have low financial values, but in their emotions (feelings of violation), and in their social functioning (fear of people, of going out, and so on). The list can be extended to any victim, visible or invisible. There is a dimension here rarely touched upon in reports which the Association of Directors of Social Work's policy statement of victims is intended rectify:

> The victim perspective should form a core part of the content of Social Work Supervision in the Criminal Justice System ; SERs should in all appropriate cases, outline the fact that the victim perspective will be pursued in proposed Social Work Supervision and that this perspective has been addressed in the preparation of the report.(ADSW Policy on Victims, 1996, para 2)

This awareness of the victim's interests and suffering needs to be enhanced considerably in assessments and in programmes of intervention, including reparation and compensation, and displayed in reports (see Chapter 7, and also the NOS).

Dangerousness

Every offence, to a greater or lesser degree, carries an element of dangerousness or risk. Car theft which actually results in no substantial material or bodily hurt nevertheless carries an inherent dangerous element. The sexual assault which stops short of rape has a provisional danger of rape because few offenders would lay claim to being in full possession of their faculties in such a situation. The staff in a bank that is being robbed do not know whether the pistol is real or merely a replica. Policy makers and sentencers have exercised their minds on the difficult question as to whether and how dangerous offenders can be identified (see, for example, The Butler Committee, 1975, Cmnd 6244, SACRO 1992). A key priority for government policy is that such people should be incarcerated for long periods and subject to intervention programmes in custody or be subject to strict supervision and surveillance when in the community (see *Commitment to Protect*, 1997). Key questions must be addressed such as:

- What are the stressors or precipitants associated with dangerous behaviour and have or can they been removed?
- What is the person's current capacity for confronting behaviour?
- How does the offender continue to view himself?
- Is the behaviour person-specific or getting back at society?
- What actually was done?
- Can we discern that he can acknowledge his own responsibility and the impact on the victim?

The *Framework for Assessing Risk* issued in draft in January 1998 as a supplement to the NOS emphasises that 'risk assessment is an important part of social work practice in the criminal justice system'. Dangerousness and risk are not in themselves highly correlated with issues that cause worry and concern. Prediction is problematic. Social workers cannot be experts in all areas of risk, and ethically it is important that the limitations of such assessment are equally recognised.

Legitimacy
The entering of lockfast premises, abuse, and the threatening of people are all examples of conduct which is beyond the bounds both of legality and legitimacy. However, there will always be debates about the boundaries of legitimacy; for example, in issues of chastisement of children and other forms of domestic violence; and boundaries within sexual relations—the concept of rape within marriage is still a relatively recent acknowledgement. At a more mundane level, report writers need to pay regard to the issue of legitimacy in assessing how far the offender went beyond legitimate conduct; for example, it stretches credulity to accept that house breakers 'were led' into crime, unless some very hard evidence can be shown of impressionable youth in the context of a group of much stronger personalities. The report writer has to exercise his own critical judgement, particularly when the only source of information comes from the offender, and must be wary of the risk of operating a 'rule of optimism' well recognised in child abuse work.

Recommendations

Sheriffs, like social workers, have held widely differing views, over the years, about recommendations in SERs, although recent evidence suggests that 'on balance the majority of sentencers were in favour of the inclusion of advice on specific sentencing options' (SWSI, 1996: para. 6.4). Equally there is a weight of opinion against recommendations on disposal:

> A report writer who, unsolicited, expresses views on the best method of disposal is going beyond his terms of reference (Lord Wheatley, 1964).

> Frivolous and incomprehensible (Sheriff in Greer and McGinley, 1979).

> The Court has repeatedly observed that it is not the function of social workers to suggest courses which might be adopted in relation to sentencing (Lord Hunter in HM Advocate v. Collins, 1982).

> Reports will provide detailed information...so that options can be fully explored. Its purpose will not be to make recommendations about sentencing or to be a plea in mitigation (Crime, Justice, and Protecting the Public, 1989 Cmnd 965).

It is concerning, in the light of this weight of judicial opinion, that the NOS should refer repeatedly and ambiguously to report writers 'recommending' disposals, and of having 'preferred options', particularly with regard to non-social work disposals. It is questionable whether the practice of 'recommending' a disposal, other than a social work disposal, has any formal judicial support. The practice

- runs the risk of bringing social workers into conflict with judges;

- encourages report writers to usurp the sentencer's function;
- assumes social workers have sufficient levels of legal knowledge and expertise.

The term '**Opinion as to Disposal**' was coined many years ago by the Streatfeild Committee (1961) which considered very carefully the parameters within which such an opinion could be given. It recognised the boundaries, both of expertise and function, of both report writer and court. A number of observations can be made:

- there is no obligation to offer any opinion—a good social enquiry report as such assists the sentencing process;
- considerable thought and caution should be exercised before offering any opinion, other than for a social work disposal and, when done report writers should explicitly acknowledge that the sentencing decision is one for the court;
- the most appropriate opinion is one relating to the person's suitability for a disposal involving social work supervision and its chances of diverting the offender from further crime;
- offering an opinion on a social work disposal is related to the social and rehabilitative possibilities of any suggested disposal—these factors do not represent the totality of sentencing considerations which the court must bear in mind.

The policy framework, discussed in Chapter 1, requires social work to provide feasible and credible community disposals for medium to serious non-violent offenders and community-based alternatives to custody for violent offenders, who are likely to face custody. It seems both logical and reasonable for social workers to articulate the most suitable social work options available to the court in these circumstances, whether or not the court is considering a community-based option, and in this context, to 'highlight' the most appropriate option, should the court wish to pursue a social work disposal. Anything beyond this specific area of expertise is likely to be inappropriate, other than to indicate the possible implications of not taking up the option of social work. It is equally important to note that where no option is made, research indicates a significantly higher risk of custody (Creamer and Williams, 1989); making appropriate social work disposals available to the court is one of the key tasks of the report writer. The task is not made easier by the fact that sentencers give no clue, in advance, to the social worker which disposal they have in mind. The concept of 'preferred options', unless related to social work disposals is likely to reinforce the views of some sentencers that social workers are encroaching on their role.

Something of these distinctions is captured in parts of NOS, which require that 'reports should comment on the possible impact or consequences of any disposal on the offender and/or his family, particularly depriving him of his liberty, or the impact of a financial penalty'. The guidance specifically requires social workers to bring to a court's attention any doubts the author has (with supporting evidence) about a person's fitness, both physical and mental, and the implications for any specific disposal, particularly custody. In these various sources, then, is more detailed and helpful guidance as to the topics on which an opinion or opinions can be offered on disposals not involving social work.

The SWSI report on SERs (1996) came to similar conclusions, which we assume will be reflected in the revised NOS on SERs in 1998:

> The term recommendation used by national standards is not helpful. We think the most appropriate form for advice is to review the pros and cons of specific sentencing options. Despite sentencers' preferences for an open-ended format, authors should be encouraged to state the community-based option or options which they consider have the best chance of preventing or reducing offending, acknowledging that the court must take wider consideration into account. If the author does not think that a given level of risk can be managed in the community he or she should say so. (para 6.11)

Use of a simple formula, consisting of 'if', 'then', 'because', may be of assistance in considering community-based disposals. This formula avoids the potential dangers of 'second guessing' the minds of sentencers, and directs the social worker towards a clear opinion, so avoiding the strictures with which this section began. It can be illustrated in the following kind of example:

IF	the court wishes to consider community service,
THEN	it should be aware of the direct effect on 'Smith'
BECAUSE	he is an ardent follower of the local football team and he would miss matches; also, he is a poor mixer and communicator, and community service may well assist his skills in these areas.
IF	the court is considering probation
THEN	'Smith' will not like the disciplinary aspects which are inherent; it will make heavy demands on him in terms of self-analysis and examination of his behaviour, and it would be a necessary requirement that he reside at home;
BECAUSE	he needs to face up to some unpleasant realities about how his behaviour affects his family (these having been documented in the earlier parts of the report) and unless he can break away from his present unstable lifestyle, the risk of further offending will remain high.

The risk in using any simple formula is that it understates the importance of creative approaches and can undermine professional decision making, precisely the complaint that can be directed toward some of the more procedural aspects of the NOS.

The argument advanced in relation to social inquiry is that it should provide an analysis based on evidence combined with professional knowledge and expertise and lead to *indicative* conclusions which require to be expressed in terms of the specific offence and the particular offender. The logic of the situation is that these conclusions ought never to be expressed as definitive conclusions relative to one sentencing option, but rather in terms of traditional social work theory as a 'differential assessment' (Siporin, 1975). In this context it is perhaps worth recalling Aristotle's comment in the Nichomachean Ethics. 'It is the mark of an educated mind to rest satisfied with the degree of precision that the nature of the subject admits and not to seek exactness when only an approximation is possible.' The end product of the social inquiry process can never be other than an approximation and it is important that not only should this be borne in mind, but also that it be clearly articulated in the submitted reports, particularly with the growing emphasis on risk assessment.

Action plans

In any exploration of community-based measures, the development of a provisional action plan is an important ingredient, and the idea receives good emphasis in the NOS. The shorthand phrase 'packages' is often used, or the concept of a 'programme of action' or 'personal change programme'. The guidance reflects an expectation that more services are being developed on a programmed basis so that when a community-based option involving social work is being considered both the judge and the offender will have as clear an understanding as is practical as to the nature and purpose of the programme proposed, the time demands and expected outcomes. Reasonable action plans can only be presented where a clear targeting framework has been established by the agency and programmes of intervention developed to address the anticipated crime-related issues for the individuals judged to fall within the target groups. While any plan has to be adapted (over time) to the individual, such an approach would allow the court and the offender to understand the core requirements, demands and intervention involved in any social work approach on offer. It can then be accompanied by a resource statement on the availability of the service and whether this can be delivered in a timescale acceptable to the court.

There are tensions and risks in this proposed practice:

- what the report writer is proposing may not meet with the court's approval and may serve to raise the expectations of the offender;
- the court may wish to impose more stringent conditions than those provisionally assessed as a 'willingness to participate in the preparation of an action plan'.

In any case, the value of action plans should be to ensure that where consent is required, the offender has made an informed choice and that judges should understand the undertaking they impose. If social workers are to meet their responsibilities they must, as far as is practicable, explore in some detail what any given social work disposal will entail both in terms of time demands, the kinds of objectives that are to be met and the kinds of activities involved as outlined in NOS. Good liaison with courts and good information is essential if sheriffs are to be familiar with the kinds of programmes on offer to certain offenders, how they operate and to what effect. Quite clearly these expectations need to be shared by sheriffs and it is essential that the Sheriff's Association endorse such an approach.

National objectives and standards—other issues

Whilst there is much in NOS especially in terms of objectives of direction and intent and practice guidance to ensure good levels of practice, a number of points require some additional comment.

Number of interviews

Although NOS do not oblige social workers to undertake a second or subsequent interview, they identify a range of circumstances where further interviews 'will normally be required'. The Inspectorate report (SWSI, 1996) found that 40% of reports were prepared on the basis of one interview, which can hardly be indicative of a thorough investigation. The reasons suggested were that many offenders were already known to the report writer and limited time was available. Clearly more emphasis is required on the need to break the habitual assumption that social enquiry reports can be prepared on the basis of one interview (Wood, 1986). NOS encourage report writers to contact the offender's family 'wherever possible'. The Inspectorate report found that this was not routinely done. The main reasons given by practitioners were issues of personal safety, the subject's refusal to agree and the lack of time.

While ideally all SER requests should involve a high quality of assessment, the growing demand from the courts for SERs means that not all will be completed to the same 'level' and there is some evidence to suggest this is creating an imbalance in the use of limited resources. It has been suggested that more time is spent on assessments than on supervision and effective forms of intervention, yet most of them are not translated into a social work disposal nor involve high risk of custody cases. Some agencies have considered experimenting with a system of priority setting which indicates the different 'level' of assessment on offer, whereby the court (and the offender) is aware of the limitations of the assessment provided. It equally may be that under such a system courts would be able to indicate at the time of request the level they expect, while some brief interviews may be done on the spot by court-based social workers (see Chapter 4). The Inspectorate report (SWSI, 1996) echoes this view and recommends that the following steps could make an impact on improving efficiency:

- provide full reports for serious or persistent offenders and short reports for less serious and early offenders;
- provide 'same day' reports where a specific and limited piece of information or advice is required; and
- make greater use of personal computers and templates when preparing reports (para 10.5)

Conclusion of interviews

The previous point takes on extra force when the Inspectorate report suggests that 'the interview should close with a discussion of...the nature of any conclusions, recommendations, and agreed courses of action which will form part of the report' (para 14.18.2). This displays an ambition that may not be possible given the limited nature of the interview. There are a number of stages in an assessment: assembling facts and information; interviewing; analysis of both; and drawing together the total body of data and analysis into an assessment (Moore, 1984). A report cannot be drawn together 'on the door step' with a quick discussion of 'recommendations and agreed courses of action'. Considerable concern must be expressed if the norm of one interview is implied as representing appropriate professional standards.

Incidence of addiction

Alcohol and/or drug misuse are present in a large proportion of situations exam-ined by SER writers. NOS draw attention to this rather neglected aspect in the coverage in reports, especially in relation to alcohol consumption—illegal drugs seem to cause a greater degree of moral panic. While addiction is not a mitigating or excusatory factor, indeed it may be viewed as an aggravating factor, examina-tion of patterns of usage and problems associated with it are important for the court in considering the risk it represents of future offending, and the availability of treatment resources which can address the problem in a particular instance. Stand-ardised tools are required to provide at least minimum data on the use of drugs and alcohol and their association with offending. The availability of a drug-assessment pack commissioned by the Scottish Office (McDonald et al, 1994) provides an opportunity for more standard information to be gathered routinely as part of the SER process. Again good IT systems are required if this data is to have any influ-ence on service provision, policy and resourcing.

Contact with third parties without the subject's consent

NOS suggests that report writers have the right to contact third parties without the consent of the subject if, after attempts to explain the needs of the court and to secure the person's agreement have failed, the writer still considers it necessary for the purposes of the report. The Inspectorate report suggests 'the issue is not whether the offender consents but what the report writer thinks the court should know...' and that 'in deciding, they should aim to be fair to the offender and sensitive to any possible adverse consequences'.

A note of caution has to be expressed. There is an alternative view which draws attention to the fact that such a right (to bypass the subject) is not specified in the legislation. Indeed the court is bound only to 'obtain such information as it can', and, moreover, the person is an adult and free to decide to accept the consequences of any non-cooperation if he is determined that the report writer should not contact a particular third party. There is a lack of detailed legal authority. For most practi-cal purposes, explanation of the issues usually serves to allay the natural anxieties of the offender in this circumstance, but in the face of informed and determined objection the report writer has a genuine problem. A better course may be to indi-cate in the report that specific areas have not been investigated due to the absence of consent, citing reasons where appropriate. This is an area that will need further debate and development as the concerns, particularly, over sex offenders (see *Com-mitment to Protect*, 1997), are leading to greater and greater expectations that so-cial workers should be able to make risk prediction on very limited investigations.

Discussions in chambers

It is widely recognised that it is not appropriate for either court-based social work staff or authors of social enquiry reports to discuss individual reports with sentencers in private before a court hearing. This practice was not uncommon in some areas in the past, but the Grant Committee (1967) made it clear that such discussions con-stitute a breach of the substantive law; 'the practice, which is not unknown, of (the probation officer) seeing the Sheriff in private when the accused and the prosecutor are not present, especially before the hearing of a case...(is) highly improper'. If direct discussion with a sentencer is required then the report writer should be present in court to speak publicly if required to do so (see Chapter 3).

Risk assessment and prediction

NOS stress the issue of interpreting the seriousness of a person's past record, and of assessing the risk of further offending. The aspiration to address issues of seriousness within reports is clear. However the criteria and the data on which to base these judgements is not. Social workers do not receive information from the prosecution which is available to the judge. What is generally known is a brief description of the offence and the number of previous recorded convictions. The issue demonstrates the difficulty of interpretation of what is serious. In many cases in summary procedure it is the persistence of the offender rather than the nature of the offence itself that is serious. Is an attempted housebreaking more or less serious than, say, taking and driving away a motor car? Are past offences to be judged on the basis of imposed penalties, or on some other criterion? Will a social work view of 'seriousness' concur with that of the bench?

The task of trying to 'read the court's mind' is ethically perilous. The report writer has typically had to rely on a subjective reading of the situation, informed only by experience and information supplied by the offender. More generally, research in the past few years has drawn attention to great disparities in sentencing, especially between areas with relatively similar crime rates.

A number of tools have been developed in the last decade to assist the strategy of 'targeting' community-based measures on cases which would otherwise have gone to prison, while avoiding net widening, such as the Cambridge risk of custody scale and the Home Office's Offender Group Reconviction Scale (OGRES, Home Office, 1996), and in Scotland Dundee University's Dunscore. While each of these tools has severe limitations, primarily because they base their predictions on 'static'(unchangeable) factors—on previous convictions which will always be present even if the offender has changed—they do provide valuable monitoring data which can make a professional judgement 'visible' in a form that allows aggregation and analysis.

More recently standardised assessment measures are being adopted, such as the Level of Service Inventory (LSI-R: Bonta, 1996), which incorporate static and 'dynamic' (changeable) factors . The information generated by such instruments allows for some estimate of the 'seriousness' of cases and can assist in determining the level of risk the offender may present to the community. This can be collated on an authority-wide basis, so that an overview can be taken to identify required changes in priority of provision. By such means profiles of high- and low-risk groups could be identified to assist objective setting and planning programmes of intervention against the existing resource/skill base. This kind of data is a pre-requisite of corporate and strategic planning, and to the management of services discussed in Chapter 2.

In addition to the above, a second set of statistical data is required, which gives, for each court district or for the social work area, the crime rates and sentencing patterns. This data is available to some degree through the Scottish Criminal Records Office in Scotland but is not readily available to criminal justice social work. Pilot projects of court information systems are underway in Scotland. In the interim, some authorities are beginning to seek access to police data which can profile offending within geographical areas and set the demand from SERs in a local context, allowing more rational planning of need against provision.

Such data could enable comparisons between the sentencing patterns of areas with relatively similar crime rates, highlighting which court areas (or even individual sheriffs) were more 'custody-prone' than others. One result of the local government re-organisation is undoubtedly the creation of a smaller data base on which such computations can be made. Social work authorities could be assisted in some degree of prediction of:

- patterns of custodial sentencing within a given area;
- court areas within the authority using custody at an above-average level, and thus in need of more effort in terms of targeting;
- the proportion of the authority's existing workload focused on people 'at risk of custody'.

Adequate information will allow some quantification of the shifts in both effort and workload required to achieve the objectives of reducing the court's use of custody and would enable resources to be used more cost effectively.

There has been insufficient emphasis on the development of information systems which support the use of risk assessment scales, nor much of any approach that takes a corporate and organisational look at the targeting of reports and intervention. We know of only one authority which seems to have invested sufficient resources to begin to establish an integrated information system recording, among other things, profile data on offenders with SER requests, worker's risk assessments scores, alcohol and drug scores, social work recommendations and court disposals, supervision planning and attendance records. These allow direct feedback to practitioners about their 'error' and 'success' rate against prediction, and allow managers to monitor assessment and supervision practices. It also provides data for managers to begin the process of targeting and rational planning. Equally important in such a development, as well as the data itself, is the fact that social workers are logging their judgements and decisions onto an IT system which can be used for individual supervision, planning and management purposes.

Such scrutiny seeks to ensure that statutory supervision is used in the higher priority cases only. A corporate approach seeks to ensure that people are kept down tariff as far as possible, rather than being drawn further into the system as a result of inappropriate social work intervention. The change of approach and thinking required is considerable.

It is disappointing, in the light of all this experience, that until the recent draft of *Framework for Assessing Risk* (SWSI, 1998), the NOS seem to have left the assessment of seriousness and risk purely at the level of the individual report writer, when clearly there is a requirement to establish information technology systems for all criminal justice teams. A dozen local authorities are taking part in a piloting exercise of risk assessment based on the framework.

Another key matter that needs urgent attention in this context of assessment is the provision of forms of early intervention, as intended by the Kilbrandon approach, such as voluntary assistance and diversion under the 100% arrangements. The 100% central funding arrangement is primarily based on the numbers of statutory orders an authority achieves, not the target groups provided with service. The resulting temptation of drawing people up into the criminal justice system to ensure the predicted income is a real danger. In order both to prevent this kind of abuse of probation, and in order to restrict the use of statutory orders, especially the more demanding ones, to cases in which the risk of custody is high, it will be important to ensure that voluntary help can be made a reality—whether it is provided by the local authority or by an independent agency. If voluntary help, in fact, comes to mean 'doing nothing', then the chances of the person re-appearing before the court, still in great need, but now at higher risk of custody, will only be increased, and the whole purpose of the exercise defeated.

Some mechanism is needed to attract funding for everyone successfully diverted from prosecution, from custody and from statutory orders. The use of risk-assessment techniques, particularly those involving the assessment of 'dynamic' (changeable) factors such as anti-social attitudes, criminal associates, as well as 'static' factors may, in the future, assist in this respect. It is to be hoped that the draft *Framework for Assessing Risk* (SWSI 1998) will result in developments in meaningful risk assessment practices.

The 'twin-track' approach—another version

The approach promoted by Rifkind (1989) and incorporated within NOS is a 'twin-track' approach. This approach seems to have found equal favour with the Labour government. On the one hand, those convicted of serious offences, particularly of violence, will expect to be dealt with very seriously, and may well be detained in prison for long periods. On the other hand, it is conceded that prisons are full of many less serious offenders who could be dealt with more effectively by community-based disposals. The social enquiry report is recognised as a key document in enabling the court to discern who could be dealt with by community-based disposals and to ensure that no custodial disposal is made for lack of a community-based alternative. Legislation has increased the circumstances when courts are compelled to use reports, particularly before anyone can be sent to custody. The White Paper *Crime, Justice and Protecting the Public* (1990, Cmd 965) suggested that the court's sentence should be the outcome of a sequence of questions:

- How serious is the offence?
- Is it more or less serious of its kind?
- Are there mitigating factors?

- Can some compensation be given to the victim?
- How much restraint on liberty is needed to punish the crime?
- If some restraints are justified, is: community service, probation, or another penalty most suitable?
- If community service, how many hours should be ordered?
- If probation, are additional requirements needed?
- Is the offence serious enough to justify a combination of penalties?
- Is the offence so serious that only a custodial sentence is justified?
- If so, how long a sentence is necessary to punish this offence? (Home Office, 1990, para. 2.19)

The social enquiry report, it suggested, will provide detailed information about how the offender should be dealt with in the community, so that the options can be fully considered. Its purpose is not to make 'recommendations' about sentencing, or to be a plea in mitigation, but to provide: a description of the restrictions on liberty which the programme would involve; information about the offence, and the offender's attitude to it; essential background information; an assessment of the offender's ability and willingness to tackle his or her offending behaviour.

The SER writer may be assisted in considering a 'twin-track' of enquiry; the first, using a subjective professional assessment, to determine whether the risk of using a community-based measure is likely to be acceptable to the court for certain target groups, particularly medium to serious non-violent offenders

TRACK ONE

IF RISK (of using a community-based measure) IS THOUGHT TO BE

UNACCEPTABLE   ACCEPTABLE

THEN:

What sentencing **objectives** is custody calculated to meet on the best knowledge available?	Is the risk (of custody): low, medium, or high?
In this situation, the report is likely to focus first on issues such as:	If **low**, then explore: financial penalties, admonition; **voluntary** assistance.
What are the effects on the victim; the offender and his/her family?	If **medium** then explore: standard/short probation; (short) community service;
The seriousness of the offence; previous like offences; previous disposals and effects; **what patterns of behaviour need to be addressed**?	If **high,** then explore: probation with conditions; intensive probation; longer community service.
Only if a community-based measure can address these issues of containment and control should one be explored;	**explore** the options available in full detail.

If uncertain as to whether the risk of custody is low, medium, or high, a reasonable approach may be to:

a) admit, in the report, to uncertainty;
b) adapt the use of the If, Then, Because, formula (above).

It is equally essential that social workers stress the limitations of any risk assessement. The court can select the appropriate measure on the basis of 'advice' that has been properly given and argued.

The second track of enquiry pursues a set of questions about the possible responses to community-based measures

TRACK TWO: Likely response to community-based measures

FACTORS INDICATING

NEGATIVE RESPONSE TO:	POSITIVE RESPONSE TO:
FINES	
Previous fines unpaid	Previous fines paid
Offending persists	Longer gaps in convictions records
HEAVY FINES	
Low income	Materially affluent
Many dependants	Few responsibilities
COMMUNITY SERVICE	
Socially unskilled	Skills to offer
High degree of personal need	Needs not an obstacle
Long/varied working hours	Regularly available
STANDARD PROBATION	
Previous poor response	Acceptance of problems
Disruptive/anti-authority	Foreseeable solutions
INTENSIVE PROBATION	
Previous poor response	Acknowledges seriousness
High predicted risk to others	Potential to comply
SPECIALIST PROBATION OPTIONS	
No discernible special need	Residential need
	Mental health problems
	Significant addiction problems
	Attendance order needed

Whilst there are risks in any formula which contains, essentially, selective examples open to varying interpretations, it is important that frameworks are developed and adapted on the basis of local empirical data, if properly costed and resourced provision is to be effective.

Chapter 6

Children who Offend

PART I: Courts and children's hearings; prosecuting children; children's hearings; reports and decision making

PART II: Disposals and outcomes; appeals; secure accommodation; integrated services

PART I: COURTS AND CHILDREN'S HEARINGS

Preamble

The fabric of social work in Scotland today can be seen as having its origins in concerns in the early 1960s with children in trouble, and, in particular, with the ways in which criminal courts at the time dealt with children who offended and appeared before them. The Kilbrandon Committee (Cmnd 2306), made recommendations which led, not only to the introduction of a distinctively new system for dealing with children in trouble, but also, consequentially, to the re-organising of all social work services under the umbrella of all-purpose social work departments—an equally distinctive Scottish arrangement.

Before the introduction of the system for dealing with children in trouble by the *Social Work (Scotland) Act*, 1968, juvenile offenders (that is, offenders under 16 years of age) were dealt with by the same types of criminal court that dealt with adult offenders. There were only a few specialist juvenile courts in Scotland and juveniles were normally dealt with by courts in buildings, or parts of them, that were separate from those involving adults; the cases were heard in private; there was protection from publicity; and the attendance of parents was essential. While identical powers were available to the courts when dealing with juveniles as were available in respect of adults (for example, probation, fines, etc.), the over-riding duty placed on all courts dealing with juvenile offenders was to act in the best interests and for the welfare of the juvenile.

Part III of the *Social Work (Scotland) Act*, 1968, replaced the former system of criminal courts dealing with juveniles by a system of children's hearings and extended their jurisdiction, under certain circumstances, to children and young people under 18 years. Part III of the 1968 Act was subsequently replaced by the *Children (Scotland) Act*, 1995 (CS Act, 1995), which now provides the legal basis for the operation of Scotland's children's hearings system. Provisions for dealing with children within the criminal justice system are contained in the *Criminal Procedures (Scotland) Act*, 1995 (CP Act, 1995).

Our concern is social work with people, whether adult or child, who are alleged to have committed criminal offences. This chapter has children who offend as its prime focus. It should be borne in mind that children's hearings have a jurisdiction which encompasses not only children who are alleged to have committed criminal offences, but also children who are deemed to be in need of care and protection and children who are regarded as being too young (legally speaking) to form the necessary intention to commit a criminal act. Indeed it was a contention of the Kilbrandon Committee that the similarities in the underlying situation of juvenile offenders who come to the attention of the authorities and children in need of care and protection 'far outweigh the differences' and that, in principle, they should be dealt with in similar ways with a focus primarily on their needs and not solely their deeds. Kilbrandon proposed an integrated system for dealing with all such children and young people since 'the true distinguishing factor...is their need for special measures of education and training, the normal up-bringing processes having, for whatever reason, fallen short' (para 15).

The children's hearing system is not intended simplistically to separate-out 'offending' and 'non-offending' children. In principle, the system is structured as a system of diversion and early intervention intended to address the needs of the whole child in partnership with parents, where possible, not simply or exclusively focusing on offending. It is, nonetheless, one of the explicit objectives of the children's hearing system to try to help young people stop offending. It is important to note that despite this decriminalising approach, for certain purposes under the *Rehabilitation of Offenders Act,* 1974 accepting or having an offence ground established at a hearing is treated as if it were a conviction and any subsequent disposal as if it were a sentence 'for the purposes of this Act (but not otherwise)' (section 3)(see chapter 13).

Scottish legal provisions make it possible, in theory, for most children and young people under the age of eighteen to be dealt with through the hearing system. Ironically, legislation following the 1968 Act has provided a series of mechanisms for dealing with more young people through the courts.

For the first twenty years since its inception in 1971, the children's hearing system had been relatively free from significant criticism. However in the 1990s there were a number of high-profile child protection cases which suggested that some serious problems existed with the system. A number of inquiries were established to consider possible improvements. These included the Clyde report on the Orkney child abuse cases (1991), the Kearney report into child care policies in Fife (1992), the Finlayson report on reporters to children's panels (Scottish Office, 1992) and the Skinner report which reviewed residential child care (SWSG, 1992). At the same time the Scottish Law Commission's report on family law (S.L.C., 1992) raised questions about the consistency of Scots law in safeguarding children's rights as outlined in the United Nations Convention on the Rights of the Child (1989), adopted by the UK government in 1991. Adoption law was also subject to review (SOED, 1993).

The White Paper *Scotland's Children: Proposals for Child Care Policy and*

Law (SOED, 1993; Cm 2286) contained proposals for significant legislative change. At the same time a major programme of research on the system was commissioned by the Scottish Office from the universities of Stirling and Edinburgh. This re-examination of child care issues and perceived problems in the children's hearing system, coincided with a strong political emphasis in the UK on law and order and a growing public concern with crime in general and with persistent young offenders in particular. Chapter 7 of the White Paper dealt specifically with children and young people who offend and was both the result of and the focus for a renewed debate on juvenile crime and the effectiveness of the children's hearing system in dealing with this group of children and young people (Whyte, 1998).

The White Paper identified tackling juvenile crime as a priority area for government and for the children's hearing system.

> Tackling offending behaviour among young people is a central part of tackling crime as a whole and the children's hearing has a vital role within this process (para. 7.8). Added emphasis will be given in training on how to deal with young offenders who appear before children's hearings (par. 7.10).

The paper emphasised that children's panel members should be well equipped by their training to deal with young people who offend and that the Scottish system should use its existing powers to deal with more 16 and 17-year-olds in keeping with the spirit of the United Nations Convention on the Rights of the Child (1989), which emphasises the special status of this group and promotes special provisions for dealing with them. With a view to strengthening the arrangements for supervision of young people who offend, the White Paper proposed the development of

> national objectives and standards for home supervision…to ensure consistency of good practices within a common framework throughout Scotland (para. 7.12) (to) enable them to be more focused to address the behaviour of the child and clarify the nature of the supervision requirement imposed (para. 7.13).

In addition, new guidance on supervision agreements was proposed with the intention of setting out

> • the purpose and specific issues to be addressed through supervision with child and family; the proposed methods by which the supervision (and others) will approach these issues; what the parents undertake to do; what the child undertakes to do;
> • the time scale for the plan; and the process for reviewing progress (para. 7.14)

Draft guidance on *Home Supervision and Contracts* (SWSG, 1996) provided an important update to practice guidance, but fell far short of the proposal for national service objectives and standards. This guidance was subsequently 'distilled' and included in *Scotland's Children, The Children (Scotland) Act 1995 Regulations and Guidance* Vol. Ch. 2. (SWSG, 1997). While this contains broad objectives of direction and intent, it does not provide national objectives or service standards. The expectation seems to be that local authorities will establish their own service standards through the development of children's plans (section 19, CS Act 1995).

Sections 7.17 -7.27 of the White Paper specifically address the issue of the persistent young offender and stress the need for intensive community-based supervision arrangements and for effective multi-agency collaboration. The paper indicates that adequate secure accommodation is already available to hearings for dealing with 'the most serious cases' (para. 7.18). It notes the very high occupancy rate (90%) and the increasing use of such resources for girls and proposes a review of the situation. The White Paper was a little more circumspect about 16 and 17-year-old offenders.

> By virtue of the seriousness of their offences and their maturity many young people should no doubt face the full rigour of prosecution and the sanctions which follow on a guilty verdict. However, there are also among this group young offenders who are *immature* and for whom a programme of care and supervision under existing powers through the hearing system might be a more effective way of changing their behaviour and reducing the risk of future offending (para 7.29) *(emphasis added)*.

No attempt was made to articulate criteria for 'immaturity', simply that

> while it would not be realistic to expect children's hearings to deal with the full range of offending after the age of 16, there is scope for them to expand their role within existing powers, provided the right resources are there to back this up. (para. 7.29)

The tension between recognising the special status and rights of youth, on one hand, and dealing with their behaviour in politically acceptable ways, on the other, remains a major pre-occupation in the UK and the general tone in recent years has been to consider more punitive ways of dealing with persistent young offenders.

(The children's hearings system came into effect in 1971. Further information and discussion of its workings can be found in Martin *et al.*, 1981; Morris and McIsaac, 1978; Moore, 1989, Cowperthwaite, 1992; Kearney, 1991; Norrie, 1997; Hallet *et al*, 1997; Whyte *et al*, 1998.)

In practice most children and young people under 16 who offend in Scotland are dealt with by the children's hearings system and do not appear in court. Nonetheless the criminal courts do at times find themselves having to deal with children.

PROSECUTING CHILDREN BEFORE THE CRIMINAL COURTS

The definition of a child in s.307(1)) of the CP Act 1995 is provided in section 93(2)(b) of the *Children (Scotland) Act*, 1995:

- a child who has not attained the age of sixteen years;
- a child aged over 16 years but who has not attained the age of 18 years in respect of whom a supervision requirement is in force;
- a child over 16 years but is not over school-leaving age in the case of child who has failed to attend school regularly without reasonable excuse; or
- a child whose case has been referred to a children's hearing by section 33 of this Act, i.e. because he is the subject of a supervision order or a care order made in England and Wales or in Northern Ireland.

The age of criminal responsibility in Scotland is eight years and section 41 of the CP Act 1995 incorporates within statute the presumption of 'non-age' found in the *Children and Young Persons (Scotland) Act* 1937, that no child under eight can be guilty of an offence. For the purpose of prosecution

> no child under the age of 16 years shall be prosecuted for any offence except on the instructions of the Lord Advocate, or at his instance; and no court, other than the High Court and the Sheriff Court, shall have jurisdiction over a child under 16 years for an offence. (section 42(1) of the *Criminal Procedures (Scotland) Act*, 1995).

Children under the age of 16 cannot be prosecuted in the District Court. The CP Act, 1995 (s.142) stipulates that summary procedures against a child must be held in private and in different rooms or on different days from the criminal courts in which adults appear, except where the child is co-accused with an adult. The scope of this section is advisory rather than mandatory (Shiels and Bradley, 1996).

Between 1971 and 1983, all children up to the age of 18, referred to in section 93 of *Children (Scotland) Act*, 1995, were included within the definition of a 'child' in section 31(1) of the 1968 Act, i.e. they could not be prosecuted for any offence 'except on the instruction of the Lord Advocate, or at his instance'. The *Health and Social Services and Social Security Adjudication Act,* 1983, (Schedule 2, paragraph 7) amended the definition by inserting the qualification 'under 16 years' after 'child'—thereby allowing those over 16 who had previously been regarded as 'children' by virtue of being under the supervision of a children's hearing to be prosecuted more readily. The same principle is maintained under the *Criminal Procedure (Scotland) Act*, 1995 (s.42) that no child shall be prosecuted except on the instruction of the Lord Advocate. Now the term 'child' refers ONLY to a person who has not attained his 16th birthday. Despite the special status conferred by the UN Convention, young people aged 16 and 17 are routinely dealt with by the adult criminal courts in Scotland. It is important to note that for the purposes of Part II, (Chapter 1 and 4) of the *Children (Scotland) Act*, 1995 which deals with services to promote the welfare of children in need and issues relating to parental responsibilities, a child is a person under the age of 18 years.

The Lord Advocate has issued instructions on which categories of offences are to be considered for prosecution in the courts. While theoretically children who offend will be reported to the procurator fiscal in the first instance, directions from the Lord Advocate ensure that they are ordinarily reported to the Principal Reporter to the children's hearings. These are normally referred to as jointly reported children.

If a child is reported for an offence that falls within the categories defined in the Lord Advocate's instructions (see chapter annexe) as meriting submission of a report to the procurator fiscal, the police are still required in terms of s.53(3) of the *Children (Scotland) Act* 1995 to furnish a copy of the report to the Principal Reporter. These two will liaise either generally, or on a case by case basis, or both, as to whether the child in question should be prosecuted before the courts, or referred to a children's hearing. In general, the prosecuting authorities observe the basic spirit and intention of child welfare legislation, and only prosecute children before the criminal courts if a special reason exists.

If, on the face of the evidence, the fiscal considers that the alleged offence is so serious that prosecution by solemn procedure is warranted, that view will take precedence over referral to a hearing. The normal procedure of reporting the matter to the Crown Office is then set in motion (see Chapter 3). The following considerations bear on the decision as to whether a child is prosecuted before the criminal courts:

- no child under the age of eight years can be prosecuted for an offence;
- no child under the age of 13 years can be prosecuted for an offence except on the specific instruction of the Lord Advocate;
- all those crimes which for an adult would involve trial at the High Court (for example, murder, rape, etc.) if alleged against a child will be reported to the procurator fiscal as well as to the reporter;
- children who are jointly involved with an adult(s) in the commission of an offence can be prosecuted before the courts, if it is considered prejudicial to separate the accused; thus, for example, a child can appear at court jointly with an adult (16 years old) if their involvement in an alleged offence requires joint consideration; as the children's hearing does not have formal power to confiscate a weapon which may have been used in connection with an offence, it can be that such a case will be prosecuted before the courts in order, in part, to ensure that such a power is available; however, reporters are often able to reach voluntary agreements with a child's parents for the destruction or confiscation of a weapon;
- as children's hearings do not have powers to order disqualification from driving, again some children may be prosecuted before the courts for this purpose, ensuring that the point at which they would normally be of an age to drive legally is delayed.

The Lord Advocate issued guidance to the police in 1987, and there has since been a significant increase in certain types of referrals being made directly to the reporter, instead of being routed by way of the fiscal.

Bringing children to court

Once a decision has been taken to prosecute a child before a criminal court, he can be:

- cited to appear on a particular date; or
- arrested but then released by the police on a 'bail undertaking' (see Chapter 3); or
- arrested and then detained in custody (whether in police cells or local authority care) and brought before the court on the next lawful day.

Thereafter he faces the normal processes of plea, trial, etc. Where a child is charged or arrested the police officer is required to notify a parent or guardian ('if he can be found') (defined by s.1(3) and 2(4) of the CS Act, 1995) and to 'warn them of their duty to attend the court' (s.42(2)(3) of the CP Act, 1995).

If a decision is taken to prosecute a child before a court on complaint or indictment, the Chief Constable is required to notify the local authority of the charge, and of the date and time of the court appearance (s.42(7) of the CP Act, 1995). The local authority is, in turn, obliged to make such investigations and submit a report which shall contain such information as to the home surroundings of the child as appear to them will assist the court in the disposal of his case, and the report shall contain information, which the appropriate education authority shall have a duty to supply, as to the school record, health, and character of the child (s.42(8) CP Act, 1995).

In practical terms this means a social enquiry report, together with a school report, is obtained. It is important to note that where the child is already in the care of the local authority, the police are under no duty to notify the parent. This responsibility may, in practice, fall on the social worker. The *Act of Adjournal (Criminal Procedure Rules)*, 1996 contains extensive rules governing the procedures to be followed during a child's appearance before the court in relation to summary matters.

On receiving notification, and in preparation of a report, the social worker should establish

- by what method of prosecution (solemn or summary) the case is being heard;
- whether the child has been cited to appear and thus not yet appeared at court, or whether he has already made an appearance and had the matter deferred;
- whether the report is prepared on a pre-trial basis, or after conviction and the specific ordering of it by the court.

Generally, a child who is arrested for an offence will be brought before a court without delay or be liberated on an undertaking (by himself or his parent or guardian) to appear at court. Where a person who is 'apparently' a child is apprehended, with or without a warrant, and cannot be brought immediately before a sheriff, subject to necessary inquiries, a senior police officer (inspector or above or the officer in charge of the police station), should liberate him on a signed undertaking by the child **and** parent or guardian that he will attend the court (s.43 of the CP Act, 1995). Any breach of this undertaking to attend is an offence subject to a fine on summary procedure not exceeding level 3. The law specifies three sets of circumstances in which the child should not be liberated where:

- the charge is one of homicide or other grave crime;
- it is necessary in his interest to remove him from association with any reputed criminal or prostitute; or
- the officer has reason to believe that his liberation would defeat the ends of justice.

Where the child is not liberated in these circumstances, the police 'shall cause him to be kept **in a place of safety other than a police station**' (s .43(4) of the CP Act, 1995) until he can be brought to court. It should be noted that although the statutory definition of a place of safety in s.93(1) of the *Children (Scotland) Act* 1995 **includes** a police station, s.43(4) specifically **excludes** this as acceptable accommodation. In principle, the local authority should be involved in providing this place of safety in **all** cases. However the legislation leaves plenty of scope for poor child care practices by exempting the police from seeking a place of safety from social work if

- it is impracticable to do so;
- he is so unruly a character that he cannot safely be so detained; or
- by reason of his state of health or of his mental or bodily condition it is inadvisable so to detain him.

The specification of these exceptions, nonetheless, require the senior police officer to certify to the court the reasons for resorting to detention of a child in police custody rather than the preferred option. Should a child be held in a police station, the police are still obliged to keep him segregated from adult prisoners (s.42(9) CP Act, 1995) and any female child will be kept in the care of a woman (s.42(10) CP Act, 1995). It is important for social work to liaise with police to establish and monitor local practices.

As a further safeguard, the law requires the Principal Reporter to be notified of children kept in a place of safety if it is decided, subsequently, not to proceed with the charge (s.43(5) of the CP Act, 1995). It is then for the reporter to decide whether or not further action is required under section 63 of the *Children (Scotland) Act*, 1995. Anecdotal evidence suggests that only a small minority of young people are provided with an alternative to police detention and that there is a growing problem of children being detained in remand centres on unruly certificates that needs to be addressed by improved liaison and better protocols between social work and police.

If a court, in summary or solemn procedure, remands a child for any purpose (for example, committing the case for trial, or deferring to obtain reports) similar special considerations apply to the place where the child is to be detained in the interim, where he is not released on bail or ordained to appear:

a) '…if he is under 16 years of age the court **shall**, instead of committing him to a prison, commit him to the local authority which it considers it appropriate to be detained—
   (i) where the court so requires, in secure accommodation within the meaning of Part II of the CS Act, 1995; and
   (ii) in any other case, in a suitable place of safety chosen by the authority'

aa) '…if the person is over 16 years of age and subject to a supervision requirement, the court **may**, instead of committing him to prison, commit him to the local authority which it considers appropriate, to be detained as mentioned above in sub-paragraphs (i) or (ii) or paragraph (a) above. (s.51(1)(a)) of the CP Act, 1995 as amended by s.56 of the Crime *and Punishment (Scotland) Act,* 1997)

   'if he is…over 16 years of age to whom para. (aa) does not apply, or a child under 16 years of age but over 14 years of age who is certified by the court to be unruly or depraved, and the court has been notified by the Secretary of State that a remand centre is available…he **shall** be committed to a remand centre instead of being committed to prison. '(s.51(1)(b) as amended).

Where a child under 16 is detained under section 51, there is no specification for any pre-conditions to be met before detention in secure accommodation. Since the court is ordering detention until trial or conviction, the time limits on the use of secure accommodation set out in regulation 5 of the *Secure Accommodation (Scotland) Regulations* 1996 (S.I. 1996 No.3255) need not apply. It is rather strange that only a sheriff can make an unlimited order; the authority of the person in charge of the secure accommodation to release the child is unclear. It is important to note these important distinctions in the legal categorising of children and young people. Local practices should be monitored, particularly with regard to those offenders aged 16-18.

Prior to the child's appearance before a sheriff, the fiscal and the reporter should already have considered whether the appearance is necessary and whether or not the child can instead be dealt with by a children's hearing. The same should be true for a young person between 16 and 18 years who is subject to a supervision requirement. However s.46(5) of the CP Act, 1995 indicates that failure to consult would not invalidate the proceedings.

The arrangements for liaison between reporters and fiscals seem to vary greatly across the country as do the rates of 'retention' of jointly reported cases. No empirically-based criteria exist to assist in weighing up the best interests of the child and the public interest. Issues of age and persistence may be more significant than risk to the public. This is an area that needs some urgent attention.

Where the fiscal has decided to retain the case and the child has been detained in police cells, the fiscal will have received the relevant unruly certificate for production in court. Where the case is dealt with on summary proceedings, the case should be heard in private (s.142 of the CP Act, 1995). If the fiscal intends to oppose bail because of the nature of the offence or because of unruliness, he should have established with the local authority before the case is called that suitable remand facilities are available.

Non-availability of a place of safety should never be an adequate ground for the court granting an unruly certificate. Courts need to be convinced that the **child is unruly or depraved**, and any allegation that this is the case brought, for example, by a social work authority can be subject to rebuttal by the child and/or his parent. While the nature of the offence may point to the child being unruly or depraved, this is not the test; it is **the nature of the child** himself that must be assessed by the court. There is virtually no independent empirical data on these children to establish whether factors other than offending are used to justify the label 'unruly and depraved'. The SWSI review *A Secure Remedy* (1996) estimated that in 1992-93, 500 young people were held in police custody on unruly certificates despite guidance indicating that these young people should have been in a place of safety under the supervision of social work. Statistical data indicates that, although small in number, there was a 35% rise in the use of these certificates between 1994 and 1995 (SWSG, 1995). This is an area that has been neglected by social work until recently.

A review by one group of local authorities identified that 49 unruly certificates had been dealt with by the 'out of hours' team in 1996, likely to be an under estimation as no data was recorded by field teams; of these 49, 31 were already in residential care and more than half of the incidents were associated with alcohol and/or drug misuse. None of the authorities had any written procedures or guidance in relation to unruly certificates or to the detention of children in general. Possibly of greater surprise was the fact that the local reporter's office did not have figures. Each police division gathered its own. No centralised data was available at police HQ. These issues are the same as those raised by Denham (1984) who noted 'the lack of integrated information on young persons certified unruly' (p.2) and that 'the number of certificates issued was uncertain as a result of inconsistent recording practices'(p.9). By 1992 the Skinner Report, when recommending the need for a review of secure accommodation, insisted that the review should inform 'consideration of what further may be done to reduce the number of unruly certificates' (recommendation 44). The concepts of 'unruly' and 'depraved' and existing provision and guidance which allows children aged 14-16 to be sent to a remand centre or prison are urgently in need of review in the light of the European and UN Conventions. Courts are not the only agencies to use 'places of safety' and these are dealt with under the provisions for Child Protection Orders later in this chapter.

Disposal by courts of cases involving children

Children who offend, in some very specifically defined circumstances, may find themselves appearing before an adult criminal court; otherwise their alleged offence is regarded as a basis for referral to a children's hearing (known as a 'ground of referral' (section 52 of the *Children (Scotland) Act*, 1995). The court 'in dealing with a child who is brought before it as an offender shall have regard to the welfare of the child and shall in a proper case take steps for removing him from undesirable surroundings' (s.50(6) of the CP Act, 1995). The court will have before it (by virtue of section 42(8) CP Act, 1995) all necessary social enquiry (social background), school, and, where necessary, any other specialist reports. It may also defer the matter to obtain the advice of the children's hearing before reaching its decision.

It is very exceptional for a child to appear before the High Court, and this is likely only in those rare cases which involve an unlawful killing. If the circumstances demand the equivalent to a sentence of life imprisonment in respect of an adult, the court will impose a sentence of detention **without limit of time** (s.205 of the CP Act, 1995). Otherwise, where a child is convicted on indictment and the court is of the opinion that no other method of dealing with him is appropriate, it may sentence him to be detained 'for a period' which must be specified in the sentence. During this period the child is liable to be detained in a place and on conditions as the Secretary of State directs (s.208).

It has been held that where a child sentenced under this provision is then ordered to be detained 'without limit of time' as the specified 'period', this is a competent sentence and is, in effect, a life sentence (RJK. v. HM Advocate 1993, S.L.T 237; Nicholson 1992:76). For example a court might sentence 'for a period of 12 months', another for 'a period of 18 months' and another for 'a period without limit of time'. Each of these examples would be competent under section 208 although the latter would be very rare indeed. It is also possible for the court to impose a non-custodial disposal or to remit the matter to the children's hearing for disposal.

More typically, children appear before the criminal courts because they are charged with an adult. Again, the courts may defer the matter to obtain the advice of the children's hearing before making a decision. One disposal open to a court is to remit the matter to the children's hearing for **disposal**, even though the prosecuting authorities have previously determined that the case was one for prosecution in the courts. In general, a court may make any order on a child it could make in the case of an adult, EXCEPT that:

- it cannot impose a community service order;
- it cannot make a probation order that includes a requirement for unpaid work;
- it cannot sentence a child to adult forms of imprisonment: any removal from home has to be in terms of an order for residential training under s.44 if the case is one on summary procedure, or an order for detention under s.208 if the case is one on indictment.

Where a sheriff imposes detention (s.44 of the CP Act, 1995) it is the duty of the local authority within whose area the child lives to provide suitable accommodation. If the child is not ordinarily resident in Scotland, the responsibility is likely to fall on the authority in which the offence was committed or in the case where a number of offences were committed in different locations, on the authority within whose area the court presides.

The local authority has the same powers and responsibilities as those regulating a supervision requirement with a condition of residence under section 70 of the *Children (Scotland) Act,* 1995, which includes authority to restrict the child's liberty as seems appropriate (s.70(4) of the same Act). The main effect is that the child is treated as a 'looked after' child, imposing duties and responsibilities on the local authority including the preparation of a care plan and regular reviews. A hearing can specify residence in secure accommodation under s.70(3) and (9) of the CS Act, 1995. While different terminology is used, it can be assumed that detention under s.44(6) of the CP Act, 1995 is likely to mean secure accommodation.

It is important to note that s.44 restricts the summary court to a residential order of up to one year. The disposal is subject to the normal early release provisions of the *Prisoners and Criminal Proceedings (Scotland) Act* 1993 (see Chapter 11) and allows for release at half the period specified (s.44(6)(a) CP Act, 1995). However the local authority may review the case **at any time** and, 'having regard to the best interests of the child and the need to protect the public', grant early release, conditionally or unconditionally (s.44(6)(b)). The release of a child who is sentenced to detention under s.208 CP Act, 1995, however, is determined by the Secretary of State.

Where a sheriff is considering using powers under s.44, it is to be hoped that advice of a children's hearing will be sought and that the case may be remitted to the hearing for disposal(s.49). Advice **must be sought** where the child is subject to a supervision requirement (s.49(3)(b)). Where a child is subject to a supervision requirement and is detained under s44, the supervision requirement is suspended until the period of detention is completed (either at the expiry of the full term or at earlier release (s.44(6)(a)) CP Act, 1995). Nonetheless the local authority retains a statutory duty to review as in the case of any child subject to a supervision requirement under s.73(6) of the CS Act, 1995 and has discretionary powers to conduct reviews 'at any time' under s.44(6)(b)of the CP Act, 1995, for children detained.

It is important to note that courts can fine, defer sentence, make orders for absolute discharge, or admonition, and can make probation orders on children. If the matter is remitted to the children's hearing for disposal, then the powers of disposal are those available to the hearing in the normal way. Moreover, the court passes total responsibility, as it were, to the hearing, in that the hearing becomes the tribunal that deals with a 'breach' of any order made. If the child commits a further offence, the fact of being subject to an order of the children's hearing does not prevent the possibility of him being dealt with for that fresh offence by the court, if the specific considerations set out above, which justify such a course, apply, or if he has attained the age of 16 years. Equally where a probation order is made by a court then any subsequent offence will be dealt with by the court.

Attendance of children at court

Children may have to attend courts in capacities other than as offenders. The law governs the attendance of children at courts:

- no child under the age of 14 years (other than infants in arms) shall be permitted to be present in court during any proceedings against any other person charged with an offence unless his presence is required as a witness or 'otherwise for the purpose of justice' (for example, to be identified in the process of evidence being given) (s.50(1) CP Act, 1995).
- where a child appears in any proceedings relating to an offence against, or conduct contrary to, decency or morality, the court may direct that all persons not officers of the court, counsel or solicitors, and persons directly involved in the case, be cleared from the court during the taking of the child's evidence (s.50(3)).

Courts attempt to be sensitive to the trauma faced by a child having to give evidence of this kind, especially if the child was the victim of, or witness to, a sexual or violent offence. Bona fide representatives of newspapers and news agencies need not leave the court but are subject to the over-riding consideration that nothing published shall lead or lend itself to an identification of the child.

Sections 271 and 272 of the CP Act, 1995 make it possible, when a child is cited to give evidence, 'on application', to appoint a *commissioner* to take evidence by video link or for evidence to be taken in court while the child is screened from sight of the accused. The court must consider 'the possible effect on the child' and 'whether it is likely that the child would be better able to give evidence' if the application is granted. In considering whether to grant an application the court *may take into account* (emphasis added), where appropriate:

- the age and maturity of the child;
- the nature of the alleged offence;
- the nature of the evidence which the child is likely to be called upon to give; and

- the relationship, if any, between the child and the accused (s.271(8) CP Act, 1995).

Schedule 1 of the *Criminal Procedure (Scotland) Act*, 1995, provides a list of offences which allow a court to proceed in the absence of the child/victim if that presence is not essential to a just hearing of the case. The offences include

1. any offence under Part I of the *Criminal Law (Consolidation) (Scotland) Act*, 1995:
   - procuring (unlawful sexual intercourse or for the purpose of prostitution) (s.7(1));
   - procuring by threats etc. (s.7(2)(3));
   - incest (s.1);
   - intercourse with a step-child (s.2); or of a person in a position of trust with a child under 16 (s.3);
   - unlawful sexual intercourse (or attempted) with a girl under 16 (s.5);
   - indecent behaviour towards a girl aged between 12 and 16 (s.6);
   - abduction (or unlawful detention) with the intent to have sexual intercourse of a girl up to **18 years** (s.8);
   - permitting a girl under the age of (a) 13 and (b) 16 to use premises for sexual intercourse (s.9);
   - causing or encouraging the seduction or prostitution etc., of a girl under the age of 16 (s.10);
   - allowing a child aged between 4 and 15 to be in a brothel (s.12);
   - procuring or being a party to the commission of a homosexual act in certain circumstances involving a child under 16;
2. any offence under sections 12, 15, 22 or 33 of the *Children and Young Persons (Scotland) Act*, 1937 i.e.:
   - cruelty to a child under 16 (s.12)
   - causing or allowing person under 16 to be used for begging (s.15);
   - exposing children under 7 to risk of burning or scalding (s.22);
   - allowing a person under 16 to take part in performances endangering life or limb (s.33);
3. any other offence involving bodily injury to a child under the age of **17 years**;
4. any offence involving the use of lewd, indecent or libidinous practice or behaviour towards a child under **17 years**;
5. taking, distribution, possession or publication of indecent photographs of children under the age of 16 (s.52) *Civic Government (Scotland) Act,* 1980.

It should be noted that the legislation on which Schedule 1 is based includes **three notable exceptions to the definition of a child as someone under 16 years**. If an adult is convicted or found guilty of any of the offences listed in this schedule, or an offence under section 21 of the *Children and Young Persons Act*, 1937 or any offence in respect of a female aged 17 years or over which constitutes the crime of incest, the court may refer the child who was the victim of the offence, or any child who is or is likely to become a member of the same household as the person who has committed the offence, to the Principal Reporter, and the offence will constitute the ground of referral to a children's hearing.

Children who offend and are involved with the children's hearings system occasionally have to attend court. There are normally two situations in which this arises:

- where the child or the parent ('relevant person' see below) deny the grounds of referral for which they have been referred to the hearing; or exceptionally where the child is deemed unable to understand the grounds of referral); and
- where there is an appeal, either on the grounds of alleged irregularities in the conduct of the hearing, or against the hearing's decision.

These situations are dealt with later in this chapter. In the first, the issues are purely legal and no reports from social workers are required or called for. In the second, the reports on which the hearing based its decision will be part of the subject matter of the appeal. In both of these situations, the child and his parent(s) have full rights to be at the court hearings, whether legally represented or not.

Attendance of parents at court

If a child is prosecuted before the courts, section 42 of the CP Act, 1995 requires his parent or guardian to attend if the parent or guardian 'can be found and resides within a reasonable distance'. Attendance must be for all stages of the proceedings, unless the court is satisfied it would be unreasonable to require their attendance (s.42(2)). Parents must also be warned by the police after any arrest of their child that they are liable to attend. Even if the father is not the parent or guardian having actual possession and control of the child, his presence may nonetheless be required. (It has been known for fathers serving prison sentences to have their presence required, and for them to be escorted to court by prison staff.) The only exception allowed in respect of the attendance of parents is the situation where, prior to the institution of the proceedings, the child has been removed from them by an order of the court. In any case, where the local authority has parental rights and responsibilities (for example, by virtue of an order under section 86 of the *Children (Scotland) Act*, 1995) the presence of the supervising social worker will be necessary. The court is entitled to hear, first hand, from a person with direct responsibility for the care of the child, whether or not this is the supervisor.

While parents cannot be fined under the CP Act, 1995 there remains a power to order a parent or guardian to provide financial security for their 'cooperation in securing the child's good behaviour' (s.45 of the CP Act, 1995). This can be done if the parent, having been required to attend court, has failed to do so. An order 'shall not be made unless the parent or guardian has been given the opportunity of being heard' (s.45(2)). Where any security is forfeited, the sum may be recovered from the parent or guardian (for example, by civil diligence or imprisonment) as if the parent or guardian had himself been convicted of the offence with which the child was charged. This power is rarely used (Nicholson, 1992).

Attendance of social workers

In any case where a child is prosecuted before the courts and where detention is under consideration there is an obligations on court officials, especially the procurator fiscal, to notify the social work authority of the prosecution of any child. The circumstances are likely to justify the presence of a social worker both during the journey to the court and throughout the court proceedings to assist the child and parents. The development of Appropriate Adult Schemes in Scotland (see Chapter 12) should assist in the prosecution process. Arrangements should be made as a matter of routine when children under the age of 13 are being prosecuted before the courts. In any case in which the child is already subject to the supervision of the children's hearing, the presence of the supervising social worker is likely to be important. In particular the matter of escort arrangements needs careful attention in any case where a child protection order, or residential supervision requirement, is in force. Where, for example, the child faces serious charges, and the parent(s) is/are incapable of providing appropriate support, the social worker's attendance provides an important service, particularly where the child is 'looked after' by the local authority.

CHILDREN'S HEARINGS

Most children in Scotland who offend are not prosecuted before criminal courts but are dealt with by the children's hearings system.

The reporter

A key figure in the juvenile justice system in Scotland is the reporter. The office did not exist prior to the implementation of the children's hearing system by the *Social Work (Scotland) Act,* 1968. It is a tribute to the foresight of the Kilbrandon Committee that the term which was coined in its report should survive the long debate and appear both in title and in substance as the committee thought it should. The office is unknown in English and Welsh procedures, and derives rather from the links between Scots law and the European family of laws.

The concept of the office of reporter could not have been understood without reference to the system of public prosecution by procurators fiscal. Indeed some have suggested that more recent interest amongst fiscals in the diversion of adult offenders from prosecution (see Chapter 7) has been stimulated, in part, by the way that reporters have developed the tradition and the role in the juvenile context.

The office of Reporter is intended to be free from administrative and political interference, and to give the office holder security in exercising discretion and decision making without fear or favour. The office was established by section 36 of the *Social Work (Scotland) Act,* 1968. The *Local Government (Scotland) Act,* 1994 established the Scottish Children's Reporter Administration (SCRA) and from 1 April, 1996 created, for the first time, a centralised non-departmental government service under a **Principal Reporter** as recommended by the Finlayson Report (1992). Prior to this, reporters had been employed by regional local authorities.

The duties of the Principal Reporter (a term which covers all reporters since they act under powers delegated to them by the Principal Reporter) are set out in the *Children (Scotland) Act,* 1995, in various statutory instruments and, in particular, *The Children's Hearings (Scotland) Rules*, 1996. The reporter has a number of functions:

- to act as a filter in respect of children referred to the children's hearing system;
- to be the administrative arm of the system;
- to act as the community watchdog in respect of the observance of the statutory rules governing the workings of the system;
- to act as legal representative of the hearings when matters have to be referred to the courts for various reasons.

The legislation permits the Secretary of State to prescribe qualifications for the reporter (s.40 of the CS Act ,1995). To date, at least, he has elected not to do so. In practice reporters are drawn from a range of backgrounds including law, education and social work on the assumption that they need an amalgam of skills.

Referrals to the reporter

When a child who is alleged to have committed an offence is referred by the police (or any other person) to the reporter, the reporter's task is to decide whether or not the child may be in need of compulsory measures of supervision and brought before a children's hearing. Referral from the police is an official and documented one, and there are parallels between how the reporter responds and how a fiscal might respond; the reporter has no power to make formal disposals, such as supervision, but has to decide on how to process the matter. He can decide that a hearing is not required (s.56(4) CS Act, 1995) and take no further formal action. In dealing with a child who is referred in respect of an alleged offence, the reporter has to satisfy himself on two counts:

- that on the evidence there is, in law, a prima facie case to answer (which is not quite the same as proof that 'he did it');
- that on the evidence available the child is in need of compulsory measures of supervision.

He may be satisfied on the first count, but not on the second and consider that various forms of action short of compulsory measures of supervision may be an adequate response.

The term 'no further action' has come to be used for a range of informal action undertaken by the reporter as part of his role in diversion and early intervention. He may see the child and his parents informally; ask the social work authority for information; and make various arrangements with the agreement of parents and child, for example, for the confiscation of weapons or for making restitution.

The reporter may decide to refer the case to the local authority for 'advice, guidance and assistance' (s.56(4)(b) of the CS Act, 1995) and suggest a period of voluntary assistance. It should be noted that despite this power, any action agreed is **a voluntary measure**. Families should be clear about the legal and ethical basis of this contact. The term voluntary supervision, much used in the past, should be avoided as it implies a legal status and gives a weight to the help provided that has no basis in law and suggests that the social worker has some authority as supervisor other than the agreement of child and family. Guidance now refers to '**voluntary agreements**' (SWSG, 1997) and distinguishes this help from that provided under section 73(12) CS Act, 1995.

By these strategies the reporter acts as a diversion agent, and many children referred on the grounds of an alleged offence (approx. 60% in 1995) never appear before a children's hearing. To assist in his decision, the reporter may request a report from the local authority to provide information on the child and the child's social circumstances. The local authority has a duty to provide this information. The scope of investigation at this initial stage is very wide-ranging. The CS Act, 1995 simply indicates that the report may contain 'such information, from any person whomsoever, as the Principal Reporter thinks or the local authority think, fit' (s.56(2) CS Act, 1995).

If, on the basis of the evidence, the reporter is satisfied on both counts, that at least one of the grounds specified is established, **and** that the child may be in need of compulsory measures of supervision, he then has the responsibility of

- arranging a hearing (s.56(6));
- requesting a report from the local authority under section 56(2), if he hasn't already done so;
- requesting supplementary or additional information from the local authority (s.56(7)); disseminating information and reports to members of the panel, who will hear the case; and
- notifying the child and his parents of the time, date, and place of the hearing.

At the hearing itself, the reporter has no decision-making function. He may advise either the members of the hearing, or the child and his parents, about legal or procedural points at issue.

Grounds for referring children to a children's hearing

The statutory grounds on which a child may be considered in need of '**compulsory measures of supervision**' (no longer compulsory measures of care as in the 1968 Act) and referred to a children's hearing are contained in section 52(2) of the *Children (Scotland) Act*, 1995. At least one of the following conditions must be satisfied: that the child

a) is beyond the control of any relevant person;
b) is falling into bad associations or is exposed to moral danger;
c) is likely—
   (i) to suffer unnecessarily; or
   (ii) be impaired seriously in his health or development, due to a lack of parental care;
d) is a child in respect of whom any of the offences mentioned in Schedule 1 of the *Criminal Procedure (Scotland) Act*, 1995 (offences against children to which special provision apply) have been committed;

e) is, or is likely to become, a member of the same household as a child in respect of whom any of the offences referred to in paragraph (d) above have been committed;

f) is, or is likely to become, a member of the same household as a person who has committed any of the offences referred in paragraph (d) above;

g) is, or is likely to become, a member of the same household as a person in respect of whom an offence under sections 2A to 2C of the Sexual Offences (Scotland) Act 1976 (incest and intercourse with a child by step-parent or person in position of trust) has been committed by a member of that household;

h) has failed to attend school regularly without reasonable excuse;

i) has committed an offence;

j) has misused alcohol or any drug, whether or not a controlled drug within the meaning of the *Misuse of Drugs Act* 1971;

k) has misused a volatile substance by deliberately inhaling its vapour, other than for medicinal purposes;

l) is being provided with accommodation by a local authority under section 25, or is the subject of a parental responsibilities order obtained under section 86 of this Act and, in either case, his behaviour is such that special measures are necessary for his adequate supervision in his interest or the interest of others.

Section 52(3) notes that the term supervision may include measures taken **'for the protection, guidance, treatment or control of the child'**. It is important to note that Chapters 1 and 2 of the *Children (Scotland) Act* 1995 refer not to parents or guardians but to **relevant persons**, as in (a) above which is normally a parent but may be a range of people who have parental responsibilities or rights, or who ordinarily have charge of, or control over, the child. A relevant person is defined by section 93 of the CS Act, 1995 as

• any parent with parental responsibilities and rights under the Act. This will always include a child's mother, and father, if he is married to the mother. It will not include an unmarried father, unless there is a court order giving him parental responsibilities and rights or he has signed a written agreement with the child's mother under section 4 of the CS Act, 1995 . A residence order saying the child should stay with him will bring with it these responsibilities and rights;

• any other adult who has parental responsibilities and rights. This could include e.g. grandparents, who have a residence order, or a relative or friend appointed as guardian in a parent's will or by the court, or any adult who ordinarily is in charge of or has control over the child.

The grounds of referral set out in the CS Act, 1995 are similar to those previously contained in the 1968 Act with some additions and changes. There is a new ground that the child has misused alcohol or drugs, (j), which was designed to bring Scots law into line with article 33 of the UN Convention on the Rights of the Child. The incest ground (g) now covers both boys and girls, and may also be used where intercourse takes place between a child and an adult in a position of trust in relation to the child. Previous grounds which talked about a child in the care of the local authority whose behaviour required 'special measures of adequate care and control' has been amended; the Act now refers to a child being provided with 'accommodation by the local authority', or for whom the local authority has parental responsibilities.

It is important to note that the 'proof' required for ground (i) must satisfy the criminal and not the civil standard required in the other grounds (s.68(3)(b)). An offence must be proven '**beyond reasonable doubt**', while the other grounds are subject to the civil test on 'balance of probabilities'.

The existence of a ground of referral does not in itself indicate that the child is in need of compulsory measures of supervision. Section 53(1) of the *Children (Scotland) Act*, 1995 provides that:

> where information is received by a local authority which suggests that compulsory measures of supervision may be necessary in respect of a child, they shall
> a) cause inquiries to be made into the case unless they are satisfied that such inquiries are unnecessary; **and**
> b) if it appears to them after such inquiries, or after being satisfied that such inquiries are unnecessary, that such measures may be required in respect of the child, give to the Principal Reporter such information about the child as they have been able to discover.

The local authority, on receiving information, has an obligation to investigate (not defined) to determine whether or not compulsory measures of supervision may be necessary.

This provision can involve social workers in a range of activity. Whilst an offence may be only one part of the evidence that social workers consider, it may support a view that the child is in need of compulsory measures of supervision. It is surprising that, other than in a few special projects dealing with persistent offenders, the police report is normally not available to the social worker.

Any other person who has 'reasonable cause' to think a child may require compulsory measures of supervision *may* (and in the case of the police *shall*) give that information to the reporter (s.53(2)). This right or duty to give information exists only insofar as the person has reasonable cause to believe that one or more of the grounds of referral apply. Norrie (1996) suggests that there is no right to give information when there is no reasonable cause for this belief. While it is not the aim of the Act to discourage the passing of information to the reporter, these words ensure that anyone acting maliciously in giving information is not completely immune to legal redress. Where police are required to make reports to prosecutors they are also required to make reports to the reporter.

Section 53(4) of the CS Act, 1995 introduced a new and highly significant provision. Not only are the police obliged to pass information to the reporter to assist him in deciding whether or not it is necessary to arrange a hearing, but the prosecuting authorities are also obliged to pass on to the reporter any evidence they hold when the reporter is trying to establish a ground of referral before the sheriff, whether on initial application or on a rehearing of the evidence. This has often happened in the past, informally, as a matter of practice rather than obligation. The section is qualified in two ways; firstly, the obligation only exists when the evidence is such that it may assist the sheriff in determining that a ground is established or not and when the reporter has made a request to be supplied with the evidence; and, secondly, when the prosecutor believes that he need not retain the evidence for use in proceedings that have or are going to commence (Norrie, 1996:98).

The issue of procedures and, in particular, time delays involving passing information and decision making were raised as a concern by SASD's *Speedy Justice for Children* in 1986. One of the first actions of the present administration in 1997 was to order a review of the efficiency and effectiveness of procedures within the hearing system. The report *Just in Time* (SCRA, 1997) recognises the contribution that timeliness of communication and decision making can make to the best interests of children and young people. The report makes a number of constructive and important recommendations aimed at improving communication with families, improving frequency of reporting, in particular that the police should avoid 'batching' (and holding back) referrals; national guidelines on police warnings; criteria for prompt referrals from schools for non-attendance; more flexible contact between reporters and fiscals especially with regard to jointly reported cases; better national and local liaison between fiscals and reporters; better integrated recording and information systems, particular with regard to resource availability; and criteria for priorities and fast-tracking.

Of more fundamental significance are the recommendations for national standards for processing children and 100% central funding for services to the hearing system to address speedily and effectively the behaviour of young people who offend and who are at risk of being dealt with in the adult system (recommendation 58). We wholeheartedly support such a proposal.

The hearing

The concern of the children's hearing system is with children who are in need of 'compulsory measures of supervision' (s.52(3) and 93(1) of the CS Act, 1995). The alleged commission of an offence is only one of a number of grounds of referral on the basis of which children can be referred to a children's hearing. Section 52(1) says simply:

> The question of whether compulsory measures of supervision are necessary in respect of a child arises if at least one of the conditions mentioned in subsection (2)…is satisfied with respect to him.

The CS Act, 1995 proceeds from the premise that if the ground of a referral is established, then this *may* be a point for social intervention in a variety of forms, blanketed in the term 'compulsory measures of supervision'. Supervision may include 'protection, guidance, treatment, and control' (s.52(3)).

The *Children (Scotland) Act,* 1995 identifies three overarching principles which must guide decision making by hearings or courts:

- where a children's hearing (or a court) determines any matter with respect to a

child, 'the welfare of the child throughout his childhood shall be their or its paramount consideration' (s.16(1);
- a children's hearing (or sheriff), 'taking account of the age and maturity of the child, shall, so far as practicable' give the child the opportunity to express his views if he wishes and 'have regard' to these views (s.16(2));
- no supervision requirement or order shall be made unless the hearing (or sheriff) consider that 'it would be better for the child that the requirement or order be made than that none should be made at all' (s.16(3)).

The first principle emphasises the **paramount principle** of the welfare of the child. The 'best interests' of the child is central to the whole Kilbrandon philosophy. This is somewhat undermined by section 16(5) which indicates that a hearing (or court) may make a decision which is not consistent with the paramountcy principle, if they consider it necessary to protect the public (implicitly from the child concerned) from serious harm. It is worth noting the phrase 'throughout his childhood' recognises the importance of considering the longer-term effects of any decision and is particularly relevant to the duty on local authorities to provide services, in some circumstances, up to and beyond the age of 21 (s.29 CS Act, 1995).

The second principle gives the child the right to have his views taken into account and is designed to bring Scots law into line with Article 12 of the UN Convention on the Rights of the Child. It should always be the intention of any children's hearing to encourage the child to express his views and to engage in discussion on the decision. The principle, however, applies equally to courts.

The third overarching principle is one of minimum or non-intervention. The Kilbrandon approach emphasises early intervention on a voluntary basis. The legislation warns, however, against over-enthusiastic interventionism without the chance of a positive outcome. The minimum or non-intervention principle amounts to a presumption that matters are best left as they are if intervention is unlikely to make things better or if doing nothing is no worse. The onus is on anyone seeking intervention by a court order or a decision of a children's hearing to justify why intervention is necessary. This principle also places responsibility on social workers to demonstrate that their proposed intervention is likely to be effective. There is scope for some concern that local authorities might use this principle to justify their non-intervention for resource reasons. Doing nothing by default is equally concerning.

The child who is referred on the basis of an offence is in exactly the same position as a child referred on any other, non-offence, ground. The question of punishment is not an issue. The commission of an offence, which in an adult, would lead to criminal prosecution, constitutes a ground for referral and, if established, authorises the hearing to impose compulsory measures of supervision. We have already noted that the reporter's role has developed in ways which seek to ensure that informal and voluntary measures are considered first, before recourse is had to compulsory ones. The aim is to reach a decision and disposal calculated to serve the child's best interest, whatever the initial ground of referral.

The principles on which the hearings operate require children's panel members to work in partnership with families, seeking, where at all possible, to arrive at a decision on the basis of a round-table discussion involving parents and child. Much of this entails a free flowing discussion to establish what is in the child's best interests; ensuring that parents and child understand the proceedings and the reasons for the decision; and that they are party to plans for any planned future intervention.

The responsibility for the conduct of the hearing rests with the chairperson. The reporter's task is to advise the hearing on legal and procedural matters, and to record the reasons for the hearing's final decision which must, at the end of the hearing, be made out and signed by the chairperson. The chairperson's main responsibility is

- to ensure that the grounds of referral are understood and accepted;
- to ensure that the substance of any decision is declared, providing it is not detrimental to do so;
- to facilitate this round-table discussion;
- to enable members of the panel to question, discuss, and exchange views with the child and his parents, and
- to enable the child and his parents in their own words and their own way to be heard and to comment on the issues which led to the referral, and any matters raised in the various reports on which the panel members may comment;
- to ensure that the reasons for the decision are explained and understood.

The children's hearing is constituted by three people, one of whom must be a woman, drawn from the children's panel.

Attendance at a hearing

The *Children (Scotland) Act,* 1995 restates two important principles of a hearing:

- privacy of the proceedings should be respected (s.43(1));
- numbers of people attending should be kept to a minimum (s.43(2)).

To ensure privacy section 43(4) provides for members of the press, who have a right to attend under s43(3)(b), to be excluded from all or part of a hearing to allow a child to express views to the hearing or where the press presence is causing or is likely to cause distress to the child. The chairperson may explain, afterwards, the substance of what took place during their absence (s.43(5)). In practice it is most uncommon for the press to show much interest in cases before the children's hearing. In addition a member of the Council of Tribunals or of the Scottish Committee of that Council has the right of attendance.

It is an offence to publish any information about proceedings at a hearing or before a sheriff which could identify a child, his/her home or school (s.44). However, 'in the interests of justice', the ban on publishing information can be dispensed with by a sheriff, the Court of Session in appeal matters, or the Secretary of State (s.44(5)).

The CS Act, 1995, as well as placing a duty on the child to attend, gives the child, for the first time, the **right of attendance** (s.45) and the **right to be heard**.

The child's attendance can be dispensed with (s.45(2) by a hearing (not by a re-porter), only if considered unnecessary, e.g. in Schedule 1 cases or where attend-ance is considered to be 'detrimental to the interests of the child'.

The Act places 'business meetings' at any time before a hearing on an official footing (s.64(1)), for purposes such as dispensing with attendance. Child and par-ents must be informed that a business meeting is to take place, the matters it will deal with and that they have the right to pass their views to the meeting via the Principal Reporter (s.64(2)). Apart from the child, the Act gives any 'relevant per-son' rights to attend a hearing (s.45(8)).

It is a fairly common for children to appear with mother, but without father, and the provisions of section 45(8)(b) allows for this. However, hearings have been known to insist on the attendance of a particular parent and there is, equally, power to require attendance as there is to dispense with it. Hearings have the power to exclude a 'relevant person' (parent etc.), and any representative, from any part of a hearing in order to obtain the views of the child or where the person's presence is 'causing, or is likely to cause, significant distress' (s.46(1)). The chairperson has a duty to explain, after the exclusion, 'the substance of what has taken place in his absence' (s.46(2) CS Act, 1995).

In general, the decision as to who shall attend is one for the chairperson. Sec-tion 43(2) requires that the 'chairman shall take all reasonable steps to ensure that the number of persons present at a children's hearing at any one time is be kept to a minimum'. People who may be present are:

- a representative of the social work authority;
- members of the Children's Panel Advisory Committee;
- panel members in training;
- any approved student or researcher;
- anyone whose presence may be justified by special circumstances.

The discretion allows for the presence of, say, a teacher, a youth club leader, a member of staff from a residential home, etc., who may have a specific contribu-tion to make to the discussion.

Given the insights which school reports provide into important areas of the child's life and behaviour, (Moore, 1989:26) it is regrettable that so few teachers attend hear-ings. It is perhaps paradoxical that a social worker, who may only have seen the child and his parents on one or two occasions, (and fathers, perhaps, not at all), should be so regularly in attendance, yet the class teacher, who has everyday contact is, generally, absent. There is an argument for including teachers in the listing of people who may or even should be present when dealing with school-aged children.

Before a hearing can proceed, it is necessary for the child and relevant person (parent) to understand and accept the ground(s) of referral as stated (s.65(5)). The chairperson of the hearing must explain (not simply read) these grounds to estab-lish that they are understood and accepted. Section 65(6) empowers a hearing to proceed where 'the child and the relevant person accept the grounds in part' and the hearing considers it proper to do so.

Where the ground of referral is that the child has committed an offence, the ground must be stated by the reporter in the referral, and communicated to the child and his parents in writing prior to the hearing, not less than seven clear days before the date of the hearing. Where the referral is in respect of a child who is already subject to a supervision requirement, the hearing shall review the original supervision requirement before dealing with any new referral (s.65(2)). The grounds must be stated in the form provided for by the *Children's Hearing (Scotland) Rules*, 1996, 'that he has committed the offence specified'. In support of this stated condition the reporter must employ the same standards of specification as would the prosecution in a criminal case, so that the specification might read:

> that on the 12th November, 1997, between the hours of 6.00 p.m. and 10.00 p.m. at 6, Highgate, Seatown, he did steal £20 in money the property of John Smith of the said address; this being an offence of theft.

Rule 11 gives the child and parents a right, separately, to be represented at the hearing to 'assist the person whom he represents in the discussion of the case of the child'. There is no provision for paid legal representation at hearings. The representative need not be legally qualified and, sometimes, it can be helpful for a child or young person to take a friend or supportive adult of their choice, to give them more confidence to speak. Written information from reporters should inform families of this right and they should always be asked by a social worker if they have considered bringing a representative and whom they would like to take with them to a hearing (Cleland, 1995).

Norrie (1997) goes further and suggests that the lack of legal aid provision is 'unjustifiable' and the 'failure to allow paid legal representation amounts, it is submitted, to a breach of Article 40 of the UN Convention' (p.5). This article provides that children who are accused of a crime are to have legal assistance in preparing and presenting their defence. While there is no need for adversarial representation in a hearing with regard to the adjudication of legal facts, clearly there is a role, given the extensive powers that hearings have to remove children's liberty, to assist the child and/or parents, many of whom lack confidence or skills, to speak for themselves. It is not our view that a lawyer is required but the lack of financial provision means that families who would want to be represented by a lawyer cannot. This cannot be acceptable.

The child or his parent(s) may refuse to accept the ground of referral. Section 65(7) allows that either may refuse, thus allowing for one of those rare examples in practice, where a child can act contrary to the wishes of his parent(s), with the result that the parent has to shoulder the subsequent responsibility and expense. The denial equates to a 'not guilty' plea in court. The child may, in effect, be saying, 'didn't do it'; or, more simply, 'prove it', given that the responsibility for proving anything rests with those who bring the case.

In the event of a denial, the hearing can do one of two things:

- **discharge the referral**, in which case the child and his parents leave the hearing and that is the end of the matter. It should be borne in mind that members of the panel may have already received and read reports designed to assist them in disposing of the case, and this may influence a decision to discharge the referral, even where a ground is being denied; or

- **make application to the sheriff** for a finding as to whether the ground for referral is established. This involves the reporter presenting the case to the sheriff on the panel's behalf seeking to establish the ground and rebut the denial. The sheriff hears the application in private, within 28 days of it being lodged. If he decides that the ground is not established then the application is dismissed and the referral regarded as discharged. If he finds that the ground is established, then the matter must go back to the hearing for consideration and disposal (s.68(10)).

The child and the relevant person may be entitled to legal aid under section 29 of the *Legal Aid (Scotland) Act*, 1986, as amended by s.92 of the CS Act, 1995, and are entitled to legal representation in the event of the matter going before the sheriff to make a finding on the ground of referral (s.68(4)). As in any children's hearing, they also have the right to 'be represented by a person other than a legally qualified person' (s.68(4)). In hearing such matters in relation to offences, 'the standard of proof required in criminal proceedings shall apply' (s.68(3)).

Once the child is back before the hearing, if the sheriff accepts that the ground of referral is established, the child or young person stands in the same relationship to the hearing as if he or she had accepted the ground(s) from the outset.

Most cases do proceed without having the matter determined by the sheriff, but there are no circumstances whereby the child and/or his parents may be denied the exercise of their right to have the matter decided by the sheriff.

When grounds of referral are accepted or established the hearing can

- continue the case to a subsequent hearing;
- discharge the referral; or
- make a supervision requirement.

REPORTS AND THE DECISION-MAKING PROCESS

There are two distinct phases to decision making in the children's hearing system. The initial consideration by the reporter is pre-occupied with two questions— namely, is there a prima facie case, and is there a need for compulsory measures of supervision. This may include police reports, police subject sheets, witness statements, school reports, social work reports, psychological reports, psychiatric reports, assessment reports, case conference minutes, information from case records, reports relating to Matrimonial Proceedings and Adoption Proceedings. Then there is the phase of decision making by the hearing if one is convened.

Initial investigation

Section 56 of the *Children (Scotland) Act*, 1995, places the responsibility for initial investigation of the case with the Principal Reporter, and the decision as to whether or not to proceed to a hearing. Rather strangely these decisions are not governed by the three overarching principles outlined above since these apply only to decisions by hearings and courts. The Principal Reporter is called upon to make 'such initial investigation as he thinks necessary' (s.56(1)). Further, 'he may request from the local authority a report on the child' (s.56(2)) detailing any circumstances relating to his social background that he considers necessary. It has long been the practice of reporters to call for reports for this purpose, but the practice has been put on a statutory footing for the first time and the local authority is now obliged to conform to the reporter's request. This investigation also provides an opportunity for social workers to consider early preventive intervention (see chapter 2). Section 53(3) also places a requirement on the police to make available to the reporter 'any report required'.

Any decision is the reporter's, and his alone. Section 56(6) is quite clear that 'where it appears to the Principal Reporter that compulsory measures of supervision are necessary in respect of the child, he shall arrange a children's hearing'.

Social workers when requested to supply information to assist this phase of initial investigation are being asked to act as the investigative arm of the Principal Reporter. The aim of any report or information which is submitted, is to assist the reporter in making his decision as to whether a child may be in need of compulsory measures of supervision and needs to be taken before a hearing.

Section 63 makes special provision for children arrested by police. No equivalent provision existed in the 1968 Act. This section was introduced to the Act at the last minute and shows a lack of parliamentary scrutiny. It is one of the most peculiar sections within the CS Act, 1995. A child can come to the attention of the reporter under section 53 or by being held in a place of safety by the police. Unlike the s.56 provision, the reporter has limited powers to release the child and instigate investigation. Section 63 requires the reporter to arrange a hearing to determine whether or not to continue the place of safety by granting a warrant and, bizarrely, whether the child should be referred to a hearing. The hearing must be arranged not later than the third day rather than on the 'first lawful day' (in practice hearings are likely to be held the next day). In no other circumstance does a hearing have the role in deciding whether or not a child may be in need of compulsory measures requiring a hearing, normally at the discretion of the reporter. Because of the timescales the hearing will have limited information on which to make a decision. This section is a mess and in practice police are likely to arrest children and release them without ever notifying the reporter, which is equally unacceptable.

The hearing

If the reporter arranges a hearing to consider the case, the law is equally explicit that 'he shall, where he has not previously done so, request a report' (s.56(7)) and may request supplementary or additional information to any report supplied to assist in the initial investigation. The procedure (rule 6) requires that the reporter give members of the hearing notice of the time and place of the hearing, 'whenever practicable at least seven days before the date of the hearing', and give them 'not later than **three clear days** before the date of the hearing':

- a copy of a report from the local authority on the child and his social background;
- a copy of the statement of the grounds for referral;
- a copy of any judicial remit or reference, or of any reference by a local authority;
- where the child is subject to a supervision requirement, a copy of that requirement;
- where a safeguarder has been appointed, a copy of any report which the safeguarder has obtained.;
- any views of the child given in writing to the Principal Reporter.

It is the duty of the local authority to supply the report which will contain information from any person the Principal Reporter or the local authority may think fit. The *CS Act*, 1995 guidance providing reporters with information on children who offend is limited. In the absence of satisfactory guidance on reports for children who offend, it is quite appropriate for the *Scottish Children's Reporters Administration* (SCRA) to issue its own requirements to local authorities. The right of the Principal Reporter to indicate to the report writer the possible sources of information is not one generally acknowledged. It does, however, have the potential for positive cooperation between the two. In the course of his investigation, or as a result of other information he has already received, the reporter may well be able to indicate particular lines of investigation for the report writer to pursue.

It is important to note that frequent complaints about late social work reports do not reflect a lack of sympathy for hard-pressed social workers. There is a statutory obligation on the reporter to give panel members **at least three days** to examine the reports. The regulations recognise that if a hearing is to be conducted with due consideration to the needs of the child this preparation time is essential. Social workers should give similar consideration to panel members. In addition to the social work report, the panel members will have a report from the child's school, and, if the matter has been previously continued for residential or other specialist reports, comprehensive information from these kinds of sources.

Safeguarders

The *Children Act*, 1975 (s.66) made provision for the appointment of a safeguarder in children's hearings system, which came into effect in 1985 with the insertion of s.34A in the 1968 Act. Section 41 of the *Children (Scotland) Act*, 1995 now enables a hearing, or the sheriff in proceedings before him, to appoint a person (usually a lawyer or a social worker) 'to safeguard the interests of the child in the proceedings'. The provision in the 1968 Act was permitted when there was, or might be, a conflict of interest on any matter relevant to the proceedings between the interests of the child and those of his or her parents. The CS Act 1995 does not specify why the appointment is necessary except that it must be in the interests of the child. This might be because of a conflict of interest between child and parent or social work or for some other reason. Safeguarders cannot be appointed in emer-gency proceedings such as **Child Protection Order** (CPO) hearings, or in prac-tice, where a hearing or sheriff disposes of a case. Given the findings of the SWSI review on secure accommodation (see below), there may be a place for use of safeguarders in such cases.

Once appointed, a safeguarder is entitled to receive any information or docu-ments which the reporter makes available to the hearing. The safeguarder may submit a report to the hearing. He or she is entitled to be present and to take part in the discussion, to be informed of the decision and to appeal against the decision. In proceedings before the sheriff, the safeguarder may elect to become a party to the proceedings. If he or she elects not to do so, he or she must submit a report.

The right of refusal to cooperate

At the stage of **initial investigation**, the child and his parent(s) have a right to refuse to co-operate in the provision of any report, or to give information to the investigating social worker. Their position is analogous to that of a person who has been reported with a view to prosecution but has not yet heard if prosecution is, in fact, to be initiated. However the statute places a duty on the local authority to pass information to the reporter at this stage. Information may already be on file. Some judgement may be needed to balance the contribution social work can make to assist the reporter in his decision making and, where applicable, the basic principle that information given in confidence should not be divulged without the permis-sion of the person who has given it (see also Chapter 14).

The social worker will, in any event, need to explain to the family the basis of the reporter's request, the way the information will be used, and what will ensue if the child and his parent(s) or relevant person give information, or refuse it. If the parent and/or child refuses to co-operate, **the social worker's responsibility to report is fulfilled by reporting this fact alone to the reporter**. There is no pres-sure to produce a report in the event of a child or his parent(s) denying the ground of referral, other than to report the fact of the denial. It would also be inappropriate, for example, to compile a report on the basis of existing information without at-tempting to discuss this with the family. Whatever the inconvenience, the adminis-tration of the system is secondary in importance to the primary responsibility to acknowledge and safeguard the rights of the citizen. The fact that the system has a welfare focus does not negate this principle. The rights and principles are very much analogous to those which apply in relation to reports for adult criminal courts.

It is then a matter for the reporter to decide which course of action to take. In practice the reporter will have written to the family and in situations of non-coop-eration with social work, the reporter may be able to gain sufficient information directly from the family or to influence the family's attitude to co-operating in the process.

Once the reporter has decided to convene a hearing, it is important that the reporter's notification reaches the family prior to the report writer's first approach. The initial contact should start by clarifying with the child and his parents whether they intend to accept or deny the ground of referral. It is not part of the social work task to persuade people in either direction, but explanation, information, and discussion of the options, consequences, and alternatives is very much part of the role at this point.

Parental access to children's hearings papers

In exercising his duty to investigate the cases of children referred the reporter may gather information from many sources. Some of the information gathered will be subject to the requirements of confidentiality. Any information which would normally be treated as confidential for this reason can only be disclosed if the client consents, or if the requirement of confidentiality is superseded by the direction of a court or by a recognised higher duty such as prevention of child abuse or neglect. Section 42(2)(d) of the CS Act, 1995 makes provision for 'making available by the Principal Reporter, subject to such conditions as may be specified in the rules, of reports or information received by him to:

    i)   members of the children's hearing;

    ii) the child concerned;

    iii) relevant person; and

    iv) any other person or class of persons so specified.'

This provision is, in part, a response to issues raise by the case of McMichael v UK (European Court of Human Rights, 24 February, 1995). It was held that '...a failure to disclose the contents of such vital documents as social reports was capable of affecting the ability of participating parents to influence the outcome of a case and this was a violation of Article 6(1) and article 8 of the Convention' (Lister, 1995).

Prior to the CS Act, 1995, in the case of Kennedy v A, 1986 (SLT 358, p.359) it was noted 'that it was abundantly clear from the *Children's Hearing (Scotland) Rules*, 1971 and in particular rule 6(3), 17(3,19(4) that the sheriff had no power to direct that the children's hearing should make available documents to the parents: the principles of natural justice had to yield to the interests of the child and in any event could not be invoked to produce a result contrary to the clear provisions of a statutory instrument.'

Under Rule 19(3) panel members have a duty to disclose the substance of reports which is material to the disposal providing 'its disclosure would not be detrimental to the interests of the child'. It had become standard practice, generally, throughout Scotland to show the social work report to the child and his parents before the hearing and to allow them to read it. The European court ruling, however, indicated that all reports **should be available** to the child and relevant person(s) in advance of the hearing. Natural justice would suggest that, in principle, this should be done on a par with the rights to hearings; at least 3 days in advance of the hearing.

Section 42(2)(d) of the CS Act, 1995 requires that what are commonly referred to as panel members' papers will be made available to relevant persons. However, under pressure of the European ruling, the practice of giving each parent of the child exactly the same reports and other information as hearing members was implemented, rather hurriedly, on 1 October, 1996, under interim guidance, before the implementation of the relevant part of Act on 1 April 1997. It is the responsibility of reporters to provide the relevant information.

These rules in practical terms require social workers to provide composite reports from the relevant agencies, providing a full up-to-date history of the situation, rather than a limited update of previous reports, as was the practice prior to October 1996. One of the practical outcomes may be that many people, professionals included, may be reluctant to divulge information which they believe may subsequently be made accessible to a third party. Making reports available to parents and children, while laudable in principle, creates many practical risks with regard to confidentiality, and the ability of parents or children to understand what is written and to use the information appropriately. Social work assistance may be sought in making sense of the material made available. There will be circumstances in which parents, themselves, may not wish details of their circumstances to be made available to another parent or even to their child. These are the hazards of an open information system.

These provisions, while consistent with the requirements of the European Convention, simply highlight that the provisions of the Convention are not sufficiently child-centred and, in some senses, have resulted in poorer practice in Scotland. It was becoming good practice to assist children put some of their views and feelings in writing to hearings. This practice of trying to ensure the child's views are made clear to the hearing is in danger of being killed off. If a child writes 'I don't want to stay with my dad' and this is passed to the parent in advance of the hearing, the consequences for the child could be significant. The hearing must be a 'safe' place for the child. Provision is required, urgently, to allow reporters or hearings some discretion to withhold information from relevant persons where it is clearly not in the best interests of the children to reveal it.

Although relevant persons are not subject to specific controls, they are subject to general legal provisions in how they deal with information:

- from 1 April, 1997, under the children's hearing's rules, it is an offence to publish any matter intended to, or likely to, identify such a child—the definition of publication is wide and covers informal sharing of information with a relatively small number of people;
- law of defamation;
- law of copyright—in practice all reports will be copyrighted to safeguard against misuse;
- alleged breaches of confidentially can be reported to the procurator fiscal or to reporters for consideration

The situation, however, remains complex. At the present time, records held by reporters do not come within the scope of the *Access to Personal Files Act*, 1987 and neither that Act nor the *Access to Personal Files (Social Work) (Scotland) Regulations*, 1989 place any duties upon reporters to disclose information held by them in pursuit of their statutory functions (see Chapter 14). Some of the information gathered by reporters may be related to the child's welfare and needs, which will be given to a hearing and therefore passed to parents; some may provide evidence that will help prove a formal ground of referral, which will not be disclosed; some may fall into both categories.

If the reporter provides information, for example, to social work and they, in turn, receive a request for access to such information, they must inform the reporter and seek his consent to disclose the information. The reporter can refuse access to information which in his view would cause serious harm to the health or emotional condition of the individual who is subject of the information, or some other person, cause disclosure of the identity of a third party, or prejudice the prevention or detection of crime or the apprehension of offenders.

It is clearly the intention of the CS Act, 1995 to increase the family's access to such information. Good practice has long recognised that sharing information, areas of concern, future plans in relation to compulsory measures of supervision with a child and family, the stated goals, and specification of access and so on, can lead to a much closer involvement of family members in the proceedings at a children's hearing.

The new provisions should reduce the possibility of variable practice between report writer and panel members. In the future, there should be a fairer balance of power in the hearing. Parents will be aware of the issues under discussion and, in the main, will be better empowered to take an active part in the discussion and decision-making process.

Use of the reports at the hearing

Reports will thus be in the hands of the members of the panel, and the family, at least three days in advance of the hearing, so that they will come to it prepared and possibly influenced by the information, in advance of any discussion that may take place at the hearing itself.

While the published regulations and guidance (SWSG, 1997) make only limited comment on report content, the earlier draft guidance on Home Supervision and Contracts (SWSG, 1996) suggested that reports should cover

- reason for referral including:
     stage of development of the child;
     specific problems or difficulties giving ground for concern;
     family composition and circumstances;
     child's social network, interests and abilities,
     nature, scope and importance of any previous social work programme
- content of assessment;
- risk assessment;
- proposals for programmes, form of supervision, frequency of contact including any proposed supervision agreement;
- advice on the extent to which voluntary measures are likely to be effective and, if appropriate, reasons why the use of compulsory measures might be more

likely to achieve the desired result; and
- options which the hearing may wish to consider for decision they might make and the facilities likely to be available to implement their decision (p.19).

In addition to a social work report, a report from the child's school should always be provided and should include:

- as full a picture as possible of the child's situation as seen in his behaviour and performance at school (separating fact and opinion, as far as possible);
- comment on any difficulties the school may be having with the child's progress and behaviour;
- information and advice about the educational provision which will be available to the child and on the kind of support the education service can offer.

The function of the report writer is to advise on the child and his social background and to offer views and opinions from a professional standpoint designed to assist the tribunal make a decision in the best interests of the child. The decision should be arrived at by a process of round-table discussion, and the report writer, if invited by the chairperson, will have the opportunity to elaborate on and clarify any matters raised by the report, to assist the family express their views, if required, and assist the hearing members in their decision making, detailing any options that may have been advanced in the report. It is rather surprising that empirical studies, though now very dated (Bruce and Spencer, 1976, and Martin *et al.* 1981), indicated that social workers seemed to contribute little to the actual processes of the hearing.

The responsibility for arriving at a decision, and for communicating it to the child and his parents, rests exclusively with the panel members at the hearing. The hearing can be continued for further investigation, and the child can be required to 'attend or reside at any clinic, hospital, or other establishment during a period not exceeding twenty-two days' (section 69(3) CS Act 1995). This provision is backed by the power to issue a warrant for detention if such a course is necessary.

PART II: DISPOSALS AND OUTCOMES: DISPOSAL POSSIBILITIES

What can be included within the parameters of 'protection, guidance, treatment or control' as elements of 'compulsory measures of supervision' is very wide (s.52(3) CS Act, 1995). However, since its inception, the system has been haunted by a spectre of 'too few community-based resources'. At the same time evidence suggests that the provision of more residential, or even semi-secure measures, will not of itself solve this problem, and there is a school of thought which suggests that if these are provided they will simply be filled, not necessarily by those who really need them.

If a hearing does not discharge a referral it is empowered to make a **supervision requirement** under section 70 of the CS Act, 1995. A supervision requirement is a statutory order made by the hearing. It can require a child to reside at a named place or comply with any condition specified. Supervision can and should be tailored to the specific and assessed needs of the child, as they have emerged from the reports, assessment and the discussion.

Guidance on home supervision (SWSG, 1997:40) identifies key principles and objectives of effective supervision including 'to reduce offending behaviour where this is the issue' and 'to provide programmes of supervision which will maintain the confidence of the panel members and the public in the effectiveness of home supervision as a decision of the hearing'. Supervision if it involves an outdated 'report once a week, all is well' routine will, for the majority, be of little value in achieving such objectives, save perhaps as an 'insurance policy' and form of surveillance. It is very disappointing, therefore, that in relation to children who offend, the guidance on frequency of contact for the first three months is only 'at least fortnightly contact'. **It is difficult to envisage that a fortnightly contact will be sufficient to provide an effective programme of intervention** for a young person truly in need of compulsory measures of supervision, seriously caught up in offending.

If the preparatory work has been done at the report stage, and if the discussion at the hearing has been constructive, then the hearing members ought to have a clear view of what the supervision conditions should be. Conditions ought to be positive; designed to enhance social skills and adult/parent-child relations; improve educational performance; control deviant behaviour and associations; provide opportunities for socially acceptable leisure activity. Many of the resources do not require high cost provision but they do require professional expertise, imagination, energy, good planning and commitment and the ability to recognise and mobilise existing community resources. Opportunities should be available for young people to make good any wrong that they have done, where this is possible, for example, by direct reparation or through mediation, or simply by writing a letter of apology, as an important stage in supervision. It is important that young people are not simply 'done to' but also have the opportunity to give help to others (see the 'what works' literature; McGuire, 1995; Gendreau and Ross, 1987; Andrews and Bonta, 1995).

Some children who come to a hearing on offence-related grounds are heavily underachieving, educationally and socially. The emphasis on social education and early intervention was central to the Kilbrandon Committee's thinking. The principle of early intervention and the kinds of services that research suggests are effective are well documented. Many of these services should be available to children at risk of offending **before** they come to be in need of compulsory measures of supervision. Research (for example, Farrington, 1996) indicates that there are numerous tried and tested forms of intervention associated with effective outcomes against control groups, including

- intensive home visiting;
- parenting skill education;
- school intellectual enrichment programmes;
- skill enhancement programmes;
- school organisation and curriculum development;
- peer influence resistance strategies;

- buddying and mentor programmes;
- anti-bullying programmes in school.

There is still a great need for education, social work and other local authority services to recognise the strength and potential, the one of the other, in the provision of structured joint programmes, particularly for the older child caught up in offending. Supervision conditions ought to identify these areas, and make possible, particularly through social work and educational services, the necessary inputs to help bring about the desired changes. Statutory responsibilities are laid upon the **whole local authority** (not simply social work) to plan the provision of 'relevant services' (s.19, CS Act, 1995) and demand **cooperation from education, social work, police and housing and assistance from health and voluntary sector services**. It remains to be seen how well this can be realised to provide well co-ordinated, collaborative and multi-disciplinary provision, anticipated by the Kilbrandon report as essential if children and families are to be helped effectively.

Supervision may impose further requirements, rather as a probation order can, for the child to

(a) reside at any place or places specified in the requirement; and
(b) comply with any conditions contained in the requirement (s.70(3)).

Subsection (a) includes foster placements and residential establishments, and secure accommodation (with the agreement of the chief social work officer) subject to the specific criteria laid down by the legislation. Subsection (b) may include a requirement to 'regulate the contact with the child of any specified person or class of person' and for the child 'to submit to any medical or other examination or treatment' (s.70(5)). This latter provision clarifies the law on medical care but remains subject to the provisions of section 2(4) of the *Age of Legal Capacity (Scotland) Act*, 1991 in that for any child 'with sufficient understanding to consent', 'the examination or treatment shall only be carried out if the child consents' (s.90(b) of the CS Act, 1995). It is important that conditions imposed in supervision orders are:

- worded in such a way as to stand the *test of legal scrutiny*, particularly bearing in mind the possibility of appeal (see later in this section);
- *capable of being supervised*; 'shall not consume alcohol', or 'shall attend school regularly' sound well-intentioned, but are meaningless without strategies to put them into effect;
- *accountable to the hearing*; while day-to-day case management and resource allocation rests with social work, the decision makers, *to whom the supervisor is ultimately accountable, is the hearing* and not the authority. This principle is reinforced by section 70(7) which allows the hearing to determine a date, in advance, for reviewing the supervision.

If supervision is to be effective in reducing offending behaviour it is important to focus clearly on the nature and consequences of the presenting problem which will often be offending behaviour. Research suggests that effectiveness is likely to be greatest where those involved

- have the support and confidence of the family in identifying the nature and consequences of the problem;
- listen carefully to and communicate directly with the child;
- emphasise problem solving, changing behaviour and developing personal or social skills;
- plan their work and carry it out in a systematic way;
- use a variety of methods of intervention;
- use authority positively;
- have access to a wide range of other resources;
- use a multi-disciplinary approach.

If the nature and scope of provision is supervision by one 'all-purpose' child care social worker utilising 'talking' approaches only, there is little reasonable chance of achieving the objective of reducing offending behaviour. A full assessment of the nature of the offending behaviour, as well as the circumstances of the child, is essential. Where offending behaviour is a central issue the factors to be considered should be

- the nature and consequences of the child's behaviour;
- the impact of the behaviour on others, particularly if this involves physical harm;
- the child's attitude to their offending: do they accept that it is a mater of concern?;
- the likelihood of the child being in a position that triggers offending behaviour (i.e. with offending peers);
- whether the pattern of behaviour has been one of escalation;
- whether relevant adults take a view that the behaviour is serious or whether they collude with the behaviour;
- behaviour related to addiction or misuse of drugs or alcohol; and, in particular
- levels of parental supervision.

There is nothing in the CS Act, 1995 to indicate what effect making a supervision requirement has on the statutory rights of the parents of the young person. It is to be assumed that parents retain all their normal rights and responsibilities including rights of contact. However court interpretation of the equivalent provisions in the 1968 Act suggest that when a supervision requirement is in place, this takes precedence over the private law rights of parents and effectively suspends them in relation to parents' right to have their child reside with them (s.2 of the CS Act, 1995).

Similarly the general duty on a local authority to promote regular contact between child and parent (s.17) does not apply to a panel when they decide on a supervision requirement. An access condition, for example, in a supervision requirement, in effect, gives the local authority the right to regulate contact as part of their duty to implement the requirement under section 71. Furthermore in Kennedy v M, 1995, it was held that even if the hearing makes no particular condition regarding access, they can still provide that this be left to the discretion of the social work authority.

Duration of supervision

Supervision requirements made by children's hearings are of a different order from sentences imposed or orders made on children who offend by the criminal courts. The latter are normally for a fixed period set by the court. The hearing, on the other hand, is empowered to take wide sweeping measures for the welfare of children, and the length of supervision can often exceed what, in respect of an adult offender, would be very lengthy periods. The main difference, however, is that the hearing has to review all supervision orders it makes, regularly and systematically, and that the child, and indeed others involved, can apply for a review even before they would otherwise normally be due.

Section 73(3) states that 'a supervision requirement shall cease to have effect in respect of a child not later than on his attaining the age of 18 years'. However, because this could mean a very long time for some children, section 73(1) makes a specific stipulation that 'no child shall continue to be subject to a supervision requirement for any period longer than is necessary in the interests of promoting or safeguarding his welfare'. Section 73(4) goes on to state that the local authority should take active steps to advise the Principal Reporter with a view to the case being reviewed, so that the hearing can have the opportunity to continue, vary, or discharge the order. This requires social workers to pay close attention to orders, particularly those relating to secure care, as the statute intends that, where possible, positive action be taken to activate a hearing review rather than simply await the stipulated periodic review of the case.

The supervising social worker, or, if the child is subject to a condition of residence, the key worker, has the job of advising the hearing of progress, change, or deterioration in the child's circumstances or conditions. If issues have been raised at the hearing or in subsequent reviews then the worker/representative has a duty to give an account of how these issues have been addressed, and of the responses made by the child to the intervention that has been attempted. There is an in-built flexibility to the system which calls for a dynamic and not a static approach to the problems of children who have been defined as being in need of compulsory measures of supervision.

Reviews

Section 73 of the CS Act, 1995 deals with formal reviews. Where an order remains in force for a period of one year without review, that order will automatically cease to have effect. The legislation intends, however, that reviews should take place regularly, as appropriate, and lays down specific requirements. Section 73(4) of the CS Act, 1995 requires a relevant local authority to refer cases to the Principal Reporter where they consider a requirement ought to 'cease to have effect or be varied', when a condition is not being complied with.

In practice this means that the supervising social worker can call a review at any time, and must account for the reason in open session, since the child and his parents must be present. Review can result from a desire to terminate the order on the grounds of good progress, to have further conditions imposed, for the deletion of existing conditions, or to vary an order in more substantial ways, for example, by substituting a residential condition. The supervising social worker has to produce the evidence in support of any proposal. The requirement for a review may come from the local authority in a more formal sense, for example, the authority may wish to delete a residential condition because the child has come into its care by virtue of other circumstances, or to transfer a child from one establishment to another (s.72 covers emergency transfers) or because the authority intends to apply for 'parental responsibilities and rights', or to place the child permanently for adoption. If a relevant person intends to take the child to live outwith Scotland, they must give notice in writing to the Principal Reporter and to the relevant local authority 'not later than twenty-eight days before so taking' (s.73(7)).

The child and/or his parent or relevant person may also request a review of a supervision requirement. It is important that they have information from reporters and from the local authority clarifying their rights and a clear explanation so this right can be exercised. The stipulated periods for review are

at any time at least three months after
    (a) the date on which the requirement is made; or
    (b) the date of the most recent continuation, or variation, by virtue of this section of the requirement.' (section (73(6))

The Principal Reporter can, in effect, arrange a review at any time. However he **must** call a review if a referral is received from

- a local authority under subsection (4) and (5) above;
- a child, parent or relevant person under subsection (6) and (7); or
- where a review date has been determined by a hearing (70(7));
- where, in any other case, the requirement will expire within three months.

The final provision is intended to avoid the problem of requirements lapsing after 12 months because no-one else has initiated a review.

The CS Act, 1995 introduced, for the first time, a right for a child, parents or relevant persons to apply under section 65(7) or 65(9), for the review of the ground of referral itself (section 85). Where a sheriff has found grounds of referral established, application can be made to have this decision reviewed if new evidence is available which would have been admissible at the time of the original application. The new evidence must be 'credible and reliable' which 'would have been admissible in relation to the...original application' and 'that there is a reasonable explanation for the failure to lead such evidence on the original application'(s.85(3)).

Transfers of orders

The situation for children who are under supervision and move across the border is one which involves social workers, initially, in the role of advising their opposite numbers of the procedures, then in assessing the situation, and, finally, in effecting the transfer. The provision for transfer arrangements to be made by the Secretary of State is located in sections 33 of the CS Act, 1995. The statutory instrument, *Children and Young Persons*, 1996 no. 3267 (s.255) contains reciprocal arrangements whereby care etc. orders in England, Wales and in N. Ireland which 'appear to correspond generally to a supervision requirement', can be dealt with as if they were supervision requirements under section 70(1) of the CS Act 1995. Similarly supervision requirements and parental responsibilities orders can be transferred to England, Wales and N. Ireland.

APPEALS AGAINST A CHILDREN'S HEARING'S DECISION

If a child or his parents or relevant person wish to **deny** the ground of referral they have a right to do so, and the matter will go before the sheriff to be determined. The sheriff may also become involved if the child or his parents (relevant person) **appeal** against any decision of the hearing, regarding a supervision requirement or warrants (but not Child Protection Orders).

All decisions of a hearing have legal effect and can be far-reaching for the child and family. The integrity of the system, as a system of justice as well as welfare, depends of the appeal mechanisms laid down by the Act and the associated rules and regulations. The statutory basis for appeals is located at section 51 of the CS Act, 1995. Decisions of hearings can be appealed against to the sheriff. Decisions of the sheriff, whether on appeal from the hearing or on an application for the establishment of a ground of referral, can be appealed against, either to the sheriff principal or directly to the Court of Session; in turn, decisions of the sheriff principal can be appealed against, with leave of the sheriff principal, to the Court of Session. No appeal from the Court of Session to the House of Lords can be taken.

Parents or relevant persons have the right to appeal and a child can appeal on his own behalf if he has the legal capacity, normally if over the age of 12 or if possessing a general understanding of what it means to appeal (see Age of *Legal Capacity (Scotland) Act* 1991 s.2(4a and 4b)). If a safeguarder has been appointed he or she may sign an appeal on a child's behalf, acting effectively as the child's legal representative (*Act of Sederunt —Child Care and Maintenance Rules*) (S.I. 1997, no 291))

- **Appeal against the Hearing's decision** Section 51 allows that a child and/or his parent or relevant person may decide, within a period of three weeks from the date of the decision, to appeal against the decision of a hearing.

While the emphasis in the hearing is on a round-table discussion, and the hope that a decision is reached by mutual debate, a point is reached where a decision has to be made, and that decision, ultimately, is the responsibility of the hearing members alone. If the child and/or his parent do not agree they can appeal against the decision. It could be, for example, that they accept the need for supervision, but not a residential condition; or that they object to the particular residential establishment that the hearing intends to name in the requirement. They can appeal against the core of the decision, or against some specific element within it. There is a separate right of appeal to the Sheriff Principal, either on a point of law or in respect of irregularity in the conduct of the case (s.51(11)(a)).

- **Irregularities in procedure** As examples of irregularities in procedure which might provide good grounds of appeal, one could specify:
  a) a failure to notify parents of the date of a hearing;
  b) failure to take account of the whole facts of a case
  c) failure to provide relevant information (panel members papers); and
  d) a failure by a hearing to state reasons for its decision.

Procedure at appeal

In the first instance, an appeal against a decision of the hearing is to the sheriff, who will hear the case in chambers. In all such cases the reporter is required to furnish the court with all documents and reports relating to the case, and with the chairperson's written reasons for the decision. The sheriff may hear evidence from, or on behalf of the parties in relation to the decision. The sheriff may also examine the reporter, and the authors or compilers of any reports or statements, and may call for further reports which he 'considers may assist him in deciding the appeal'.

Possible outcomes

Under section 51 the sheriff may do several things on appeal. He may

- confirm the original decision

If the sheriff is **satisfied that the decision of the hearing is not justified** in 'all circumstances of the case' and allows the appeal, he may

- recall a warrant;
- direct that a condition attached to a requirement shall cease to have effect;
- allow the appeal and discharge the case.

In any case 'as he thinks fit', he may

- remit the case with the reasons for his decision to the children's hearing for reconsideration of their decision—for example, if the appeal had been against a particular residential establishment being named in a requirement, the hearing would have to consider an alternative establishment;
- discharge the child from any further hearing or other proceedings in relation to the grounds of referral of the case—in short, this frees the child from any further proceedings whether by a hearing or by a court; or
- substitute for the disposal by the children's hearing any requirement which could be imposed by them under section 70 of this Act (s.51(5)(c) CS Act, 1995).

The provision under section 51(5)(c) was enacted, with little support from those giving evidence, because of government concerns that there should always be a court-based forum available to make final decisions about children and to allay anticipated criticisms in relation to the European Convention on Human Rights.

This is a major and worrying departure from the original Kilbrandon principle of separating adjudication from disposal, described by the former Lord President, Lord Hope, in 1991, as 'the genius of Kilbrandon'. It could undermine the balance between hearings and the courts. As Norrie (1996:90) put it, 'if judicial decision making is seriously considered to be more appropriate than letting a children's hearing make decisions then the whole children's hearing system ought to be abolished forthwith and all children in need of compulsory measures of supervision given the "benefit" of a judicial determination...Not only is the provision bad in principle but it is likely to prove bad in practice'.

The provision in the CS Act, 1995 means that rather than examining whether or not a hearing comes to a reasonable view, the sheriff can decide what is 'in the best interest of the child' himself. It is likely that practice will vary in different courts with some sheriffs taking the view that they are better qualified to make decisions than hearings, and others happy to leave disposal to hearings. It may be a matter of debate as to whether sheriffs are as well qualified as panel members in determining the most appropriate disposal in a child's best interest. In any case it demands, for ethical reasons if for no other, that sheriffs undertake substantial formal training in child-care matters, at least equal to that of panel members, to equip themselves should they decide to undertake this duty. It remains to be seen how often this power will be used and it is hoped courts will rarely seek to make decisions themselves. In Parliament, government stated that this power 'should be used sparingly and that a sheriff should think carefully before interfering with the decision of a children's hearing' (Cleland, 1995:28).

In the nature of court business, appeals take time. Section 51(9) permits that where an appeal is lodged, the child or his parent (relevant person) may make application to a hearing for the suspension of any supervision requirement appealed against. It is left to the discretion of the hearing either to grant or to refuse this application.

If the appeal is against the decision of the hearing and there is no further appeal against the sheriff's decision on the matter, the sheriff's decision is binding both on the hearing, on the child and on his parents (relevant person). Where the sheriff considers the appeal to be 'frivolous' (section 51(7)), he may order that no appeal can be made against any subsequent decision by a hearing to continue the supervision requirement, which was the subject of that appeal, until after the expiry of 12 months from the date of his order.

In addition to the right of appeal to the Sheriff Principal, on a point of law or on the ground of an irregularity in the conduct of the case (s.51(11)(a), there is a final appeal from the sheriff or Sheriff Principal to the Court of Session. This can be lodged either by the Principal Reporter (acting on behalf of the hearing), or by the child and/or his parents; or by both. No further appeal is competent. On deciding an appeal, the Sheriff Principal or the Court of Session **must** remit the case to the sheriff for disposal in accordance with any directions given. These appeals must be made within twenty-eight days of the decision appealed against.

POWERS TO DETAIN CHILDREN IN SAFE PLACES

A place of safety

A place of safety is defined by section 93 of the *Children (Scotland) Act*, 1995, as 'a residential or other establishment provided by a local authority'; 'a community home within the meaning of section 53 of the *Children Act*, 1989'; 'a police station' (note this exclusion from s.43(4) of the CP Act, 1995), or 'a hospital, surgery, or other suitable place, the occupier of which is willing temporarily to receive the child'. Sections 57-60 of the CS Act 1995 sets out the law on child protection orders.

Following the Orkney Inquiry, the CS Act, 1995 changed the law significantly on removing children from places where they may be at risk. The Act is more specific than in the past about when emergency measures can be taken, what conditions can be attached to orders and how long they should last. The view of the Orkney Inquiry was that the former place of safety order was too easy to obtain from Justices of the Peace (JPs). Place of safety orders were replaced by **child protection orders** (CPO) and the role of JPs in this provision was minimised. The procedures are complex and it is highly unlikely, whatever the explanatory information available, that disadvantaged families will be able to exercise their rights without appropriate legal advice and representation. Indeed social workers themselves are likely to require access to good legal advice. A detailed discussion can be found in the in the regulations and guidance (SWSG, 1997, Volume 1 *'Support and Protection for Children and their Families'* pp.58-64).

These procedures have been developed primarily with the child at risk of abuse in mind. They should, nonetheless **apply equally for children who offend**, otherwise administrative and legal processes will single out children who offend in ways contrary to the spirit of the system, in practice channelling 'difficult' children through the procedures of the CP Act, 1995 and its provision for place of safety orders and unruly certificates. The basic criteria which have to be satisfied before any order is granted is that

- there are reasonable ground to believe that a child is being so treated (or neglected) that he is suffering significant harm or will suffer such harm, if not removed and kept in a place of safety, or kept where he is being presently accommodated; and
- an order is necessary to protect the child from such harm (or such further harm) (s.57(1)).

The application must be heard by a sheriff. Anyone can apply including a concerned relative or friend, teacher, police officer or other person wishing to protect the child, including a local authority (s.57(1)). There is a duty (s.57(3)) on the applicant to state the grounds on which the application is made and provide such supporting evidence (documentary or otherwise) to enable the sheriff to determine the application.

In addition to the criteria above, a sheriff can grant a CPO, specifically in favour of a local authority if satisfied that:

- they have reasonable grounds to suspect a child is being or will be so treated (or neglected) that he is suffering or will suffer significant harm;
- they are making (or 'causing') enquiries to allow them to decide whether they should take any action to safeguard the welfare of the child; and
- those enquiries are being frustrated by access to the child being unreasonably denied, the authority having reasonable cause to believe access is required urgently. (s.57(2))

The 'test' for these orders is whether there are **reasonable grounds** to believe the child is suffering '**significant harm**'. There is an immediacy about the legislation that requires the harm to exist rather than something that may occur sometime in the future. It remains to be seen how this will be interpreted in practice. Practice has developed in some authorities for solicitors to make application on behalf of their authority under section 57(2), in effect taking control away from social work. Where it is the social worker's judgement that has led to the local authority's application, it is the social worker's professional judgement that is being tested and they should make the application and presentation, assisted by solicitors as required.

The sheriff has power to set 'such terms and conditions' as he considers appropriate. However, the key powers set out in section 57(4) can

- require the child to be produced;
- authorise the removal of the child to and retention in a place of safety by the applicant;
- authorise prevention of removal of the child;
- provide that the location be kept secret from any person or class of person specified in the order.

The sheriff **must** consider if it is necessary to give directions to the applicant with regard to regulating contact between the child and certain adults, including parents (s.58(1)), or directions relating to the exercise of parental responsibilities (s.58(4)). The reference to 'class of person' may be, for example, siblings, grandparents etc. However the sheriff's directions could, equally, prevent contact with a particular person, such as an alleged abuser or offender, and could make contact subject to certain conditions, such as social work supervision. Direction can be sought from the sheriff in relation to

(a) any examination as to the physical or mental state of the child;
(b) any other assessment or interview of the child; or
(c) any treatment of the child arising out of such an examination or assessment. (s.58(5)).

The implication seems to be that any such action should be sanctioned by the sheriff. This seems a rather burdensome responsibility to place on an applicant at a time which is meant to be a real emergency. Similarly the legislation seems unclear about what happens if the parent or relevant person refuses to comply with any directions given. It may be social workers will have to return to the sheriff as the case develops as concerns become clear and the facts become known. In practice, because of the emergency of the situation, the local authority may have to assume that the direction places a duty on them to fulfil it. If the applicant is not a local authority, the local authority and the Principal Reporter must be notified 'forthwith'.

Any child on a CPO is deemed to be 'looked after' by the local authority in terms of section 17. This means the authority has a duty to safeguard and promote his welfare, to promote contact between the child and parents, where this is in the child's interests; to take account of the child's views, and those of his parents or relevant persons before making decisions; and to take account of religion, race and culture. Any direction in relation to medical assessment or treatment requires the consent of the child, unless the doctor assessing capacity is of the view that the child does not understand the 'consequences'.

The reporter may discontinue the order and liberate the child where he believes the criteria for a CPO are no longer satisfied or that the conditions or directions attached are no longer appropriate (s.60(3) CS Act, 1995). This provision constitutes something of an additional safeguard for the individual child although is likely to be used rarely. While in such cases it is clearly the reporter who is responsible for the liberation and any subsequent problems, it is unlikely that reporters would come to such a decision without close liaison with social work management and the social worker's assessment of the possible consequences .

Once a CPO has been granted, if the reporter does not liberate the child and if there has been no application to the sheriff to set aside or vary the order, the Reporter must arrange a children's hearing on the **second working day** after the implementation of the order (s.59(3) to decide whether to continue it or not or to vary any direction attached (s.59(4)). There is no flexibility in this for the reporter to consider factors such as the mental state of a parent etc.

The decision of this initial children's hearing is an interim one whether or not to continue or vary the order until a later children's hearing sits to consider the formal 'grounds of referral' in respect of the child, as in any normal situation. The children's hearing to consider the grounds of referral should take place by the **eighth working day**. Normally, therefore, a CPO, if continued, will be expected to last only up to 8 days.(s.65(2)). If the hearing is unable to dispose of the case it can then continue for a further 22 days up to a maximum of 66 days under section 66 of the CS Act, 1995. Where there is an initial children's hearing and it continues the order, the same people have the right, similarly, to request the sheriff to set aside or vary the order . This applications must be made **within two working days** of the continuation (s.60(8)(b) CS Act, 1995).

It should be noted where the child, parents, other relevant persons, and the applicant for the CPO exercise their right to ask a sheriff to set aside or vary a CPO or any condition or direction within it, the sheriff will deal with the whole matter and there will be no initial children's hearing to consider continuation or variation of the CPO (s.60(7)). Where an application is made to the sheriff to set aside or vary a CPO, in any of these circumstances, it shall be '**determined within three working days**' (s.60(8)). The applicant is required to notify the Principal Reporter who may arrange a hearing to provide advice 'to assist the sheriff in his determination' (s.69(10)).

The sheriff can do several things under section 60(11) to 60(13):

- confirm the order and/or any direction;
- vary the order, the directions or any conditions;
- give new directions;
- recall the order;
- cancel directions.

Although the CPO is in itself an emergency provision, the legislation recognises that in some rare circumstances it will not be possible physically to bring a case before a sheriff. In such cases, Justices of the Peace (JPs), who are not involved in granting CPOs, may authorise an **emergency order** for removal or detention of a child in a place of safety in special circumstances. The JP may authorise the applicant (an individual or a local authority) to remove or prevent removal of a child from a safe place if

- it is not practicable in the circumstances to obtain a CPO from a sheriff. (s.61(1)); and
- the conditions for granting a CPO are satisfied.

The JP's authorisation expires as soon as the sheriff decides on the CPO application or after 24 hours, whichever is earlier (s.66(4)(b)), or within 12 hours if no arrangements have been made to remove the child or prevent the child's removal (61(4)(a)).

A police constable also has authority to remove and keep a child in a place of safety for up to 24 hours if he 'has reasonable cause' to believe

- the conditions for a CPO are satisfied;
- it is not practicable in the circumstances to make an application to the sheriff;
- it is necessary to remove the child in order to protect him from significant harm (s.61(5)(6) CS Act, 1995).

The test remains 'significant harm' and this is not intended to remove from the streets children who offend.

Warrants

There are a number of points at which warrants may be sought or issued in respect of children. Each provision has time limits: section 45 warrants last for seven days, section 66 warrants last for 22 days and can be continued up to a total of 66 days, and section 69 warrants last for 22 days and can be granted an unlimited number of times. Distinguishing between them is not straightforward (for a detailed discussion see Norrie, 1997). If a child is considered likely to fail to attend a hearing in the future a choice of provision seems to be offered, but only one can or should be used in any one type of hearing. Norrie suggest that when the case is being continued after consideration, section 69 seems to be the appropriate provision and where grounds are denied or not understood and are sent to a sheriff for proof, section 66 ; in all other cases section 45 is likely to be used (Norrie 1997:158).

i) By a hearing

* to secure the attendance of a child at the hearing and for his detention for that purpose (s.45(4)and (5)); in effect there are two types of warrants—those where the child has failed to attend and those where it is anticipated that the child will not attend. These warrants last for up to seven days;
* for continuation for reports or further assessment, particularly, where a child fails to conform to a direction;
* in relation to a Child Protection Order that has already been taken out, and may renew that warrant for a second period of 22 days up to a maximum of 66 days;
* for secure care to be used in the context of detention as outlined in the section below on this specific topic.

ii) By the reporter

* The hearing may act in many of these instances on an application by the reporter so his part is crucial. We noted that he has powers to liberate children taken into places of safety if he thinks that compulsory measures of care are NOT justified. He may also be required to seek warrants from the sheriff in relation to matters referred to the hearing, as indicated above.

iii) By the social worker

The need to apply for a warrant for the detention of a child can arise quite unexpectedly in the course of other work; for example:

* a home visit for a social enquiry report on an elder sibling discovers that the mother's new boyfriend is a man with convictions for Schedule 1 offences; action needs to be taken to decide the position of the younger siblings who fall within the age group for consideration by the children's hearing;
* a child under statutory supervision who leaves home with no indication as to his intended location; the social worker may need to have a warrant if the parents cannot secure his quick return so that the problems of delay and drift are avoided; the warrant can be withdrawn if the child does re-appear.
* within the terms of a Child Protection Order, the social worker, in conjunction with the chief social work officer, may be considering the use of secure accommodation and require a warrant for the purpose.

iv) By the sheriff

* where the child fails to attend a hearing for determination of a ground of referral that has been denied;
* where the reporter applies for an extension to a Child Protection Order beyond the time limit permitted to a hearing;
* where a child has been detained by the hearing pending an appeal against the hearing's decision, the sheriff may recall the warrant if he allows the appeal;
* he may grant an unruly certificate for the detention of a child aged 14 to 16 in a remand centre or in prison in a case where that child is being prosecuted before the courts, as opposed to being referred to the hearings;
* he may grant an appeal against the making of an order for secure accommodation.

A children's hearing may deal with a child who is referred to it on a variety of grounds. The alleged commission of an offence is but one of these grounds. Whatever the grounds, the hearing has powers to detain children, and these powers are defined and structured to meet situations which require, in the interests of the particular child and the wider administration of justice, that children be detained. The power of the children's hearing to detain children referred to them is a matter of some complexity.

In respect of a child who simply fails to turn up for an arranged hearing (where failure is clearly not the result of some ordinary mishap) a children's hearing can issue a warrant for his apprehension and detention in a place of safety for a period **not exceeding seven days**. When a child 'cannot immediately be brought before a children's hearing, the Principal Reporter shall, wherever practicable, arrange a children's hearing to sit on the first working day after the child was so found' (s.45(7)). The warrant lapses after the day on which the hearing first sits to consider the case (s.45(6) CS Act, 1995).

When a children's hearing is unable to dispose of the case (s.66), for example, where the grounds require to be established, the hearing may grant a warrant if:

- there is reason to believe that the child may not attend at any hearing of his case; or
- fail to comply with a requirement under section 69(3) of this Act; or
- it is necessary that the child should be kept in a place of safety in order to safeguard or promote his welfare.

Warrants may contain such conditions as appear to the children's hearing to be necessary or expedient; may require the child to submit to medical or other examination and treatment (subject to the child's consent under section 90); and can regulate contact with certain persons (s.66(4)).

Beyond this, a child can only be detained for a further period on the application of the Principal Reporter on 'cause shown'; in other words a child cannot be detained simply as a matter of administrative convenience. It is wrong in principle, for example, for detention to be prolonged because a social worker has not managed to get a report done. Only real difficulties which emerge in the course of the children's hearing's deliberations, or the absence of information which is vital to the decision making, are likely to be advanced as reasons justifying applications for continued detention in the child's interests.

Finally, section 69 of the CS Act, 1995 deals with the situation where grounds are accepted or established and more information is needed to allow the hearing to make its decision. The hearing can be continued without issuing a warrant, but a warrant can be issued where

- it is necessary to safeguard or promote the child's welfare; or
- the hearing believes that the child may not attend the subsequent hearing (69(7) CS Act 1995).

A warrant under this section is limited to 22 days. This procedure can be repeated as required. Warrants issued by children's hearings or by sheriffs can, for example, contain requirements for 'placing' and 'keeping' (note not 'detaining') a child in secure accommodation (s.66(6)) providing the legal criteria are met and subject to the agreement of the chief social work officer.

Where '*a person who is apparently*' a child is apprehended, with or without a warrant, and cannot be brought immediately before a sheriff, the police (an officer of the rank of inspector or above or the officer in charge of the police station), subject to inquiries, should liberate him on a signed undertaking by the child and parent or guardian that he will attend the court (*Criminal Procedure (Scotland) Act,* 1995 s43).

The law specifies three sets of circumstances in which the child should not be liberated where:

- the charge is one of homicide or other grave crime;
- it is necessary in his interest to remove him from association with any reputed criminal or prostitute; or
- the officer has reason to believe that his liberation would defeat the ends of justice.

Where the child is not liberated in these circumstances, the police 'shall cause him to be kept in a **place of safety other than a police station**' until he can be brought to court. In principle, the local authority should be involved in providing this place of safety in all such cases. However the legislation leaves plenty of scope for poor child care practices by exempting the police if

- it is impracticable to do so;
- he is so unruly a character that he cannot safely be so detained; or
- by reason of his state of health or of his mental or bodily condition it is inadvisable so to detain him. (s.43(4) of the *Criminal Procedure (Scotland) Act,* 1995)

This is a grey area which, until recently, has been neglected both by the Scottish Office and by local authorities. Guidance is poor and outdated, nor is there is anything in statute to define what is 'impracticable' or what is meant by 'unruly'. As we noted previously, section 43(1) of the CP Act, 1995 explicitly **excludes police stations** from the definition of a place of safety in section 93(1) of the CS Act, 1995 in these circumstances and s.43(4) of the CP Act, 1995 provides exceptions. Courts, of course, may remand children in a remand centre or in secure accommodation. While these are much less frequent in their usage there is anecdotal evidence that the number of children being held in such circumstances is growing. It is important that good protocols exist with the police and good information systems are available to monitor these practices .

Where children are detained in police custody they must be segregated from adults and the senior police officer must certify the reasons for resorting to this practice. This certificate must be produced to the court when the child first appears. As a safeguard, the law requires the Principal Reporter to be notified of such children if it is decided not to proceed with the charge (s.43(5) *Criminal Procedure(Scotland Act,* 1995)). It is then for the reporter to decide whether or not further action is required under the *Children (Scotland) Act,* 1995 (s.63).

SECURE ACCOMMODATION

New arrangements for the provision for secure accommodation were introduced by section 8 of the *Health and Social Security Adjudications Act*, 1983, and were subsequently amended by the *Law Reform (Miscellaneous Provisions) (Scotland) Act*, 1985. Secure accommodation is currently defined by section 93 of the *Children (Scotland) Act* 1995 as 'accommodation provided in a residential establishment, approved by the Secretary of State in accordance with regulations under section 60(1)(bb) of the *Social Work (Scotland) Act*, 1968 or under paragraph 4(2)(i) of Schedule 4 to the *Children Act*, 1989, for the purpose of restricting children's liberty'.

The regulations require not only that secure units have to be registered, but that euphemistically named quiet rooms, isolation wings, close support units or whatever, come under similar scrutiny. The aim is to ensure that Scottish legislation is compatible with the European Convention of Human Rights, and that **no child is placed in secure accommodation except on the authority of sheriff or a children's hearings**.

Two legal principles drawn from Article 37 of the UN Convention on the Rights of the Child are intended to direct practice:

(b) No child shall be deprived of his or her liberty unlawfully or arbitrarily. The arrest, detention or imprisonment of a child shall be in conformity with the law and shall be used only as a measure of last resort and for the shortest appropriate period of time.

(c) In particular every child deprived of liberty shall be separated from adults unless it is considered in the child's best interest not to do so.

When approved, the UK government reserved the right not to apply rule (c) 'where at any time there is a lack of suitable accommodation or adequate facilities for a particular individual...'. An Inspectorate report and review of secure accommodation (SWSI, 1996) instigated by the White Paper *Scotland's Children*, states categorically that 'at the moment **these two principles are not being met**' in Scotland (para. 73). It is important to note that the *Secure Accommodation (Scotland) Regulations*, 1997 which set out the effect of the arrangements, subject to section 75 of the CS Act, 1995, stress that

- the use of secure accommodation for children is seen to be a very exceptional measure;
- only those children who genuinely need secure accommodation are placed and kept in it;
- where it does prove necessary to use secure accommodation, the length of time during which a child stays within it is minimised;
- the use of secure accommodation is seen in the context of an appropriate child care (and not punishment) framework, consistent with the welfare principles within the legislation.

A child may be placed in secure accommodation under a supervision requirement made by a children's hearing or, under certain circumstances, by a court under Parts V and XI of the *Criminal Procedure (Scotland) Act*, 1995.

Section 70(9) and (10) of the CS Act, 1995 (supervision requirements) also deals with the use of secure accommodation. Where a children's hearing is satisfied that it is necessary to make a supervision requirement with a condition residence, they may specify in the requirement that the child be placed and kept in secure accommodation, 'during such period as the person in charge of that establishment, with the agreement of the chief social work officer of the relevant local authority, considers necessary'.

It is important to note that children's hearings have no power to require that a child be *kept* in secure accommodation, rather they simply authorise the *placing* of the child there (Norrie, 1996). While the distinction may appear semantic, in practice, establishments have open and closed accommodation and the actual decision to place and keep a child in secure accommodation rests with the person in charge of the establishment, who must obtain the agreement of the chief social work officer. Before granting such authority, however, the hearing must be satisfied that one of the following conditions exists:

- the hearing must have made a supervision requirement with a condition that the child resides in a named residential establishment; **and either**
- the child having previously absconded, is likely to abscond unless kept in secure accommodation, **and** if he absconds, it is likely that his physical, mental or moral welfare will be at risk; *or*
- is likely to injure him or herself or some other person unless kept in such accommodation.

This subsection applies to supervision requirements and to warrants requiring placement in secure accommodation. Any assessment or report must be specific about the evidence for, or nature of, the judgement that one of the conditions exist. The law and the interests of the children requires that these criteria are met rigorously. It is difficult to imagine how one can rigorously demonstrate the second condition, unless the child has already absconded before **and** put himself at risk in the specified manner. The issue of moral danger is one that panel members may, justifiably, have anxieties about, but the possibility of such danger **alone**, does not justify the use of secure accommodation under this legislation. The disproportionately high numbers of girls in secure accommodation in Scotland may reflect discrimination towards girls in this regard.

The welfare principle in section 16(1) of the CS Act, 1995, which is at the heart of the legislation, applies. The interplay between the provisions under sections 16 and 70(9) and (10) are not clear. Norrie (1996) indicates that the phrase 'injure himself or some other person' refers to personal injuries, and not economic injuries such as damage to property. While it can be argued that a child who, for example, steals cars is likely to cause himself or others physical injury, a child who commits a criminal offence that does not put either himself or other people at risk of physical injury is probably outwith this provision. Any argument that this is a threat to moral welfare amounting to an 'injury' is too wide an interpretation (Norrie, 1996:149). It is worth noting that research data suggest that most offences involving those under 16 tend to be non-violent.

The criterion of injury to others may open the door more to issues of public protection under section 16(5) than 'best interests of the child' and raise concern that secure accommodation could be used for persistent offenders whether or not there is any evidence that they may 'abscond' and 'injure' themselves or others. Any action by panel members under 16(5) 'which would not be consistent with their affording paramountcy' would be a negation of the Kilbrandon philosophy and would signal such a fundamental change in the role of hearings as to question its very existence. **It must surely always be possible to act within the ethos of this system and safeguard the best interests of a child while safeguarding the public.**

Section 75 allows the Secretary of State to make regulations with respect to secure accommodation for children who are subject to supervision requirements with a condition of residence, but for whom a hearing has not issued an authorisation for placing in secure accommodation for children who are otherwise 'looked after' in terms of the *Children (Scotland) Act,* 1995 and for children placed under sections 44 or 208 of the *Criminal Procedures (Scotland) Act* 1995. The **66-day limit** for keeping a child in a place of safety (s.66(8), CS Act, 1995) applies to children kept in secure accommodation under this provision.

Regulation 5 provides for children to be kept in secure accommodation for a **maximum period of seventy two hours** (excluding Sundays and public holidays) either consecutively or in aggregate in any period of twenty eight days, without the authority of a hearing or a sheriff. A chief social work officer and the person in charge of the residential establishment providing secure accommodation can place a child who is subject to a supervision requirement, as an **interim placement,** in secure accommodation providing the criteria in section 70(10) CS Act, 1995 are met and where they consider it in the best interests of the child. The chief social work officer should 'so far as is reasonably practicable, seek and take into account the views of the child'. The parents or guardian must be informed in writing and the child must be referred 'in any event within twenty four hours of the placement' to the Principal Reporter informing him in writing of

- details of the placement and any subsequent placement or release;
- the reasons that it was in the child's best interests and appropriate to his or her needs;
- the views of the chief social work officer and person in charge as to the continuing need for the child's placement in secure accommodation.

The reporter should arrange a review within seventy-two hours of the placement, or if this is not reasonably practicable within a further period of twenty-four hours.

Where a hearing makes a child subject to a supervision requirement with a secure condition or continues such an order, the reporter should arrange a review **within three months**. If the child has not been placed or kept within secure accommodation within the preceding six weeks of it coming into effect, the child or his parents or guardian may write to the Principal Reporter requesting a review.

This must be arranged within twenty-one days of receipt of the request. Local authorities have a responsibility to instigate frequent reviews of children who are looked after by them.

Detention under the Criminal Procedure (Scotland) Act 1995

When a child appears before a sheriff in summary proceedings and pleads or is found guilty of an offence to which s.44 of the CP Act, 1995 applies, the sheriff may order him to be detained in residential accommodation provided by a local authority for a period not exceeding a year. The child can only be placed in secure accommodation if and when the chief social work officer and the person in charge are satisfied that the requirements discussed above are met. Where a child is committed or remanded by a court to be taken to a place of safety or to be detained as a fine defaulter in a place chosen by the local authority, he cannot be placed in secure accommodation without the consent of the chief social work officer and the person in charge.

Courts have the power under s.51(1)(a)(i) of the CP Act, 1995, to commit or remand a child directly to secure accommodation. The responsible local authority has no discretion to move the child out of this accommodation even where it believes that such a placement is no longer required (regulation 14). When a child is detained under section 205 or 208 of the CP Act, 1995, (cases involving murder or on indictment) the Secretary of State is responsible for determining where he is placed and under what circumstances (see circular 26/93).

Secure Accommodation (Scotland) Regulations 1997 require that for children detained in secure accommodation under the *Criminal Procedure (Scotland) Act*, 1995 reviews should be arranged

- within seven days of the placement irrespective of whether the child is still held in secure accommodation;
- at such time as seems necessary or appropriate in the light of the child's progress;
- in any event at intervals of not more than three months.

Regulation 15 indicates that in carrying out a review with regard to the detention of a child in secure accommodation, advice should be sought from 'a secure placement review panel'. This panel should be established by the local authority responsible for the management of the establishment and should consist of 'at least three persons'

- none of whom may be the chief social work officer or person in charge of the establishment providing the secure accommodation;
- one of whom must be an independent person who is neither a member of the Council nor an employee of a local authority or the residential establishment.

This panel should be provided with all the relevant facts in order to offer informed advice about

- the necessity for such a placement;
- whether the placement is in the child's best interests;

- whether this particular placement is appropriate to the child's needs;
- the implication of the above for the current placement.

INTEGRATED SERVICES

Interface of the children's hearing and criminal justice systems

There are no technical reasons in Scots law why most young people under 18 years should not be diverted from the adult criminal justice system and dealt with by the hearings system. It was clearly the intention of the 1968 Act that they should normally be dealt with outwith the adult system.

Section 49 (3) of the *Criminal Procedure (Scotland) Act,* 1995 requires the Sheriff Court and empowers the High Court to refer young people subject to supervision, except in respect of an offence where the sentence is fixed by law, to the Principal Reporter to arrange a hearing for advice, who can then remit the case to a hearing or dispose of it. In addition to this provision, section 49(6) of the *CP Act,* 1995 makes specific provision for summary courts to seek advice from the children's hearings on disposals when dealing with most young people up to within six months of their 18th birthday and under certain circumstances to remit them directly to the hearing system for disposal if they so wish. *National Objectives and Standards for Social Work Services in the Criminal Justice System* (NOS) recognise that

> a substantial proportion of the offenders coming into the criminal justice system will be 16 and 17-year-olds. Many will already have been in trouble with the law and will previously have been dealt with by the Children's Hearings...and that the powers outlined above are also not widely used (General Issues: Para 133).

Anecdotal evidence suggests that the system is not fulfilling its responsibilities in practice to these young people; neither is Scotland recognising the special status of 16 and 17-year-old offenders, intended by the UN Convention, by dealing routinely with them in the adult criminal courts.

Kennedy and McIvor (1992) examined 182 Social Enquiry Reports (SERs) requested from one regional social work department in a six month period on 127 young people aged 17 (52%), 16 (45%) and 15 years old (3%). The offences were mainly of dishonesty (69%) and other non-violent crimes such as breach of bail (19%). Fifty three percent of the sample had previous appearances in the children's hearing system, (66% of those 16 years and under and 42% of those 17 years old); all but one had been on some form of supervision in the past. Most had been discharged at 16 with their offending unresolved. The young people were found to have been referred repeatedly to the reporter. The study concludes that within the hearing system 'there is a lack of resources geared at addressing offending behaviour and the factors which surround it'(p.45) and suggests that the circumstances of some young people deteriorate following discharge from the hearing system, particularly those who have been in residential care, placing them at high risk of custody. Johnstone's study (1995) of 107 SERs on 16-year-olds in another jurisdiction in Scotland had similar findings. NCH intensive probation project in Edinburgh (1996) notes 66% of its referrals have previously been subject to supervision requirements.

Statistical data shows that the hearing system deals with very few young people in this age group. In 1995, of the 25,735 referrals to reporters on grounds of offences, only 321 related to 16-year-olds and 117 to 17-year-olds (Scottish Office Statistical Bulletin, 1997:12). The adult court seldom refers or remits young people to the hearing system except where required by law and few SERs recommend this to the courts. While criminal court references to the hearings for advice increased from 353 in 1993 to 456 in 1994 (a rise of 29%) they remain small in number and only 172 cases were remitted to the hearings for disposal in 1995 (Scottish Office Statistical Bulletin, 1997:23). Of the 163 boys and 8 girls under 16 dealt with in Scottish courts in 1994, only 27% were remitted to a hearing for disposal. Most were dealt with directly by the courts and were admonished, discharged, placed on probation or fined. Fourteen per cent (23 boys and 2 girls) were subsequently detained. Neither the prosecution process nor the outcome in most cases indicates that these young people were considered such serious offenders or of such significant risk to public safety that they had to be dealt with in the adult criminal system.

Henry McLeish, the Minister of Home Affairs, recognised in a speech to justices (February 28,1998) that 'where a youngster is involved (in prosecution) the decision is even more crucial because (it) will affect the rest of their lives'. He repeated the policy outlined in the *Scotland's Children* (1993) by emphasising that there 'is no question that society expects those who commit serious crime to be treated with the full severity of the law and sometimes that expectation must take precedent over the age of the offender'. He commented that 'some argue that the absence of court-based punishment for offences does not send a strong enough signal to the child or the community. I would argue that the powers of a hearing are wide-ranging and can have a significant impact on the life of a child and his family'. He acknowledged that the 'majority of young offenders are...involved in less serious crime' but not the contradiction that they should be prosecuted in the adult court at all.

The limited empirical data discussed above gives some weight to the view that the most persistent offenders are discharged prematurely from the system only to face the full force of the adult system shortly afterwards. Available statistical data gives some support to the view, not so much that the hearing system is unable to deal with the young person in this age group who offends, but that it simply does not do so. Intentionally or otherwise, it normally passes them readily to the adult system. The adult system, in turn, does not seem to view the hearing system as an obvious route for dealing with those under 18 years appearing before it. Section 32 of the *Crime and Punishment (Scotland) Act,* 1997 is intended to assist in addressing this issue. It introduces a new provision within the *Social Work (Scotland) Act,* 1968 (section 27(1))

    aa) making available to any children's hearing such reports relating to persons aged 16 and 17 years in relation to the commission of an offence, as the hearing may require for the disposal of the case;

ab) making available to any procurator fiscal or the Lord Advocate such reports as the procurator fiscal or the Lord Advocate may request in relation to persons who are charged with an offence

This is intended to improve the operation of diversion of young people from the adult system and to make available to children's hearings information and services provided under the 100% funding arrangements.

Experience suggests that many young people who are 'jointly reported' are vulnerable young persons of questionable maturity, who have failed to resolve long standing difficulties in their lives. The designation 'jointly reported', in many if not most cases, should trigger special provisions which recognise their 'special status' and high risk of criminality and custody (Whyte *et al*, 1998). The transfer of these young people to the adult criminal system (which is the common practice) is more a counsel of despair than a constructive and cost-effective response to young people. There may well be a need for specially designated staff drawn from both child care and criminal justice social work with special skills in managing control issues while providing evaluated programmes of intervention based on principles of effective intervention with these very difficult, disruptive and highly vulnerable young people.

The apparent failure of the courts to utilise fully existing provisions within Scottish legislation lies partly with the lack of credible provision, but may also lies, to some degree, with the Crown Office. Procurators fiscal would seem to prosecute 16 and 17-year-olds unless special circumstances indicate they should be dealt with by the hearings (Murray, 1988). It is likely that fiscals have insufficient information on the social circumstances of young people under 18 years coming to their attention, which would allow them to apply the White Paper's 'test' of maturity or to assist them make an appropriate decision in balancing public interest with the welfare of the young person. We welcome the amendment to section 27(1) of the *Social Work (Scotland) Act*, 1968 and suggest that co-ordinated reports from both child care and criminal justice social work are required to assist procurators fiscal and reporters in their decision making and to alert social work services to possible ways of providing credible and effective services for these 'special status' young people. Research on mental health diversion (Duff and Burman, 1994) noted that it was more work for fiscals to divert cases than to prosecute them. While there is no data to indicate this is true with regard to children, there may need to be very visible 'gains' for fiscals if they are to maximise the potential within the system and to operate within the spirit of the UN Convention.

The CS Act, 1995 makes a final special provision under section 73(12) where a review is arranged because a supervision requirement is about to expire as the child is about to attain the age of 18; the children's hearing **must** consider whether voluntary supervision and guidance (as distinct from voluntary assistance) is still required. Where they do consider it necessary the local authority **must** offer supervision and guidance 'the child is willing to accept'. While this is a slightly odd provision, which in practice may have little effect, it does recognise the ongoing needs of young people beyond the age of 18 and that the local authority should exercise its powers to assist such vulnerable young people.

National Objectives and Standards specifically addresses some of these concerns:

Because of their lack of maturity or particular factors in their social background and experience of life it may be preferable to continue to deal with some 16 and 17-year-old offenders in the Children's Hearing System and to make greater use of the opportunities for doing this which are contained in the current legislation...Experience has shown a tendency for offenders in this category to progress fairly rapidly to custody once they enter the criminal justice system (General Issues: para 134).

An authority's strategic plan should specifically state its policies for this group and the services to be provided for them. Certain types of probation programmes are more suited to these offenders...It is necessary that the development and provision of service for young offenders in the criminal justice system should be complemented by the development and provision of services to the Children's Hearing so that a full range of options is open to the courts and Children's Hearings for dealing with 15-17-year-old offenders. Local Authorities should therefore plan the provision of services for 15-17-year-olds as a whole and co-ordinate their plans for services to the Children' Hearings with those for services to the courts and prosecution system (General Issues: para 135).

Where programmes are provided for this group as part of a probation orders consideration will be given to incorporating within such programmes young offenders placed on supervision by the Children's Hearings. SWSG agreement must be obtained to such proposals and SWSG will agree with authorities a cost-sharing arrangement whereby local authorities meet the marginal costs of incorporating these young offenders into the programme (General Issues: para 136).

Some 16 and 17-year-old offenders appearing before the adult court may respond better to a supervision requirement...Consideration should be given to recommending in appropriate cases that the court remits the offender to the Children's Hearings for advice/disposal. Some guidance on criteria which would guide such recommendations is offered at...section on Social Enquiry and Related Reports (NOS: Probation section 17).

Special consideration will be required in the light of the provisions of the *Sex Offender Act*, 1997 (see Chapter 11). While most children who fall into this category in Scotland are dealt with by children's hearings and will not be subject to registration requirements, those prosecuted and convicted in the courts are subject to these arrangements (section 3(3) of the 1997 Act).

Provision of assistance and accommodation

Children (Scotland) Act, 1995 promotes a corporate approach to service provision within which young people who offend have to be located. Local authorities have a duty to prepare and publish service plans (s.19 of the CS Act, 1995) for all children in their area giving details of 'relevant services' (defined in terms of Part II of the CS Act, 1995 and the 1968 Act and other legislation under which local authorities provide services) and to publish information about relevant services which are actually provided in their area (s.20). Local authorities are required to consult Health Boards, voluntary organisations, Principal Reporter, chairmen of children's panels, housing associations etc. They have a range of duties and responsibilities to children 'looked after' by them. Section 26 of the CS Act 1995 empowers a local authority to provide 'accommodation', on a voluntary or compulsory basis, for children looked after by them. This can be provided by placing the child with

- a family (as defined by s.93(1)(a) and (b);
- a relative;
- any other suitable person;
- a residential establishment; or
- **other arrangements as appropriate**.

The accommodation can be in any part of the UK. The CS Act, 1995 places a general duty on the local authority to

- safeguard and promote the child's welfare including preparation for leaving care;
- provide family support services;
- promote contact between the child and his/her parents;
- take account of the child's view (normally 12 or over);
- have regard to the child's religion, race, culture and linguistic background;
- review the child's care at regular intervals (ss.17 and 31).

In addition to the general duty to promote welfare under section 12 of the 1968 Act, section 22 of the CS Act, 1995 amends and extends section 12 clarifying local authorities' powers to promote the welfare specifically of 'children in need' (those under 18 years), 'in kind or exceptionally in cash'. Many young people who come to the attention of criminal justice will fall into this category. The CS Act, 1995 places a duty to safeguard and promote the welfare of any child in need in their area and so far as is possible and consistent with that, promote the upbringing of the child by his/her family. It is important for criminal justice social workers to provide adequate data for their child-care colleagues, who are responsible for planning and developing policies and services for the needs of young offenders . The definition of a child in need is contained in s.93(4)(a) of the CS Act, 1995: 'he or she is in need of care and attention because

i) he is unlikely to achieve or maintain or to have the opportunity of achieving or maintaining a reasonable standard of health or development unless there are provided for him, under or by virtue of this part, services by a local authority;
ii) his health or development is likely significantly to be impaired or further impaired unless such services are so provided;
iii) he is disabled, or
iv) he is adversely affected by the disability of any other person in his family.

The remainder of s.12 of the 1968 Act empowers local authorities to provide assistance for those of 18 or over where that assistance is needed for the individual and not in relation to children within a family. The local authority has a duty under s.25 of the CS Act 1995 (for those under 18) to provide accommodation for any child in their area who needs it because

- no-one has parental responsibilities, or
- he or she is lost or abandoned or
- the person who has been caring for the child is prevented permanently or not and *for whatever reason* from giving the child suitable accommodation or care (replaces s.15 of 68 Act)

Local authorities also have power to provide accommodation for any child in their area if they think this is necessary to safeguard or promote the child's welfare. They are also empowered to provide such accommodation for anyone between 18 and 21.

Throughcare and aftercare

In addition to the general duties, local authorities have more specific duties of 'after care' for anyone under 19 years who was looked after at any time after she/ he ceased to be of school age (s.29(1)) of the CS Act, 1995. Local authorities are empowered to provide advice, guidance and assistance (s.29(2)) for this same group when they are over 19 but less than 21 **if they apply** for it. Local authorities are also empowered to provide this same group with financial assistance, until they are 21, towards the expense of education and training and to make contributions towards accommodation and maintenance (s.30). If the finance is made available it can be continued beyond 21 for the completion of education or training.

Many young people leaving care experience difficulties. It is now well recognised that those who, for example, have experienced secure care because of their offending will have particular difficulties returning to the community and making a successful transition to independence. Preparation for young people leaving care is particularly important if a career of crime is to be avoided. This needs to be an integral part of the care planning and not left until they are due for discharge.

The all too common practice of terminating supervision for those nearing their sixteenth birthday, when they are, clearly, still caught up in offending and facing adversity, on the pretext that they have 'outgrown the system' or 'we cannot do any more for them', will further disadvantage these young people in terms of the opportunities provided by the CS Act, 1995. While the potential 'benefits' do not justify continuing with compulsory measures when they are no longer necessary, it should be noted that ending a supervision requirement before the age of sixteen will make it more difficult for such young people to claim the help and services which could be made available under these provisions. In the event, it is up to social workers to encourage young people to make use of the extensive range of powers under the legislation and to claim all the help they can . Written information on their rights should be available to all young people leaving care and discharged from the hearing system.

Provisions for 'advice, guidance and assistance' under section 17(2) cover all 'looked after' children and are governed by *The Arrangements to Look After Children (Scotland) Regulations*, 1996. Volume 2 (chapter 7) deals with Throughcare, which is defined as 'the process by which the local authority plans and prepares the young person they are looking after for the time when he or she will cease to be looked after'. Aftercare is defined as the 'provision of advice, guidance and assistance when a young person ceases to be looked after'.

There is no longer ambiguity within the legislation. Aftercare duties and responsibilities for young people lie with the local authority as a whole and not one particular department. The Guidance supports the idea of an **Interagency Throughcare and Aftercare Panel**, stressing that 'the social work department of the local authorities have the lead responsibility, but in discharging it they should involve other relevant departments, agencies and organisations, making full use of the duty to collaborate set out in the Act'. 'The panel could promote communication between agencies and help develop a common understanding of concepts and language used such as "vulnerable". It could also facilitate the monitoring and evaluation of services, recommend action to be taken by specific agencies and stimulate joint initiatives.' In the initial draft of the Guidance the vulnerable nature of many young people was recognised with reference to research which indicates that **a young person formerly looked after is 70 times more likely to end up homeless than other young people and is likely to lack many of the basic skills required to maintain independence**.

The regulations require the local authority to produce a care plan and the legislation requires the local authority 'so far as is reasonably practicable' to ascertain the views of the young person, their parents (undefined in this part of the Act) and any other person considered relevant when doing so (s.17(3)of the CS Act, 1995). Great emphasis is placed on this being a working plan and not merely a paper exercise and it should:

- include a preliminary assessment of follow-on accommodation and support needs;
- make specific proposals;
- clarify the objectives and responsibilities of social work staff and the potential role of other agencies;
- ensure a young person's access to information, support and preparation that he or she requires to make a positive transition to independence;
- identify a designated key worker with overall responsibility for co-ordinating services including follow-on accommodation, support and care management;
- record the expected contributions of housing and education departments, (including career and employment advice), housing associations, health and voluntary support agencies.

It is suggested that every care review after the young person's 14th birthday should consider planning for the future. Once the young person is no longer looked after, although not subject to this review process, the guidance suggest that the co-ordinator arranges ongoing informal reviews to allow monitoring and evaluation of the young person's progress and the provision and adjustment of services available under the legislation.

The Guidance makes specific reference to children who are 'looked after' as a consequence of their offending and suggests that to 'make the best use of the flexible provisions in the law, local authority children's and criminal justice services should be co-ordinated' taking account of the provisions in para. 132-136 of the General Issues section of National Objectives and Standards. The Guidance also suggests that where a social worker with child-care responsibilities has an active interest in the young person's aftercare, consideration should be given to their writing any SER and supervising any order. While it is crucial that this work is co-ordinated and joint assessment undertaken, it seems quite inappropriate to consider that a child-care worker should supervise the order.

The ambition of the *Children (Scotland) Act*, 1995 is to be applauded. The resources required to make the proposals a reality, however, are not in evidence. The experience of the *Children Act*, 1989 in England does not give grounds for optimism. There is a greater case than ever before for providing 100% funding for services to children and young people who offend.

A critique: beyond care

The introduction of the CS Act, 1995 and the associated guidance should have tightened up procedures. Practice wisdom suggests that many children 'placed' do not meet the criteria for secure accommodation in any strict sense and are placed there because panel members or social workers feel they 'have tried everything else', or because of the limitations of mainstream residential units in providing structured care for difficult and often damaged teenagers. It remains a matter of speculation if any improvements have occurred since the inception of the Act. Questions have to be asked when girls, who represent such a small proportion of children referred and coming to hearings, represent such a high proportion of children who require secure accommodation and have their basic civil rights to liberty removed 'in their best interest'.

It has been argued that, despite the children's hearings' philosophical base, more children per head of population are locked up in Scotland, than anywhere else in the UK (Stewart and Tutt, 1987). While this conclusion may result more from the way statistics are generated than reality, it warns against complacency in Scotland. Whatever the welfare needs, the formal removal of liberty is a serious matter and requires strict principles of justice as well as welfare to apply. It remains to be seen whether evidence of improved practice in this area will emerge as a result of legislative changes.

The Inspectorate review on secure accommodation (SWSI, 1996) provided a worrying picture. It estimated that Scotland has proportionately 30% more secure places than England (para. 85). Most places are used for young people aged 15-18; they are generally full and in constant demand; and the number of young people being *kept in prison* in Scotland is increasing (para. 74). There is no independent empirical data on the use of such accommodation or on its outcomes and this too is now required as a matter of some urgency.

The review suggested that secure care is being used because of a lack of appropriate alternatives in the community and because other systems have failed to deal with difficult behaviour from its onset (para. 75). Many of the children identified were already in the long-term care of the local authority when placed in secure care (para. 51) and most were placed by children's hearings (para. 35). At the same time, the report suggests, as have other commentators (Littlewood, 1996), that there are few apparent differences between many children in secure care and children in other forms of care.

The White Paper *Scotland's Children* recognised that 'the children's hearings need to have available to them a full and effective range of resources' (para 7.17) for young people who persistently offend. The review suggests that scarcity of normal resources has the knock on effect that 'far from being used as a last resort, secure care is being used to make up for there being fewer residential school places' (para. 77) and limited community-based resources. It sensibly avoids any knee-jerk reaction to recommend more secure care and confirms the view put by the White Paper 'that there is considerable scope for improved local multi-agency collaboration in providing effective services for children who present special problems in the development of normal personal self-control' (para. 7.26).

It is difficult to believe that Scottish children should have a greater need for secure facilities than children elsewhere in the UK. Social workers, in particular, have to question why this may be the case and what strategies their authorities have to minimise the use of secure accommodation. One might speculate that despite the Kilbrandon principles and the hearing system, children who offend persistently are not being provided with adequate services to address their needs, in particular their offending behaviour, within their communities. Many may be at risk of being 'abandoned' to secure accommodation because of the inadequacies of local residential units and intermediate provision and their inability to address the presented problems.

The legislation and the regulations give a great deal of discretion to 'the person in charge...with the agreement of the chief social work officer' to keep or remove children from secure accommodation. Intensive community-based support units and well structured, adequately staffed, residential units are required for these, the most difficult and vulnerable young people in our society.

The hearing system relies on a series of checks and balances. To secure care, the gatekeepers—sheriffs, panel members, police and chief social work officers—must operate consistently and make explicit criteria for placement. An improved review system is required which promotes vigilance and allows justice and care to operate more effectively. The SWSI review recommends the establishment of a National Planning Group 'to oversee the planning, management and development of secure units and the care and education services for young people with behavioural problems which include offending. More attention is needed to the development of effective early intervention services' (recommendation 28).

FOOTNOTE

Lord Advocate's guidelines

Children who have committed certain offences will be reported to the procurator fiscal for consideration of a prosecution in either the High Court of Justiciary or the Sheriff Court. These offences include:

1. Treason, murder, rape, deforcement of messengers and statutory offences for which the statute only makes provision for prosecution on indictment, or for a penalty on conviction on indictment, such as possessing firearms with intent to injure, use of firearms to resist arrest, carrying firearms with criminal intent; intercourse with a girl under 13 years of age.

2. Culpable homicide, attempted murder, assault to the danger of life, sodomy, assault and robbery involving the use of firearms, attempted rape, incest and related offences.

3. Other offences which are normally prosecuted on indictment such as assault to severe injury or permanent disfigurement, assault with intent to rape, serious assault and robbery (in particular involving the use of weapons other than fire-arms), assault with intent to rob involving the use of firearms, fire raising and malicious mischief causing or likely to cause great damage to property or danger to life, all Misuse of Drugs Act offences involving possession of Class A drugs and possession with intent to supply and supply of *any* controlled drug.

4. An offence alleged to have been committed by a child aged 15 years or over which, in the event of conviction, obliges or permits a court to order disqualification for driving. Minor Road Traffic Act offences carrying a liability to discretionary disqualification should not normally be reported.

5. An offence alleged to have been committed by a child over the age of 16 years who has not attained the age of 18 years and in respect of whom a supervision requirement of a children's hearing is in force; offences committed with an adult.

6. Any other offence which in the opinion of the Chief Constable is so serious as to warrant the instruction of solemn proceedings by the Lord Advocate in the public interest.

7. An offence alleged to have been committed by a child in respect of whom a report cannot be submitted to reach the reporter at least six clear weeks before attainment of the child's 16th birthday.

Chapter 7

Community-based Measures

Diversion; reparation; community measures available to courts; fines; supervised attendance orders; caution; compensation; restriction orders; anti-social behaviour; community protection orders

INTRODUCTION

A key platform of Labour government policy is the promotion of community-based measures. It is an important part of the policy that these disposals are not seen solely as alternatives to custody but as credible mainstream disposals in their own right against which consideration of custody is a last-resort alternative. It is important to distinguish these community-based disposals from those which are directly alternatives to custody. Disposals such as community service and probation with a requirement of unpaid work are identified within the legislation as measures available for 'an offence punishable by imprisonment'. Research, to date, has suggested that the range of 'non-custodial measures' available appears to have had limited effect on the levels of custodial sentencing. The emphasis in current policy is that custody should be 'used sparingly' and reserved for those offenders who present a serious risk to the public; and that, essentially, for the rest, various forms of community-based measures are intrinsically the preferred penalty or disposal— not because they are 'alternatives to custody'. The impact of policy in the eighties throughout the UK was summed up by Lord Bingham, the Lord Chief Justice, at a Police Foundation meeting in July 1997 (see Chapter 1).

He suggested that the main challenge for the Labour government is to steer public and political debate on crime away from an obsession with sentencing, in particular the use of custody, towards prevention and the use of community disposals and diversion. This chapter deals with community-based measures other than probation and community service.

DIVERSION

The concept of diversion can be used in a broad sense to describe strategies to re-route people out of the criminal justice system as a whole, not just to engineer a shift away from current levels of the use of custody. The introduction of Scotland's children's hearings system was a major diversionary measure in itself. It simply took the responsibility for dealing with 'children in trouble' away from the criminal justice system, and set up an alternative tribunal system with quite differently articulated values and procedures. The introduction of 'fiscal fines' by section 56 of the *Criminal Justice (Scotland) Act,* 1987 and their further extension by section 302 of the *Criminal Procedure (Scotland) Act,* 1995, are intended to reduce the pressure of criminal business in the lower courts (see Shiels and Bradley, 1996: 283).

There can be various motivations for the introduction of diversionary measures: economic, social, or humanitarian. A diversionary measure may be established to relieve workloads of procurators fiscal; to avoid 'stigmatising' offenders, improving their chances of re-integration; to help the vulnerable offender, and to treat with humanity those offenders who are not fully responsible for their actions. There is some recognition in these strategies that the criminal justice system is one which can further damage individuals who get into trouble, and often does little to remedy, effectively, the harm that individual offenders have done to others. At a more practical level, the pressures on court business, and the huge expense of court time and of building more prisons as a response to lawbreaking, is once again creating economic motivations to find new ways of dealing with offenders.

This section is mainly concerned with *secondary* diversion to social work, that is, measures which give courts opportunities to divert people from custody. However, there has been a development in social work's involvement at the level of *primary* diversion, that is, at the stage which seeks to avoid the necessity for court proceedings at all. Attempts to deal with crime at an informal community level, or without recourse to formal agencies at all, are outwith the scope of this text.

Measures examined under this heading have their legislative basis in section 27(1) of the 1968 Act as amended by the *Crime and Punishment (Scotland) Act,* 1997 and under section 12 of the 1968 Act, to 'promote social welfare...on such a scale as may be appropriate...' . The amendments extend 100% central funding for certain services to support the further development of diversionary services.

The amended section 27(1)(aa) is intended to bring 16 and 17-year-olds who offend and are dealt with by the children's hearings within the ambit of 100% funding by 'making available...such reports...as the hearing may require for 'the disposal of a case'. Section 27(1)(ab) will extend the scope of diversion, in general, by 'making available to any procurator fiscal or the Lord Advocate such reports as...(they)...may request in relation to persons who are charged with an offence'.

The particular emphasis in these amendments was outlined by the then Minister for Home Affairs (Fraser, 1993). Diversion pilot projects were to 'explore the potential of social work service for reducing the costs to the criminal justice system by intervening early to the minimum extent necessary to resolve problems linked to alleged offending' and to 'include supervision for 16 and 17-year-old offenders referred by the courts to the children's hearings for disposal' (see Chapter 6).

The police

The police play a key role in the development of strategies to divert juvenile offenders both from custody and from court appearances. This involves shared working between reporters, local authority social work, the police and other relevant agencies. The scope for a similar approach in relation to adults in trouble is still under development. However, government policy on crime prevention encourages local authorities to play a central role in bringing together the relevant agencies for this kind of shared approach and to explore the scope for social work specialist staff to be involved in crime prevention. If social work is to enhance its community involvement role in relation to crime, it needs more formal links with the police and to establish its role in the local authority crime prevention strategies. A corporate strategy, involving local authority social work and other services, the police, health and the voluntary sector is required to target, for example

- young adult offender, particularly those at the interface of children's hearing and adult systems who are a prime 'target' of government policy;
- alcohol and drug misuse as a major factor in crime.

The procurator fiscal

Social work involvement in diversion has been primarily in the form of shared working with the procurator fiscal. The second report of the Stewart Committee (Cmnd 8958, 1983) advocated the adoption of diversion to social work as one of a number of diversionary strategies which should be available to procurators fiscal. The Stewart Committee suggested that 'more frequently, perhaps, it will be an offender's personal or social circumstances that cause concern, and the prosecutor may wish to investigate the possibility of making a referral for counselling or practical assistance'(para. 3.29). The report indicated that 'in minor cases, where...stresses are identified, we are of the opinion that an early offer of assistance by a social worker or volunteer helper may prove a constructive alternative to prosecution. We consider this alternative would be appropriate where the public interest and the individual interest are best served, not by prosecution and punishment, but by encouraging and assisting the alleged offender to conform to accepted standards of behaviour'. It is worth noting the emphasis on the role of the 'independent' sector in criminal justice provision, for example, in providing volunteer help as a means of diversion.

Diversion schemes developed their own characteristics and ways of working. Many years ago the Ayr scheme (Moody, 1983) began to operate what came to be known as the **waiver** method of diversion. Under this method the case was marked 'no proceedings' at the point at which it was decided to divert the individual to social work. In effect prosecution was waived unconditionally and the offender put in touch with social work. This freed the offender from the possibility of future prosecution and thus enhanced the voluntary nature of co-operation. In the **deferred** method of diversion, advocated by the Stewart Committee, and more commonly in operation, prosecution becomes conditional on a satisfactory outcome to any arrangement made and allows the fiscal to make a decision about prosecution in the light of the accused person's response. Diversion schemes have sought to maximise the potential of both approaches by having a mixed approach.

Research evidence has suggested some reluctance on the part of fiscals to operate more 'adventurous' diversion, particularly for people with mental or psychological problems (Duff and Burman, 1994). This raises an important policy issue
about the role of diversion against concerns for public interest. The fiscal's con-
ceptions of public interest in the past has tended to focus more on retributive and
denunciatory aspects of decision making rather than on restorative and reparative
ones, argued Moody and Tombs (1982). There is little opportunity to debate or test
in public how fiscals determine whether or not prosecution is in the public interest,
and what interpretations they use. The only mechanism, given that fiscals are responsible to the Lord Advocate, is that of the Parliamentary Question, somewhat
cumbersome for the purpose. Policy on diversion has to operate alongside, for
example, sustained campaigns to have domestic violence taken seriously and so
prosecuted as a matter of public policy as a means of denouncing the violence that
is involved. A victim perspective should be an important element in diversionary
practice.

In the main, the Stewart Committee did not seek to determine what prosecution
policy should be on particular offences or issues. It was more concerned to explore
ways in which some less serious matters might be dealt with, other than by the
expenditure of court time.

One important implication of diversion for social workers arises when a social
enquiry report is requested on someone who previously has been diverted. The
authority is likely to have information about the diversion. Any charge which results in diversion as an alternative to prosecution, technically, can only be referred
to as an **alleged** offence. Information on personal and social circumstances, gathered during the intervention, are likely to be relevant background material in considering any subsequent offence, as is the person's response to any social work
help in consideration of community-based measures as a potential disposal by the
court.

A social enquiry report for the court cannot avoid making reference to the contact over diversion and the reasons for it. The alleged offence which led to diversion cannot be presented as part of a list of previous appearances: the alleged offender has not been required, as part of the diversion, in any formal sense, to admit
to the offence, even if he acknowledges to the social worker that he 'did it'. In
addressing this matter in a report it may be helpful to consider

- the reasons the authority was involved;
- the circumstances of, and background to, the alleged offence;
- the reasons for diversion, and the method employed;
- the way the person was helped, and his response;
- the implications of the above for disposal.

The Review of Criminal Justice Social Work Services (SWSG, 1997) indicated
government's intention to establish nineteen pilot diversion schemes in 1998, funded
under the 100% arrangements, in various locations throughout Scotland to be used
for less serious offences. Some of the pilot projects will focus on particular groups,

such as drug users, using both waiver and deferred prosecution methods. Programmes are expected to last between 6-8 weeks. Some projects will focus on a specific approach to intervention such as mediation or reparation to the victim. 'They are aimed at less serious offenders where the grounds to prosecute exist but to do so may not be in the public interest. These cases may be suitable for assistance or support to address the behaviour which underlies their offence' (SWSG, 1997).

Reparation and mediation

Reparation and mediation are key concepts in restorative, as opposed to retributive, justice. Marshall (1992) has suggested that an important aspect of their appeal lies in their potential to meet several aims:

- providing the opportunity to compensate victims;
- making offenders personally accountable for their actions;
- offering the possibility of reducing recidivism;
- diverting from formal procedures and sanctions;
- reducing costs and burdens on the courts.

Reparation is a form of making amends by an offender, usually through the intervention of a third party (mediation); **directly** to the victim to compensate for the offence in some way, for example, by financial compensation, an apology; or **indirectly**, where reparation is made to some other person or organisation, often determined by the victim, for example by a donation to charity. The criminal justice system provides for financial reparation to be made, in some circumstances, to victims as part of a court order (see below on compensation and restitution). Generally reparation schemes have been established in recent years:

- to explore ways of making amends other than by financial compensation (for example, by making an apology, undertaking some form of personal service, by arranging meetings between offenders and victims); and
- using mediation as a basis for such reparation, rather than a court order.

Reparation need not be confined to the stage of primary diversion. However experimental schemes of reparation and mediation in Scotland have tended to involve work at this stage. Some schemes have attempted to explore the possibilities for mediated reparation at the secondary stage—for example, as part of social enquiry report preparation or as part of a probation order.

Mackay suggests the chief benefits that can be achieved by Reparation Agreements...are:

- the ending of feuds or their prevention;
- the negotiation of financial or material amends;
- avoidance of the inconvenience of court appearances;
- the possibility of improving or restoring relationships;
- the chance for the victim to face the offender personally;

- the pre-emption of retaliation. (1988: 38)

Mackay argues that reparation brings values into play, such as the ideas of forgiveness and reconciliation, that do not sit easily with the dominant political views on responses to crime. This may be one reason why government policy has not placed much emphasis on reparation and mediation until recently.

The concept of **mediation** in criminal justice systems, carried out by trained mediators (bearing in mind that the diversion schemes often involve serious elements of mediation) are still relatively new and not yet tried and tested. Marshall viewed mediation as 'the injection of a third party who represents the principle that ordinary people can, with a little assistance, solve their own problems in conjunction with one another. Each offender, in effect, represents a unique set of problems to be solved...The mediator is a catalyst for community action...The mediator's role is to encourage and help those involved deal with the problem creatively and constructively themselves...' (Marshall 1994:3).

The potential of such approaches remains under-developed in Scotland. Warner's evaluation of two schemes in Edinburgh and Glasgow (1992) concluded that, while the potential of reparation and mediation is great, the practice has been somewhat limited, involving relatively small numbers and cases where it is questionable if prosecution would have been pursued.

COMMUNITY-BASED MEASURES AVAILABLE TO THE COURTS

Absolute discharge

The effect of an absolute discharge is that the person leaves the court without any penalty being imposed, even though guilt has been admitted or proved. The law states that the court may make such an order, provided that the penalty is not otherwise fixed by law, 'if it is of the opinion, having regard to the circumstances, including the nature of the offence, and the character of the offender, that it is inexpedient to inflict punishment, and that a probation order is not appropriate' (section 246 of the *Criminal Procedure (Scotland) Act*, 1995).

The order of absolute discharge is available to courts hearing cases both on solemn procedure and on summary procedure. In cases on solemn procedure, section 246 (2) makes it clear that such an order is made 'instead of sentencing him'. In cases of summary procedure, an order of absolute discharge is made 'without proceeding to conviction" (section 246(3)). It is possible to appeal against the original conviction (s.247(3). Section 247 further adds that the original conviction does not count 'for any purpose other than the purposes of the proceedings in which the order is made, and of laying it before a court as a previous conviction in subsequent proceedings for another offence'. In practice absolute discharges made by solemn courts are counted as convictions for the purpose of the current and future prosecutions; in summary proceedings absolute discharges are regarded as convictions in the event of future prosecution (s.247(4)) even though the order is made without proceeding to conviction.

An order of absolute discharge can be referred to in any subsequent criminal proceedings, but in all other aspects a conviction is not recorded against the person. It is possible to make an order of absolute discharge, AND to order forfeiture of an article (for example, a knife) at the same time.

Admonition

An admonition involves the person leaving the court without any penalty being imposed. However, the admonition represents a warning, **and does involve a conviction**, whichever method of procedure is being used. Section 246(1) of the *Criminal Procedure (Scotland) Act*, 1995, says a court 'may, if it appears to meet the justice of the case, dismiss with an admonition any person convicted by the court of any offence'.

Because an admonition involves recording a conviction, technically it does represent a breach of probation by further offence if the person is already subject to supervision, and the necessary action has to be taken by the supervising officer. There are some important complexities about its use as a penalty as the outcome of breach of requirement of probation proceedings (see Chapter 8).

Deferring sentences

Section 47 of the *Criminal Justice (Scotland) Act*, 1963 empowered courts to defer sentences, although the practice seems to have been well established before that time. The power to defer sentence is **now located** in the *Criminal Procedure (Scotland) Act*, 1995, section 202.

It is important to note the distinction between adjourning a case before sentence (s.201), for example for reports, and a deferred sentence. There is no restriction on the length of time for which sentence may be deferred and it may be deferred more than once. The power is expressed in general and wide-ranging terms: 'it shall be competent for a court to defer sentence after conviction for a period and on such conditions as the court may determine'.

Section 202 (2) and (3) makes it possible to return a person to court, either by a warrant for his arrest, or by citation, if it comes to the attention of the court that deferred that he has been convicted of a further offence in another court during the period of deferment and 'may deal with him in any manner in which it would be competent for it to deal with him on the expiry of the period of deferment'. If the court that deferred sentence convicts the offender of a further offence 'it may deal with him for the original offence in any manner in which it would be competent for it to deal with him on the expiry of the period of deferment, as well as for the offence committed during the said period'.

The deferring of sentence is not a substantive disposal. It is exactly what its name suggests, a deferring of sentence. People do not 'get' deferred sentences as the final disposal of their cases; the possibility remains of imposing a substantive disposal at the termination of the period of deferment.

A deferment of sentence is linked with the general condition 'to be of good behaviour' but sentences can be deferred for a variety of reasons. Deferrals are commonly used for purposes such as:

- to test behaviour over a specified period of time;
- to see how a person responds to a recently ordered period of supervision;
- to enable a person to perform a specific task or service related directly to the circumstances of an offence; a typical example is to enable the offender to make restitution; more unusual examples have included writing an essay on hooliganism, baking cakes for older people, buying a gift for a spouse who had been a victim;
- to enable the person to receive help or treatment.

The completion of conditions creates an expectation that the offender will be dealt with more leniently, though no promise of a particular disposal should ever be made. Even if the condition is complied with, the final disposal will not necessarily be admonition. Sentences of imprisonment and fines after periods of deferment successfully completed have been held on appeal not to be excessive. A deferred sentence is less likely to be used for a very serious offence. The most frequently used periods of deferment are 3, 6, and 12 months.

There is no objection in law to longer or to repeated deferments, but in practice courts do arrive at a point at which sentence has to be imposed. Indeed one complaint about the frequency with which the deferring of sentence is suggested by both defence agents and social workers, is that the options at the end of the period can often be perceived by courts as being less than at the original point of conviction. The chief complaint is that deferring is often suggested for the lack of anything better, and appears to duck the main issue that faces the court—namely deciding disposal. If, however, a clear case and specific purpose can be made for a period of deferment then an argument for its use can be advanced.

There are many promising examples of short social work programmes coupled with a deferring of sentence, for example, the court requiring people to attend an alcohol education programme within a set period of deferment. There seems particular merit in the development of this idea in the context of current policy to reserve the heavier or more costly orders (such as probation) for the more serious or needy cases. Normally when sentence is deferred for social work, a supplementary social enquiry report will be requested for the court diet to which sentence is deferred.

Social work services provided as part of a deferred sentence are not, however, funded as part of the 100% arrangements. Consequently practice varies greatly in Scotland. Some authorities encourage the use of deferment to provide social work assistance as a means of avoiding low-tariff probation disposals, while others are reluctant to provide any service under this provision. Different sheriffs, equally, have differing views on the use of deferrals.

Should an SER writer want to encourage a court to defer sentence, particularly for social work involvement, National Objectives and Standards (NOS) indicate that the writer should clearly indicate

- the proposed purpose;
- an appropriate time period;

- expectations of the offender; and
- the nature of the service available .

At the date of the deferred hearing, the prosecutor will inform the court of any convictions against the person which have been recorded in the interim, and of any outstanding charges that may be faced.

THE FINE

The fine is the most frequently used (between 70%-80%) of all disposals (Statistical Bulletin, 1990-1997). Its use is not confined to first or early offenders. The fine is both a versatile and a successful measure and it has been argued that 'the fine is popular on grounds other than its reforming effect, but it is the only sentence for which there is evidence that it may reduce the number of subsequent convictions' (Pease, 1980:151). It is an important part of the social work task to give full and detailed information in social enquiry reports about income and financial circumstances and commitments and to offer advice to the court. This is emphasised in NOS and details should be verified wherever possible.

While the concept of 'unit fine' (fine in proportion to means) considered by the conservative government in 1988 (Rifkind, 1989), and included in the 1990 Act was never implemented, it remains an important aspect of fining that the amount of the penalty should reflect the circumstances of the individual and their ability to pay. This is crucially important given the numbers receiving custodial disposals for fine default. It is important for social workers to be aware of who is more likely to default, for example for the most part, fines in relation to *Road Traffic Act* offences are paid in full and within the time periods allowed by the courts. Nonetheless despite a significant reduction in the problem of people admitted to prisons for non-payment of financial penalties throughout the 1990s, a colossal 44% of all admissions to Scottish prisons in 1992 and 38% in 1995 were for fine default.

Some people simply cannot pay given their circumstances; some people refuse to pay, either because the amount or equity of the particular fine is not accepted, or because of adherence to a criminal value system that is beyond the influence of either social work or the court. It was concern about the rising proportions admitted to prison for fine default in the 1980s that a report on the subject (ADSW, 1987) made many recommendations for change. Subsequent legislation introduced a number of important changes into the ways that the payment of financial penalties are enforced.

Imposing fines

Until 1982, legislation on fines referred to a specific amounts of money, shown in figures, and maximum fines as '£x or £y'. The *Criminal Justice Act*, 1982 introduced a new approach to defining and calculating fines in the various legislative. In place of fixed values, it introduced a **Standard Scale** for summary courts, whose levels could be varied subsequently in line with inflation and other considerations.

These provisions, as subsequently amended and extended, are now contained in section 225 of the *Criminal Procedure (Scotland) Act*, 1995.

Any new legislation enacted since 1983 will refer instead to a particular **level** on the Standard Scale; the maximum level chosen is intended to reflect the seriousness of the offence. The maximum level of fine that can be imposed in respect of statutory offences will be (in cases under summary procedure) on the notice of penalty (see Chapter 3).

The Standard Scale at present is:

Level	
1	£200
2	£500
3	£1,000
4	£2,500
5	£5,000

The **maximum** levels of fine which the various courts can impose are:

High Court	unlimited amount, subject to statutory maxima
Sheriff Court	
on solemn procedure	unlimited amount, subject to statutory maxima
on summary procedure	level 5
District Court	level 4

Courts may impose fines for any offence for which the penalty is not fixed by law. The maximum amount of the fine is limited by:

a) the maximum power of the court, as set out above; and

b) in the case of statutory offences, the maximum set out in the statute which creates the offence with which the court is dealing.

Some statutes permit that both fines and imprisonment can be imposed for the same offence. It is generally regarded as unwise to impose both a fine and a probation order at the same time (that is, in a case where a person is facing more than one charge), even though there may be no legal obstacle to the combination. It is possible to include restitution as a requirement within the probation order, if the court considers that the individual victim of the offence should receive financial compensation from the probationer.

The means of the offender

The law insists (section 211(7) of the *Criminal Procedure (Scotland) Act*, 1995) that the means of the person, 'so far as known to the court' shall be taken into account in determining the amount of any fine. This can be seen as underlining the principle of individualised justice. Unless there is a social enquiry report available, the court usually has to rely on the accused's lawyer, if he has one, or on a series of direct questions to the person in the dock to ascertain his financial position. There have been some experiments in which people have been asked to give this information routinely on a written form in advance of any hearing, to improve the administration of justice. People pleading guilty by letter usually send in a completed 'means form' with their letter plea.

In a summary case, the court has power to have the offender searched and any money found on him at the time of his apprehension can be applied by the court towards payment of the fine, unless:

- the court is satisfied it belongs to someone else;
- the court is satisfied the loss of such money would be more injurious to this family than imprisonment or detention (s.212 (2)).

The person can apply, either orally or in writing, that any money found should not be applied towards the fine, and the court may make various enquiries on receipt of such an application (s.212(4)).

Time to pay
The court MUST allow at least seven days to pay a fine, or the first instalment (s.214), UNLESS:

a) the offender appears to have sufficient means to enable him to pay forthwith— this includes arranging for money to be brought from home, work, or a bank account, for example); or
b) he does not ask for time to pay—though the court can nonetheless still allow time to pay rather than permit the person to 'do time' at public expense;
c) he has no fixed abode—the definition is left to the interpretation of the courts, and it may well be that a social worker's knowledge of the facilities available to, or used by, people in this predicament can help both the person and the administration of justice;
d) the court is satisfied for any other special reason that no time should be allowed —a typical example is of someone who is already serving a prison sentence.

The court may allow further time to pay on application by, or on behalf of, the offender (214(7)). In all cases where time to pay is not allowed, the court must state and minute its reason for its decision (section 214(3), CP Act, 1995).

Fixing an alternative prison sentence in default of payment
The court must NOT, when allowing time to pay, fix an alternative (prison) sentence in the event of future default of payment (section 214(4)), UNLESS:

- the person is present before the court; and
- the gravity of the offence; or
- the character of the person; or
- some other special reason

...makes it expedient to impose such an alternative without any further enquiry— that is, without convening a subsequent court, commonly known as a means or fines enquiry court (see below), and again the reasons must be stated and minuted.

Arrangements for payment
Usually the court orders payment of a fine either within a stipulated period (for example, three months), or by instalments—the latter typically being expressed in

terms of a weekly or fortnightly amount (especially if he is receiving state benefit paid at this frequency). The court can specify a starting date for payment by instalments which is longer than seven days after the hearing, for example, if a first wage packet is not due within that time span.

If the offender is already paying a previous fine, whether by instalments or within a stipulated period, the court needs to specify whether payment of the new fine should commence on completion of the existing one, or concurrently with it.

Special arrangements apply to young offenders as far as ordering an alternative sentence of detention in the event of default is concerned, and these are included in the sections below relating to Fine Supervision, Means or Fines Enquiry Reports and Supervised Attendance Orders.

Nicholson (1992) has usefully drawn attention to the period of time it should take for a fine paid by instalments to be paid off in full. Two High Court pronouncements are quoted which reflect rather differing views. In one case a fine was reduced because it would take an unemployed person over a year to pay at the set rate; in another case two years was seen as not too long in view of the need to make the person face up to their responsibilities regarding the seriousness of the offence. Cases like these reflect attempts by sentencers in dealing with people of limited means, to find a balance between an amount which will reflect the seriousness of the offence without being so unrealistic as to invite non-payment, and consequently result in custody.

In October 1990, government announced its intention of deducting unpaid fines from people receiving social security benefits at source. Courts will not normally resort to this until they have considered a Means or Fines Enquiry Report, and the provision does not necessarily obviate entirely the possibility of imprisonment, or a Supervised Attendance Order (see below).

Social and Means Enquiry Reports will therefore need to distinguish carefully between those elements within state benefits that are designated (in the theoretical calculations on which these benefits are based) as being, on the one hand for the individual's necessities, and, on the other, as being for expenditure on the person's dependants. Familiarity with welfare benefits rates or access to this information is indispensable for social enquiry report writers.

Fine enforcement and supervision

Provision for fine supervision was first made in 1963. The provision is now located at section 217 of the *Criminal Procedure (Scotland) Act*, 1995. The provisions apply equally to cases on solemn procedure and on summary procedure. The duty on social work authorities to provide services in connection with fine supervision is located within section 27 of the *Social Work (Scotland) Act*, 1968. Social work services related to means and fines have been a neglected area of practice for many years. It is likely that the contribution, particularly of court-based social work services, to the wider assessment of means and to the provision of fine supervision will be a matter of review by central and local government in the light of the introduction of supervised attendance orders. Nonetheless extensive legislative provision exists.

Fine supervision can be ordered in relation to people of any age. It can provide a means of entry for the social worker into issues of family interaction and budgeting, where information suggests there may be problems in making payment.

The law requires that young offenders (that is, people aged 16 but under 21) must be placed on fine supervision before any period of imprisonment can be ordered in default of payment (section 217(4)), UNLESS the court is satisfied that it is impracticable to place them under supervision. No definition of 'impracticable' is given in the Act: in common sense terms the young person who is of no fixed abode is difficult to supervise in this way. While the absence of supervisory resources on the part of social work ought not to be used by courts as an excuse for avoiding this requirement, in practice this has often been the case. Section 217(5) requires that the reason for a determination of 'impracticability' be minuted by the court. The intention and spirit of these provisions is that young people should not end up in custody unnecessarily on account of fine default. A report on fine default over a decade ago (ADSW, 1987) highlighted that a large proportion of those being received into prison for fine default were indeed young people. This has remained a significant though reducing problem in the 1990s.

Fine supervision should not be regarded as a kind of mini-probation. If probation is needed, then that is what should be ordered. The duties of the appointed supervisor are cast in narrower terms than those of the officer supervising a probation order. The duties in relation to fine supervision are defined by section 217(8) of the CP Act, 1995) as:

- to communicate with the offender with a view to assisting and advising him in regard to payment of the fine; and
- to report to the court without delay as to the conduct and means of the offender if payment is not made.

The law requires the Clerk of Court to give the person a copy of the order placing him or her under supervision (section 217(7)). In practice the person will probably get a letter from social work acknowledging the situation and inviting them to make an appointment with a social worker to discuss the matter.

Fines enquiry reports

Court systems are efficient at identifying default and will take action immediately. If there is a default on payment, and a failure to respond either to warning letters by the court, or to the advice of the supervisor, the defaulter will be cited to appear at a Fines Enquiry Court (formerly known as Means Enquiries), and the court must 'take such steps as may be reasonably practicable to obtain from the supervising office a report...'. A formal notice requiring a report will be issued (section 217(6)).

Although a report may be given either orally or in writing, as far as the legislation is concerned, the general principles applicable to social enquiry reports (the right of the subject to know the contents of the report; the importance of the writer's presence in court etc.) should apply in this instance also. The report should contain information about:

- basic/elementary details of the home circumstances of the subject;
- details of any employment, together with information about the frequency of any job changes, duration of periods of employment; efforts to find work; employment rates and prospects in the locality (especially during the period of supervision);
- full information about income, expenditure, and responsibilities for dependants, and other financial commitments;
- response to, and use of, fine supervision and the issues addressed; opinion as to whether supervision will be, or has been, effective in facilitating payment of the fine.

A fine supervision order stays in force until:

- the order is transferred to another court area, if the subject moves residence, though in this case the new court may, and often does, order the continuation of the supervision, if no other circumstances have changed; or
- some other court order is made in respect of the fine, such as imprisonment if there is further or continued default; or
- a supervised attendance order is made; or
- the fine is paid in full; or
- the fine is remitted to nil.

The fine supervision order is something of a hybrid. It is not a probation order, and is not primarily concerned with goals such as preventing further offending or helping with the totality of personal and social problems. Consent to a fine supervision order is not necessary; neither can the offender be compelled to receive visits from or make visits to the supervisor. On the other hand, it is very clearly directed to avoid the use of custody for fine default, in a situation where a high proportion of prison admissions are for that very reason.

The order is a function which has not been given great priority by social work. This was reflected by the establishment in 1984 of an experimental scheme of Fines Enforcement Officers . These officers were appointed by the courts and focused more on enforcement than supervision. Research by Nicholson and Millar (1989) pointed to considerable promise in reducing the number of persons dealt with by alternative methods for fine default; it also highlighted the familiar problem of the link between low incomes and fine default, and commented 'the scope of fines enforcement officers may be restricted by certain offenders with very poor financial means making rational decisions to serve time (in prison) rather than pay their fines irrespective of any advice and assistance that fines officers could offer'. This system was never fully developed. A few fine officers, as they are now known, still exist and provide a valuable function. Most have been phased out. Fine supervision is generally carried out by criminal justice social workers in the field, largely as an administrative exercise, where the person will be contacted and invited to make an appointment.

Once time has been allowed for payment of a fine (where no alternative of imprisonment in the event of future default has been fixed) no order for imprisonment in default of payment can be made without a further court hearing (section 216 of the *CP Act*, 1995). These hearings are normally referred to as Fines Enquiry or Means Enquiry courts.

It is possible for a person to apply to a court, either orally or in writing, for a variation in the arrangements originally ordered for the payment of the fine (section 216). In this event, it is not necessary to convene a court, and the matter is dealt with by court officials, in consultation with the appropriate judge if necessary. The person then receives a written notification of the decision reached. The court must allow further time, unless it is satisfied that failure to pay has been wilful, or that there is no reasonable prospect of payment if further time is allowed (215(3)). Supervising officers can make good use of this provision if it becomes evident from contact with the person that the order for payment originally made by the court was unrealistic or uninformed, and if there is a real possibility that payment would be made if a more reasonable arrangement were to be substituted. A warning letter may be issued if payments slip behind, before reaching a decision to cite the defaulter to a Fines Enquiry Court. In practice any slippage usually results in a citation.

Once it is decided to order an investigation into the means of a defaulter, the procedure is to issue a citation requiring him to appear at court. If he does not appear, it is competent for the court to issue a warrant for his apprehension; for example, someone who moves address and fails to notify the court to which a fine is owed, may find himself liable to arrest, because he has not received the citation to court. The police treat these warrants with some discretion, and often arrange for the person to come to a subsequent hearing. However, it is quite legitimate to detain a defaulter in custody if a warrant is in force, and it can be that people who owe fines can form part of the more familiar daily court proceedings, rather than appearing before a court that is doing nothing other than dealing with default cases. Unless the court has a report, the investigation of means and circumstances, which is the essence of the hearing, can only be by a series of direct questions to the defaulter, without any real independent verification. The possible outcomes from the Fines Enquiry Court are to:

- vary the period of time originally allowed for payment;
- vary the arrangements for paying instalments;
- order fine supervision, together with any such variation in arrangements for payment;
- continue such supervision, together with making any variation to the arrangements for payment;
- make a supervised attendance order;
- order a period of imprisonment to be served in the event of payment not being made, or made on time, in the future;
- order a period of imprisonment to be served immediately on account of the default;
- reduce or remit the fine to nil;
- take no action.

A period of custody, whether immediate or to be served in the event of future non-payment, **cannot** be ordered in relation to young offenders UNLESS they have previously been under fine supervision, or the court is satisfied that it is impracticable to place them under such supervision. The ordering of imprisonment, whether immediate or in the event of future non-payment, terminates any existing fine supervision.

Fines and financial penalties (including caution and compensation orders)

Periods of imprisonment in default

The periods of imprisonment to be served in default of the payment of financial penalties are (section 219 of the *Criminal Procedure (Scotland, Act,* 1995):

Amount of Penalty		Maximum Period of Imprisonment
Not exceeding	£200	7 days
Exceeding	£200 but not £500	14 days
Exceeding	£500 but not £1,000	28 days
Exceeding	£1,000 but not £2,500	45 days
Exceeding	£2,500 but not £5,000	3 months
Exceeding	£5,000 but not £10,000	6 months
Exceeding	£10,000 but not £20,000	12 months
Exceeding	£20,000 but not £50,000	18 months
Exceeding	£50,000 but not £100,000	2 years
Exceeding	£100,000 but not £250,000	3 years
Exceeding	£250,000 but not £1 million	5 years
Exceeding	£1 million	10 years

It should be noted that these amounts can now be changed by statutory instrument in the same way that levels of fine on the standard scale can be changed.

Part payment

If a financial penalty has been paid in part before any alternative period of imprisonment in default comes into effect, the period of that imprisonment will be reduced proportionately (s.214). Equally a prisoner can secure his release if the unpaid part is paid into the prison on his behalf—for example, by a friend, or family member.

Remitting fines

Any fine may be remitted, i.e. cancelled, either in whole or in part at any time (section 213). Persons, including young persons, who are serving sentences of imprisonment or detention may make written application to have their unpaid fines remitted or, more usually, to be allowed to serve the alternative of imprisonment or detention concurrently with the sentence they are serving. Not all offenders will be aware of the court's power to deal with outstanding fines in this ways, and written information could be helpful.

SUPERVISED ATTENDANCE ORDER

Rifkind (1989) and subsequent government ministers have acknowledged the problem of custody resulting from fine default and the high proportion of the prison population resulting from fine default and often for less serious offences. Despite the emphasis in policy and legislation aimed at avoiding custody resulting from fine default, the policy failed to reduce custody figures throughout the 1980s and has shown only limited success in the 1990s. As early as 1970, the Wooton Committee expressed concern that non-custodial disposals should be truly non-custodial and that offenders should not be committed to prison for failure to pay fines solely for want of the financial means to do so. During the early development of community service, there was some speculation that a community service order might have been used to work off unpaid fines (Scottish Council on Crime, 1974). **The Supervised Attendance Order** (SAO) was created instead.

The SAO was introduced by the *Law Reform (Miscellaneous Provisions) (Scotland) Act,* 1990, section 62 and schedule 6, now sections 235-237 and Schedule 7 of the *Criminal Procedure (Scotland) Act,* 1995, as an additional measure to help deal with the problem of fine defaulters. The legislation took effect on April 1, 1991 and, initially, was available to those courts, when and where local authority arrangements for the operation were approved by the Scottish Office. Originally three pilot SAO schemes in Strathclyde, Tayside and Highland were in operation by 1992. In principle government made a commitment to make SAOs available to all courts across Scotland by Spring 1998, for offenders over age 18 years, providing 4,500 orders a year at the cost of £2m. There were 7,509 receptions into prisons for fine default in 1995.

National guidelines for the operation of SAOs were introduced in 1992 as the pilot schemes were extended, to ensure consistency of approach regarding expectations and measures of compliance. NOS are expected to be issued in June 1998. The key objectives set are to

- extend the community-based sentencing options available to the court by serving as a disposal to be used:
    for persons who fail to pay a fine; and
    for offenders aged 16 and 17 whom the court considers unable to pay an appropriate fine;
- to instil discipline in the offender by requiring him or her to attend regularly and punctually, behave satisfactorily and participate fully;
- provide constructive activities for offenders to undertake with the aim of encouraging personal and social responsibility and self respect;
- supervise offenders firmly and fairly and follow-up non-compliance promptly.

The philosophy of SAOs, like community service, is a fine on time in the way that a traditional fine is on income. The punishment element is contained in the time required for the activities, and in the essential discipline of regular attendance, prompt time-keeping and satisfactory performance. There is also the sanction of prompt application of disciplinary or breach proceedings which can result in the imposition of a custodial sentence. NOS suggest the activities to be provided should be categorised under 3 broad headings:

- activity of an educational nature broadly relevant to the offender's personal circumstances;
- activity designed to stimulate interest and encourage the constructive use of time;
- activity involving unpaid work in the community.

A Supervised Attendance Order under section 235 can **only be made** where the offender is of or over 18 years of age and a financial penalty has been imposed **and, either** the court has ordered imprisonment in default, **or** there has been a failure to pay, either in whole or in part.

It is important to note that an order may only be made when 'the court considers a supervised attendance order **more appropriate than** the serving of, or...the imposition of, such a period of imprisonment' (235(3)(c)). Where a supervised attendance order is made following action to order a period of imprisonment in default, the effect of the order is to discharge the fine. This raises some questions about the status of SAOs; on one hand they are clearly alternatives to custody but are imposed on offenders whose offence originally attracted a fine and would not have attracted custody. The intention is to reduce the number of people imprisoned for default, and the influence of the community service order as a model is apparent. This is not necessarily intended to be a 'next step' in a staged process of dealing with default—the threat of imprisonment is still there, and is intended to be a real deterrent. It remains to be seen, in practice, whether SAOs will reduce custody or, unintentionally, increase the risk of custody for non-serious offenders.

An SAO is defined as 'an order made by the court in respect of an offender requiring him:

a) to attend a place of supervision for such period of not less than 10 hours and not more than
   i) where the amount of the fine, part or instalment which the offender has failed to pay does not exceed level 1 on the standard scale, 50 hours; and
   ii) in any other case, 100 hours as is specified in the order; and
b) during that period, to carry out such instructions as may be given to him by the supervising officer' (s.235(2))

The order requires the offender to attend a place of supervision for between 10 and 100 hours (subject to a limit of 50 hours where the outstanding amount is up to level 1 on the standard scale (£200)).

The *CP Act*, 1995 extended the arrangements to provide that, under s.235, SAOs may be used as an alternative to, or replacement for, imprisonment for fine default where the offender 'is or over the age of 18 years'. In its original form the legislation required the court to obtain consent of the offender prior to making the order. The offender's consent is no longer required and no pre-sentence assessment is required. This creates practical difficulties in matching the offender to a suitable programme since social work has no say in who it gets an SAO.

The initial findings from a pilot project in Tayside (1994) provided encouraging results, in that it was estimated that about 50% of people in default, who otherwise might have been imprisoned, were given SAOs. The order proved particularly popular with sheriffs for 16 and 17-year-olds during the pilot, and a practice developed, whose special provision is now included in section 236 of the *Criminal Procedure (Scotland) Act*, 1995.

Under the special provision made in the legislation for **16 and 17-year-olds** in section 236, 'the court, having determined the amount of the fine, if it considers that the offender is **likely to pay** within 28 days **can**

i) impose a fine; **and**
ii) subject to paragraph 1 of Schedule 7, make a supervised attendance order in default of payment within 28 days' (236(3)).

The order comes into force unless the fine has been paid in full. If it has been 'part paid' then the hours required under the SAO are reduced in proportion to amount paid (236(5)). If the court considers the offender is **unlikely to pay**, it **shall** make an SAO (236(6)). The first pilot project for this service was introduced in Dundee in 1997. At the time of writing only two pilots are operating. Until this provision is fully implemented, 16 and 17-year-olds can only be dealt with under section 237 and, consequently, can only be made subject of an SAO after further time has been given to pay and if he is in default at the end of that period.

Where any offender has been granted 'time to pay' a fine under section 214 (see fines above) the court may impose an SAO in default of payment (s.237) with the same rules for part payment as above.

Where more than one supervised attendance order is in force, the court may order that the hours are served concurrently or consecutively, PROVIDED that the total number of hours served does not exceed the permitted maximum. Currently the maximum number hours is 100. However Schedule 7 of the Act contains power for the Secretary of State to increase that maximum by way of Statutory Instrument, if developing experience appears to justify it. In practice, there is no mechanism for identifying when an offender has multiple orders other than by asking the offender. Since neither consent nor a pre-sentence social work assessment is sought prior to making the order, it is not uncommon for an offender to have a number of orders made by different courts totalling more than the 100 hour maximum. Clarification is required as to whether they should be treated concurrently or returned to court by social work as incompetent.

The requirements of the order are to be completed within 12 months, but if they cannot be completed, for valid reasons, then the order remains in force until they are. There are requirements similar to those in probation and community service orders for the person to notify any change of address and to be available, and important provisions for the person under supervision, or the supervisor, to ask for a variation in the terms of the order, or to revoke the order under schedule 7(5) of the CP Act, 1995. Two criteria should inform an application:

• circumstances have arisen which affect the capacity of the offender to comply with all or part of the order;
• the court should consider amendment or revocation in the interests of justice.

The CP Act, 1995 does not specify the necessary grounds for revocation or amendment. It is to be assumed that, for example, if the offender is moving to England for legitimate reasons and it is not possible to complete the order more quickly than planned, the supervisor will have to apply to the court to review the order. NOS suggest that the most likely grounds for making an application will be:

- an illness (medically certified) extending over a sufficiently long period to prevent the offender from performing the order satisfactorily;
- a period of custody served during the currency of the order which prevents the offender from carrying out the order;
- a move to a place where there is no SAO scheme or where the scheme is unable to accept the transfer;
- employment requirements which make it impossible for the offender to attend to carry out the order.

If the court is satisfied with the application it may

- vary the number of hours;
- extend the 12-month period allowed to complete the order;
- revoke the order; or
- revoke the order and impose a period of imprisonment, not exceeding three months in the sheriff court and 60 days in the district court.

NOS identify key performance indicators for the service:

- the court will send the local social work department a copy of the order, with a copy of the complaint/indictment and the list of any previous convictions libelled, within 3 working days of the order being made;
- The supervising officer, who must be an employee of local authority social work must interview the offender within 7 working days ;
- Arrangements for starting the order should be made no later than three weeks from the date the supervising officer received the order;
- Completion reports should be submitted to court within 14 days of the completion of the order.

Where the offender fails to attend, the supervising officer must follow up the absence 'normally within 4 working days' of being informed and make a decision on whether or not the absence is acceptable. The rules are very similar to community service, and absences due to ill health, for example, require medical certificates. A system of cautions and formal warnings operates, when explanations for absences are considered unacceptable up to a third unacceptable absence, when the order is suspended and breach proceedings instituted. Breach proceedings can, however, be instituted at any time.

Failure to comply leads to the person being returned to court, either by citation, or by warrant. Failure to comply with the order, including failure to complete the hours within the given period, can result in the court:

a) revoking the order; and

    b) imposing such imprisonment or detention not exceeding
        i) in the case of a sheriff court, three months and
        ii) in the case of a district court, 60 days; OR
    c) varying the number of hours in the order. (Sched. 7 para. 4(2))

It is important to note that the period of imprisonment for breach of require-ments could be much greater than any period of imprisonment that would have been imposed for fine default (see maxima set out in s.219 above). It has been suggested that some defence agents are loath to recommend SAOs for this reason since breach could attract a higher penalty than had the offender simply defaulted and been sentenced to custody, e.g. £200 = up to 7 days. Breach applications must be accompanied by a report providing information about

- when and where the offender was required to carry out the activities, what they were and how the offender responded; and
- how well overall the offender complied with the requirements of the order.

As for any breach in other types of orders, witnesses and satisfactory evidence are required. There is no guidance within the procedures when an order is sus-pended, pending the outcome of a breach, and another order is made by a different court during that period.

Supervised Attendance Orders are transferable to other areas, in the event of the person changing his or her address, with the usual proviso about the availabil-ity of an appropriate facility in the area to which the person is moving. The Secre-tary of State for Scotland has powers to designate certain courts where SAOs must be made instead of sentencing the fine defaulter to custody. No courts have been designated in this way.

SAOs appear to be **a distinctively Scottish innovation.** Section 27 of the *Social Work (Scotland) Act*, 1968, is amended to include the duty of supervising such orders along with probation and after-care responsibilities of local authority social work departments.

The order contains an amalgam of elements drawn from both previous and existing practice:

    a) The independent sector has played a significant role in running the schemes to date, and one of the successes of the pilots has been the involvement of APEX in providing employment training opportunities within the context of SAOs.
    b) The intention of the SAO is to provide a very direct alternative to a period of imprisonment that would otherwise result and, in this sense, has the same thrust as the introduction of the community service order.
    c) Like fine supervision, the order does not require consent. The focus, however, is not now on payment, in that the order is intended to **substitute** for pay-ment—**doing hours instead of paying money**.

NOS outline the types of activities that should be the focus of time spent:

- activities relevant to the financial circumstances of the offender, including rel-evant issues which may contribute to not paying fines;

- activities relating to the development of life skills and solving problems;
- activities which challenge anti-social attitudes and assumptions;
- activities designed to stimulate and encourage the constructive use of time;
- unpaid work in the community involving group and individual assignments.

NOS recommend that those undertaking SAOs for the first time should be involved in a 'core induction module' which should include debt advice and financial management. As regards unpaid work in the community, NOS offers little guidance to distinguish this from community service. It will be important to see whether this provision simply becomes an alternative to existing community-based measures, even in lieu of them, or has a genuine effect in serving its main objective of reducing the numbers sent to prison and of having some impact on the problem of fine default.

The formal requirements placed on the offender are

- to attend as ordered;
- to carry out such reasonable instructions as may be given by, or on behalf of the supervising officer;
- to notify the supervising officer as instructed, in particular, of any change in address or employment;
- to notify the supervising officer without delay of any change in the times of employment.

It is to be hoped that the SAO can be developed as a simple, pragmatic, and workable solution to the problem of fine default. Despite systems of fines enquiry and fine supervision, receptions of fine defaulters to prison between 1993 and 1997 were equivalent to 30%-40% of those received under sentence. This is a situation where imprisonment seems unnecessary and inadequate to deal with what are often only relatively small amounts owed by defaulters. However there is concern that, cast as 'alternative to custody' (rather than a 'community disposal') for an offence which did not originally and would not normally attract custody, use of SAOs may escalate offenders up the tariff. It remains to be seen whether the normal stages of fines enquiry and supervision, where the level of social work input is often minimal, will continue to operate meaningfully.

CAUTION
(pronounced '*kay-shun*')

Courts may require people to lodge a specified sum of money as a security for their future good behaviour. This money is referred to as **caution**. An order for caution will stipulate:

i)   the amount of money to be found: on indictment 'as the court considers appropriate' (s.227); in Sheriff Summary courts this may not exceed the level 5 of the standard scale (s.5); and in District Courts it may not exceed level 4 of the scale (s.7);

ii) a period of time within which it must be lodged with the Clerk of Court;

iii) a period of time, not exceeding one year, during which the person must be of good behaviour.

The person who is of good behaviour over the specified period may recover the money from the Clerk of Court at the end of the period, and will also receive interest on it, calculated at the prevailing rate of deposit. However, any further offence committed during the period makes the person liable to forfeit the money, and the initiative in making a motion to this effect usually lies with the prosecutor (at the time the new offence is being dealt with).

It is not possible to order the payment of caution by instalments. Courts sometimes ask social work to help resolve these matters, but any assistance offered is voluntary. Non-payment of caution within the period allowed is treated as a non-payment of fine (section 5(2) and 7(6) of the *Criminal Procedure (Scotland) Act, 1995*). The procedures for enforcement, and the fixing of alternative periods of imprisonment in default, are operated and calculated as discussed above in relation to fines. This means, for example, that Fine Enquiry Courts have to be held.

Caution, as well as being a separate order in its own right, can also be included as a requirement in a probation order. Caution may be required, at the discretion of the court, for any offence for which imprisonment is not being imposed, and without regard to age or any other consideration.

COMPENSATION

The Compensation Order was introduced by section 58 of the *Criminal Justice (Scotland) Act*, 1980 and is now located in ss.249-253 of the CP Act, 1995. Before the Act, courts had sometimes deferred sentences to allow for compensation to be paid to a victim, and determined the final disposal in the light of the response made. The 1980 Act enabled courts to make compensation an order, and thus to try to ensure that, in appropriate cases and circumstances, individual victims can be compensated financially by the offender. Important features of the compensation order are:

i) it can be imposed **in addition to** other penalties, as well as instead of them, including custody;

ii) if a choice has to be made as between fine and compensation, **compensation should be preferred** (s.250)(1);

iii) imprisonment is available as an (ultimate) sanction in default;

iv) all the procedures applicable to the enforcement of fines (and supervision of their payment) **apply to compensation orders**.

The compensation order is available to courts both on summary and solemn procedure and to the district courts. The court must take the person's means 'as far as known' into account when determining whether to make an order, and in deciding the amount (section 249(5)). There is no limit to the amount of compensation which may be ordered in cases on solemn procedure. In cases on summary procedure, the maximum amounts are:

• in Sheriff and Stipendiary Magistrates Courts an amount not exceeding the maximum of level 5 on the standard scale;

* in District Courts an amount not exceeding the maximum of level 4 on the standard scale.

These amounts apply to each offence, and not necessarily to any cumulative total, if more than one offence is under consideration. Section 250(3) declares that 'for the purposes of any appeal or review, a compensation order is a sentence'.

The fact that compensation orders can be made in addition to other penalties reflects the concept that most crimes have two victims—society in general, and an individual who has been harmed or who has suffered as a result of the offence. Thus an offender may be ordered both to undertake unpaid work for the community and to make financial amends to a victim as a result of an offence. However in the assessment of the 'means' of a person who is serving or is to serve a period of imprisonment or detention, 'no account shall be taken of earnings contingent upon his obtaining employment after release' (s.249(6). **There are two exceptions** to this principle of being able to combine compensation with other penalties:

a) compensation orders cannot be combined with an order of absolute discharge; and

b) a compensation order cannot be made simultaneously with a probation order; however, it is possible to include **within** the probation order a requirement that financial amends are made to an individual victim; traditionally this was described as a **requirement for restitution**.

Payments under a compensation order are made to the Clerk of the Court and not to the individual victim (section 249(9)). Where restitution is a requirement of probation, the supervising officer is responsible for arranging the receipt of the money and for payment to the victim. It should be noted that local authority funds under section 12 of the *Social Work (Scotland) Act)* 1968 cannot be used for this purpose.

In a case where both fine and compensation are ordered, any payments received go firstly towards the compensation (s.250(2)). If property that has been taken is recovered, but damage has been caused to it in the meantime, 'that damage (however and by whomsoever it was in fact caused) shall be treated...as having been caused by the acts which constituted the offence' (s.249(3)).

A compensation order **cannot** be made in respect of:

i) loss suffered in consequence of the death of any person; or

ii) injury, loss, or damage due to an accident arising out of the presence of a motor vehicle on a road, except under the heading of subsection (2) discussed above (s.249(4)).

Some recent imaginative attempts by sheriffs to innovate on compensatory sentencing have been stamped out on appeal by the High Court. In two instances sheriffs, instead of imposing fines or ordering compensation orders to victims, ordered that compensation should be payable to local charities. Because the charities had no direct connection with the offence, the High Court ruled these disposals as incompetent (HM Adv, v Nelson , 1996, SLT. 1073).

Compensation orders and civil damages

Victims are not prohibited from taking action in the civil courts, even if a compensation order has been made by a criminal court. Section 253 deals with the relationship between amounts ordered by the civil courts and those ordered by criminal courts. The damages in civil proceedings are to be assessed without regard to the compensation order—that is, by the criteria ordinarily used by the civil courts (section 253(2)). The civil court's assessment may well exceed the amount of compensation ordered by the criminal court. However, the civil court's actual award of damages will be restricted to the amount by which they exceed the amount paid under the compensation order.

The situation where all or part of the compensation order remains unpaid and damages are awarded in civil proceedings is dealt with by subsection 3 of section 253. The aim of this subsection is to preserve the power of the criminal court to imprison for non-payment, without preventing the injured party, in a civil case, from recovering the full amount of his loss. These provisions do not apply if the compensation order is no longer outstanding, e.g. if the offender has been imprisoned for non-payment. Finally, if the civil court assesses damages at a level **lower** than that ordered to be paid in compensation by the criminal court, the offender can apply to the criminal court for a review of the compensation order (section 64). Some examples may clarify the implications of these sections:

a) James Smith is ordered by a criminal court to pay £500 compensation, and pays it in full. The victim takes the matter to a civil court which assesses damages at £750. The only order the civil court can make is for £250—that is, the difference.

b) Smith pays nothing of the compensation, and serves time in prison as a consequence. That is the end of the matter as far as the criminal court is concerned, but the civil court can make an order for the full £750 damages (which it has assessed).

c) Smith pays £250 of the compensation order but suffers no penalty for his default. The civil court assesses damages at £250 only. In this situation the civil court cannot make an order for damages to be paid.

d) Moreover, if the civil court assesses damages at only £250, Smith can now apply to the criminal court for the amount of his compensation to be reduced—and, if successful, may avert the risk of the amount he still owes under the compensation order being enforced.

The Criminal Injuries Compensation Board

The Criminal Injuries Compensation Board was set up to make payments to the victims of crime or to the relatives if the victim had died as a result of being the victim of criminal activity. It is not empowered to compensate for loss in respect of property offences. The offender does not require to be apprehended or convicted for a claim to be considered. Awards can only be made where the value of the claim is £1000 or more. This figure is varied upwards from time to time, although the appropriate figure is always the one applicable when the incident giving rise to the claim took place. Any award made will be reduced by any amount awarded by the courts.

Victims support schemes

In a number of areas, victims support schemes are well established, using volunteer helpers to visit and assist people who have been the victims of crime. The policy statement on Victims (ADSW, 1996) indicates that 'concern for victims of crime should be a major consideration' for social work and that a 'victim perspective should form a core part of the content of supervision of the offender' (paras 1.1-2.1). While most of the work of the supervisor will be on behalf of victims rather than directly with victims, there is scope for social workers to make referrals to such schemes, and indeed to learn from the experience of these schemes of the effects the crimes of their supervisees are likely to have had on their victims.

Confiscation orders

The court has the power to make a confiscation orders under s.6(3) of the *Proceeds of Crime (Scotland) Act,* 1995. As the legislation suggests, proceeds from crime, for example, drug crime, can be confiscated, including cars, planes or even houses, following a disclosure of the offender's assets to the court.

RESTRICTION OF LIBERTY ORDERS

The *Crime and Punishment (Scotland) Act*, 1997 (s.5) amended section 245 of the *Criminal Procedure (Scotland) Act*, 1995 by making provision, under sections 245 A to F for **restriction of liberty orders (RLO)** including **electronic monitoring** or tagging (s.245C). Section 5 of the 1997 Act was partly implemented in July 1998 (S.I. 1997 No.2323). Pilots are under way in Hamilton, Aberdeen and Peterhead.

The government, in their review of criminal justice services (SWSG, 1997), indicated that these provisions will be introduced in the Autumn of 1998. It is expected that the orders will be similar to the 'curfew' orders introduced by the *Criminal Justice Act*, 1991 in England and Wales and to the provisions under the *Criminal Justice and Public Order Act*, 1994 for curfew orders with electronic tagging. The legislation makes provision for an RLO 'where a person of 16 years of age or more is convicted of an offence other than an offence the sentence for which is fixed by law' and the court is satisfied that this is 'the most appropriate method of disposal'. The order may restrict the offender's movement to a total of '12 hours in any one day', by requiring him to be in a specified place, such as at home, for set periods of time in each day or in each week, or equally to be absent from specified places, such as football grounds, for similarly specified periods of time. Section 245C makes provision to include electronic tagging in an RLO, 'a requirement that the offender shall, either continuously or for such periods as may be specified, wear or carry a device for the purpose of enabling the remote monitoring of his compliance'. An order may be made for any period up to 12 months and the offender **must agree** to comply with the order and its conditions and the court is required to explain 'in ordinary language' the effect of the order and its requirements and the consequences of non-compliance.

An RLO can be made **concurrently with a probation order** having 'regard to the circumstances, including the nature of the offences' and 'having obtained a report as to the circumstance and character of the offender'(s.245D(1)). Failure to comply with probation order requirements are dealt with in the normal way (s.232(2)(c). The legislation makes provision for the court to exercise its powers under s.245(F))2)(b), which deals with breach of an RLO, and/ or, under s.232(2)(c) failure to comply with the RLO as a requirements of a probation order.

Before making an RLO the court must 'obtain and consider information about the place' and about 'the attitude of the person likely to be affected by the enforced presence there of the offender'. The wording indicates this 'person' may well be a parent or partner, for whom restriction may cause difficulties. The legislation does not specify who should provide this information and it clearly distinguishes between the 'person responsible for monitoring' and 'the officer of the local authority who is to supervise' when an RLO is imposed concurrently with a probation order. There was some hint when the previous government used private security agencies to pilot electronic tagging in England, that a private agency might be established to take on all the functions of RLOs. It is likely, however, that assessment in Scotland will be by way of an SER and that criminal justice social work will have a role in RLOs. It is equally likely that any requirement for remote or electronic monitoring will be carried out by a private security agency, with the necessary equipment and technical expertise, as an addition. The Secretary of State will provide regulations to determine which courts the order will be available to and which 'class' of offenders it will apply to (s.245A(8)).

RLOs may be varied on the application of the offender or the person responsible for monitoring compliance, by amending, deleting or inserting requirements or by revoking the order (245E).

Breach provisions, as a result of failure to comply, allow the court to continue, vary or revoke the order and or impose a fine not exceeding level 3 on the standard scale. Where the court decides to revoke the order it may 'dispose of the offender in any way which would have been competent at the time when the order was made'. Where the offender is subject to a probation order, s.245E(2) indicates that the court 'shall' before disposing of RLO 'discharge the probation order'. This provision, rather strangely, seems to assume that failure to monitor (for example, by tagging) is deemed equally a failure to supervise. Normal documentary evidence is required to prove any breach.

Electronic tagging has been available in the USA, Canada, Australia and New Zealand for many years as a means of house arrest or home detention, and has been piloted in recent years in England. Different programmes seem to vary in size, scope and target group. Some countries use electronic monitoring as part of a non-custodial sentence, which seems to be the intention in Scotland, while others use it for offenders originally sentenced to imprisonment but released under restriction. In countries where it is imposed as a community disposal, it has generally been used for socially stable offenders with jobs, homes and families, who have committed non-violent property offences or driving offences: most such offenders, in Scotland, would have been considered appropriate candidates for fines, probation or community service orders.

Home Office research (Mortimer and Mair, 1996) indicated that while over half of those tagged had been in custody before and over three quarters had received other community disposal, the most common offences for which an order was imposed were theft (25%), burglary(17%), driving while disqualified(14%) and drug offences(12%). During the pilot period 24% had their orders revoked, usually for missing curfew periods or for removing or damaging the tag.

There has also been some debate about unit costs of the order. The Home Office estimated the average monthly cost at £675 compared to £1,555 per month for a category C prison and the cost of an order at £2,295 compared to £2,425 for probation and £1,773 for community service. However others suggest that when start up costs are added, the pilot costs were between £10,000 and £14,000 per person (Penal Affairs Consortium, 1997). No doubt economies of scale will require more people to be monitored to bring down the unit costs, once the investment has been made.

The Penal Reform Consortium have highlighted the kinds of difficulties associated with the pilots:

- wearing anklets had a stigmatising effect, publicly identifying the person as an offender;
- some participants noted that it was very difficult to obtain employment while on electronic monitoring;
- some family members found the long curfews a definite strain after a time and considerable friction and family disruption may be a potentially serious consequence.

Baumer and Mendelsohn (1992:65) reviewing research in the USA concluded the 'incapacitative and public safety potential of this sanction have probably been considerably overstated...at best the electronic equipment can only identify the presence or absence of an offender...and suggests that the primary target population for home confinement will continue to be "low risk" offenders who are not thought to be a threat to public safety...as an alternative to secure custody (it) appears to be limited'.

The jury is still out, as far as research is concerned, on the ability of court-ordered electronic monitoring to divert offenders from crime or from custody. While one can envisage certain circumstances in which this form of monitoring might be a useful tool, the circumstances may be limited compared to the necessary start up costs and potential benefits.

ANTI -SOCIAL BEHAVIOUR

A greater recognition of the needs of victims and communities, and media attention to issues of anti-social behaviour such as 'stalking' has resulted in provisions in law and proposals for a number of criminal and/or civil orders that are intended to be preventive and protective measures. They have important implications for social workers in the criminal justice system, both as SER authors and as supervisors.

The *Protection from Harassment Act*, 1997 sections 8-12 applies to Scotland and introduces a new order, known as a '**non-harassment order**', which can be made in both civil and criminal courts. The Act makes breach of an order (s.9) an offence punishable on indictment, by up to five years imprisonment, or by a fine, or both; and on summary conviction, by up to six months imprisonment, or a fine up to the statutory maximum. Harassment includes psychological harm, such as alarm and distress, and can result, not only from breach of the peace, but also from statutory offences such as abusive and malicious telephone calls (Brown, 1997).

Despite the Lord Advocate's expressed view 'that the common law of Scotland is adequate to deal with the menace of stalking', Scottish provisions were included in the Act. Section 8 deals with obtaining a non-harassment order in the civil court, and section 11 inserts a new section 234A into the *Criminal Procedure (Scotland) Act,* 1995. The initiative to ask for an order lies with the prosecutor and not with the court. Where a person is convicted of an offence 'involving harassment of a person', the prosecutor may apply to the court to make a non-harassment order. The court must be satisfied that making the order is appropriate to protect the victim from further harassment. As a civil order the standard of proof is a balance of probabilities.

The Act is silent on the issue of corroboration, implying that corroboration is not required. Orders made by criminal courts may be appealed as sentences (s.234(3) and revoked or varied (but not to increase their length) either by the prosecutor or the person against whom the order is made. Commentators (Sinclair, 1998) suggest that in practice, the legislation is little different to the existing powers of interdict (which includes the power of arrest), with the exception that the creation of a criminal offence for breach of a civil order may make the remedy more effective than interdicts.

This view was confirmed by the McKinnon case in 1998. The judges, in an appeal case, placed strict limits on when protection can be given to victims using these orders. They took the view that a non-harassment order could not be granted if an offender was convicted only of a single incident, and previous convictions could not be used to establish a 'course of conduct'. The Lord Justice-General, Lord Rogers recognised that this controversial decision would restrict the usefulness of such orders but took the view that they were only available in very limited circumstances. The offender was jailed for three months for breach of the peace, but a non-harassment order was refused. The ruling suggest that an offender would need to be convicted of an offence involving at least two incidents.

In addition to non-harassment orders, the *Crime and Disorder Act* (s.26) makes provision for an offence of **racially aggravated harassment**, intended to protect members of 'racial groups' from racially motivated crime. A 'racial group' is defined by reference to race, colour, nationality (including citizenship) or ethnic or national origins.

There are proposals to introduce an **Anti-Social Behaviour Order** (ASBO) in the *Crime and Disorder Act*, 1998 (sections 18 and 21), as a response to a spate of well-publicised anti-social housing cases. The consultation paper indicated that the order is intended 'to tackle the problem of threatening and anti-social neighbours'; and 'the unacceptable level of anti-social behaviour and crime on Scotland's streets'.

Critics suggest that the order will provide little that existing provisions cannot already meet, and risks seeing people as the problem rather that focusing on the problems which people create (Collins, 1997). A parallel is drawn with the statutory offence of vandalism (now section 52(1) of the *Criminal Law (Consolidation) (Scotland) Act*, 1995), which has added little to the common law of malicious mischief and has had little impact on vandalism. Anti-social behaviour can at present be tackled by applying to the civil courts for an interdict to prevent future behaviour or can be prosecuted as a breach of the peace under common law, or be addressed under the harassment legislation discussed above. It is the government view that these measures are insufficient and that the ASBO is required to prohibit a named individual or individuals (who may be part of a household or a group) from behaving in a disruptive and anti-social manner. It is hoped the order may prove more useful than the remedy of interdict.

The orders will only apply to those aged 16 years or over. The kind of behaviour expected to be the focus of the orders are repeated unreasonable conduct which has a significant or substantial effect on the normal life of a neighbourhood, or which intimidates members of a community. It is expected that only local authorities will be able to seek these orders through civil procedures. Where local authorities receive complaints and are unable to resolve matters by advice, conciliation or where, having consulted with the procurator fiscal, criminal action is considered impractical, they can apply to court for an ASBO. The local authority will be required to consult the police before applying to ensure that all relevant information and available options for dealing with the problem have been considered. Normal appeals will be available both to the applicant and the defendant.

Breaches of the order, however, will be an offence. It is expected that breaches on indictment will attract penalties of up to five years imprisonment and/or an unlimited fine. In the absence of a reasonable excuse, if the 'anti-social' person does anything expressly prohibited by the order it will be an offence. If what is done is charged as a separate offence, the court will 'have regard' to the fact that it was committed while subject to the order. Detailed guidance is expected to be provided on implementation of the legislation.

COMMUNITY PROTECTION

A further civil order, a **Sex Offender Order**, is to be introduced by the *Crime and Disorder Act,* 1998. The order is aimed at people who have served a prison sentence for a sex offence (no matter when the offence) and who are likely to be unsupervised within the community, whose behaviour is continuing to give cause for concern or are judged by the police to represent a risk of potential criminal behaviour. The order will require an application to a sheriff by the police, in consultation with local authorities and other relevant agencies, and will allow for monitoring and the control of activity. The person subject to the order will be required to notify changes of address etc. as required under the *Sex Offenders Act,* 1997 and, therefore, the order could be used to plug a gap by applying these conditions to offenders who completed their sentence before the Act was implemented. As a civil order the standard of proof is a balance of probabilities. Equally, because it is neither a conviction nor a sentence, no conditions of treatment or supervision will be possible.

A further order is proposed by the *Crime and Disorder* Act, 1998 (s.72), a **Drug Testing and Treatment Order** (DTTO). It is intended to assist the courts deal with drug misusers who commit crimes in order to fund their misuse. It will give the court the power to impose drug testing and treatment by placing a drug dependent offender on a programme of treatment for the addiction which has contributed to their offending. The **consent of the offender will be required.** While the court will be able to specify some of the terms surrounding the treatment and will be able to review progress through pre-determined court hearings, it will have no power over the treatment content as such. Regular and random drug testing is expected to be an integral part of the order. However it is proposed that the court will have no power to impose a further sanction on the offender on the basis of failed tests alone. The court will be able to amend the details of the order with the consent of the offender. However, refusal on the part of the offender will mean a range of sanctions, including custody, can be imposed.

The DTTO will be available free standing or **concurrently with probation and or/a restriction of liberty order**.

Finally

The existence of this wide range of community-based disposals adds an extra dimension to the task of social enquiry report writing and to the important tasks highlighted, which will require increased levels of specialisation.

There is, then, the much more complex issue of assessing the risk the offender poses to the community and exploring the relevance of these community-based measures in meeting the court's concerns in sentencing. The potential for combining surveillance mechanisms, such as spot checks, random drug testing and electronic surveillance, with professional social work help has still to be tested. We have lessons to learn from the USA, where these mechanism were used extensively and operated with minimum or no constructive professional help and proved ineffective (Petersilia and Turner, 1993).

The range of disposal, in combination, raises fresh challenges to find meaningful ways of helping offenders change their behaviour which can be demonstrated as effective in contributing to the strategy of community safety.

Chapter 8

Probation: Old Concept, New Application?

Historical perspective; current situation; legislation; requirements; breach; transfers, variation and discharge

Social work in criminal justice and criminal law are inextricably bound together. The essence of probation work is that a legal order depends on its having a social work content to be meaningful. Aspects of the legal order and understanding of its social work content have changed over time in line with requirements of government policy. Some understanding of probation's history, and the core values that have inspired its practice are important if the social work profession is to maintain an independent or objective stance on the nature of probation practice within the framework of National Objectives and Standards (NOS) to which they are being asked to adhere.

One of probation's greatest virtues is its adaptability and flexibility in the face of a range of human situations and sentencing concerns. Its practitioners need a degree of imagination and creativity that no textbook or guidance can supply; a sense of vision, enthusiasm, experimentation and purpose is also required (Wood, 1991).

The *Criminal Procedures (Scotland) Act*, 1995 provides the legislative framework for probation in Scotland. The CP Act, 1995 retains Scottish probation practice in a recognised form, now distinct from English legislation and practice, and despite the terminology employed in NOS which referred to probation as a 'sentence' of the court, probation in Scotland remains 'instead of sentencing'. It is important to recognise that Scottish probation orders remain just that: an 'order' (and not 'sentence') made under the terms of the *Criminal Procedures (Scotland) Act*, 1995. The fact that from 1995 a probation order follows conviction in both summary and solemn proceedings (a change from previous legislation) creates no conflict in adhering to social work principles in the supervision of offenders.

The introduction of 100% central funding and NOS has provided a new impetus and new opportunities to test the relevance of probation practice against the demands of a modern criminal justice system. In the past Scottish social workers were accused of being more creative in finding ways of saying 'no' to probation than in developing its use in a positive direction. This is no longer the case. Between 1989 and 1995 probation orders increased from 3,753 to 6,071, an increase of 61%. However there has been no corresponding decline in the prison numbers which grew from 13,652 to 16,267 in the same period (Statistical Bulletin, 1997). The major challenge for social work remains to demonstrate that probation is being used effectively for medium to serious offenders and is having an impact on the custody figures in Scotland.

AN HISTORICAL PERSPECTIVE

The work of King (1969), Bochel (1976) and Haxby (1976) examines the origins of probation and the efforts of penal reformers and religious charitable societies at the turn of the century in relation to England and Wales. The influences leading to legislation and service provision in Scotland is less well documented.

The first legislation for probation on both sides of the border was the *Probation of First Offenders Act*, 1887. This was later extended by the *Probation of Offenders Act*, 1907. Some essential **principles** are reflected in the idea to which this legislation gave effect. A central idea is that of **holding back from punishment** for a period of time and putting the person in trouble under the supervision of a person responsible to the court for providing both supervision and the help. From the beginning, the combination of a legal device (originally a bond or recognisance) with the work of a caring individual supervising the order, was the essence of probation; both elements are inseparable. Successful completion of probation should result in the avoidance of punishment and the person 'living down' or 'making good' for his offence.

The *Probation Act,* 1907 defined the duties of probation workers, in a succinct and memorable phrase, as to 'advise, assist, and befriend' those in their charge. Nicholson (1992) also points out that the original Act expected the probation workers to find employment for their probationers, where appropriate. The importance of employment, or at least employment training, is a feature of service provision that is again gaining prominence in partnership with the voluntary or independent sector. During the first decades of this century, it was the practical and organisational aspects of probation that were developed. The insights of the behavioural and social sciences began to influence the work and a separate organisation for probation was established. The language of 'rehabilitation' came to be substituted for that of 'reform'. Today the medical language of 'rehabilitation' seems less appropriate than the language of 'social inclusion' or 'social re-integration', now being adopted by most local authorities.

The *Criminal Procedure (Scotland) Act*, 1995 provides much of the current framework of probation legislation. A probation order is made **'instead of sentencing'** in both summary and solemn procedure (s.228). Section 228 defines probation as:

> an order requiring the offender to be under supervision for a period to be specified in the order of not less than six months and not more than three years.

The professional status of probation officers was enhanced by the Morison Report (1962, cmnd 1650), which included Scotland within its remit. The Committee's definition of probation reflected the importance of the concept of supervision:

> we understand by probation the submission of an offender whilst at liberty to a specified period of supervision...during this period the offender remains liable, if not of good conduct, to be otherwise dealt with by the court.

The organisational arrangements for probation in Scotland are located within the *Social Work (Scotland) Act*, 1968, in particular, section 27. It is important to emphasise that section 27 is underscored by section 12, which places a duty on local authorities 'to promote social welfare'. This locates probation clearly as a social work service, a welfare rather than primarily a punishment exercise, where the object is to 'help' the offender change as a means of protecting the public and the victims of crime. The Dewes Report (1995) recommendation to remove the requirement for probation officers to be qualified social workers in England, has not been adopted in Scotland, further distinquishing policy and practice, north and south of the border.

Whilst there was no avowed intention to diminish the understanding of probation or to weaken its practice in relation to adults, the 1968 Act did dispense with a number of organisational links that had, previously, kept courts and probation officers in close relationship. In particular, following the implementation of the 1968 Act, the worker was no longer an officer of the court but an agent of the court, in exercising statutory duties on behalf of the local authority.

Two important factors have been significant to the changes implemented in probation practice in Scotland. The first, a very broad one, 'the collapse of the rehabilitative ideal' opened up a debate about the purpose and value of criminal justice social work services. More broadly it was paralleled by the collapse of the 'welfare consensus' in wider social and political spheres. The second, more specific to Scotland, was the failure over a period of 20 years to create organisational arrangements, professional, managerial and financial, within the framework of the 1968 Act, to produce criminal justice services, in particular probation, that inspired the confidence and use of the courts. The Kilbrandon 'one door' philosophy came to be particularly associated with the local 'all-purpose' area-based social work team as the basic unit of service delivery and contact with the public. To the area team, came all referrals representing the wide-ranging needs of the community. The theme of promoting welfare was paramount. While one objective of all purpose departments was to break away from an earlier pattern, in which some families were in contact with numerous social workers from a number of different departments, it is important to note that there was nothing in the policy to indicate that the worker (as opposed to the agency) should also become 'all-purpose'. Indeed, within its terms of reference, the Kilbrandon report envisaged a highly trained practitioner with specialist skills, whose location in the local authority would make it possible to co-ordinate the use of a wide range of provision, as well as collaborate with other professionals; thus accessing the most comprehensive service available for the service user. In practice, the norm came to be 'one general practice worker to one person or family', with that worker taking on most of the tasks involved.

Criminal justice social work and the use of probation got lost in this system. Courts got little feedback on what was happening in probation practice, where it existed, and an increasing number of instances came to their attention in which nothing much at all was being done, which dented confidence in the use of the measure. 'Offender work' as it was commonly known, was low priority, except where a few individual workers managed to carve out a space to specialise, or where special projects existed. When pressures of work grew, or expenditure was reduced, there was little protected time for probation work. Even today there is limited published research into what happens within a probation order in Scotland, and little promotional publicity from social work authorities about achievements in this area of work.

THE CURRENT SITUATION

It is not possible to understand the current situation for probation in Scotland without reference to the agenda set south of the border, however unpopular that frame of reference may be to our readership. One cannot approach the issues of probation without acknowledging that the substantial shifts in policy that characterise the administration of probation in England and Wales mark a significant departure from that of Scottish policy and practice, while similarly demanding efficient and effective probation practice. There has been a concerted attempt to move probation in the directions of:

- being a 'high-tariff' community-based disposal;
- focusing on 'confronting offending', rather than merely advising and assisting;
- being for protection of society and on behalf of the victims of crime;
- targeting young offenders and more serious offenders, particularly those at medium or high risk of short periods of custody;
- demonstrating effectiveness and value for money.

The elements of professional, even individual, autonomy that characterised the 'officer of the court' model of probation are all but gone, having given way to the implementation of corporate and strategic planning subject to NOS. There is now a greater degree of direction from central government than there has ever been. In the current arrangements 100% central funding is available to designated areas of provision; all other services have to be met from the local authorities' budgets.

Organisation and referrals within social work

100% central funding of criminal justice social work services created the opportunity for a break with patterns, both of organisation and, crucially, of thought that had dominated since the establishment of 'all-purpose' social work departments in 1969. The establishment of specialist criminal justice teams in local authorities, the publication of national service objectives and service standards; Social Work Inspectorate reports; and the evaluative studies commissioned by the Scottish Office on the operation of NOS (Paterson and Tombs, 1998) have all gone a considerable way to improving relationships with the courts.

The introduction of NOS and associated changes set the stage for the provision of probation services in which a culture of commitment to the work, and an expectation of excellence, could become the norm, instead of an occasion for surprise, as had so often been the case when the service was provided by 'general practitioner' social workers.

NOS require the worker to have a high degree of legal knowledge, familiarity with courts and the criminal justice system, well developed skills in assessment relevant to the workings of the system and a range of methods of intervention. While the services remain an integral part of local authority social work provision whose duty to the community is to 'promote welfare', criminal justice provision as it emerges is very different from what went before. Crime and criminal behaviour is a central concern of social workers and the primary legitimacy for their intervention. This had tended to be downplayed in the overarching welfare approach of the past. The creation of specialist services and well informed practitioners better recognises that offence-led probation is an ethical and anti-discriminatory mechanism, which ensures that people do not get drawn unnecessarily into criminal justice services, to meet supposed needs unrelated to their offending.

With the change in emphasis has come the need for new forms of intervention, of case recording and of data gathering, reflecting the primary concern with crime and with offending behaviour. It provides the justification for 'targeting' attention and resources on certain offenders, and for the objectives of the work undertaken to be directed towards changing criminal behaviour and influencing, for good, patterns of offending. There are, equally, risks in this rapid change, that the pendulum could swing too far in the opposite direction, to the exclusion of any concern with individual offenders' needs and other wider social issues of poverty and disadvantage.

Data providing evidence of demand, response and outcome will become the basis for local authorities to demonstrate value for money (or 'best value'), to demonstrate effectiveness, and to influence policy and decision making in the future. In addition to local agency data, there is an urgent need to establish a national core data base (see McAra, 1998). The approach has been to seek a Scottish solution to a Scottish problem.

Most local authorities now have specially designated criminal justice social work staff. New organisational solutions and methods of co-ordinating work are required if changes to patterns of practice and organisation are to avoid fragmentation of provision. Managerial expertise in the field of criminal justice social work is essential. There are signs that co-ordination and collaboration within social work across child care, adult services and criminal justice remain problematic. Shared working is generally set, in principle, as a model of good practice in most areas of social work practice. The challenge to managers is to develop mechanisms to ensure that the integrated structure of social work is not simply theoretical, but one that can be operated in reality.

NOS (Organisation and Management section) stresses that the services '...should be fully aligned with systems for the organisation and management of all social work services provided by the local authority, including arrangements for strategic oversight and review of social work services generally'; 'the roles...must be clearly stated, in terms of service delivery, management, co-ordination, policy planning, service development, monitoring and evaluation...'; and in wanting the best of all possible worlds 'maximum use should be made of those resources available elsewhere in the local authority or in the wider community where needed...'. There

should be 'scope for social workers providing centrally funded services to undertake related work in individual cases (e.g. where within an offender's family there
are difficulties such as mental health or addiction problems) and for other staff...to
participate in this area of work...'. The NOS remain silent on how this might happen in practice.

The maintenance of good practice and the survival of integrated services may
depend on the commitment of politicians, managers and practitioners alike, and on
opportunities such as the interchange of personnel between criminal justice units
and other parts of social work service. Opportunities for secondments and exchanges
may be required for practitioners, and for promoted post holders. All new 're-
cruits', at whatever level of seniority, should, as part of induction, spend time in
each of the service sections. Where general practitioners are in use, they will need
ready access to specialist consultants to support and oversee their work.

Professional responsibility and National Objectives and Standards

'The supervision of offenders placed on probation requires a wide range of professional knowledge and skill' (NOS, Probation section). The question is whether the
detail and content of the NOS is sufficient to enhance that professionalism and
whether re-organised local authority bureaucracy can produce the flexibility, innovation, and the levels and quality of practice that are required.

The terms 'bureaucracy' and 'bureaucratic' tend, all too often, to be used in a
derogatory way, denoting 'red tape', defensive decision making and unnecessary
levels and layers of control. Merton (1957:189) noted 'if the bureaucracy is to
operate successfully, it must attain a high degree of reliability of behaviour, an
unusual degree of conformity with prescribed patterns of action...and the methodical
performance of one's duties'. Alongside this well-recognised problem is the role
of professionals within bureaucratic organisations (Stevenson et al, 1978). NOS
add a further layer which can be interpreted either as bureaucratic control or professional direction and safeguard. It is heartening that NOS (Probation section)
emphasises that 'the term "standard" is used to establish benchmarks...the term
does not imply the rigid application of rules and procedures'.

Probation and punishment

NOS (Probation section) outlines a three-tiered approach within probation: 'standard' probation; probation with requirements; and 'intensive' probation. The reasons and objectives for this approach can be understood in terms of government's
twin-track approach (see Chapter 1), which seeks to 'use prison sparingly' (NOS,
General Issues) only for the most serious offenders, and to have available a range
of community-based disposals for other offenders. This will require ways of distinguishing or grading the different types of probation and other community-based
social work disposal. The policy and legislation intends that community service be
used only where prison would otherwise ensue (see Chapter 9). Probation's very
versatility means it has the potential to be used across a wide range of situations:

'standard' probation for less serious situations, up to 'intensive' probation for serious offenders.

In Scotland probation orders continue to be made 'instead of sentencing' (section 228, CP Act, 1995); the sentence or the punishment is turned away from for a time, and can be avoided altogether if the outcome is successful. The issue is not to suggest that probation is undemanding—the opposite is true; or that it is not experienced as a sanction or punishment by the probationer—the control elements and time demand often will be; simply that at the heart of probation is the notion that supervision and help are combined as an alternative to sentence. The essential character of probation remains the **combination** of control and help. If one takes undue precedence over the other, the true value (and probably any beneficial effect) of probation is lost. Probation is not custody in the community.

Distinctions between different types of probation may reflect differences in degrees of help provided but, equally, should reflect greater demand of time from the offender and may involve more surveillance and monitoring. 'Probation combines control in the form of obligations placed on offenders which will include **restrictions on their personal freedom**, with opportunities and assistance for them' (NOS probation section). Probation should normally only be used where there is a need for **both**. Restriction, however, is not the prime reason for imposing the order, just as punishment per se is not the main objective and character of the order. These are important principles that deserve prominent underlining.

One difficulty associated with the welfare approach of the past was to view a probation order as a device to ensure an individual received a service and some courts made orders if they wanted to 'do somebody some good', in the hope that the use of a statutory order would guarantee some attention from social work. Social work values stress the importance of minimum intrusive intervention and diversion from formal systems, where appropriate. The principle remains that voluntary measures of assistance, embodied in section 12 of the 1968 Act, should be used, if at all possible. Probation, however, is a compulsory order and, therefore, should be reserved by social workers and sentencers, where elements of risk are present, or where control is required along with assistance for personal change. Intensive probation should be reserved for high-risk offenders, where any personal change programme will be combined with significant demands on the offender's time.

The problem of 'net widening' (drawing people into formal criminal processes to their ultimate disadvantage) has been well documented on both sides of the border (McMahon, 1993). The danger is that failure on the part of the offender to respond positively to probation may result in a more severe sentence for breach than the original offence merited. So there are good reasons for not imposing requirements and levels of contact that are not justified by the person's offending behaviour.

In the current system, there are dangers that authorities, in order to meet their

annual 'targets', will draw people, unnecessarily, into probation. Some imagination in the 100% funding arrangements is required to allow costs to be met where
a service is offered on a voluntary basis (e.g. on deferral of service) which otherwise might have led to some statutory intervention. Equally local authorities, if
they are serious about their crime prevention role, must make some preventive
services available on a voluntary basis.

The **three-tiered approach** to probation identified in the NOS—standard probation, probation with conditions, and intensive probation—is in need of further
clarification in terms of the seriousness of the offending to which each should be
geared. A range of requirements, from the reparative (for example, restitution or
compensation and unpaid work), to personal change and educational approaches,
through to treatment approaches in instances of addiction and mental illness, and
monitoring and surveillance on behalf of the community, can be contained within
a probation order. The intensity of supervision, in any case, cannot in itself be
legislated for, but has to be left to the professional supervising the order against
some assessment of the risk the person presents to the community and the objectives set for the specific order. This is probation's versatility and adaptability. It is
perhaps a satisfying comment that the law of the land contains the dilemmas, perhaps even tensions, of a measure like probation that does not 'fit' readily into a
punishment or tariff model.

Probation existed before the current policy was promoted. To retain its essential qualities will, in some measure, depend on the vision, concept, and commitment that social workers and their managers bring to it. It is not possible to practice
probation, to implement NOS, and operate within the legislation on one hand, without a concept of social work and effective help on the other; nor is it possible to
practice probation solely motivated by a concern for welfare but without an understanding of the law, its procedures, and the workings and needs of the courts, victims and the community.

Action plans

NOS (Probation section) emphasises the importance of an **initial** action plan which
incorporates the legal requirements of the order. 'The plan should set out what will
be done during the course of the order to address the problems and issues associated with offending behaviour with the aim of reducing the risk of re-offending'.
McIvor and Barry (1998) found that most probation files contained action plans
suggesting that these are completed and recorded at some stage during the supervision period.

One reason for the emphasis on action plans is the need to convince courts that
something purposeful will happen when they make a probation order. Legislation
requires that the court should be 'satisfied that suitable arrangements…can be made'
(*Criminal Procedure (Scotland) Act,* 1995, section 228(2))

NOS emphasise the importance of a three-month initial phase of supervision
which provides the opportunity for a fuller assessment, confirming or adapting the
initial action plan. Three months does not seem, particularly, in the longer orders,

an unrealistic management and practice objective for making a start on the perceived problem areas in the probationer's situation. NOS underline the point that the action should be focused on the offending and programmes should be aimed at assisting the cessation or reduction of that offending.

The importance of matching supervision style to the learning style of the probationer is recognised by many commentators (see 'responsivity' principle, Chapter 2). Efforts to match supervisors and probationers have to acknowledge the often illusive nature of professional relationships in the context of providing well structured programmes of intervention and opportunities for personal change. An important way to convince sentencers about the value of probation is to provide information and promotional accounts of work carried out, information on particular programmes and evidence of outcomes.

THE LEGISLATION

Using probation

Availability
Probation is available for people of both sexes, of virtually all ages, of every conceivable kind of criminal history, and for almost all crimes and offences.

- A probation order can be made in respect of any person who has attained the age of criminal responsibility. In Scotland, that means aged eight and over *(Criminal Procedure (Scotland) Act*, 1995, section 41). Children can sometimes be prosecuted before the adult courts (see Chapter 6), and probation is a possible disposal.
- A probation order can be made in respect of any offence for which the penalty is not fixed by law. There are very few offences which carry a fixed penalty: at one extreme, murder carries a fixed penalty of life imprisonment—but culpable homicide does not carry a fixed penalty; at the other extreme, many road traffic offences carry fixed penalties.
- The law makes no reference to previous convictions as a bar to the use of probation; in the past probation has often been used only for first offenders, for certain types of offences, for people who have not been to prison before, or for people who have not been on probation before.

The criterion suggested by the legislation is that of *expediency*. The governing sections which allow for the making of probation orders state that the court may, 'if it is of the opinion that **it is expedient to do so**', make a probation order (emphasis added). There is an open invitation to 'creative interpretation'.

The Morison Committee (1962) concluded that there was an a priori case for the use of probation when four conditions existed:

- The circumstances of the offence and the offender's record must not be such as to demand, in the interests of society, that some more severe method be adopted in dealing with the offender. (In this context it is important to note government's policy that only the most serious and/or violent offences should attract periods of imprisonment.)

- The risk, if any, to society through setting the offender at liberty must be out-weighed by the moral, social and economic arguments for not depriving him of it.
- The offender must need continuing attention, since otherwise…a fine or dis-charge will suffice. (Note that this was written before the introduction of super-vised attendance and community service, but the principle holds good.)
- The offender must be capable of responding to this attention whilst at liberty. (This puts a very heavy burden on any social worker who reports that probation is 'inappropriate' because it is alleged that the person will not respond, as this view may amount to a passport to imprisonment as far as some offenders are concerned.)

The *Criminal Procedure (Scotland) Act*, 1995 (s.228) provides for orders of not less than six months and not more than three years. There is scope for extensive periods of supervision for high-risk offenders. In practice data suggests that in 1994, 58% of orders were for less than one year, 38% for less than two and only 4% were for over two years. This may well indicate that despite the increase in use of probation its full potential, particularly for offenders who otherwise would re-ceive custody, is still under-utilised. *A Commitment to Protect* (SWSI 1997:22) suggests that rather than sentence certain categories of sex offenders to short peri-ods of custody, lengthy periods of supervision under a probation order might offer better protection to the community, particularly if a personal change programme is part of the order.

The *Criminal Procedure (Scotland) Act,* 1995 section 228 (1)(a) requires the court to obtain a report before making any probation order. Section 203 also re-quires the courts (except district courts) to obtain reports before disposing of any case involving anyone subject to supervision under section 27(1)(b)(i) to (vi) of the 1968 Act, which as well as probation and community service, includes super-vised attendance orders and prison licence (see Chapter 5).

Explanation

The legislative requirements in s.228(5) of the *Criminal Procedure (Scotland) Act,* 1995 place responsibilities on the court (not the social worker):

- the court must explain the effect of probation to the offender;
- the explanation must be in **ordinary language;**
- the explanation must include reference to any additional requirements which it is proposed to include;
- the explanation must specifically refer to the offender's liability to be sentenced for the original offence if he *either* commits another offence whilst on proba-tion, or fails to keep any of the requirements of the order;
- the offender must express his willingness to comply with all the require-ments, that is to say, with the standard requirements applicable to all proba-tion orders (see below) and any additional ones that the court may propose to insert.

Whatever guidance, advice, or suggestion that may have been included in a social enquiry report, it is the court that is making the proposal for probation to the prospective probationer. The person must consent to the order and is entering into an undertaking with the court. The undertaking necessarily involves contact with a social worker. The importance of the person fully understanding what he is undertaking is self evident. The following example is adapted from one used by Avon magistrates' court (Anthony and Berryman, 1998: 233).

Probation Order

We intend to put you on probation for ... months/years for the offence of ... Before making this order I (the sentencer) will explain what it means and then ask you if you agree to the order being made.

Being on probation will restrict you personal freedom and you will be supervised by a criminal justice social worker.

You will be supervised in order to

- stop you offending
- protect the public from you;
- help you change your ways;

While you are on probation, you must keep in touch with your supervising officer. Make sure that he or she knows where you are living, and carry out any instructions he or she gives you as part of the probation order.

Under the conditions of the probation order, you must

- attend any groups your supervising officer tells you to attend;
- live at...;
- attend (groups) meetings of...;
- get medical treatment at...;
- get treatment for your alcohol or drug dependency by...

If you do not keep to any of these conditions, you may have to come back to court and, in addition to the order being continued, be fined, have the conditions changed, or be sentenced in some other way.

We can also look again at our decision to put you on probation if you or your supervising officer ask us to review the matter.

Do you understand what a probation order is?

Do you agree to the order being made?

We place you on probation for...months under the conditions already explained.

Please see the social worker before you leave the court.

Modern concepts now cast the courts as the service user and in this instance it is the local authority that is contracted to provide a service, rather than, perhaps, the individual supervisor. We still await the probationer who uses as a defence to any alleged breach of probation on his part, that the local authority failed to honour its contract in providing an effective service. The probationer can often feel relatively powerless, yet any failure on his part may lead to prosecution for breach. It is now relatively less hard to define the obligations on supervisors and authorities since the introduction of NOS and they can more readily be taken to task for falling down on the job.

Effects of probation

As we noted probation is an order, not a sentence, and people are not 'sentenced' to probation in Scotland, they are simply placed on probation. This is an important legal distinction between probation orders in Scotland and elsewhere in the UK, both on solemn and summary procedure, in that the person stands convicted of the offence but the order is made 'instead of sentencing him' (section 228 (1) of the *Criminal Procedure (Scotland) Act,* 1995. The legislation goes further and indicates that this conviction 'shall be deemed not to be a conviction for any purpose other than the purposes of the proceedings in which the order is made, and of laying it before a court as a previous conviction in subsequent proceedings for another offence' and 'shall in any event be disregarded for the purposes of any enactment which imposes any disqualification or disability upon convicted persons, or authorises or requires the imposition of any such disqualification or disability' (Section 247(1)(2)). For all practical purposes probation counts as a conviction. These legal niceties, however, represent an important statement about the nature of probation suggesting a completely different model of criminal justice from the crime-punishment model which has dominated political ideology.

It is sometimes said people are given a 'chance', or even another chance when placed on probation. The danger in this way of thinking is the notion that probation is in lieu of something worse, or that you only ever get one chance. An important corollary of the present policy and the strategy of a three-tiered structure to probation is that it clears the way for the repeated imposition of probation. If it works once, it could well work again; if it failed before, then, in any event, this only puts it in the same league as many other measures, including prison, and merely represents a challenge to learn the lessons of previous attempts.

The effect of probation is that successful completion of the order means that the probationer receives no sentence per se for the original offence. The court retains its right, if the person commits another offence, or is brought back to court for not keeping one of the requirements of probation, to impose sentence in respect of the original offence, as if the probation order had never been made.

Sections 53 and 54 of the *Criminal Justice (Scotland) Act,* 1980 made it possible for a probation order to be made after a period of deferred sentence. Section 55 of the 1980 Act made it possible for a probation order to be combined with a period of disqualification from driving: this matter is now governed by Road Traffic regulations.

The legal status of probation orders can be a fact to be borne in mind when a court is dealing with a person for more than one charge. Whilst it may be technically competent to order probation on one charge, and other measures in relation to other charges, there are a number of points to be made:

- It is inappropriate to order both probation and a custodial sentence (however short) simultaneously; however, instances have been known of the courts putting someone on probation who is due to be released very shortly from an existing custodial sentence.

- Careful consideration needs to be given if unpaid work is a possibility as a condition of probation. Some people can cope well with the two demands; but for others it can present a problem. NOS indicate that the order should be an option, only where the person is at serious risk of custody, and is only appropriate where the offender will benefit from the probation supervision. If the person has the scale of problems and represents a degree of risk such that probation is called for, then it is the primary measure to use, and the offender should be given as much opportunity as possible to succeed.
- Again it can be counterproductive to combine probation with a fine, even if technically competent; experience indicates that the latter can be a counterproductive influence on the course of the order, particularly if it is a heavy one.

Format of the probation order

The statute determines that the format of a probation order 'shall be as nearly as may be in the form prescribed by Act of Adjournal' (section 228(3) of the *Criminal Procedure (Scotland) Act,* 1995). The CP Act, 1995 ensures that the following arrangements shall be included:

- the name of the local authority area in which the person resides or is to reside;
- provision for the person to be under the supervision of an officer of the local authority; moreover, NOS (Probation section) insist that 'the responsibility for supervising probation orders will be held by a professionally qualified social worker';
- provision, if the person resides or is to reside in a local authority area where the court making the order does not have jurisdiction, for the order to name the appropriate court for that area of residence, and to require the local authority in that area to arrange for supervision;
- the court must be satisfied that suitable arrangements for supervision can be made by the local authority, in whatever area.

Though the responsibility falls to the local authority to arrange for supervision, it is still significant that **legislation consistently refers to 'an officer of the local authority'**, not simply 'the authority or even the 'chief social work officer'. This emphasises the individual responsibility placed on the supervising officer, which is appropriate given the nature of probation.

Serving the order

The CP Act, 1995 requires the Clerk of Court to give copies of the probation order to the probationer; to the supervising officer; and to any person in charge of an institution in which a probationer may be required to reside (for example, a probation hostel, or a mental hospital). In practice, it is normally the supervising officer who will serve the order. This is an opportunity to underline the point that the contract is with the court, and only consequentially with the social worker. The importance of serving and explaining the order is paramount. It has been argued that the order is not completely made until this is done. The order should be served at the earliest possible moment. It is certainly better practice that the supervisor serves the order than the report writer (if the two are different) as suggested in NOS.

The probationer should sign one of the copies of the order to the effect that it has been served on him, and the date recorded; this signed copy is then retained by the supervisor. The importance of speedy administration is greater when the probationer is to reside in a different area. The court-based social worker should notify the appropriate office in writing the same day as well as attending to practical matters such as fares and subsistence, if appropriate, and provide the probationer with the necessary instructions for contacting that office.

Appeals

It is possible to appeal **against conviction** for an offence on which a probation order is made, if the original plea was one of not guilty and the person feels the conviction is still wrongful. However the notion of appealing against the imposition of probation as a disposal is rather incongruous, given that the person consented to be placed on probation. The High Court, sitting as an Appeal Court, may quash a sentence and pass another sentence and, in practice, may make a probation order. The period normally runs from the date the order is made.

REQUIREMENTS OF PROBATION

The essence of probation as a legal order depends on it having a social work content to be meaningful. The CP Act, 1995 requires that supervision must be available before an order can be made. The law also can dictate to some degree the structure and content of supervision, in the form of the various requirements included in probation. It is important that courts understand the practical implications of any requirement made and that supervising officers address the aims and pre-occupations of the courts if additional requirements are inserted. Both the legislation and NOS have done much to reinforce this point.

Standard requirements

There are some requirements which are **common to all probation orders**. In Scotland these are (following the Act of Adjournal):

- to be of good behaviour;
- to conform to the directions of the supervising officer;
- to inform the supervising officer at once if he changes his place of residence or place of employment.

NOS stress that home visiting on a regular, and indeed unpredictable, basis throughout the order is an important aspect of probation practice. There are growing physical risks for social workers making home visits and special safeguards are required.

It is important to note that powers are available to bring probationers who are not co-operating back before the court though they have neither been convicted of a fresh offence, nor have broken one of the specific extra requirements. The clearest example is the probationer who simply disappears from contact, and is thus in breach of the third standard requirement set out above (not informing the supervisor of a change of address). However it is open to the supervisor to regard some flagrant item of bad behaviour or failure to conform to the supervisor's directions as a breach of requirement of probation. The problem of defining and interpreting good behaviour or a reasonable direction is obviously one of subjectivity, but it is important to note that the powers are there, and are intended to be used as appropriate. It is clear that control as well as help is intended to be a feature of probation, and the supervisor has responsibilities to the court, the community and potential victims, as well as to the probationer.

Extra requirements

There are general powers to include additional requirements in a probation order and specific powers to include particular kinds of requirements as formal conditions of an order. If social work is serious about the effects of net-widening, then general requirements within a standard order should be considered before any specific conditions are applied; for example, it should not be necessary to have a formal condition to provide supervision on a group-work or programme basis; this can be agreed with the probationer and the court as the appropriate standard means of supervision in any given case from the outset.

General power to include extra requirements

Section 229(1) of the CP Act, 1995 provides the court with a general power to include extra requirements in a probation order. This allows the content of probation to be tailored to the individual case and circumstances with which courts are confronted. Requirements must meet two common-sense criteria:

- they must be reasonable and legally enforceable; and
- they must be capable of being supervised.

It is important to distinguish between the various working agreements of supervisors and probationers, and legally defined requirements which are enforceable by law. The law provides a guiding principle concerning requirements:

as the court, having regard to the circumstances of the case, considers—
(a) conducive to securing the good conduct of the offender, or for preventing a repetition by him of the offence, or the commission of other offences. (Section 229(1)).

Employment

Under early probation legislation, finding work for probationers was one of the duties of probation officers. In the past some Scottish orders included the requirement that the probationer 'should use his best endeavours to obtain and maintain himself in regular employment' as a method of bolstering the probationer's incentive to stay in work, and to encourage the use of training and resettlement facilities of the Department of Employment or other similar agencies. There was a time when three refusals to take jobs offered by a Job Centre, or after interviews arranged by the supervisor, would have been regarded as a sufficient basis for breach of requirement proceedings to be instituted. All of these practices fell into abeyance for the good reason that meaningful employment and training opportunities became scarce. McIvor and Barry (1998:33) found that over a third of probation orders had employment as an objective for male offenders. This was viewed as an area where least progress was made. There is much scope within developing policies of 'welfare to work' and the New Deal, for the establishment of training opportunities for all unemployed probationers as an integral component of the provision rather than as a requirement of any sort.

Caution

Caution, although a free-standing disposal (see Chapter 7), can be included as a requirement in a probation order. The probationer is required to lodge a sum of money with the Clerk of Court within a stipulated period as a security for his good behaviour during the course of the order. If the order is completed successfully, the probationer is repaid the money, together with accrued interest. The Clerk of Court will require confirmation from the supervising officer that all the requirements of the order have been met. A requirement for caution could be used if there are doubts about a prospective probationer's level of motivation and to ensure that he has (literally) an investment in its successful outcome. In practice it is seldom used in this context.

Compensation or restitution

This has been part of probation practice for many years. The *Criminal Justice (Scotland) Act* 1980, introduced a specific compensation order as a disposal in its own right (now section 249 of the CP Act, 1995). A compensation order can be made alongside any other disposal except probation (section 249(2)). This exception is because compensation can be an additional requirement within a probation order to pay 'either in a lump sum or by instalments for any personal injury, loss or damage caused (whether directly or indirectly) by the acts which constituted the offence' (section 229(6) of the CP Act, 1995). A practical point is that compensation, when a requirement of probation, is not paid into court by the probationer as it would be in the case of a separate order, and so it is important to establish at the start of the order who is to be the beneficiary.

Section 228(7)(a) stipulates that any compensation requirement shall be met within 18 months of the making of the order or not later than 2 months before the end of the period of probation. Failure will be regarded as a breach of requirement and could bring the entire order into question. Whether the supervisor agrees to accept the responsibility of collection, or leaves the probationer to comply without interference, some oversight is necessary in terms of supervising the requirement.

Reparation and mediation

There is a growing interest in schemes of reparation and mediation (see Chapter 7), which involve some personal form of recompense (not necessarily financial), negotiated between a victim and offender. There is no legislative bar to including reparation within probation. Most formal schemes for reparation and mediation established in Scotland operate at the pre-court stage of proceedings.

The emphasis on supervision operating 'on behalf of victims' (ADSW, 1996), creates an expectation that concern for the victim should feature, explicitly, as part of standard probation practice, and there is no essential reason why formal legislation or extra requirements are required to create opportunities for offenders to 'make amends' or to 'make good' in some way for their offence where this is practical. There are many ways of interpreting the phrase 'confronting offending behaviour' which could be developed in this way as a humane, constructive, and reconciling approach to supervision, which is focused on re-integration.

Criminal associates

Whilst it is a stated requirement of prison licences in Scotland that the licensee should choose his or her company carefully, the use of a requirement in probation is likely to be rare. The topic of choice of associates is likely to be part of a standard action plan. While the reasonableness of a requirement could be demonstrated in some instances, the practicalities of enforcement and of proving any breach are unworkable. If a situation did arise of serious concern to the supervisor the order could be returned to court on 'cause shown' and a more specific requirement considered.

Abstention from alcohol and drugs

Any requirement to refrain from the consumption of alcohol outwith the probationer's own home or from the use of drugs runs into similar practical difficulties of enforcement as the choice of associates—though often the two may be related. A general requirement included in a standard order may help support the probationer's self discipline, provide a valid reason to resist the pressures of 'associates', or confirm agreement by the probationer to participate in a programme designed to deal with alcohol or drug misuse. In practice, a formal requirement is only likely to be required where treatment (medical or social), in the context of hospital, clinic, or other centre is proposed. It remains to be seen how Drug Treatment and Testing Orders will be used alongside probation.

Formal requirements specified within the legislation

Probation is a community-based measure. Nonetheless the possibility of a **requirement of residence** may be important in convincing courts that a person need not be sentenced to imprisonment. In a democratic society, any requirement that seeks to govern a person's place of residence is a major encroachment on civil liberties and needs careful definition. Consequently specific provision is made in legislation and section 229(2) and (3) of the *Criminal Procedure (Scotland) Act,* 1995, provides for residence as a formal and additional requirement within a probation order.

The probationer must not only consent to the general terms of any probation order, but also to the specific details of any formal requirement of residence. Before making any such requirement, the court MUST 'consider the home surroundings'. The person in charge of any residential facility within which a probationer is required to reside should receive a copy of the probation order authorising that residence, before admitting the probationer. The establishment must agree, in advance, to accept him and the report writer must make known to the court the precise terms of admission and the rules of any particular regime. The essential ingredients of any requirement relating to residence are:

- the period of residence 'shall, not extend beyond 12 months from the date of the requirement or beyond the date when the order expires' (229 (3)(b)); also 'the period for which he is so required to reside shall be specified in the order'. This can be varied subsequently on application from the supervisor if circumstances appear to warrant it;
- The institution or place must be named in the order; the wording should be very specific—'x hostel or house; y street; z town': the wording may include to 'sleep there each night unless permission to absent himself has previously been given.

The requirement to reside in a hostel usually requires obliges the offender to abide by the rules of the hostel. Before any probationer can leave or be discharged from a place at which he has been ordered to reside, an application has to be made **to vary the order to** remove the requirement. This can be used to restrict the probationer who, it is felt, needs to be kept away from certain locations.

In the past a requirement to 'reside where approved by the supervising officer' was often considered inappropriately draconian. However the provisions of the *Sex Offender Act* 1997, which have introduced requirements for registration and monitoring, and the allied policy outlined in *A Commitment to Protect* (SWSI 1997), suggests that greater use of this kind of requirement in community disposals might be likely in future for certain offenders. If probation orders are to be used effectively with sex offenders, then it can be expected that restriction of residence, and even of movement e.g. not living near a primary school, participating in youth clubs, among other things, will become issues for probation supervision.

Requirements of treatment for a mental condition

The inclusion of a requirement in a probation order of treatment for a mental condition is governed by section 230 of the *Criminal Procedure (Scotland) Act*, 1995. The legislation specifies:

- the treatment must be for a mental condition (not a physical one);
- the treatment must be one of three broad types of treatment specified by the section.

The court must first obtain the evidence of a (single) registered medical practitioner approved for the purposes by the *Mental Health (Scotland) Act*, 1984. As for any probation order the court is required to ask for a report before placing the individual on probation. The evidence for the condition must show two things:

- the mental condition 'requires and may be susceptible to treatment';
- the condition 'is not such as to warrant his detention in pursuance of a hospital order' under Part V of the *Mental Health (Scotland) Act*, 1984 (sections 58-60 of the CP Act, 1995).

The period of treatment will be under the direction of either a medical practitioner or a chartered psychologist and shall not extend beyond 12 months from the date of the requirement. These conditions rule out the possibility of a requirement where the condition is not susceptible to treatment or where the treatment period is likely to be in excess of 12 months. However treatment can be as an in-patient, an out-patient or as a patient living in the community (s.230(2)). The treatment, which must be specified in the order, must be one of the following:

- treatment as a resident in a hospital within the meaning of the *Mental Health (Scotland) Act,* 1984 and not the State Hospital;
- treatment as a non-resident at such institution or place (for example, a specialist clinic) as may be specified in the order;
- treatment by or under the direction of such medical practitioner or chartered psychologist as may be specified in the order.

Beyond this, the nature of the treatment need not be specified in the order. However section 232(5) recognises that any refusal to undergo any surgical, electrical or other treatment will not be seen as failing to comply if in the opinion of the court the refusal is 'reasonable having regard to all the circumstances'.

The court shall not make a probation order containing a requirement for treatment for a mental condition unless it is satisfied that arrangements have been made for the intended treatment. If the treatment is to be undertaken as a resident, the court must be satisfied that arrangements have been made for the probationer's reception and escort to the facility. Also, in this instance, the hospital authorities will require a copy of the probation order before the person can be admitted.

Before the *Mental Health (Scotland) Act,* 1984, the role of the supervising officer in cases involving treatment for a mental condition, particularly when in-patient treatment was involved, was largely nominal and administrative. The legislation cleared the way for a much more integral role on the part of the supervising officer. Given that hospital social workers and mental health officers are officers of the local authority, there is considerable scope to call on their expertise and familiarity with the procedures of mental hospitals.

Considerable scope is given to the clinician responsible for providing the treatment. Arrangements can be made for a part of the treatment to be given in a different place from that originally specified in the order. Section 230 enables these kinds of changes to be accomplished with much greater administrative ease than was previously possible. The overriding qualification is that these changes cannot be made unless 'the probationer and any officer responsible for his supervision agree'. Whereas formerly, the medical practitioner had to notify the court of any important changes, that responsibility now lies with the supervising officer and, in effect, requires the clinician to keep the supervisor fully informed as to the progress of treatment. The clinician's responsibility for the purely psychiatric or psychological aspects of the treatment remains their prerogative. However, the real strength of this measure lies in the possibility of an inter-disciplinary, community-based approach to the mentally disordered offender.

Studies, such as Cooke's study in Scottish prisons (1994), which indicate that a significant proportion of those in custody experience psychological disturbance, and that the disturbance often pre-dates imprisonment, question the appropriateness of dealing with such people in prison; there is scope for the expansion of this aspect of probation practice. Classically, those addicted to alcohol or drugs, compulsive offenders, the sexually deviant, have all been considered the kinds of people who might benefit from aspects of treatment provided in this way. Moreover, especially for those who may spend some time as an in-patient, the task of re-integration within the community, more typically associated with prison throughcare, becomes an important part of work under a probation order.

Requirement to perform unpaid work

The possibility of including a requirement in a probation order that a person perform a period of unpaid work of benefit to the community was formally introduced by section 7 of the *Community Service by Offenders (Scotland) Act,* 1978. 'Section 7' orders, as they became known, are dealt with under section 229(4) of the *Criminal Procedure (Scotland) Act,* 1995. The CP Act, 1995 requires that a probation order with a condition of unpaid work can only be made where 'an offender (over 16 years) has been **convicted of an offence punishable by imprisonment**'. While the provision makes no stated requirement, as is the case for a community service order, that the alternative for the offender is a custodial sentence, this would seem to be implied. Briefly, a requirement in a probation order for unpaid work must specify:

- the number of hours to be worked, which must be not less than 40 nor more than 240 (300 in solemn procedures);
- that the hours must be performed within 12 months of the order being made, even if the order itself is for a longer period—unless extended by the court under section 240(1)(a);
- that the probationer reports to an officer of the local authority specifically designated for community service purposes; this may or may not be the same officer nominated to supervise the whole probation order.

It is implicit that the unpaid work should be for the benefit of the whole community, and not for an individual who may have been affected by the original offence. The wording of the requirement may be in terms such as:

shall perform x hours of unpaid work for the benefit of the community within 12 months as directed by the local authority officer designated for community service purposes.

It should be noted that section 229 of the CP Act, 1995 contains a number of restrictions on ordering requirements for unpaid work in a probation order:

- no person aged under 16 can be made subject to such a requirement;
- the person must consent;
- arrangements are in force to enable cross-border provision; either in respect of persons residing north or south of the border (as the case may be) or moving

after the making of an order. It may be worth noting at this point that no problems exist between the Scottish order, made instead of sentence, and the English provision of probation as a sentence of the court.

- the court has to know that a scheme exists in the area where the person resides or is to reside and that work is available;
- the court must consider a 'report by an officer of the local authority about the offender and his circumstances', together with an assessment as to his suitability for community service.

Day training centres

No power exists in Scotland, equivalent to those in England and Wales, for establishing day centres though it is consistent within the wide powers given to local authorities under the *Social Work (Scotland) Act,* 1968 (as amended) that such centres could be established and used. This kind of development may result from the expansion of 'supervised attendance orders' in respect of fine defaulters, (s.235 to 237 of the CP Act, 1995, Chapter 6). Some intensive probation projects have established these kinds of resources.

Concurrent orders

Restriction of Liberty Orders (RLO) can be made concurrently with a Probation Order by virtue of section 245(D)(1) of the CP Act, 1995. Failure to comply with probation order requirements can be dealt with under section 232(2)(c) in the normal way. The legislation makes provision for the court to exercise its powers under s.245(F))2)(b) which deals with breach of an RLO. Failure to comply with the requirements of the RLO similarly means the court can exercise its powers under s.232(2)(c) (see Chapter 7).

It is expected that Drug Treatment and Testing Orders, Anti-Social Behaviour Orders and Non-Harassment Orders will also be available concurrently with probation. It will be important to ensure that offenders are not simply set up to fail by the application of additional provisions. In any case, since these additional orders focus more on restriction than help, it is important to ensure that positive help is made available to the offender in conjunction with any restrictions to avoid the poor outcomes well demonstrated in the USA of restrictive measures without positive help (Petersilia and Turner, 1993).

NATIONAL OBJECTIVES AND STANDARDS

It is important to distinguish between that which is contained in legislation, and that which has been set out in National Objectives and Standards (NOS) as good practice. Despite the frequent use of the term 'must', NOS do not have the force of law. However they do carry much weight— not least, that coupled with the system of 100% central funding, service standards are subject to inspection; their legal status, at the end of the day, is that of guidance.

Reviews of probation

NOS impose obligations on local authorities to have formal reviews, involving both the probationer and the supervisor's line manager, in which progress in meeting agreed targets is established and plans for the next phase of supervision agreed. The guidance specifies that formal reviews of progress should be carried out at three and six months, and where the length of the order permits, six monthly there-after. The review will be minuted and countersigned by the probationer. Research supports the view that the outcomes of a programme of intervention are signifi-cantly better when the programme is focused and well structured, involves multi-ple methods and is multi-disciplinary. The most successful outcomes are associ-ated with programmes which have clearly stated and measurable objectives; which are understood both by the practitioner and the participant; where practitioners are sufficiently trained and know what they are doing; where the intervention has a chance of achieving its objectives (i.e. it is relevant), and where some evaluative information is gathered to check that they have actually done what was agreed. These are the elements of programme 'integrity' (Andrew's *et al* 1990).

While there is no legal obligation on the probationer to countersign any record that is kept of work under the probation order, the review provides an opportunity for the probationer, the manager and the supervisor to examine the objectives set, the service delivered to date to achieve these objectives, and any interim assess-ment or evaluation of progress made. McIvor and Barry (1998:24) found that 51% of initial reviews were carried out within the time period specified by NOS but suggest some 'reluctance on the part of social workers to convene formal reviews', and that intervention aimed at directly addressing offending behaviour featured in 70% of orders; 'the most striking feature (was) that the majority of work with probationers was undertaken by social workers or by other agencies on a one-to-one basis'. Where there was limited evidence of targeting, NOS were least often met and practice appeared more closely aligned to a welfare model with emphasis on the probationer's problems rather than their offending. In most cases the super-visor assumed the sole responsibility for providing services. Where use of other agencies was most often made was in the provision of services related to employ-ment, alcohol, drug and health issues.

The main aim of the guidance is that good practice should be encouraged as a norm rather than set out in rule form as a minimum requirement. Good manage-ment will insist on holding supervisors to account for their practice, and will look for proof of it in the form of written records, including regular reviews involving the supervisor, the probationer, and any other relevant person as required. There is always a risk that the benchmark of a three-month review could become the mini-mum necessary to meet NOS in a bureaucratic and procedural sense.

Intensive probation

NOS promote the concept of intensive probation in a specific way. Intensive pro-bation in other countries has tended to be developed within a context of probation as a punishment, with the 'intensity' relating to the restriction and the surveillance demands made on the offender. Intensive probation need not, of course, be puni-tive delivery. **Most research indicates that the more punitive the supervision the less effective it is in terms of reducing re-offending** (Palmer 1993) and that the most effective programmes combine intensive monitoring with constructive help aimed at changing behaviour. Intensive probation should, however, by definition, be intensive and involve significant time demand. Commentators suggest that intensive programmes should 'occupy 40-70% of the offender's time' over a period of 3 to 9 months (Gendreau et al, 1994:75).

There has been little discussion in Scotland about the meaning of 'intensity' and there is none within the guidance, on whether the intensity of such probation should relate to the amount of contact or to the nature of the intervention or both. Nor has there been discussion on the role that restriction or 'time demand' should play, if any, where the offender is viewed as a risk to the public. It seems rather incongruous that most intensive probation is being delivered by the voluntary sector in a format that looks more like well-resourced standard probation, than anything that is intensive in terms of its aims and objectives regarding community safety or its targeting of serious offenders. The intensity of intervention needs to be the minimum necessary to achieve the objectives set for the individual probationer. In some instances this will be very intensive.

If probation is to develop as a credible option for very serious offenders, the full scope of probation provisions, from 6 months to three years, needs to be utilised. In 1994 only 4% of orders were for more than three years. It seems important, whatever the degree of intervention, that if a three-tier structure of probation is to be meaningful, the term 'intensive probation', itself, needs 'to be used sparingly' and reserved for those high-risk offenders who may well be facing custody or for those who already have a record of failure in standard probation and in probation where specific conditions were applied. Otherwise, sentencers will go straight for 'intensive probation' as a first option, as they often do with community service, because it has become associated with a service that is meaningful and credible both to sentencer and offender.

BREACHES OF PROBATION ORDERS

There are two **types of breach of probation**. In any reference to breach of probation it is essential to be aware of which type is under consideration. The two will be dealt with separately, and it will be helpful to social workers if they think in terms of the separate types of breach, rather than the general heading of 'breach of probation'.

The two types of breach are:

• breach of requirement of probation; and
• breach by further offence.

The legislation for breach is set out in sections 232 and 233 of the *Criminal Procedure (Scotland) Act*, 1995.

Breach of requirement of probation

Anything contained in the order to which the probationer should adhere is a requirement of the order and any failure on his part to do so constitutes a breach of requirement. As noted earlier, probation orders contain some standard requirements; over and above that there are wide powers for additional requirements to be included.

Any breach of requirement immediately entails a decision on the part of the supervising officer as to the response. Doing nothing, whether by design or default, is one response, and the probationer will draw his own conclusions about the importance of the breach, and indeed, of the order, from any inaction on the supervisor's part. There are various possibilities intermediate between taking no action and taking the probationer back to court.

Warnings

NOS stipulate that formal warnings should be issued to probationers for failure to comply with the requirements of their orders and that breach proceedings should be initiated in the event of non-compliance following a maximum of two formal warnings; 'all warnings must be put in writing' (NOS Probation section). In practice, practitioners have discretion on when a warning becomes a formal warning, which requires written expression. McIvor and Barry (1998:34) found that 46% of probationers had received at least one formal warning for non-compliance during their orders.

Consultations

Consultation with colleagues and/or a line manager over breach is obviously to be recommended. Some sentencers are prepared to have informal discussions with supervisors, which may be helpful in coming to a decision; for example, sentencers may have a view of the original offence, their purposes in making the order, and may be ready to reconsider this if there has been some good progress in the meantime. At this stage, however, the court has no power to instruct the supervisor on the response to make to the breach; **this is only a consultation**. Formal proceedings in court for breach can only be instituted at the initiative of the supervising officer. Consultation with the procurator fiscal may, also, be helpful where breach proceedings are being considered, in order to discuss the adequacy of the evidence available to the supervisor, and what might constitute best evidence. Fiscals and court-based social workers have also been known to be helpful in drafting the wording of the grounds to include in any formal allegation of breach.

If proceedings for breach are initiated, it is important that the grounds are accurate, and valid, in terms of the requirements of the order. **Action plans are working agreements and not, in themselves, requirements of the order**. The importance of the probationer having understood the original terms of the order to which he agreed in court and of these having been spelled out in 'ordinary language' at the time, is of crucial importance to breach proceedings.

Which court deals with which breach?

The legislation simply refers to the 'appropriate' court without it always being readily apparent which court that is, although there is a definition of 'appropriate' court in section 228(4) of the CP Act, 1995. Briefly, this means the court which is named in an order, or amendment to an order, where the offender resides outwith the jurisdiction of the court making or amending the order. The legislation gives both the appropriate court and the court which originally made the order the power to deal with breaches. All High Court breaches, of whatever kind, must be referred back to the High Court—in effect to the Clerk of Justiciary in Edinburgh, who will consult the appropriate judge and advise accordingly. Otherwise the court which holds the order, whether it be the court which made the order or another court, and by definition a court of similar standing, is empowered to deal with any breach.

The supervisor has the responsibility of safeguarding the authority's responsibilities, and the court of origin, where it differs from the court dealing with the breach, should be advised of the progress of the order and any subsequent breakdown. These exchanges are important to the development of a dialogue with the courts and to the court's confidence in criminal justice practice. It is worth noting that the CP Act, 1995 (s.108) enables prosecutors to appeal against 'too lenient sentences', including supervised release orders, refusal of a non-harassment order, community service orders, decisions to remit to children's hearings and probation orders. The importance of this lies in the expectation that sentencers should not be 'soft' and this may be a consideration in the treatment of breach proceedings.

While English courts may amend Scottish probation orders to take account of individual circumstance, **no English court may terminate a Scottish order**. Scottish courts of the appropriate standing, may terminate English orders. Where the breach is of a nature which calls into question the existence and continuation of the order, the following considerations apply:

- if the matter is urgent (for example, the probationer has vanished without trace, or is considered a danger to the community), and a warrant for his arrest is likely to be required, then action should begin with the holding court; once arrested, any issue of referring to the court of origin can be resolved;
- if the probationer can be cited to appear, but is not co-operating with the order, then the court of origin, and if possible, the sentencer who made the order, should be consulted. In making the order, indications may have been given by the court as to the consequences of any breach. The court can then instruct either that the probationer be brought back directly before it, or that the holding court should deal with it in the first instance.

Where the 'appropriate' court which deals with a breach of requirement is not the court which made the original order, the court of origin should be advised of the outcome, with a brief précis of the order's progress and the background to the breach proceedings. Where a breach by further offence occurs, there is some value in having this dealt with, if possible, by the sentencer who made the order in the first place, particularly if return to court for the breach is likely—in smaller courts this may occur as a matter of course. It is important to note that only the court of origin or the 'appropriate' court can deal with a breach by further offence and not the court which is dealing with the offence itself (unless they are the same).

Possible outcomes

For breaches of requirement the court has powers to:

- **impose a fine** not exceeding level 3 of the standard scale, this being the maximum whether the procedure is solemn or summary, and allow the order to remain in force;
- **make a community service order** in addition to the probation order providing the conditions for making a CSO are satisfied; in this situation section 238(1) of the CP Act, 1995 requires that a community service order should only be made for an offence punishable by imprisonment i.e. as an alternative to custody, so the breach of requirement of probation must be regarded as sufficiently serious to warrant a custodial disposal. Any breach of a probation order calls into question the existence of the order, and it can be argued that this, therefore, is of itself, justification for using a community service order;
- **vary any requirements of the order** (or add new ones), except that:
  a) the order cannot be extended beyond three years from the date it was originally made; and
  b) a requirement for medical treatment cannot be inserted, on the application of the supervisor, after the order has been in force for more than 3 months;
- if the order is varied in any way, the supervisor (technically the chief social work officer) will receive 3 copies of an **amending order** from the court; these set out the new arrangements, have the same status as the original order, and need to be served on the probationer in the same way that the original one was;
- all the above may be taken by the court. Implicit in the legislation is that the court may decide to **take no action,** in which event the disposal is recorded as 'no order'.

If the court wants to let the order continue, these are the only possibilities. Often courts want to give a warning, but if admonition is announced, this is a disposal in its own right, and has the effect of terminating the order; a verbal warning can be given, but the formal device to give effect to it, if the order is to continue, is 'take no action' on the breach. Instances have been known of orders being terminated inadvertently.

If the court feels that the breach of requirement is of such gravity as to call the whole probation order into question, it is possible to **terminate the order** and deal with the original offence as if the order had never been made. All the sentencing possibilities that were open to the court at the time remain open to it now, though it can be the case that events during the order may affect the sentence that is now imposed.

Action by supervising officer

To bring an allegation of breach of requirement before the court, the supervisor (or the chief social work officer or his appointee) needs to lay information that a breach has occurred. The evidence of one witness is sufficient to proceed (section 232(3)). This is a relatively recent development introduced by the *Criminal Justice (Scotland) Act,* 1995 to make the process of breach more straightforward, and one has to assume, to encourage greater use of breach in Scotland. The essential stages include:

Laying information

The onus of proof in any criminal case is that the prosecution must prove its case 'beyond reasonable doubt'. Consultation with the procurator fiscal, especially as to the adequacy of the evidence to support an allegation of breach, is to be recommended. The Thomson Committee on Criminal Procedure (1975) recommended that the procurator fiscal should be responsible in all respects for 'leading' on breach of probation matters, including the prosecution in court, and the administrative arrangements. There is no legal obligation on fiscals to do so, though most do take this responsibility. The supervisor should provide the prosecution evidence and give information to the fiscal for use in court and to present the case. In areas where the fiscal does not take this responsibility, the authority may choose to instruct its legal services section to appear on the supervisor's behalf.

The supervisor will prepare information, which contains the grounds alleging the breach of requirement. This provides the basis of the allegation (for example, 'failed to report') and is the essential starting point of the subsequent proceedings. The fiscal will advise on the nature of evidence, for example, office callers' book, copies of (registered) letters sent, and so on. Another question to be determined is the method of bringing the probationer before the court. There are two possibilities:

i) **Citation:** this is the normal and preferable method, and is used when the probationer has a fixed place of residence. He duly receives a letter signifying that an allegation of breach has been made, and that he must come to court on a specified date and answer to it. If he contests the allegation, the court may need to fix a later date for the 'proof' to take place.

ii) **Warrant:** this is used when the probationer has left without trace. The court authorises his arrest and detention. When arrested (in whatever part of the United Kingdom) he will be brought back to the court in his normal area of residence to be dealt with for the breach. The supervisor must be ready to attend court in person as soon as this happens. Occasionally the period of probation has expired before such a warrant can be executed: in this event the supervisor should discuss the matter with both fiscal and court, as warrants, once issued, are not lightly withdrawn. Indeed, given the present policy on probation being pursued by the government, it seems likely that the breach would still be pursued.

Attendance at Court

The supervising officer is expected to attend the appropriate court (that is, the holding court, or the court of origin, as the case may be) in person, at any hearing of a breach case. If the probationer denies being in breach, the court will generally fix a later date for proof of the breach. The supervising officer will have to attend to:

i) give evidence in support of the allegation in any contested case; in this respect she takes her cue from the leading of the fiscal, but is liable to cross-examination by the defence; where the fiscal has declined to prosecute then either a member of the department's legal services department may appear to lead the presentation of the case, or the Clerk of Court will give such 'lead in' clues as to procedure as may be helpful;

ii) assist the court's disposal of the case ONLY if the allegation is admitted by the probationer or proved against him. Often in breach cases the court simply looks to the supervisor for a lead, but it is important that the supervisor draws attention first to the issue of whether the probationer is admitting the breach, as this can be overlooked.

If the breach is admitted, or proved, it may be that a continuation for reports is advisable before disposal is decided, particularly if the probationer has had to be arrested on warrant. In other situations (for example knowing beforehand that a breach will be admitted) it may be possible for a view to be formed, or a report prepared in advanced.

It is important to give the background to the specific allegation, and to give a reasonably comprehensive account of what transpired during the probation period. It is helpful if at the time of reporting the breach even prior to the information stage, the social worker gives an indication of what might be a suitable disposal in the event of the breach being admitted or proved. The supervisor will continue to have responsibilities to the probationer, as well as to the court, throughout the proceedings. Post-sentence and throughcare considerations will apply in the event of a custodial sentence being imposed (see Chapters 4 and 11).

Breach by further offence

The commission of a further offence during the period of probation is automatically a breach of probation, which has to be brought to the attention of the court (section 233 of the CP Act, 1995). There is no discretion open in this matter. At present this probably means that the court-based social worker will examine the court list of cases to be heard in sufficient time to check it for people currently on probation before the court sits. It may well fall to court-based staff to notify supervisors that a probationer is in further trouble. The use of information technology will soon make this detection process straightforward and it is expected that court's administration will identify and action breaches by further offences as a matter of course.

An offence committed before the person was put on probation may not come before the court until he is already on probation: this does **not** count as a breach by further offence, even if the offence occurred after that in respect of which the order was made. However, a person may come before a court **after** the period of probation is terminated but for an offence committed **during** the probation period: this **does** count as a breach by further offence. Someone who is on probation at the time he commits a further offence faces the prospect, if convicted, of receiving **two** sentences—one for the new offence, and one for the offence in respect of which the order was first made.

Outcomes

Basically there are only two outcomes possible in an instance of breach by further offence. Either the court takes no action in respect of the breach, or it sentences in respect of the original offence. In notifying the facts of a breach by further offence, the supervisor will include, along with any notification, their professional view, or the view of the court which dealt with the new offence, if known, as to the future of the probation order.

Action of supervising officer

Once it has been confirmed, either by the supervisor, or by the court, that a breach has occurred, and that the person should be brought before the court for breach by further offence, the essentials of procedure are as follows:

- The supervisor should bring the matter to the attention of the procurator fiscal. He, in turn, will satisfy himself that the commission of the further offence can be proven by reference to court records, which he may need to obtain for the purpose.
- The supervisor will co-operate with the Clerk of Court to put in motion the issue of a citation or warrant, as the case may be, to bring the probationer back before the court.
- The procedure in court is much as before; the allegation needs to be put to the probationer, and, if necessary, proved. If it is known in advance that the allegation is to be admitted (as is most likely) then this is one of the few instances in which preparation of a pre-trial-type report is in order (see Chapter 5). The report will normally focus specifically on the questions of progress during probation, the fresh offence, and the issue of examining possible disposals.

If the person is sentenced for the original offence, the order is terminated. If the decision is to sentence only for the new offence then the person is still on probation, and supervision resumes instantly assuming the disposal for the new offence is compatible with probation (e.g. admonition, fine etc.).

The procedure is less complex where a custodial disposal is imposed in relation to the new offence, by a court which is not the 'appropriate' court, for a breach of probation. In practical terms this terminates the order. The situation is one in which the procedure simply represents an administrative tidy up, necessary only because the court dealing with the new offence did not have power to deal with the original offence on which the order was made. In this situation, the presence of the probationer in court is not required, and the court is simply invited to discharge the order in the light of the new circumstances.

In the recent past social workers seemed reluctant to instigate breach proceedings. McIvor and Barry (1998:34) found the 32% of orders had been breached and were re-sentenced for the original offence. Of these, 60% received a custodial sentence. Only in 25% of breaches was the order continued. Clearly the consequences of breach can be severe for the offender.

Breaches involving courts in England and Wales

An essential principle in Scotland is that the 'appropriate' court has all the powers and responsibilities to deal with breaches of that order, whether they are breaches of requirement or breaches by further offence. The system in England and Wales, however, makes a much greater play of distinctions both between different levels of court, and between different areas. For present purposes there are two levels of court in England and Wales—Crown Courts, and Magistrates' Courts—and the basic system is that a Magistrates' Court for the probationer's place of residence supervises on behalf of the court of origin, **whatever its level**. All Crown Court orders are held by local Magistrates' Courts, whose powers in relation to them are limited in some respects. However, the English system contains powers to facilitate an easy committal from one level to the other.

A probation order made in Scotland on a person who resides, or goes to reside, in England or Wales will be supervised (held) by a Magistrates' Court for the area, whatever the level of court making the order in Scotland. Court areas in England and Wales are known as Petty Sessional Divisions, and the supervising probation officer will be an officer assigned to that Petty Sessional Division. The National Association of Probation Officers publishes a directory annually of all the Divisions, and the probation offices within their area. The larger areas have officers specially designated for Court Liaison purposes.

The supervising Magistrates' Court has powers only to vary the requirements of the order (e.g. place of residence). **It has no power to deal with any breach**. This must be sent back to the court of origin. For example, in an order made in Glasgow, transferred to Perth, and then transferred to St. Albans, it would be appropriate for the supervisor to liaise with the last point of contact in Scotland, i.e. Perth, to establish the correct location of the court to deal with this matter. There can be some urgency, if the subject is remanded in custody in England. Section 234 of the 1995 Act sets out the arrangements for probation orders on people residing in England and Wales.

Unlike Scotland, probation has the legal status of a sentence in England and Wales which complicates the powers available within the respective jurisdictions. Where an order has been transferred from a court in England and Wales, the court in Scotland may not exercise any power under sections 232(2(b)), 233 or para. 1 of Schedule 6 of the CP Act,1995, i.e. any power to sentence the offender for the offence for which the order was originally made (either failure to comply with a requirement of the order or for the commission of a further offence) or to discharge the order. If the offender fails to comply with such an order or the court in Scotland is of the opinion that it is in the interest of justice that the order should be revoked under paras. 7 or 8 of Schedule 2 of the *Criminal Justice Act,* 1991, then the court in Scotland may require the offender to appear before the court which made the order. A Scottish court supervising an order made in England or Wales CAN discharge that order, either on the grounds of good progress, or in the event of the probationer receiving a substantial custodial disposal in respect of some new offence.

TRANSFER, VARIATION AND DISCHARGE OF PROBATION ORDERS

Amendments and discharge of probation orders are dealt with by section 231(1) of the 1995 Act, detailed in Schedule 6 of the Act.

Transfer of probation orders

Transfers of probation orders are, or become, necessary in two main sets of circumstances:

- *Instant transfer*: when people offend away from their normal area of residence and are put on probation by a court which does not have jurisdiction in the area where they live, then the order is made out directly to the court for the person's place of residence. Such an instant transfer is also necessary when a person, though appearing before a court which does have jurisdiction in his normal place of residence includes in the order a condition that he reside in some other area (for example, a probation hostel outwith the area of the court's jurisdiction).
- *During the Order*: this becomes necessary if the probationer takes up residence in a place outwith the jurisdiction of the court which holds the order. Such a move usually arises as a result of a change in the domestic circumstances of the probationer, but could result, for example, from an application made by the supervisor that the probationer should be resident in a hostel in a different area outwith the court's geographical jurisdiction.

Instant transfer

The formalities of transfer in such an event are as follows:

- *Probationer resident or to be resident in Scotland*: The Clerk of the Court which makes the order, or of the appropriate (holding) court, will require the name of the local authority area in which the probationer lives, or is to live, in order to 'cause copies of the probation order to be given to the officer of the local authority who is to supervise the probationer and to the person in charge of any institution or place in which the probationer is required to reside under the probation order'. The Clerk is also responsible to 'cause' a copy of the order to be given to the probationer or 'sent to him by registered post or by the recorded delivery service'—delivery by the Post Office will be seen as evidence of receipt. The assumption would seem to be that orders are served directly on probationers but in exceptional circumstances they may be sent by post. Should the postal service become common practice it is important that practitioners make suitable arrangements to serve the order.
- *Probationer resident or to be resident in England or Wales*: The court will require the name of the appropriate Petty Sessional Division—that is the area of jurisdiction of the Magistrates' Court—and will send copies of the order to the Clerk, to the Justices for that Division, and to the Chief Probation Officer for that area. The order will require that the probationer will be 'under the supervision of a probation officer appointed or assigned' to that Division. The Magistrates' Court supervises on behalf of the Scottish Court irrespective of the level of court in which the order was made.

Transfer during the currency of the order

A transfer of probation becomes necessary if the probationer moves residence during the currency of the order, or if application is made to vary the order so that he is required to live elsewhere. **In this instance the responsibility falls on**

the supervising officer to initiate the administrative proceedings to put the transfer into effect. As a matter of good professional practice, the supervisor should first contact the relevant social worker (in Scotland) or probation office (in England) in the new area, to ascertain:

- that the probationer is, or will be, resident at the new address;
- that arrangements can be made for his supervision;
- that all the requirements currently in the order can be complied with in the new area; if they cannot, a variation of the order to remove what cannot be enforced or supervised will first be necessary (see below).

Probationer moving within Scotland

The supervisor must apply to the court which holds the order (i.e. the local one) for a transfer to a new area within Scotland, providing the name both of the court and of the local authority area to which transfer is to be made. (Sometimes the move may be within the one local authority area, but to a different court area). The probationer has discharged his responsibilities by notifying the change of address, and is not involved in any proceedings. The Clerk of Court in the new area will issue an **amending order**. Four copies of the order 'together with such documents and information relating to the case' are sent by the Clerk of Court to the clerk of the sheriff or district court (as the case may be) in the probationer's area of residence, one copy to the local authority, and two copies to the supervising officer, 'one of which the supervision officer shall give to the probationer'. The arrival of new or amended documentation provides an opportunity for the new supervisor to review and/or re-establish the working agreement for probation supervision. In the instance of orders made by the High Court, that court holds all its own orders, and the Clerk of Justiciary is required to send to the chief social work officer, 'three copies of the amending order together with such documents and information relating to the case as is likely to be of assistance to the chief social work officer'. The chief social work officer, in turn, shall send two copies to the officer supervising the probationer, 'one of which the supervising officer shall give to the probationer'.

Probationers moving to England or Wales

The supervisor applies, as above, to the court which holds the order, but only needs the name of the Petty Sessional Division for the new area. The order will be supervised by the Magistrates Court for the new area, and will require the probationer to be under the supervision of a probation officer 'appointed or assigned' to that division.

Transfer to England and Wales of probationers aged under 18

The *Criminal Justice Act*, 1991 introduced Youth Courts which deal with offenders aged over 16 but under 18. The provisions came into force in October, 1992. Community-based penalties can be imposed by these courts on offenders aged 16 and 17, including probation, and community service. Previously there were problems transferring probation orders made in Scotland in relation to 16-year-olds to England and Wales, in that, until the 1991 Act, juvenile courts had jurisdiction in relation to 16-year-olds, and could not make probation or community service orders in respect of them. The arrangements for transfer from Scotland to England are set out in Schedule 3 of the *Criminal Justice Act*, 1991 Part II, and sections 228(2)(b) and 234 of the *Criminal Procedure (Scotland) Act*, 1995 . The legislation also incorporates arrangements for the transfer of probation orders which include requirements for unpaid work, but indicates that the maximum number of orders permitted in this circumstance is 100 hours. Part I of the same Schedule sets out arrangements for courts in England and Wales to make probation orders on people resident or to be resident in Scotland. The appropriate court (for purposes of supervising the order) is defined as being a court of summary jurisdiction, in practice the sheriff summary court, even if the offender is convicted on indictment, though it must be a sheriff court in this latter circumstance.

In the rare circumstances of a person under 16 years of age being put on probation by a court in Scotland (see Chapter 6), and (even rarer) being, or intending to be resident, in England or Wales, the contact will need to be with an appropriate court, and the issue of this latter court not having powers to make probation orders remains. Schedule 5 of the *Children and Young Persons Act*, 1969, contains provisions which allow for the (English or Welsh) Youth Court to accept the situation and make a supervision order under the Act in place of the Scottish probation order.

Variations of probation orders

A variation of probation refers to a change in one of the substantive requirements in the order, as opposed to the essentially administrative nature of transfers. A variation represents a change in the content of the order, and its importance approximates the making of the order in the first place. Accordingly, the probationer must be present in court and agree to the proposed changes of requirement and content. Variations are ordered by the court which holds the order, and it is, therefore, necessary to make arrangements with the Clerk of Court for the probationer to be formally cited to appear. It is worth noting that orders made in the High Court have to go back there for a variation to be made, if such is required or proposed. Variations can be ordered in either of two situations:

- in proceedings for breach of requirement (above); or
- on the application of the supervisor; this requires the preparation of a formal application and submission of this to the court so that the Clerk of Court can arrange a hearing and cite the probationer to attend.

The following variations are possible:

Cancelling any of the requirements in the original order. In this instance the presence of the probationer is NOT necessary, as his consent is assumed. A variation to cancel a requirement is necessary where, for example, there has been successful conclusion to a requirement of treatment for a mental condition; or good progress during a period of residence in a probation hostel. A variation to cancel can sometimes be necessary as a preliminary to the transfer of an order, if some aspect of the contents of the order cannot be complied with in the new area.

Inserting any requirement, additional to, or in substitution for, an existing requirement. Any such additional requirement must have been legally possible at the time the order was originally made. It should be noted that a requirement for treatment for a mental condition can only be inserted within three months of the making of the order. The initiative for the inclusion of additional requirements rests mainly with the supervisor. The following provisos apply to variations of probation:

- no variation shall reduce the period of probation;
- no variation shall extend the period of probation beyond three years from the date of the original order;
- the same rules apply to the insertion of requirements for:
  —hostel residence
  —treatment for a mental condition
  —unpaid work

as would have applied at the time the order was made.

Once a variation has been ordered by the court, copies of orders, also known as **amending orders**, will be issued by the Clerk of Court. These need to be served on the probationer, signed and countersigned as if the order were newly made. Copies of the amending order will also be required by a hospital, hostel, or placement agency if the new requirement inserted relates to them.

DISCHARGE OF PROBATION

Early discharge is integrally part of the purpose of probation, both in general terms, and in any particular case. The possibilities of discharge seem to be relatively underused. Occasionally discharge becomes necessary for purely administrative reasons, and the exercise is one merely of tidying up, in situations where

- The probationer is sentenced to a substantial period of custody for a fresh offence committed whilst on probation, and the court imposing the custodial sentence cannot deal with the original offence for which the order was made. The supervisor simply applies to the court which holds the order. The presence of the probationer in court is not required.
- A court dealing with a further offence, though competent to deal with the original offence, neglects to do so, often through administrative oversight, and a similar situation to the above arises.
- A court dealing with a further offence makes a new probation order in respect of that offence, but, again through oversight, neglects to announce a decision about the offence for which the original order was made; again it is necessary for the supervisor to tidy up the completion of the first order.

Of more significance is the possibility of discharging the order in advance of the due date, on the grounds of good progress. The significance of this for the probationer is immediate: a discharge of the order is equivalent to successful completion, and he escapes both any possibility of another penalty for the original offence, and is no longer bound by the requirements and restrictions of probation.

There is no legal bar to applications at any stage in an order. NOS, however, suggests that at 'the halfway point in the probation order...supervisors should consider, in the light of the progress made, whether there is scope to make use of Schedule 6 of the *Criminal Procedure (Scotland) Act*, 1995 which provides for the discharge...of probation orders.' NOS also suggest some criteria for discharge; that 'an application for the early discharge of an order on the grounds of good progress is appropriate where the offender has not re-offended during the currency of the order, has successfully completed the tasks associated with the Action Plan, and when no further work on issues associated with offending behaviour is considered necessary...it should also indicate to the court the frequency of contact which will be maintained during the final phase of the order if an application for early discharge is not accepted'.

A discharge of probation may be initiated in either of two ways. The authority lies in paragraph 1 of Schedule 6 of the *Criminal Procedure (Scotland) Act, 1995*.

- The probationer may apply to the court. This is rare, and there is some reason for thinking that probationers are not systematically informed of their rights to make such an application. They can be given the information without any offer being implied or promised. The probationer is entitled to receive the supervisor's help in making such an application, even if she intends opposing it. She receives a citation to attend court and answer the probationer's application. The court has power to discharge an order, even in the face of opposition from the supervisor.
- The supervisor may apply to the court. Before doing so, an independent check with the police and/or the procurator fiscal may be in order to ensure that no outstanding matters embarrass the application for early discharge. In this event the probationer's presence is NOT necessary. If the application is granted, copies of an order discharging the order need to be served on the probationer. Then the matter is complete.

Satisfactory completion

A final report must be submitted for the appropriate court and sent to the Clerk of Court holding the order, no later than two weeks from the date the order is terminated. The report should summarise the progress made on completing the action plan and should include any relevant information about the offender's conduct during the course of the order. A copy of this report should provide important feedback to the original SER author.

It is important that at the completion of the order the offender is reminded of the legal implications of having been on an order with respect to the *Rehabilitation of Offenders Act*, 1974.

If authorities are serious about measuring effectiveness, in the absence of a national data base, this is also an opportunity to seek the offender's permission to make contact with him in 6, 12 and 24 months to gather information, in confidence, on his progress.

It is to be hoped that in the, not too distant future, more systematic follow-up work will be carried out to identify patterns and trends in outcomes for different kinds of offenders and different kinds of programmes. It is essential for authorities to generate follow-up data, particularly conviction rates, for a minimum of two years, now a standard measure in most research.

Chapter 9

Work and Service by Order of the Court

Policy; community service orders; unpaid work as a requirement of probation orders; amendments.

PURPOSE AND POLICY

The power of courts to order offenders to undertake unpaid work or service for the benefit of the community had its origins in concerns of the mid 1960s with the numbers of people (then) in prison, and the idea was first proposed by the Report of the Advisory Council on the Treatment of Offenders, 1970 (the Wootton Report). The prime purpose for its introduction was that it should constitute an alternative to a short prison sentence. The *Community Service by Offenders (Scotland) Act*, 1978, now consolidated in the *Criminal Procedure (Scotland) Act*, 1995 was enacted to enable courts to make a **community service order** (CSO) requiring people to perform a specific number of hours of unpaid service for the benefit of the community.

Prior to the 1978 Act, The Scottish Office funded four regional social work departments to introduce experimental schemes for community service; these were established from 1976 onwards. As no legislation was available for the purpose at the time, the courts in Scotland ordered unpaid work as **a requirement inserted in a probation order**. When the *Community Service by Offenders (Scotland) Act*, 1978 was introduced it provided BOTH for a separate community service order AND for unpaid work as a requirement in a probation order.

Differing views on the merits of the two approaches emerged. There seemed no clear philosophy behind the 1978 Act's inclusion of both methods; rather it may have simply been a reflection of existing practice. There was some disquiet among members of the judiciary about the inclusion of community service in a probation order, when it was clear that the community service order would feature as a penalty in its own right; as a result the Act emerged from parliamentary debate with both a community service order and a requirement for unpaid work in probation.

The Wootton Report had discussed both possibilities, and thought that there were some advantages in community service being a requirement of a probation order. However, the view which prevailed was that there were more attractions in having community service as an order in its own right. In practical terms there seems to be little differentiation in seeking to give effect to the legal distinction between community service in the separate order, and unpaid work as part of probation. Statistical data suggested that only a small proportion of work ordered by courts was under the aegis of a probation order. Nonetheless the legal distinction exists and has been maintained.

The original intention was to use CSO as an alternative to custody; however, research demonstrated that this was not the case in practice. Research (McIvor, 1992) examining the nature of practice and its outcomes suggested that, though reasonably popular as a disposal, that the use of community service was having limited impact on custody.

It is also worth noting that the community service initiative was the first example of ring-fenced money from central government provided to ensure that community-based measures for offenders were provided by social work departments. The introduction of community service and unpaid work was the model on which the 100% central funding for criminal justice social work was based and was a harbinger of things to come, in ways that could not have been anticipated at the time.

Community service is now available across the whole of Scotland. Since 1989 community service orders have grown from 4,135 to 5,506 in 1995. Since there has been no corresponding decline in custody it has to be questioned how effective it has been **as an alternative to custody**. National Objectives and Standards (NOS) dealing with community service and unpaid work as a requirement of probation were published in 1989 by the Secretary of State. These were revised and up-dated in 1996.

A central concern of the Wootton Committee was that community service/unpaid work should be an alternative to a prison sentence. However, at the outset, the legislation did not require that the courts impose a prison sentence, and then substitute some order for work or service. The 1978 Act allowed courts to make a community service order 'instead of any other way of dealing with him' (section 1) leaving a vast area of discretion in the courts' interpretation of circumstances in which community service or unpaid work is an appropriate disposal.

New legislative provision attempted to prevent the use of community service for a range of petty offenders, and to reserve this community-based disposal for those at serious risk of a custody. Legislation was necessary, in part, because community service had become, in practice, the only community-based disposal involving social work departments, which seemed to have the confidence of the courts. (see Statistical Bulletins 1980-1997). Change came in the form of the *Law Reform (Miscellaneous Provisions) (Scotland) Act,* 1990, which sought to strengthen the original policy intention by amending section 1 of the 1978 Act, and required that a community service order be made **as an alternative to a term of imprisonment or detention** (section 62(3)).

Section 238 of the CP Act, 1995 now indicates that community service must be used for a person **'convicted of an offence punishable by imprisonment'** and **'the court may, instead of imposing on him a sentence of, or including, imprisonment or any other form of detention, make an order'**. Section 229 (4) which deals with probation with a requirement for unpaid work, uses the former phrase, 'convicted of an offence punishable by imprisonment' but not the latter, although this would seem to be implicit. Thus the legislation provides two legal alternatives to custody, one the disposal of community service and the other an equally high tariff disposal, a probation order with a requirement for unpaid work used 'instead of sentencing'.

The interpretation by a court of what circumstances justify a prison sentence to which community service might be the alternative is still an area of considerable discretion, flexibility, and variation. There is evidence to suggest that there are still problems in trying to ensure that community service is used, in practice, in the way the legislation intends. Sheriffs in Scotland have wide-ranging powers to use custody for most crimes, powers that seem well used in relation to persistent, rather than necessarily serious, offenders, many receiving short periods of custody. There is little evidence to suggest that community service, though growing in use, is having any real impact on the short-term custody figures and it is still an open question whether those receiving community service would indeed have been facing custody.

Few people are likely to appeal against the imposition of community service, so whether or not a custodial sentence was in prospect can seldom be tested. However provisions under the CP Act, 1995 for the High Court to provide sentencing guidelines in appeals (s.197 of the CP Act, 1995) may, in time, clarify the nature and intention of the legislation. In the meantime, it may simply be the case that all the CP Act 1995 does is to underline a policy intention on the part of the legislators. In one case (Giusti v. Walkinshaw, 1996, S.C.C.R. 61) the decision was clear that if a judge discounts imprisonment as a sentence, then a CSO should also be discounted; however, in another, (McD v. Orr, 1994, S.C.C.R. 645) the High Court held that although imprisonment was not an appropriate sentence, a CSO could still be made.

Whatever else, the penal system's track record is far from impressive and research reviews, particularly from abroad (Andrew's *et al* 1990, Lipsey 1991) suggests that community-based programmes are significantly better in terms of reconviction in the medium term. When one considers the relative costs of prison at around £2000, and CSO at £95 **per month** (1997 figures), it becomes increasingly difficult to understand the court's reluctance to use community-based options as a serious alternative to custody.

Government's policy initiative has not been fully thought through (see Chapter 1). On the one hand there is an attempt to reduce the prison population by seeking to persuade courts that community-based measures are preferable as the normal penalty, except for the most serious matters which require long sentences; legislative provisions specify that some measures (community service orders and probation with a requirement of unpaid work) should ONLY be used as an alternative to a custodial sentence. On the other hand, it is understandable that government are reluctant to be seen to interfere too much with the sentencing process and the independence of the Scottish judiciary. The judiciary themselves need to comment on the policy objectives set by government for the provision of community disposals and alternatives to custody and why they seem to be have limited impact on custody figures. Alternatively government may require to limit the availability of custody to the courts.

In the past there was some frustration on the part of courts that schemes for community service were frequently over-subscribed. This has not been the case for many years and there is need for greater specification on the use of CSOs and requirements for unpaid work.

Community service is popular with sentencers and seems to be understood by the wider public. It seems an attractive penalty, and has ingredients within it which appeal to a variety of sentencing considerations (retribution, reparation, rehabilitation, and basic humanity).

NOS identify the aim as 'to provide Scottish criminal courts with a credible community-based penalty by requiring those found guilty of imprisonable offences and who would otherwise have received a sentence of imprisonment or detention to undertake unpaid work for a specified number of hours for the community'. Any benefits to the individual person that may result from the experience of giving service, or sense of satisfaction from the task undertaken, are secondary considerations as far as sentencing is concerned. In relation to requirements for unpaid work within probation orders, NOS indicates that when an additional condition is being considered the SER author should be satisfied that

- the offender can benefit from the supervision, assistance and control which a probation order offers and is therefore suitable for probation;
- the offender is at serious risk of a custodial sentence;
- the offender is suitable for community service and a work placement is available;
- neither probation without a requirement to undertake unpaid work nor a community service order alone is likely to be acceptable to the court, given the seriousness of the offence and the circumstances surrounding it.

THE COMMUNITY SERVICE ORDER

Community Service Orders are made in Scotland under 238 of *Criminal Procedure (Scotland) Act,* 1995. They can be made on any person 'of or over 16 years of age convicted of an offence punishable by imprisonment, other than an offence for which the penalty is fixed by law' and 'instead of imposing on him a sentence of, or including imprisonment or any other form of detention, make an order'.

The order must specify the number of hours which the person has to perform. This number may not be less than 80, and may not exceed 240 in summary (300 in cases heard on solemn procedure). The hours were increased in 1996 as part of an emphasis on the 'demanding' nature of CSO by the previous government (Circular SWSG 15/96). The hours must be completed within 12 months. The order remains in force until the hours have been completed, or the order revoked (see below for the circumstances in which this may happen). The Act makes provision for an order to be made by a district or a sheriff court but few district courts have access to a scheme reflecting the intention of reserving CSOs for serious offenders.

A number of provisos apply to the making of orders under section 238:

- the person must consent to the making of the order;

- the court must have been notified by the Secretary of State that a scheme exists in the area in which the person resides or is to reside;
- the court must have considered a report 'by an officer of a local authority' about the person and his circumstances, together with an assessment as to his suitability for community service;
- **that it must be an alternative to a term of imprisonment or detention**.

Little guidance is provided within NOS as to who is considered 'suitable' for CSO. The person will receive a copy of the order, which contains a number of detailed requirements to be adhered to. The central one is to perform the specified number of hours of service at such times as the officer may instruct. Others requirements derive from this, and have to do with the mechanics of making arrangements for the service to be performed (s.239 of the CP Act, 1995). They are:

- to report to the local authority officer appointed for community service purposes;
- to notify without delay of any change of address or in the time, if any, at which he usually works.

It is worth remembering that, at the same time as making a community service order, a court may also order:

- the person to find caution;
- the person to pay compensation to a victim;
- any period of disqualification appropriate to the offence;
- any order of forfeiture of any article featured in the offence.

The order does not contain any generalised commands to 'be of good behaviour' or 'to conform to the directions of the supervising officer'. Advice may be given and sought informally, but only non-acceptance of the specific legal requirements can be a ground for breach. All of this is different in the case of unpaid work as a requirement of a probation order, dealt with below.

An order made under section 238 of the *Criminal Procedure (Scotland) Act,* 1995 is a conviction. The normal rehabilitative period (before it becomes spent) is five years. A person performing community service discharges his responsibilities to the court immediately the number of hours specified is satisfactorily completed within the 12-month period.

Breach of a community rervice order (section 238 order)

A person who commits a further offence while subject to a community service order is not in **breach of that order per se**, though it may be that the sentence he receives for that further offence may require other action to be taken in respect of the community service order (see aggravated offences below).

The only breach proceedings that can arise relate to a breach of requirement of the order (section 239(4) of the CP Act, 1995). A breach of requirement may be constituted by:

- a failure to perform the work as instructed;
- a failure to complete the number of hours within the 12-month period;
- a failure to report or to perform the work satisfactorily;
- a failure to report any change of address, employment or employment circumstances.

NOS set out a framework of discipline to be applied consistently in the interests of justice. Disciplinary procedures are liable when the offender fails to comply with the following requirements without reasonable excuse:

- failure to attend;
- lack of punctuality;
- failure to report as required by the community service officer;
- failure to notify a change of address without delay;
- failure to notify a change in employment circumstances without delay;
- failure to perform work to a satisfactory standard (para 77).

When absence from work is considered unacceptable, the guidance requires the officer to set a series of formal warnings in motion and limits discretion to two such absences. On a third, the guidance requires that breach proceedings are instituted and the order suspended. As with other breaches of requirement, on the third failure the guidance requires the institution of breach proceedings and suspension of the order.

Judgements on satisfactory work performance standards are inevitably subjective. NOS emphasises that the standards must be set at an attainable level and that the context of the placement agency is important. Some guidance is offered to assist in applying consistent criteria:

- **quality of performance**—the work done and the manner in which it is done conforms to the standards laid down by the placement agency;
- **work effort**—offenders are expected to apply themselves energetically to the demands of the work required of them by the placement agency;
- **behaviour and attitudes**—offenders are expected to conduct themselves in such a way as to demonstrate respect for the rights of others and willingness to co-operate with others in the placement agency.

It is the supervisor's responsibility to decide whether a breach has occurred and whether return to court is the appropriate response to that breach. Only if the supervisor initiates proceedings for breach can the person be brought back to court.

Once a decision has been taken to bring the person back before the court for an alleged breach, the procedure follows the pattern of that for breach of **requirement** of probation (see Chapter 7). It should be noted, however that the term 'appropriate' court defined in s.245(5) differs in meaning from that in a probation order (s.228(4)). When the High Court makes the order, it is the appropriate court, otherwise it is the court which has jurisdiction over the place where the order is carried out.

Information has to be laid and the court arranges for the person to appear before it and answer the allegation. One witness alone can represent an adequate standard of evidence of proof of breach of requirement, although corroborated evidence is always to be desired. Previous requirements for evidence had occasionally deterred some agencies from providing placements, but the *Law Reform (Miscellaneous Provisions) (Scotland) Act,* 1990 Act clarified that the local authority officer can be the main provider of evidence about instructions and failure to keep them, rather than agency personnel having to take time out to give evidence in court. Even so, the fullest corroborative evidence available, in the best traditions of Scots law, are required, since the person's liberty may be at issue.

Circular DSW 2/1989 insists that people on community service need to produce a medical certificate if they cannot undertake their work or service due to sickness. Self certification is not acceptable. There are provisions for the authority to refund the person the cost of the doctor's fee, though the circular is silent on any provision about making a loan to those whose income may preclude them first having to paying the fee from their own pocket. Authority staff are required to retain the certificates in the event of this being a contested matter in any breach proceedings. The Circular also gives very specific guidance on how many unacceptable absences can be allowed before breach proceedings are initiated. If the allegation of breach is admitted or proved, the court can do one of four things:

- impose any penalty in respect of the original offence that it might have done at the time had it not made a community service order; in view of the 1990 Act's insistence that a community service order should only be made as an alternative to a custodial sentence, logic suggests that the penalty for breach should be a custodial sentence. However, in practice it seems that the law is to be interpreted more flexibly, and that courts need not impose a custodial sentence for a breach of requirement;
- impose a fine not exceeding level 3 and let the order continue; again the imposition of a fine for serious non-compliance demonstrates the ambiguity of the legislation with regard to the imposition of order only as an alternative to custody;
- vary the number of hours, **except** that the overall total ordered must not exceed the maximum allowed, and let the order continue;
- take no action, and let the order continue.

For community service to have credibility both with the courts and the community, it is important to apply rigorous standards. However the requirement of NOS to suspend orders can create inequalities and difficulties for the offender, when one option within the breach procedures is continuation and/or variation of the order; the time gap between suspension and the breach being heard is important. The time gaps vary greatly between courts and, in some instances, it can be three months before a breach is heard, making the likelihood of continuing the placement thereafter limited. It is important that standards are equally applied to court administration to ensure some equity in this matter or it will continue to result in slippage of social work standards, whereby only those that are judged unlikely ever to complete the order or those that are 'not wanted' will be breached.

UNPAID WORK AS A REQUIREMENT OF PROBATION

Community service was first used in Scotland as a requirement of a probation order, prior to the enactment of the *Community Service by Offenders (Scotland) Act*, 1978. The legislation for probation at the time, the *Criminal Procedure (Scotland) Act*, 1975 contained provisions allowing courts to include extra requirements in a probation order relevant to the purpose of probation; and it was under this heading that requirements for community service were first made. There was unease, initially, at the strategy of introducing something as demanding as community service under a rarely used part of probation legislation, particularly as the measure was considered quite different, philosophically, from the prevailing concept of probation.

Section 7 of the 1978 Act introduced specific legislation for unpaid work as a requirement of probation. Section 229(4) the *Criminal Procedure (Scotland) Act*, 1995, now deals with the main issues relevant to probation and unpaid work. As noted above there remains some ambiguity in the status of this order. The legislation indicates that it should be used only for people 'convicted of an offence punishable by imprisonment' but does not specify, as with a CSO, that the alternative for the offender is custody. This, however, would seem to be implied. NOS supports this contention, indicating that this provision should only be available for those at serious risk of a custodial sentence, **and** where the offender can benefit from the probation component.

In both cases, section 238 orders and section 229(4) orders, the social work authority will arrange or provide placements. No formal differentiation is made in the way work is organised between the two orders, though it could be a matter of debate as to whether the various philosophical considerations surrounding the two orders should lead to some differentiation.

The person subject to a community service order has no responsibilities under the order, other than to perform the work satisfactorily within the 12-month period. However, the person who is subject to a probation order with a requirement of unpaid work is subject to all the other obligations and requirements of a probation order since unpaid work is but one component of a larger order (see Chapter 8).

The *Criminal Justice Act*, 1991, introduced arrangements for probation orders made in Scotland, which include a requirement for unpaid work, to be transferred to England and Wales if the offender is, or is to be, resident, there. The arrangements are set out in Schedule 3 to the 1991 Act, Part II; these provide that the number of hours acceptable in England and Wales shall not exceed 100 hours (see above). These arrangements came into effect in October, 1992.

Breaches of requirements to perform unpaid (probation orders)

A person who is subject to a probation order with a requirement of unpaid work and who commits a further offence is in breach of the basic probation order. The situation is the same for any person on probation who commits a further offence; the legal position on breach of probation by **further offence** is dealt with in Chapter 8. A person who fails to carry out the unpaid work, or fails to complete it within 12 months, or to perform it satisfactorily, is in **breach of requirement** of probation. NOS requirements are the same for unpaid work as a requirement of probation as they are for CSO in relation to sickness certificates, and number of unacceptable absences prior to breach proceeding etc.

Community Service Orders made as a result of Breach of Requirement of Probation

If there is confusion over the reasoning behind having two methods of ordering service/work, it could be argued that the 1978 Act compounded the situation by making provision for a (separate) community service order as a possible penalty for a breach of requirement of probation, without prejudicing the continuation of the basic probation order, now s.232(2) of the CP Act, 1995. Before the 1978 Act there were limited possibilities available in the event of a person being brought back to court for breach of a probation requirement, whilst still leaving the order in force. Anything other than a small fine tended to lead to the termination of the order.

It is possible for a court in dealing with this breach, as with any breach of requirement of probation (s.232(2)):

- **either** to vary the probation order by including a requirement for unpaid work and thus allowing both for the probation order to continue in force and for a substantial period of work/service to be performed;
- **or** to make a community service order, as an alternative to custody for the breach, though this would terminate the probation order.

Section 232(2)(d) also allows the court, in the event of dealing with a breach of requirement of probation, including a situation in which the requirement breached might be one to perform unpaid work, to make a community service order, **and** leave the original probation order in force, thus maintaining all the other requirements for, and purposes of, that order. The outcome, in theory, could be two entirely separate orders, a community service order and a probation order, running in tandem, **except** that the one (the community service order) has been made in respect of a breach of requirement of the other (the probation order).

This is likely to be a very rare occurrence. Supervisors considering initiating breach proceedings in respect of a section 229(4) order are unlikely to seek such an outcome and, since a community service order should only be made 'for an offence punishable by imprisonment', the breach of requirement of probation in respect of which any community service order was made, would have to be very serious.

The only grounds for initiating breach proceedings in a community service order are for breach of requirement of the order (i.e. failing to perform the work, or to perform it satisfactorily, or within the 12-month period), whereas in a section 229(4) order, a further offence constitutes an automatic breach of the probation order. If the breach is admitted or proved, the court can impose a fine, vary the (rest of the probation) order in some other way, or take no action, as above. If the court decides to terminate the order and deal with the original offence, then the 'original' offence, in this context, is the breach of requirement of probation.

Dealing with breach by aggravated offence

The *Criminal Justice (Scotland) Act,* 1995 section 40, now sections 233(3) and (4) and 241(1) and (2) of the *Criminal Procedures (Scotland) Act,* 1995, introduced a radically new concept into proceedings for breach, in respect of section 229(4) and section 238 orders respectively.

Where the subject, 'during the period when the community service order was in force **or within three months following the expiry of that order'** is convicted of an offence 'in any place where unpaid work under the order was being or had previously been performed', the Act empowers the court, where the fact is libelled or specified, to '**have regard to the fact** that the offence was committed in those circumstances'. In other words if they commit an offence in any place where the work was performed up to three months after the end of the requirement, which could be beyond the expiry date of the probation order, this will be treated as an aggravation for the purposes of sentence. The facts have to be libelled or specified. Any reference to community service would imply previous convictions and may contravene sections 101(1) and 166(3) of the CP Act, 1995 (that previous convictions are not normally made known to the court). It would seem that for a court to have regard to the accused's behaviour as a statutory aggravation, the Crown will have to be circumspect in drafting the charge or place the single charge on a separate indictment or complaint if there are several charges (Shiels and Bradley, 1996:236)

NOS (CS section) stress the importance for supervisors of making sure that people subject to either section 238 or section 229(4) orders are well informed about these provisions, since clearly these matters will be given serious weight by sentencers.

Terms of service/work and administrative arrangements

The CP Act, 1995 sets out details governing the actual performance of the service/ work, and these apply both to section 238 orders and to section 229(4) orders.

The court has to concern itself with the following details:

- the person must consent to the making of the order/requirement;
- the number of hours must be specified (80 to 240; 300 in solemn procedure);
- that the person is 'suitable' to undertake the service/work;
- that a report as to the person's suitability has been obtained;
- that opportunities for work/service are available;
- that a scheme/arrangements exist in the area where the person resides or is to reside that are approved by the Secretary of State.

NOS identifies four sets of circumstances in which an assessment of suitability may be provided to the court where:

- the social worker preparing the SER initiates an assessment for suitability;

- the court requests both an SER and an assessment for suitability;
- the court requests an assessment for suitability having received an SER;
- the court requests only an assessment for suitability.

A copy of the order for work/service should be given by the Clerk of the Court to the offender on the day of the imposition or alternatively sent by recorded delivery to the last known address. A copy of the order is also sent to the chief social work officer.

NOS stress that all offenders should be seen by the community service officer within one week of the date of disposal and that the offender should sign and date two copies of the order to the effect that he understands what is entailed. It is the responsibility of the officer to explain to the offender, in detail, the nature of the order and to check that he understands his obligations and rights. Work should normally begin within two weeks and not later than three weeks from the date of disposal.

It is important to note that all offenders are subject to the order from the point of disposal, and offenders should not leave court in doubt as to the requirements of the order, and of the 'contract' with the court to which they have consented, including full information about the consequences of breach of the contract or non-compliance with the order.

A very distinctive feature of CSO is the considerable number of 'placement' opportunities provided for people in trouble by a wide range of agencies in the community. Supporting these agencies is an important task for social work staff as is ensuring the safety both of the offender and of the agency and its users; clarifying responsibilities that go with participation in a measure of criminal justice; and making sure the person performing the work/service in the agency understands their responsibilities.

Legislation says little about this subject of organising placements. The CP Act, 1995 simply says that the person must 'perform for the number of hours specified in the order such work at such times as the local authority officer may instruct'(s.239(1)). However one detail is included: that any instruction shall 'so far as practicable, be such as to avoid any conflict with the offender's religious beliefs, and any interference with the time, if any, at which he normally works or attends a school or other educational establishment' (section 239(3)). Care is taken to ensure unpaid work does not interfere with the regulations of the Department of Social Security (e.g. the '21 hours' rule). NOS stress that while 'there is no reason why an offender should not be instructed to work for more than 21 hours in any one week…regulations governing entitlement to unemployment benefit, national insurance credits and income support must…be taken into account where an offender is to be so instructed'. 'However, community service must not be seen by the offender as an exemption from seeking employment'. The New Deal regulations may raise challenges for organising placements in the future.

Someone who consents to a court making an order for community service or unpaid work, consents simply to do a set number of hours as instructed by the local authority officer. He has minimal rights (apart from the issues of religious belief and interference with work or schooling mentioned in the Act) to determine what particular piece of work or item of service he is to undertake. In practice discussion and an attempt to match the individual to an appropriate placement is the norm. NOS indicate that the officer should take into account the skills and interests of the offender and involved him in the decision making about the most appropriate placement. This, however has to be balanced with a judgement on the kinds of risk that the offender may pose to the community or to the organisation providing the placement.

Local authority personnel have been very successful in finding a wide range of placements that have both challenged the skills of people ordered to perform work or service, and serving the wider considerations of criminal justice. The suggestion in research is that where the offender is carrying out work he considers to be worthwhile and where he has direct contact with the beneficiaries of the service, the experience is likely to have the greatest impact on the offender.

In the case of 229(4) orders (unpaid work as a requirement of probation), a supervising officer will be appointed who has overall responsibility to the court for the implementation of the probation order. However, the legislation for the unpaid work requirement speaks of specific responsibilities of the local authority officer designated for community service purposes, who is likely to be a different officer. There is nothing inherently unworkable in all this, but it does require a measure of consistency and co-operation between the two.

Revocation and amendment of community service orders (section 238 orders)

The possibility of **revocation applies only to community service orders**. Two related criteria must be met, namely that circumstances have arisen since the order was made and, for that reason, it would be in the interests of justice for the court to consider amendment or revocation. There are no specified circumstances contained in the legislation. The provision for revocation may cover the following kinds of situation:

- to allow for his life circumstances changing (for example, obtaining a new job or moving to take up work) such that the number of hours originally ordered cannot be performed in the time available, or suitable work cannot be found, and it is not considered in the interests of justice to penalise the person for the changed circumstances;
- medically certificated ill-health over a lengthy period which prevent the work being carried out.

The power to revoke orders is set out in section 240 of the CP Act, 1995 and should not be used as a substitute for breach proceedings. An application for revocation can be made either by the local authority officer, or by the person performing the service. Possible outcomes of such an application are:

- the court may finish the order ahead of time, without him suffering any penalty;
- the court may vary the order by changing the number of hours, or by extending the 12-month requirement;
- the court may simply revoke the order and take no other action;

- the court may revoke the order and deal with the original offence in any way it could have done at the time had the order not been made.

If the final option is anticipated or intended, then the process has to take place on the basis of the offender having and exercising his normal right to be present at a hearing, to present his own defence and/or statement in mitigation, and to be legally represented for these purposes.

There are separate powers to amend and vary such requirements within probation orders (see Chapter 8).

AMENDMENTS

Community service orders can be amended under section 240, on application by either the supervisor or the person under supervision. Amendments may be to deal with changes of circumstance, such as a move of residence to a different court area, or to change the time scale to accommodate changes in work patterns, and so on.

Transfer of orders and cross-border issues

Courts in Scotland can make community service orders on people resident in England and Wales. The Scottish court must forward to the equivalent court copies of the orders and three copies of the amending order. The clerk of court is responsible for sending these documents. The supervising officer is responsible for transferring other relevant documents **or information to assist the new supervisor**.

Where the transfer involves a section 229 order (probation with a requirement of unpaid work) the maximum number of hours allowed for 'combination orders' in England and Wales is 100 hours. If the s.229 order exceeds 100 hours, an application to the Scottish court under Schedule 6 of the CP Act, 1995, to consider reducing the hours is required. If the court declines the application, it is not competent to transfer the order and the offender should be advised that a move before completion of the order will result in breach action.

In the event of a breach of an order which has been transferred to a court in England, Wales or Northern Ireland, under section 244 of the CP Act, 1995, that court may exercise any power which would apply for an order made in that part of the UK except the power to vary the number of hours' work in excess of that which the originating court could have ordered or to revoke the order (with or without dealing with the offender as for the original offence (NOS CS section).

Courts in England, Wales or Northern Ireland can deal with breaches of requirement of community service orders made in Scotland, **except that**, if so doing, **they cannot deal with the original offence**. They can vary the order, fine for the breach and let the order continue, but **they cannot take any course of action which would involve the termination of the order** and would have to remit the case back to Scotland if termination was thought appropriate. This applies **whatever the level of court**, for example an English Crown Court cannot terminate an order made by a Sheriff (Summary) Court in Scotland. The Scottish court might not necessarily agree with the English court's view, and, having considered the matter, might allow its continuation and return the matter to the jurisdiction of the English or Welsh court. In dealing with any cross-border matters, the Probation Directory, published annually by NAPO, is a very useful source of information about probation areas and office addresses in England and Wales.

Similarly courts in England, Wales or Northern Ireland transferring orders must forward copies of the order and three copies of the amending order to the appropriate court—High Court to High Court, crown court and magistrates' court to sheriff court. In the event of breach, under para. 6 of Schedule 3 of the *Criminal Justice Act,* 1991, the court in Scotland may not exercise any power under section 239(5)(b) or 240(1)(c) of the CP Act, 1995 i.e. revoke the order (with or without dealing with the offender for the original offence) either for failure to comply with a requirement of the order, or in the interests of justice. If the offender fails to comply with the order, or the court in Scotland is of the opinion that it is in the interests of justice that the order should be revoked under para. 7 or 8 of Schedule 2 of the *Criminal Justice Act* 1991, then the court in Scotland may require the offender to appear before the court which made the order.

Given also that English and Welsh courts can now make community service orders on 16-year-olds, another cross-border problem has been removed. However in this circumstance it should be noted that courts in England and Wales are restricted to a maximum number of hours of 120 in respect of 16-year-olds. It is suggested that, if the number of hours originally ordered by the Scottish court exceeded that maximum, then an application to vary the order to reduce the number of hours would be necessary. English courts making a community service order on a 16 year old who was resident in Scotland could not, however, make an order for more than 120 hours, even though if the same person had appeared before a Scottish court, he could have been ordered to perform up to the maximum.

Satisfactory completion

A report must be submitted to the appropriate court, and to the original SER author, on the satisfactory completion of an order. The report should outline the setting and nature of the work undertaken, the standard of work achieved and any information available on the impact of the order on the offender's attitude or behaviour or its contribution to his development of new skills or interests. It is important that at the completion of the order the offender is reminded of the legal implications of having been on an order with respect to the *Rehabilitation of Offenders Act,* 1974.

If authorities are serious about measuring effectiveness, in the absence of a national data base, this is also an opportunity to seek the offender's permission to make contact with him in 6, 12 and 24 months to gather information, in confidence, on his progress. It is essential for authorities to generate follow-up data, particularly conviction rates for a minimum of two years, now a standard measure in most research.

Chapter 10

Custodial Sentences and Prisons

Custodial sentences; young offenders; prison regimes

PREAMBLE

The extensive use of imprisonment as a penal sanction is a comparatively modern phenomenon in Scotland. Concepts of social welfare and custody are even more recent and not native to the Scottish tradition. Prisons have long received bad press. There is little disagreement that the act of imprisonment is a negative (albeit sometimes a necessary) one; the debate hinges more on whether the experience can be put to positive use. Penologists in twentieth century have been no less critical in their analysis of prison systems, in spite of the material improvements over time, than those of the previous century (Christie, 1982; Garland, 1985). The criticisms tend to be consistent over time and across national frontiers; post-war American penology demonstrated the negative effects of imprisonment, the patterns of 'inmate subcultures', the high re-conviction rates of custody and the processes of social control (Clemmer, 1958; Cressey 1961, Cohen, 1983). In Britain similar critiques and similar evidence are to be found (Cohen and Taylor 1972; Coyle ,1991).

In general terms the prison system in Scotland has evolved along similar lines to other western prison systems with its primary concern as secure custody. It has had some unique features and influences along the way, in particular, its central role within criminal justice in the early part of the century. Subsequent changes separated it from the mainstream criminal justice system and placed it under government bureaucratic control as an arm of the civil service, in what was the Scottish Home and Health Department.

While Scotland espoused 'treatment and training' as official objectives of prison in the 1960s, no attempt was made, officially, to adopt treatment as the main aim of sentencing adults. A relatively brief experimentation with extended periods of detention for persistent offenders, corrective training and preventive detention, introduced by the *Criminal Justice (Scotland) Act,* 1949, were abolished in the *Criminal Justice (Scotland) Act,* 1980. Nonetheless the rhetoric and language of treatment has lingered on and fits easily with the traditional paternalism characterising the relationship between the Scottish prison system and the prisoner (McManus, 1995).

Coyle (1991:275) suggests prison needs to be viewed, once again, as a part of the criminal justice process as a whole. He questions the degree to which 'treatment' concepts are appropriate to a penal or justice model, where resources should be available as a human right, not in the hope of rehabilitation. The first task of prison is secure custody in a safe environment through the exercise of good order, he argues; thereafter, the prison system has a responsibility to create a positive environment within which a prisoner can be encouraged to make use of opportunities, in the expectation that exercising choice will be the basis for accepting responsibility for personal change.

It is interesting to note the Elgin Committee's major concern, at the beginning of the century (1900), was with Scottish prison overcrowding and the ever increasing prison population as a result of the growing number of less serious convictions (related to alcohol misuse). This echoes very similar concerns at the end of the century. The overcrowding problems of the 1980s returned in the 1990s accompanied by the highest custody figures this century. In March 1997 prison figures reached a new daily record of 6,369. The expectation is that new records will be achieved in 1999 unless some radical change occurs.

The problems were not confined to convicted adults. Normally, adults (those aged 21 and over) are detained in separate institutions from young offenders (those aged 16 to 21). Special arrangements exist for the transfer of young offenders to adult establishments if they reach the age of 21 during their sentence. However, at the stage of remand, or prior to conviction, some young offenders can be held within the same institution as adult offenders. The *Law Reform (Miscellaneous Provisions) (Scotland) Act*, 1990, introduced further flexibility as regards the location of prisoners. The number of young offenders in adult custody in England almost doubled between 1992 and 1996; the government was found to be in breach of the UN Convention on the Rights of the Child by holding young people under 18 alongside adult prisoners; the number of girls sent to prison trebled between 1992 and 1996 (Howard League, 1997); the number of prisoners held on remand doubled between 1981 and 1996; the overall prison population increased by 53% between 1992 and 1996 (Prison Reform Trust, 1997). The equivalent data for Scotland is not readily available but every indication is that the same problem exists.

The Tory government's UK-wide response was to commit to the building of 21 new institutions at an estimated cost of £1.2 billions; a hundred million was ear marked for five new training centres for children aged 12-15, dubbed 'private child jails' (only one has been completed). Five new institutions were planned for Scotland. Predictably the government's penal policy was attacked by penal reformers. Less predictably, perhaps, was the public attack by leading members of the judiciary, on both sides of the border, including the former Lord Chief Justice (Lord Taylor), the current Lord Chief Justice (Lord Bingham) and the former Lord Justice General (Lord Hope). The Chief Inspector of Prisons (Judge Tumin), in July 1994, in a public lecture, indicated that the debate on law and order was 'driven by rhetoric' and that the belief that 'if prisons were made bad enough men would not commit crimes' had to be exposed as historically untrue. The criticism went unheeded.

By 1995 this expansionist penal policy was equally being promoted by the Secretary of State for Scotland (Michael Forsyth) as part of a 'prison works' strategy. Influenced by English proposals, the Secretary of State announced, in 1995, that three key policy initiatives would be introduced by the *Crime and Punishment*

(Scotland) Act 1997: the abolition of parole for prisoners with fixed term sentences, curtailment of remission, and mandatory life sentences for rapists and other violent offenders who had previously committed a similar offence. The 'three strikes and you're out' policy for burglars and drug dealers adopted in England was dropped in Scotland. The incoming Labour government did not implement these proposal but has not completely ruled out the possibility of future implementation. Nor has it rushed to commission new prisons other than to confirm the completion of Scotland's first privately-run prison in Kilmarnock.

It is important to consider the context in which such measures were being proposed. Scotland continued to use very high levels of imprisonment compared with other countries in Western Europe. European data placed Scotland near the top of the 'league table' for prison populations, estimated in 1995 to imprison 110 per 100,000 of the population, behind Spain (122) and Portugal (119) but ahead of England and Wales (99) against a Western European average of around 80: Germany (67), France (84) (Penal Reform Trust, 1997).

The number of persons sentenced to imprisonment and the proportion of persons with charges proved, and given a custodial sentence, has increased substantially over the last 10 years, generating a prison population which already stands at the highest level recorded this century (Scottish Office, 1996). The use of custody rose from 11% of all sheriff court disposals in 1991 to 15% in 1994 (Paterson and Tombs, 1998).

Some of the rising numbers can be accounted for by the rise in serious, violent and drug-related crime, which, in turn, has resulted in longer sentences; a higher proportion than ever before of the daily population in prisons is sentenced to more than four years. At the same time there were signs of a fall in the proportion of short sentences of up to three months, down from 61% to 53% of sheriff court disposals (Paterson and Tombs, 1998). Nonetheless short sentences still account for the vast majority of admissions to prisons in any year. Summary data on annual receptions indicate that approximately 40% are prisoners on remand and of these 90% are untried; about 60% are prisoners under sentence, and of these approximately 42% of adults and 30% of young offenders are fine defaulters. Over 90% are male (Statistical Bulletin, 1996). The White Paper *Crime and Punishment* (1996:43) noted that 83% of custodial sentences in 1994 were for less than 6 months and that 'these figures raise questions about the use of custody and whether more can be done to shake out of the prison system those who do not need to be there'.

The Chief Inspector of Prisons in Scotland (Clive Fairweather) reported on Barlinnie in 1996, that despite a large investment in a refurbishment programme, it was 56% over capacity. 'It is nothing short of a national disgrace that so many have had to endure the conditions resulting from the constant mismatch which has been created between the finite number of cells available and the burgeoning prison population which has been outwith Scottish Prisons Service (SPS) control'.

Scotland witnessed the implementation of a double strategy, on one hand support for an increase in longer prison sentences and, at the same time, support for increased use of community disposals to reduce the number of short sentences. Evidence suggests the former has been successful and the latter has still to achieve its objectives. The consequence is massive overcrowding in prisons.

No serious strategy has been developed for reducing numbers in custody, without which, any efforts on behalf of SPS to promote humane regimes will be viewed as little more than rhetoric. If the current Labour administration is serious about the promotion of community-based disposals to reduce prison populations and about creating prison regimes that can contain and provide opportunities for personal change, radical policies are required. They may need to consider ways of limiting the numbers of beds available in prisons for short-term offenders. At present where a warrant is issued, SPS will find a space. This 'open policy' is a recipe for ever-growing demand; the more new beds that are created, the more likely the prison numbers are to grow.

The *Prison (Scotland) Act*, 1989, as amended by the *Prisoners and Criminal Proceedings (Scotland) Act,* 1993 provides much of the legislative basis for the operation of prisons in Scotland.

CUSTODIAL SENTENCES: GENERAL

It is in this context that the policy of 'using prisons sparingly' is being promoted. The policy intention is that the imposition of a custodial sentence should be a last resort except for the most serious offenders who present a risk to the public. As we noted, legislation requires courts, in many instances, to consider all other options and requires them to consider reports on many offenders to assist them examine other options before imposing custody. Credible social work disposals and adequate resources to support them have a crucial part to play in targeting those receiving short sentences and the success of a community-based strategy is crucial to issues of imprisonment. Equally social work has an important role in assisting those who are admitted to custody in dealing with incarceration and in preparing for re-integration on release (see Chapter 11).

Apart from these general policy considerations, a number of factors influence the length and type of any custodial sentence that is imposed. Factors such as the level of court, the type of procedure being used, the extent of previous criminality, and the specific provisions or penalties of any particular statute will represent boundaries around the imposition of a custodial sentence (see Chapter 3).

Whatever sentence a court may impose in respect of a man, it may also impose in respect of a woman. There is only one penal institution for female offenders, which contains a range of facilities. Sentences are served in single-sex institutions, although there are staff of both sexes in those institutions. No-one can be admitted as an inmate to any penal establishment, except by express sentence or order of a court, or by administrative decision, under some statutory orders, where the court does not specify the type of institution in which the person is to be held .

Determinate sentences

The great majority of custodial sentences, whether in relation to adults or to young offenders, are determinate sentences—that is, of fixed length. All such sentences automatically carry a period of early release, dependent on the length and type of sentence. Prison Governors have power to 'award' additional days up to a sixth of the sentence (ADAs) if the person offends against prison discipline. Once discharged, providing they are not subject to any form of post-prison supervision, the person is no longer under the control of the prison or the court, and their sentence is at an end.

The 1993 Act introduced radical changes in the arrangements for parole and early release, incorporating many of the proposals of Kincraig Committee (1989) (see chapter 11).

Life imprisonment

Life imprisonment is the only indeterminate custodial sentence available to the courts in relation to adults. It is the fixed penalty for any offence of murder. The comparable custodial sentences, in relation to young offenders and children, are set out later in this chapter. The sentence of life imprisonment is also available as a penalty in some very serious cases (for example, rape). It can only be passed in the High Court. Judges of that court have power, when imposing a sentence of life imprisonment to make a recommendation as to the designated length of time which they consider the person should spend in custody prior to release on licence. The release from custody of persons sentenced to life imprisonment is a matter for the Secretary of State. This matter is discussed in the Chapter 11 on throughcare. Life sentence prisoners are informed of the sentencing judge's recommendation as to the designated length of sentence to be served and, if appropriate, when the Secretary of State for Scotland disagrees with that recommendation, and the reasons for this, as this can be the basis for an appeal by the prisoner. Knowing the probable release period (not the actual release date) in advance can be helpful to social workers in throughcare planning.

Consecutive and concurrent sentences

People who face a court on a number of charges may receive sentences of imprisonment in relation to each charge. Sentences may be imposed consecutively or concurrently, even with a sentence which the person is already be serving.

Examples

- Steven Orr receives two sentences, one of 28 months imprisonment, the other of 34 months imprisonment, to run **consecutively**. This means that he is sentenced to a total of 62 months imprisonment. This sentence could only have been imposed in the High Court, in that its total duration exceeds the powers available to the Sheriff Court.
- George Hamilton receives two sentences, one of 18 months imprisonment and the other of 21 months imprisonment, to run **concurrently**. This means he is sentenced to a total of 21 months imprisonment. This sentence could have been ordered by a Sheriff Court on solemn procedure.

- Stuart MacGregor receives two sentences of imprisonment, one of 3 months duration, the other of 6 months duration, **to run concurrently**: that means a total sentence of 6 months duration.
- Ian Thomson, who has already served 2 months of a 6 month sentence, receives a further sentence of 6 months imprisonment:
  i) if imposed **consecutively**, he will commence serving it on the expiry of his present sentence (with whatever remission he may receive in relation to that sentence); but,
  ii) if imposed **concurrently**, he will commence serving it on the day that it was ordered by the court (that is, overlapping with the sentence he is already serving).

Courts of summary procedure cannot impose sentences, which *in total* amount to more than their ordinary maximum powers; thus a district court cannot impose two 60-day sentences consecutively, and a sheriff summary court cannot impose sentences totalling more than 6 months, unless, for example, one of the sentences is for breach of bail, or a particular statute gives the court such powers (for example, parts of the *Police (Scotland) Act*, 1967).

Courts of solemn procedure can order that a custodial sentence should be back-dated, e.g. from the date that the person was committed for trial. The day on which sentence is imposed may be some weeks after that event. Thus a person who has been awaiting trial in custody for, say, 3 months, and has a 9-month sentence imposed, but backdated to the time of committal, will only have 6 months to serve as from the date of sentence. Not all sentences are back-dated but the court must always have taken account of time already spent in custody awaiting the trial.

Suspended and partially suspended sentence of imprisonment

Any sentence of imprisonment passed in Scotland takes immediate effect. There is no such thing in Scotland as a **suspended or partially suspended sentence**. However, both of these do exist in England and Wales. It may be helpful, when colleagues south of the Border are writing reports for Scottish courts, to advise them of the position in Scotland. A suspended sentence of imprisonment involves a court sentencing the person to 12 months imprisonment, but suspending the operation of that sentence for a period of 2 years, dependent on future good behaviour. The person can avoid serving time in a penal establishment, provided he commits no further offence during the operational period. Under a partially suspended sentence, a court may order that the first month of, for example, a 12-month sentence will be served in custody, but that the remaining 11 months (on release) shall be suspended. Suspended and partially suspended sentences of imprisonment are NOT available in respect of young offenders in England and Wales. A suspended, or partially suspended sentence of imprisonment, is an actual sentence of imprisonment, and will show as such on the person's list of previous convictions (see Chapter 13 on the *Rehabilitation of Offenders Act*, 1974).

Confusion has been known to occur between the deferred sentence and the suspended sentence. The deferred sentence is not a sentence at all. It is a deferring of sentence, without any question, necessarily, of subsequent imprisonment.

CUSTODIAL SENTENCES FOR YOUNG OFFENDERS.

Separate and special provisions apply to young offenders, i.e. offenders aged 16, but under 21. Convicted young offenders cannot be sentenced to imprisonment but can be made subject to a period of detention (s.207 of the 1995 Act). The basic provisions relating to young offenders are set out in the *Criminal Procedure (Scotland) Act*, 1995.

Young Offenders' Institutions

Young Offenders' Institutions were created by the *Criminal Justice (Scotland) Act*, 1963. The Act required that any offender who was not considered suitable either for Detention Centre Training, or for Borstal Training, (later abolished by the *Criminal Justice (Scotland)* Act 1980) should serve his sentence in a Young Offenders' Institution. The length of any such sentence would be fixed by the court in accordance with its ordinary powers. The prime objective was to avoid young offenders having to serve their sentences in the same institutions as adults prisoners.

Concern had been raised by a number of suicides in custodial establishments for young people, resulting in a review of Suicide Precautions at both the Detention Centre and the Young Offenders' Institution at Glenochil (Chiswick Report, 1985) Further changes were made to the sentencing of young offenders by the *Law Reform (Miscellaneous Provisions) (Scotland) Act*, 1985, whereby the court could impose detention on persons over 16 and under 21, where it could impose imprisonment on an adult. Detention means detention in a young offenders' institution— now s.207(5) of the CP Act, 1995.

The *Law Reform (Miscellaneous Provisions) (Scotland) Act,* 1990, at section 39, introduced even further flexibility for young people to be moved between different institutions by administrative arrangement (rather than by court sentence) if the circumstances of either the young person or the institution (for example, overcrowding) required it. Section 39 authorised the Secretary of State to direct that prisoners may be committed and/or removed from 'any prison to any other prison'.

Section 19 of the *Prisons (Scotland) Act,* 1989 currently enables the Secretary of State to provide young offenders' institutions and remand facilities; section 21 authorises the continued detention of a young person until 'the day immediately preceding his twenty-third birthday'. Section 20A (added by the 1993 Act) authorises detention of a person under 21 in a prison or remand centre instead of a young offenders' institution. This can only be temporary if the persons is under 18. This might, for example, be to facilitate visits, or medical or other treatment. In principle, young offenders will be detained in separate institutions for young offenders, though they may be moved between types of regime.

Young offenders convicted of murder

The *Criminal Justice (Scotland) Act*, 1980 changed the arrangements for young offenders convicted of murder. Before the Act, life imprisonment was the sentence passed on any person aged 18 and over convicted of murder, whereas offenders under 18 were sentenced to 'Detention During Her Majesty's Pleasure'.

The effect of section 43 of the 1980 Act, now section 205 of the *Criminal Procedure (Scotland) Act*, 1995, was that:

- Life imprisonment is the sentence for murder in relation to persons aged 21 and over.
- Offenders aged 18 but under 21 are sentenced 'to be detained in a young offenders' institution and shall be liable to be detained for life' (s.205(3)). We noted above that administrative arrangements exist for the transfer of young offenders who may reach the age of 21 during sentence to institutions for adult prisoners.
- Offenders under 18 are sentenced 'to be detained without limit of time and shall be liable to be detained in such place, and under such conditions, as the Secretary of State may direct' (s.205(2)). The place need not be a penal institution, especially initially if the person is quite young. There may well be various transfers and changes according to the progress and maturation of the young person. The release and supervision are operated as for a sentence of life imprisonment, and are administered under the arrangements for parole (see below).

Detention of children (by courts, as opposed to Children's Hearings)

There are circumstances in which children, that is, persons under 16, OR aged between 16 and 18 but under the supervision of the children's hearing, can be prosecuted before the courts for crimes and offences, rather than being referred to the children's hearing. In extremely serious cases a 'child' may thus become liable to prosecution under solemn procedure (see Chapter 3). Such cases tend to be very rare. Section 208 of the *Criminal Procedure (Scotland) Act*, 1995 makes provision for the detention of children who may be prosecuted under solemn procedure. The provision states that 'where a child is convicted on indictment and the court is of the opinion that no other method of dealing with him is appropriate, it may sentence him to be detained for such a period which it shall specify in the sentence; and the child shall during that period be liable to be detained in such place and on such conditions as the Secretary of State shall direct.

Courts are obliged to consider reports when dealing with children, and to have regard to their welfare. The wording of section 208 allows that the place need not be a penal institution. However, it is quite possible that the sentence, though a fixed one, will be of such duration that the child may pass into the young offender, or even adult, category during it. Again there may be various transfers to different institutions to reflect this, and these may include penal institutions. The release of children detained under section 44 is discussed in the Chapter 11.

Residential care for children

When children are prosecuted on summary procedure, they appear before a sheriff court (and never a district court). One of the disposals open to the court is to order a period of residential care. The period may not exceed one year, and must be of a specified length within that span. It is notable that, ordinarily, in an adult context, the maximum power of detention available to the sheriff summary court is six months. An order for Residential Care is made under section 44 of the *Criminal Procedure (Scotland) Act*, 1995. The place, conditions and duration of care under a section 44 order are determined by the local authority. There is no remission as of right, but the child may be released in the community, conditionally or unconditionally. The Parole Board is NOT involved in determining the release of children held under section 44 orders. The views and involvement of social workers are crucial to the effective discharge by the local authority of its duties under this section. The liaison is with the Social Work Services Inspectorate for these cases, and not with the Prison Service (as it is with section 208 cases discussed above, and with young offenders in the normal course of events). A child will not appear before a court with such a disposal in prospect without a children's hearing having tendered its advice. It requires careful consideration as to whether any advantage is to be gained by the court imposing an order under section 44 as against any course of action open to the children's hearing under section 70 of the *Children (Scotland) Act*, 1995. The use of a section 44 order is the only means by which a child appearing before a court on summary procedure can be detained, but it is no guarantee that such detention will necessarily be in a particular institution.

PRISON REGIMES

The rehabilitative ideal once expressed in prison rules that the 'the purpose of the training and treatment of convicted prisoners shall be to establish in them the will to lead good and useful lives on discharge, and to fit them to do so' has come under serious criticism in recent years (Wood, 1991; Coyle, 1991). Many politicians have argued that 'humane containment' or 'preventive detention' is all that prisons can, and indeed, should aim for. A related point is expressed in the saying that people go to prison **as** punishment and not **for** punishment.

Historically, prisoners have had few legally enforceable rights and little reference has been made in legislation to prisoners' rights; the practice assumption being that these are lost on admission and anything then granted by prison rules is a privilege subject to withdrawal by governors. The European Court of Human Rights viewed the lack of distinction between rights and privileges to be unhelpful and prison rules now attempt to distinguish between the two.

All penal establishments are under the control of Scottish Prison Service. In 1993 the Scottish Prison Service (SPS) assumed agency status under the conservative government's policy of devolved management for public bodies. SPS is run by a Prisons Board, which consists of a chief executive, a deputy, four departmental heads and two lay non-executive directors.

Opportunity and Responsibility: Developing New Approaches to the Management of the Long-Term Prison System in Scotland (SPS, 1990) reflected a radically different approach to the basic task of prison adopted by SPS, and is an important document to be considered alongside the policy on social work in prisons outlined in *Continuity through Co-operation* (SWSG, 1989). *Opportunity and Responsibility* set a new tone for future development of prison regimes. It based its approach on the philosophy of 'positive choice', a view that the prisoner is responsible for his actions, and should be encouraged to accept that responsibility. It sees the provision of opportunities and choice—for personal growth and development—as one way of assisting the prisoner accept responsibility for his actions and for personal change. This starting point is in marked contrast to a 'treatment' approach, which tended to view the prisoner, in a medical analogy, as a person in need of 'cure'. The thinking rejects any concept of 'coerced' cure and sees the goal of facilitating change as more achievable.

Whilst *Opportunity and Responsibility* is particularly concerned with the long-term prisoner (people serving over 4 years), parts of the basic philosophy are clearly applicable to all groups. It seeks to eliminate, as far as practicable, the unsatisfactory and dangerous concentration of high-risk prisoners in one or two locations, although it seems supportive of the notion of specialist resources or regimes. This may well have been influenced to a degree by the experience of the now defunct Barlinnie Special Unit, which demonstrated that the personal and social skills of Scotland's most difficult prisoners could be enhanced.

The Scottish Prison Service mission statement for 1997-98 reflects the discussion above, where a balance is sought between the primary objectives of secure containment and the secondary ones of providing opportunities for challenge and change. The mission statement identifies four key themes (COCO).

- Custody: to keep contained those committed by the courts;
- Order: to maintain good order in each prison;
- Care: to care for prisoners with humanity and with dignity;
- Opportunity: for personal development, responsibility and preparation for release.

These themes emphasise the variety of objectives that prisons, in principle, are attempting to pursue: security; creating a safe environment for staff and prisoners through the maintenance of order; meeting the primary physical and health care needs of prisoners; and issues of personal development and preparation for return to the community.

The average annual cost of a prison place in 1997/8 was £28,317, ranging from places of low security, for example, Low Moss £15-16,000, to the special regimes in Shotts and Peterhead which cost £70-80,000 per place.

SPS and the local authority

Recent developments pose challenges to social work, particularly in the light of the growing number of non-consensual supervision licences. Non-parole licences (see

Chapter 11) have grown from 398 in 1997/9 to over 500 in 1998/99 and are expected to reach 566 by the year 2000.

Social workers and their authorities are expected to develop complementary approaches and programmes, which link to the work going on in prisons, and are equally relevant to families in the community. The emphasis on collaboration between community-based social workers, their prison-based colleagues and prison staff, though crucially important and still under-developed, has partly deflected from the focus on collaboration between SPS, local authorities and voluntary sector in a more strategic way.

SPS's regime development section carries responsibility for social work provision, psychological services and the provision of development programmes. A framework for purchasing social work services issued in 1998 requires SPS to purchase key services from local authorities. In 1997/98 over £1.3 million was spent on social work services in the North East area (£300k in Edinburgh prison alone), and £1.1 million in the South West (£360k in Barlinnie prison). This is a substantial investment when compared to Health Care (£3 million) and Psychological Services (£680k). This expenditure is subject to government's 'best value' requirements, which replaced the previous administration's drive for compulsory competitive tendering. Service level agreements (SLA) will be developed between SPS, local authorities and the independent sector as providers. The culture of SLAs will demand better social work information systems to generate adequate data in order to show SPS what they get for their money. It is another matter whether SPS will consider it value for money.

SPS has produced protocols for establishing effective programmes of intervention and has set a target for 1998/99 of providing a menu of four nationally available prison-based programmes relevant to the needs and risks of prisoners including cognitive skills, anger management and relapse prevention programmes. This strategy includes specific targets to provide 450 cognitive skills programmes places and 70 sex offenders programmes places per year within prisons. It is assumed that prison staff will be the primary agent of delivery supported by specialist staff. Outcomes are awaited with some interest. Links must be created between this range of programmes and social work provision if throughcare is to be effective. In turn bridges are required between specific throughcare services and mainstream local authority and voluntary sector provision.

It is time for unitary local authorities to take their responsibilities to community safety seriously. Many existing local authority services, for example, drug services, could operate both within and outwith prisons. Prisoners need accommodation as much as social work services. Serious offenders in unstable accommodation may well pose serious risk to the community. It has to be asked why housing staff are not operating within prisons, anticipating homelessness long before release, where they could plan safe locations, as required for high risk offenders as part of their community safety strategy. In practice this will require authorities to examine their housing policies and priorities—their anti-social tenants policies may be in direct conflict with their responsibilities to community safety. The same strategy could be adopted by employment and training services. It is unrealistic to think that SPS could be expected to provide for this range of services from its budget, (unless of course it could charge local authorities for accommodating their citizenry and contributing to their local safety).

It is only by addressing the practical needs of offenders, including accommodation and employment outlined in recent evaluations (McIvor and Barry, 1998), and combining this with other offence-focused issues, that ex-prisoners are likely to engage meaningfully in personal change, particularly non-consensual offenders, and those offenders who are actually long-term prisoners but get sentenced to many short-term periods of custody with limited gaps in between, and so never require supervision and seldom seek voluntary assistance. Priorities must reflect these requirements.

Types of prison

Prisons are of various types. Section 22 of the 1993 Act allows the Secretary of State to commit any prisoner to any prison. Prison rules authorise the Secretary of State to set aside prisons, or parts of them, for particular purposes or for particular classes of prisoners. Within the rules, governors have the power to allocate prisoners within their institution as they see fit, having regard to the classification of the prisoner. Governors may classify prisoners in accordance with factors such as sex, age, offence, length of sentence, or previous record (see McManus, 1995, for a detailed discussion of material summarised below). Security classification are defined in the prison rules. They are:

Category A: *Maximum security* for prisoners who place national security at risk; are highly dangerous to the public, prison staff, their families, or to the police in the event of escape.

Category B: *Secure conditions* for prisoners likely to be a danger to the public in the event of escape.

Category C: *Minimum restriction* for prisoners unlikely to be a risk to the public.

Category D: *Open conditions* for prisoners who do not represent a risk to the pubic.

Governors must allocate a prisoner to the lowest category, give the prisoner an explanation for their classification, and keep this under review (at least annually). Untried prisoners must be allocated to category A or B. A governor must obtain the approval of the Secretary of State within 72 hours of allocating a prisoner to category A. The same approval is required to allocate a life prisoner to category D.

Security categories are a crucial determinant of many of the conditions experienced by prisoners. Most prisoners serve their sentences in closed prisons. There are, however, two 'open' prisons in Scotland, one at Penninghame, near Newton Stewart, and one at Noranside, near Forfar. Any one institution may contain a variety of sections, variously termed 'wings' or 'halls', dependent on the physical nature of the building, including remand sections, secure sections, and so on. Factors such as proximity to family, employment skills, and other more individualised factors have little bearing on the allocation of prison.

Women prisoners

Prison rules require that female prisoners are accommodated entirely separately from male prisoners. The vast majority of adult female prisoners serve their sentences at Cornton Vale prison, near Stirling. The institution also acts as the place where all young female offenders serve their sentences. The great majority of women on remand and serving periods of fine default are also detained in Cornton Vale, though there are facilities for holding small numbers in Aberdeen, Inverness and Dumfries. The overall small numbers of female prisoners makes it more difficult to provide a full range of facilities available to male prisoners. Steps have been taken in recent years to provide similar facilities for female category C and D prisoners. Subject to directions of the Secretary of State, Governors may allow women to have their babies with them in prison. There are numerous texts which suggest that women are differentially and less well treated in prison than men (Carlen, 1990). This has been the subject of a Scottish Office review (1998a).

Communication with the outside world

All incoming and outgoing mail may be subject to censorship by prison authorities The issue of censoring mail is an area that has been subject to most change in recent years, forced on prison regulations by cases decided before the European Court of Human Rights. Prisoners have the right, subject to certain restrictions, to receive and send mail and is entitled to be supplied with material for writing one letter per week with postage paid by the Secretary of State. Any other letters they may wish to write have to be paid for out of the earnings received for work done within the prison. Prisoners may ask for additional free letters in order, for example, to write to agents or social workers. These 'special' letters may be granted at the discretion of the governor.

No correspondence to or from courts shall be opened or read by prison authorities except where an officer has cause to believe that it contains a prohibited article. The prisoner must be given an explanation and the correspondence opened, but not read, in the presence of the prisoner. Governors may confiscate any prohibited article found. The content of correspondence to and from legal advisers may be opened and read where the governor has cause to believe that the contents endanger the security of the prison or the safety of anyone or relate to criminal activity. The prisoner must be informed and the letter only read by the governor or an officer specially authorised. All other correspondence can be opened by an officer, but can only be read where the officer considers that it contains material forbidden by directions in the rules. The directions allow all mail sent to or by category A prisoners to be read by an authorised officer; otherwise mail is read only where it is considered to contain material prejudicial to good order, security, and/or relates to criminal activity.

In most institutions it is now possible for the prisoner to have access to a telephone in order to assist maintaining contact with family. The calls have to be paid for from earnings for work done in prison.

Visits

All convicted prisoners are normally entitled to have a visit, for not less that 30 minutes each seven consecutive days. A prisoner whose family lives at some distance away is allowed to accumulate visits, in order to have longer one, and, alternatively, is entitled to not less than two hours in any period of 28 days. The Benefits Agency is empowered to pay extra lodgings allowance to permit an overnight stay near a prison, if the distance from home base is sufficiently great as to require one. Prisoners under 16 are entitled to a minimum of two visits of at least 30 minutes each seven days. Untried prisoners are allowed to receive a visit of at least 30 minutes each weekday, and, in certain circumstances, at weekends.

The number of visitors at any time is a matter for the governor's discretion and the Secretary of State has powers to reduce this entitlement for practical reasons. In practice, prisoners are usually allowed three adult visitors, but if children accompany adults, this number may be reduced. Visits normally take place in open surroundings, but all visits must be within the sight of an officer. Governors have the power to require any specific visit, or all visits, to take place in closed visit facilities where there is a barrier between the visitor and the prisoner, for example if there is concern about passing prohibited material such as drugs. Such orders are subject to three-monthly review. Closed visits, however, are usually reserved for those who are considered to be a security risk.

Rules allow governors the discretion to establish a system of passes and, in these circumstances, no visitor will be allowed into a prison without a pass previously sent out to them by, or on behalf of, the person they are going to visit. 'Special' visits may be granted in exceptional circumstances at the governor's discretion. These may be suggested on welfare grounds by social workers either within or outwith the prison.

Prisoners are entitled to be visited by their legal adviser at any reasonable time. The same is true for procurators fiscal, and for police, providing the person is willing to be interviewed. All visits must be within the view of an officer.

All visitors are subject to common regulations, so that, before admission, they may be asked to state their name and address and the purpose of their visit. They may be asked to deposit any article which the officer considers may be prejudicial to good order or safety. If the visitor is suspected of being in possession of prohibited material, they may be asked to consent to a search of their person, including mouth by visual examination, or personal possessions. Removal of clothing, except outer garments, is not authorised. If the visitor refuses they may be refused admission. An officer has the power to detain anyone in possession of an unauthorised article under, s.41(3) of the 1989 Act as amended by s.153(4) of the *Criminal Justice and Public Order Act,* 1994.

These general provisions apply to social workers although it is expected that visits from community-based social workers will involve liaison with prison-based colleagues. Social workers will have official means of identification with them on such visits. If it is intended that other personnel working with the social worker (for example, student, volunteer associate, or colleague from another agency) should also visit, an identity card may not be necessary, but the arrangements for these visitors should be established in advance.

Discipline

Ordinary criminal law continues to operate within penal establishments and any matter which could constitute a criminal offence may be reported to the police and dealt with in the normal way. The only material difference is that for prisoners already validly detained, trial dates may be delayed beyond the statutory limits discussed in Chapter 3. Governors have a great deal of discretion as regard reporting issues to the police. However, if a prisoner asks for the police to investigate a matter, the governor must allow this. The same applies to officers' requests. Often internal disciplinary measures are enforced. In the light of decisions of the European Court in recent years, prison rules now contain comprehensive and detailed lists of breaches of discipline, and detailed rights within the procedures are set out.

On report of a breach, governors have the discretionary power to keep a prisoner apart from other prisoners for up to 72 hours, though the Secretary of State may authorise further periods of a month at a time. Charges must be brought and normally heard within 48 hours and the offender served with written notice at least two hours before any hearing. The prisoner should have time to prepare and can present his own case, calling witnesses on his own behalf. Governors have some discretion on the use of witnesses and can allow legal representation in exceptional circumstances. The normal criminal standard of proof must be satisfied. Prisoners have the right of appeal against a finding of guilt, either to the internal complaints committee, or, where the governor heard the case, to the Secretary of State. It is important to note that visiting committees in Scotland, unlike their equivalent in England and Wales, have no jurisdiction in these matters. Punishments are also listed in the prison rules and can include caution, loss of privileges; stoppage of wages; confinement; forfeiture of the right to wear one's own clothing; forfeiture of remission for those sentenced before October 1, 1993, and additional days for those sentenced on or after that date, to a maximum of 14 days for any one offence and a cumulative maximum of one sixth of the total sentence—this in effect postpones eligibility for consideration of parole.

Visiting committees

Sections 8 and 19(3) of the 1989 Act deal with the appointment of visiting committees. Appointments under section 19(3), for institutions holding young people under 21, are made by the Secretary of State for Scotland; as regards membership, 'not less than two members shall be justices of the peace and not less than such number of members as may be prescribed by the rules shall be women'. Appointments under section 8 are the responsibility of specified local authorities, providing less than a third are members of the authority appointing them. Section 8(2) requires that rules are established to deal with the functions of visiting committees and specifies that these should include requirement for members 'to pay frequent visits to the prison and hear any complaints...by the prisoners and report any matter to the Secretary of State they consider it expedient to report'. Members are also empowered to visit the prison at any time and to have free access to any part of the prison and to all prisoners.

The general purpose of visiting committees set out in the rules is to co-operate with the Secretary of State and the governor in promoting the efficiency of the prison and to inquire into and report to the Secretary of State on any matter they are asked to report on. This includes concern about food and drink, inspection of prison records and issues of security. At least two members must visit at least fortnightly. A major role for committees is to hear complaints from prisoners, outwith the sight of an officer, unless the prisoner or member requests otherwise. Findings are recorded in the committee's minute book, shared orally with prisoners, and copied to the governor and the Secretary of State. Prisoners can ask to see the visiting committee or write to them at any time When an officer receives a request he must notify the governor without delay.

Complaints

The potential for the abuse of power in a closed institution such as a prison is well recognised, as is the willingness of inmates to complain about every aspect of institutional life. Good order requires an effective system of complaints that keeps complaints to a minimum. In 1994 SPS introduced a new internal complaints procedure headed by an independent Prisons Complaints Commissioner, with authority to make recommendations to the Chief Executive of SPS. The Commissioner has jurisdiction over all matters for which SPS is responsible, including adjudications.

Research and practice

Whatever the ambition of policy and the future success of social work disposals, prison remains, and is likely to remain, the major response to serious offenders. SPS in a bold venture has made a number of senior appointments in professional psychology, a social work advisor and a programme developer/manager, in recognition of the need to begin to provide opportunities for personal development and effective personal change as part of their throughcare strategy. This renewed emphasis on throughcare, which is more associated with personal development than punitive philosophies, may signal a new emphasis in penal policy in Scotland. Some would suggest the emphasis on sentence planning and throughcare stems more from the prison service's need to demonstrate 'quality of service' in the face of threats of privatisation by the previous government (Macguire and Raynor, 1997).

For any prison-based strategy of programme development to be effective we need to know more about how incarceration affects individuals, and the factors, if any exist, that are more likely to be associated with positive outcomes on return to the community. While every prisoner is unique and different types of offenders have different characteristics, some general principles seem to be emerging from research that give some clues as to the kind of provision required.

Research such as Zamble and Porporino's in Canada (1990) suggests that understanding coping mechanisms and adaptive behaviour may provide useful insights for the provision of services within prisons. It is well established that the way one copes with the circumstances of life is a critical factor in future adaptations. Prisonisation theories (sociology of institutions) have tended to argue that the reason for the apparent failure of prison is that prisoners adapt to their environment in ways that subsequently make it difficult for them to survive lawfully on the outside.

Early research suggested that many prisoners' ability for coping was better in prison than in the community, possibly because it is more structured and constrained than life on the outside, and so they are not quite so free to create so many problems for themselves. More recent studies suggest, however, that prisoners' coping ability is not so different in the inside than it is on the outside. The evidence suggests that the more times a person has been in prison the worse they cope with the conditions (a major justification for the role of social work in prevention of custody where possible), and that coping problems are a central cause of the maintenance and repetition of criminal acts, if not their origins. This may provide a better explanation of why those with greater or poorer criminal and custodial histories continue to do so badly.

The implications of the study were that when prison primarily constrains behaviour and responsibility, and where there are limited opportunities to change behaviour progressively, this creates a warehouse effect, a 'behaviour deep freeze', in which outside behaviours are set aside until release. The researchers argue that receptivity to change is real but it is transient; it doesn't last very long once somebody has settled down within a regime. Those who didn't settle down after a few months were found to be more likely to re-offend on release. Similarly for those whose thoughts about the future decreased or who become more immersed in the social world of prison life—in with the crowd, they were also found more likely to re-offend on release.

The implications are wide-ranging and are reflected in some SPS planning intentions. There is a need for opportunities to help the prisoner adapt to prison life and to the deprivations and strictures of prison, using induction programmes. The argument is that if cognitive programmes are to be provided, they need to start early, within a month or so. It may be too late to wait till the end in the expectation that a pre-release programme will provide adequate preparation for release. The suggestion is that the way the person adapts to community life may be affected more by how he deals with custody over time, than how he prepares for release.

SPS have developed a national induction centre (NIC) in Shotts prison to address the needs of the very long-term prisoner by locating them, immediately after sentence, in a setting in which they can adjust and come to terms with their imprisonment and where they can address their initial coping difficulties as they arise.

Specific programmes are increasingly available as part of preparation for release. These require to be carried through into the community to minimise the 'wash out' effects that are often associated with institutional programmes. Research seems to suggest that if these approaches are detached from sentence planning, the capacity of the person to adapt effectively to prison life and, where possible, to keep alive a sense of their identity outside, may undermine these efforts. A major challenge is providing an appropriate range of programmes and supporting their voluntary use.

Research like this provides major challenges to policy makers, prison and social work managers and to practitioners. How seriously are the terms **throughcare** and **sentence planning** being taken? Is it realistic to provide tailored programmes in prison which are associated with positive outcomes?

The rediscovery of 'effectiveness' (see Chapter 2) has given a growing confidence, supported by some academic evidence, that certain kinds of well-planned and
structured interventions can have a significant impact on re-offending rates. This has
challenged the 'nothing works' position and has led to a greater focus on addressing
offending behaviour, running groups to tackle drug abuse, as well as efforts to amel-
iorate the social and financial problems of resettlement. A new optimism is emerging
in prison research which stresses that the principles of effective intervention directing community-based programmes must equally apply to the provision of programmes
within prisons. While differential responses are required and different priorities (and
resources) will operate within different regimes, to be effective, intervention programmes should be designed to address, in both content and method of delivery, the
most critical factors that support and maintain criminality.

The principle of 'programme integrity' discussed in Chapter 2 should equally
apply, namely most effective programmes have clear and stated aims and objectives; the methods are appropriate to achieve the objectives; are carried out by staff
who are trained and skilled in the particular method; are adequately resourced and
managed; the programme initiators are involved in all the management phases of the
programme; and the programme is subjected to some form of ongoing evaluation—
in other words there is effective management and planning to ensure that what is
intended is actually done. (see Andrews *et al*, 1990; McGuire, 1995).

The recognition that the type and method of intervention is important, however, **has still to be support by good empirical data** either in the UK or in North
America. Research has identified numbers of factors which are associated with
supporting and sustaining criminal behaviour. Various classification systems exist
to try and distinguish between prisoners who require greater security, and those
who present a control problem as part of sentence-planning initiatives.

Management strategies for throughcare are now the subject of ongoing evaluation. Systems consist usually of three components: a semi-structured interview
schedule used to obtain background information on the prisoner; assessment of
crime-related and crime-sustaining (criminogenic) factors in which key factors are
prioritised as most significant in contributing to the individual offender's criminal
behaviour; and an accompanying intervention plan in which specific prison-based
programmes are identified to address these key factors (Baird and Neuenfeldt, 1990).

Dhaliwal et al, (1994) in an evaluation of a case-management strategy in Canada
selected 12 crime-related factors, broad in nature, to be targeted: academic/voca-
tional skills; employment pattern; financial management; marital/family relations;
companions; emotional stability; alcohol usage; drug usage; mental ability; health
(physical); sexual behaviour; and values/attitudes. The primary concern of the study
was to examine the management process: the extent to which the case-management system was used to recommend intervention programmes within prisons based
on the classification; the extent to which the programmes were then actually delivered; and what effect these processes had on recidivism. After 6 months follow up
21 of 107 (20%) had been re-incarcerated and after 18 months 40%. While earlier
studies had suggested that positive outcomes can be achieved, this study found that

the system was not very effective, and that classification for effective rehabilitation was not supported by these findings.

The important message from this research is not to revert back to intuition or to offering a fixed menu of the same programmes for all offenders, since some system of priority and targeting will be required, but that our knowledge remains very limited and new strategies need careful implementation to ensure knowledge and understanding is enhanced and also to avoid erroneous dismissal of certain approaches. **At this stage the theory seems impressive but practice results have still to become impressive**.

The more practical findings from the study were that intervention plans had not been implemented fully for a large proportion of offenders, suggesting that for many it may have been less that the classification system was ineffective but that in assessing offender needs for programme planning, the recommendations often just appear to have become part of an offender's file and nothing more. Equally a large proportion of the recommendations for programmes were judged, by independent raters, to be inappropriate for addressing offenders' crime-related needs.

McAllister's review of throughcare for young offenders (1992) suggested that practice was very patchy but there was certainly some good work going on in prison. As well as containing, prison also damages prisoners' family ties and links with the community. Programmes which try to help prisoners build links with the community are thought to help reduce subsequent re-offending (Bottoms, 1993). While empirical data is limited, research findings are consistent with concepts of control theory, which essentially asserts that people do not offend if they are in social situations that have positive meanings for them.

Some of the findings above were reflected in Gemmell's study in Scotland (1995:25) indicating 'the work between a prisoner and his personal officer, work which could have been recorded within the prisoner's personal development file, does not take place in the in-depth way envisaged by the creators of the (sentencing planning) scheme. Instead sentence planning is seen as a way of charting a prisoner's progress through the prison system'. Gemell concludes that 'the range of opportunities, which were to be made available (by Opportunity and Responsibility) failed to materialise'.

A key difficulty identified by Macguire and Rayner (1997) in the practice of sentence planning was the expectations of joint working and collaboration between social work and prison officers. Sentence planning was on the whole not undertaken collaboratively; liaison was difficult; documentation was late in getting to social workers. Social work contact with prison and community-based social workers, understandably, spent the limited time available in prison, seeing prisoners rather than developing joint plans about them. McIvor and Barry (1998), in Scotland, found that over two thirds of prisoners had received one or more visits from a community-based social worker in prison, but only about a third recalled having a three-way meeting with the community-based and the prison-based social worker. While throughcare and sentence planning as concepts command widespread support, the expectations of extensive liaison and joint sentence planning are not commonly in place.

Chapter 11

Social Work and Throughcare

Release provisions; social work in prisons; release on licence; Schedule 1 offenders; supervision in the community.

> It has been said, and well said, that it is easy to imprison a man—the difficulty is to release him: and again that the true test of a prison system is what happens to the prisoner when he comes out: and yet again that it is on release that the prisoner faces the hardest part of his punishment. All this means that whatever is done in prison may be wasted unless the hard transition to normal life is eased by a humane and efficient system of after-care. It forms an essential part of the whole system. (Fox, 1952, p.72).

INTRODUCTION

The origins of the concept of throughcare are to be found in the professional debates about the operation of prison after-care. Prison after-care was largely an activity of volunteers and voluntary societies until the early 1960s; thereafter, welfare officers within prisons were paid by central government and were, if fact, part of the prison system. The idea or ideal that after-care should begin as early in the sentence as possible has been long recognised (Paterson, 1932). Early intervention and visits or other contact by community-based officers was viewed as an essential part of providing an effective service (McAllister *et al*, 1992).

Section 27 of the *Social Work (Scotland) Act,* 1968 provided the legislative basis for statutory after-care by local authorities, but, initially, seemed to overlook voluntary assistance. The *Law Reform (Miscellaneous Provisions) (Scotland) Act,* 1990 remedied this. Section 27(1)(c) was inserted in the 1968 Act and placed a duty of local authorities to make available 'advice guidance and assistance' to people who request such a services within 12 months of release from custody.

National Objectives and Standards on Throughcare (NOS) require, as did Fox's view of 'after-care', much 'more than attention to material aid on discharge, though it includes this' (Fox, 1952:257); care, control and surveillance are held together within the definition of supervision, advice, guidance and assistance. In the 1990s social work services are intended to combine practical help for the individual and their family, while working on behalf of victims and acting to protect the public. The Leisk case (McManus, 1997) stressed the importance of public safety now placed on the role of social work supervisors in the community and the importance of working collaboratively with prison staff, with the police, and other relevant agencies.

Concepts of throughcare, resettlement and early release

Concepts of throughcare, resettlement and re-integration are integrally linked to dominant ideas of the function of prison. Traditionally, prisons sought to train and to rehabilitate, and within such a philosophy, the concept of 'after-care' seemed to find a home. Current ideas stress 'humane containment', 'positive custody' and 'opportunity and responsibility' (Coyle, 1991). There has been limited discussion until recently in Scotland on social work's contribution to throughcare and McIvor and Barry's evaluation (1998) confirmed that this area of practice was considered, by both practitioners and managers, as the least developed of all criminal justice social work services.

Revised National Objectives and Standards (NOS) on Throughcare (1996/7) re-established a clear framework for future development. The term throughcare is used to 'denote the provision of a range of social work and associated services to prisoners and their families from the point of sentence or remand, during the period of imprisonment and following release into the community. These services are primarily concerned to assist prisoners to prepare for release, and to help them to resettle in the community, within the law, whether required by statute as part of licence, or simply because the prisoner seeks such a service'.

Principles of throughcare and of integrated practice were embodied within guidance to newly established social work departments (SHHD/SWSG, 1976) in Scotland and included

- the goals of social work service with offenders are similar to those for other client groups, and include helping people…;
- for this client group, however, it is important to recognise the particular need to modify attitudes and behaviour, and to act as an agent of social control;
- social work with offenders and their families is a continuing process which may span a number of situations brought about either by statutory orders, or by voluntary referral;
- should be conceived as a process which starts as soon as sentence has been passed, is developed during detention, and is available thereafter for as long as necessary.

This historical material demonstrates that many of the current policy objectives are long-standing ones. Robertson *et al* (1983) noted 'it is evident that imprisonment per se gives rise to or exacerbates difficulties, and that ironically this may result in inhibiting the development of long-term or casework services, as does the division of responsibility for men and families. At the same time, there is evidence that, in the absence of special provision, the needs of prisoners and their families are unmet despite local voluntary initiatives'. This problem is not specific to Scotland. Any resolution has to look to more fundamental values and principles as reasons for helping people during imprisonment and on release, than the particular theories or models that have underpinned after-care in the recent past (see McAllister et al, 1992; Macguire and Raynor, 1997; Wood, 1991).

Legislative provision has been updated and guidance is in place to support new approaches to prison-based service delivery, complemented by community-based provision which must provide adequate accommodation and employment opportunities for prisoners returning to the community and specialist accommodation for high-risk offenders. Four accredited hostels are planned for this purpose in the future. Changes in legislation have replaced the previous aftercare and licence system, in so far as it existed, with a structured system of **unconditional early release** for most prisoners, supplemented by a more focused and restricted system of **conditional early release** on licence.

The concept of throughcare is more widely cast than is provided for in legislation. NOS are intended to realise the policy aspirations in practice, and contain a wealth of essential guidance. While the guidance emphasises a primary concern with 'the safety of the public', the service objectives and standards promote a reintegrative approach in that 'successful resettlement of an offender within the community is probably the best guarantee against offending'.

Social work services in prison are funded by the Scottish Prison Service (SPS) and delivered by local authority social work, on the basis of service level agreements, as part of their throughcare responsibilities. It is formally recognised that social work activity in this area cannot now be undertaken without reference to prison policy and practice on 'sentence planning' and the expectation that '...prison staff will be required to undertake more intensive work, in conjunction with social workers and other specialists,...as part of the Sentence Planning scheme'. More importantly it is hoped that the change in emphasis will represent a significant change in role and performance, and result in convincing evidence, in the shape of lower re-conviction rates, that resettlement can be effected.

LEGISLATION: GENERAL

After the 1993 Act

Two policy shifts radically affect work in the community with people discharged from penal establishments. One is the recognition that work with offenders is specialised, which finds expression in NOS and the establishment of 100% central funding arrangements; the other is the implementation of a system of early release based on the Kincraig Report's recommendations (1988, Cmnd 598) contained in the *Prisoners and Criminal Proceedings (Scotland) Act,* 1993. The emphasis here is on the impact and implications of the Act, on its influence on work in the community; on government's expectations of control and monitoring within the Act; and with the associated policy and guidance, in particular, revised NOS and *Commitment to Protect* (SWSI, 1997).

Section 27 (b) (ii) of the *Social Work (Scotland) Act,* 1968, requires every local authority to provide a service for 'the supervision of, and the provision of advice, guidance, and assistance for...persons in their area who, following on release from prison or any other form of detention, are required to be under supervision by the terms of an order or licence of the Secretary of State, or of a condition or requirement imposed in pursuance of any enactment'. The section is still subject to the limitation in that it speaks only of the period after release, and does not explicitly include the period of imprisonment itself. It is clearly the intention that NOS on Throughcare will, in this instance, take precedence over the letter of the law and promote serious activity in this field. The provision can be taken as emphasising the points that:

- the prisoner is entitled to good quality social work service;
- the entitlement extends to members of the immediate family.

Equally ex-prisoners should be afforded the same respect and attention to detail at the point of referral as would any other client seeking voluntary assistance. What may be different in their presenting situation is the critical issue of community safety. Social workers are expected to be alert to the potential risk that people discharged from prison may represent and to their role and contribution to the protection and safety of others. At the point of contact the risk may not be well defined. This has implications for social work duty systems, to ensure that non-criminal justice social workers have ready access to the necessary expertise. Voluntary agencies, too, cannot escape considerations of risk, or of public concern, especially where they are funded by local authorities or the Scottish Office to make a contribution to throughcare provision.

RELEASE PROVISIONS

The *Prisoners and Criminal Proceedings (Scotland) Act,* 1993 implemented the main provision of the Kincraig Report (1988). Parole release and supervision provisions are substantially different from those prior to the current enactment. Many categories of prisoners who were previously subject to some form of statutory supervision are now released unconditionally.

Essentially there are six categories of prisoner/detainee provided for; the Act makes greater or lesser changes to the prior arrangements. The categories referred to are:

- the voluntary referral;
- the short-term prisoner i.e. those serving less than 4 years;
- the long-term prisoner i.e. those serving more than 4 years;
- the life sentence prisoner;
- detainees under the *Mental Health (Scotland) Act* ,1984;
- children detained under sections 44 and 208 of the *Criminal Procedures (Scotland) Act,* 1995 .

Voluntary assistance

Voluntary assistance is available, in general terms, under section 27 of the 1968 Act. The *Law Reform (Miscellaneous Provisions) (Scotland) Act,* 1990 added a subsection (c) to section 27 of the 1968 Act, which states:

the provision of advice, guidance, and assistance for persons in their areas who, within 12 months of their release from prison or any other form of detention, request such advice, guidance, or assistance.

This clarifies the point that local authorities have a mandatory duty to provide an after-care service **to any one who asks for it within twelve months of release**, not just to those who qualify for statutory supervision as a part of their sentence and release provision. Subsection (c) should be seen as empowering financial assistance, where appropriate, to people on discharge from prison. NOS recognise that some prisoners, not subject to statutory supervision, will seek voluntary assistance while others may, because of their own vulnerability or the risk they constitute to others, be judged as needing assistance but unlikely to seek it. The latter will remain an important target group for voluntary assistance. The objectives of voluntary assistance are ambitiously outlined in guidance as

- to provide and facilitate a range of services for prisoners and ex-prisoners and, where appropriate, their families, to assist them to deal with any problems they may face, particularly following release;
- to assist offenders to reduce the risk of their re-offending through the provision of a range of services to meet identified needs;
- to seek to limit and redress the damaging consequences of imprisonment including the dislocation of family and community ties, the loss of personal choice, and the resultant stigma;
- to help prisoners and their families to develop their ability to tackle their own problems;
- to help prisoners and their families, on request, to prepare for release;
- to assist the families of released prisoners to adjust to the changed circumstances arising from the prisoners' return, where such a service is needed and requested;
- to assist ex-prisoners to re-integrate successfully into the community and thus reduce the incidence of crime.

It is part of the social work task to encourage ex-prisoners to seek assistance and to 'facilitate contact with the relevant local area team or voluntary agency prior to the prisoner's release to build on work already undertaken in prison'. Many local authorities work in partnership with the independent sector agencies, such as Sacro or APEX, in providing a network of accommodation services, employment training and day-care provision, all of which form an important component in the overall strategy for dealing with the problems of care and resettlement. Practical and tangible help which is meaningful to the ex-prisoner needs to be part of the formula of addressing offending behaviour. Paterson and Tombs (1997) report that ex-prisoners thought that social work concerns about re-offending after release were irrelevant.

The short-term prisoner

Section 1(1) of the 1993 Act stipulates that as soon as a short-term prisoner, i.e. anyone serving less than four years, has served one half of his sentence, he shall be released unconditionally provided that he is not subject to a Supervised Release Order (see below). The release is not entirely unconditional as the prisoner can (under s.16) be returned to serve the unexpired period of the sentence on commission of an offence 'punishable by imprisonment', between the early release date and the date by which he would have served his sentence in full. The person will also be sentenced for the 'new' offence.

Rules made under section 39 of the *Prisons (Scotland) Act* 1989, as amended by section 24 of the 1993 Act, empower governors to 'award' additional days imprisonment for those found guilty of disciplinary offences. These additional days (ADAs) must not exceed one sixth of the prisoner's sentence. In view of these provisions it cannot be assumed that the short-term prisoner will necessarily always be released at the half-way point of the sentence.

Under previous arrangements the two to four-year group were the mainstay of the parole system. At a stroke this was swept away by the implementation of the 1993 Act. This group, particularly young offenders, now represents the main group to be targeted in respect to voluntary help and assistance.

The short-term prisoner: supervised release orders

The Supervised Release Order (SRO) is a relatively new form of supervision on release from custody, introduced by section 14 of the 1993 Act, for prisoners sentenced to **'imprisonment for a term of not less than twelve months and not more than four years'** (in effect the majority of serious offenders). An amendment was made by the *Criminal Justice Act,* 1993 to make the order available for young offenders as well as adults. Section 209 of the *Criminal Procedure (Scotland) Act,* 1995 provides the current legal basis for supervised release orders, made by the court **at the point of sentencing,** if it considers it necessary to protect the public from serious harm from the offender on his release from prison. Conditions can be inserted in the order. The Crime and Disorder Act, 1998 will limit the use of SROs to convictions on indictment and will exclude sex offences.

A number of appealed cases suggest that sentences should not be modified to bring offenders within the provisions of section 209. In Maltman v HM Advocate (Aug. 22, 1997), the appeal court took the view that the matter of sentencing must be dealt with in stages, first determining whether or not custody is appropriate and thereafter the length of custody. Only then, if the sentence is within the appropriate range, should an SRO be considered. In another case where the SER made a strong recommendation for post-release supervision, an appeal to reduce a four-year sentence to bring it within the scope of section 209 was rejected.

Right of Appeals An offender may appeal against the imposition of an SRO. Similarly any decision made in respect of **requirements inserted** under section 15 (4) of the 1993 Act or any decision arrived at in respect of breach proceedings under section 18(2) are subject to appeal. An appeal must be lodged **within two weeks** of the court's decision (section 19). The court which made the order may on application of the subject or the supervisor amend, vary or cancel any requirement specified in or by virtue of the order. The terms of an SRO are dealt with in the section 'Supervision in the Community' below.

The long-term prisoner

The long-term prisoner is defined as one serving four or more years in aggregate. The qualifying date for parole is **'after half sentence'** (section 1(3)) and the prisoner can be considered for parole annually thereafter until he has less than 16 months to serve. This provision applies to prisoners sentenced on or after 1 October 1993. (For those sentenced to under ten years prior to October 1st 1993, section 22 of the *Prisons (Scotland) Act* 1989 still applies and allows the Secretary of State to release a prisoner on licence 'after one third of sentence', or 12 months, whichever is greater.) Discretionary release requires a decision from the Parole Board. The provision applies both to adult offenders and to young offenders detained under section 208 of the CP Act, 1995, and is known as a **parole licence**.

Section 1(2) stipulates that, in any case, the long-term prisoner shall be released on licence **on completion of two thirds of his sentence.** Anyone, therefore, who is not recommended for parole must serve their sentence until the two-thirds point, plus any lost remission or added days. The residue of the sentence will be 'served' in the community under the supervision of a social worker, authorised in the terms of the licence granted by the Secretary of State. A licence issued under this section is referred to as a **'non-parole' licence**.

Prisoners released on non-parole licence under section 1(2) of the 1993 Act will normally have been refused parole or will have 'self rejected' from the process. Those released under section 16(7) will have re-offended whilst on licence. It is important that the supervising officer is clear about which of these three circumstances has been involved in a case, since the route to release on non-parole licence may have a bearing on the assessment of risk. The number of prisoners released on non-parole licences is expected to grow from 398 in 1997/98 to 566 in 1999/2000.

Example: Bob McNab has served six years of a twelve-year sentence,. He applies for release on parole licence. This application is rejected by the Parole Board, having considered his response to prison and the various reports to hand. He decides against any further attempt at obtaining parole release and simply awaits his licensed release at the point where he has served two thirds of the sentence, i.e. at the eight-year point.

The licence remains in force until the 'entire period specified in the sentence' has elapsed, known as his 'sentence expiry date'. This is reckoned from the commencement of sentence and means that where, for some reason, the sentence was ordered to be from a date prior to the court's decision, because of time spent on remand, that date becomes the operative one for this purpose (section 11(1)). NOS recognise that such prisoners are 'likely to present a high risk in terms of response to supervision' and this must inform the approach adopted.

The Secretary of State is required to consult the Parole Board where he intends to impose a non-standard condition in the supervision licence. The consultation can take two forms:

- use of parole dossiers; and/or
- reports from prison staff.

If the documentation suggests the desirability of imposing any non-standard conditions, the Secretary of State may request a **Home Circumstances Report** (HCR) and a report from the social worker in the prison. Prisoners who have been released on mandatory supervision and have committed a new offence during the period of supervision for which they receive a new custodial sentence of under four years (either for the offence or for the breach, or both), are released on mandatory supervision on a **'short sentence' licence**.

The long-term prisoner: parole

The system of parole came into being in Scotland on April 1st 1968, (*Criminal Justice Act* 1968, ss.60 and 61). The authority for parole in Scotland now lies with the *Prisoners and Criminal Proceedings (Scotland) Act*, 1993.

The concept of parole has always involved a form of **'early release'**. At its core lies the concept of release 'ahead of time' and of the prisoner **'serving out his time in the community'** under supervision. However parole candidates are, and form, a highly selected group within the early release provisions. As a consequence, there is an expectation on supervisors to act, and to be seen to be acting, in ways which reflect a concern for *public protection* and *person-specific control*, which now applies to the range of licences identified above.

Parole has been defined as an 'administrative scheme...whereby a person may be released under specific conditions to serve part of that sentence under supervision in the community' (Parole Board of Scotland, 1986). Its aim was defined as giving prisoners 'the maximum chance of successful and safe re-integration into society by releasing them under supervision before they would normally be due for liberation' (ibid.). The emphasis then, as well as on risk of re-offending, was on the person's response (the training curve notion) and on their progress to an extent that further custody would not improve their prospects on release (the peak notion), and on suitable supports within the community (the re-integrative notion). The *Parole Board (Scotland) Rules* 1993 and 1995 set out the matters which may be taken into account by the Board in considering the references by the Secretary of State

- the nature and circumstances of any offence of which that person has been convicted or found guilty by a court of law;
- that person's conduct since the date of his/her current sentence(s);
- the likelihood of that person committing any offence or causing harm to any other person if he/she were to be released on licence, remain on licence or be re-released as the case may be;
- what that person intends to do if he/she were to be released on licence, remain on licence or be re-released on licence, as the case may be, and the likelihood of his/her fulfilling those intentions; and
- any written information or documents or written representation which the Secretary

of State or the person concerned has sent to the Board or which the Board has otherwise obtained.

The rules provide for prisoners to have access to reports and other information contained in their dossiers, with suitable safeguards in non-tribunal cases for withholding of information that would be potentially damaging to disclose. McAra (1998) suggested that for most cases it was the changes occurring during the time spent in custody rather than the quality of community-based services that was the key factor in Parole Board decisions. She also noted that Parole Board members lacked information about the content and process of parole supervision.

The Parole Board consists of Secretary of State appointees, including judges, psychiatrists, social workers, criminologists and business people and deals with matters of early conditional release and the recall of such prisoners. Section 20 of the 1993 Act relates to the composition and function of the Board . It simply brings matters into line with the needs of the present Act. The former local review committees which made recommendations to the Board in relation to certain individual institutions were phased out in 1995 and all decisions on release are considered directly by the Board.

Section 21 of the 1993 Act made provision for the creation of posts of 'parole advisers' 'to give advice to prisoners or **former prisoners** (emphasis added), who wish to make representation to the Secretary of State or to the Parole Board as regards any matter concerning their release on licence or return to prison or detention...'. These have not been introduced and it is to be assumed that they have quietly been dropped because of cost. Potentially this could have been an important development as it would have created a body seen as impartial and available.

Integrated approaches to parole supervision have still to be achieved. Paterson and Tombs (1997) note that communication between Parole Board members, community-based and prison-based social workers need improvement. The Board generally wanted more information about social work policy and services; social workers wanted more specific feedback about outcomes of parole considerations. Parole Board members, offenders and social workers appeared to have different understanding about the role of social work.

The long-term prisoner: life and designated life prisoner

A life prisoner is one whose sentence of life imprisonment is fixed by law. A designated life prisoner is one whose is 'sentenced to life imprisonment for an offence...not fixed by law;...whose sentence was imposed under section 205A(2) of the CP Act, 1995 (imprisonment for life on further conviction of certain offences); or...whose sentence was imposed in respect of a murder committed by him before he attained the age of 18 years'; and the sentence was determined at the discretion of the court (Section 2 of the 1993 Act as amended by section 16 of the *Crime and Punishment (Scotland) Act* 1997). The 1997 Act replaced the term 'discretionary life prisoner' with the term 'designated life prisoner'. In practice the definition refers to those who received a life sentence for a crime other than murder and to those under 18 years receiving a life sentence for murder. Thus an offence of murder carries a statutory life sentence while that of armed robbery does not. The latter may be of such a kind and quality, combined with previous record, that the court chooses to impose a life sentence. The former becomes a '*mandatory life prisoner*', the latter a '*designated life prisoner*'. The designated part is the period which the court decides the prisoner must spend in custody before release can be considered, referred to as the period for punishment and general deterrence. These prisoners are released on '**life licence**'.

Under section 1(4) of the 1993 Act (section 26(1) of the 1989 Act) mandatory life prisoners may be referred to the Parole Board by the Secretary of State for consideration, after consultation with the Lord Justice General (Scotland's top judicial officer), or in his absence, the Lord Justice Clerk and, if available, the trial judge, before reaching a decision to release on parole licence. The term 'if available' gives some indication that these procedures are not intended to be delayed unnecessarily.

Section 1(6)(a) covers a small number of prisoners, but in the nature of their criminal history, a vitally important group. Section 1(6)(a) is concerned with prisoners who are serving one or more life sentences *and* a term of imprisonment (irrespective of length). Section 1(6)(b) is concerned with prisoners serving more than a life sentence, whether the sentences have been passed at the one sentencing point or at different times. The Secretary of State '*shall not release*' such a prisoner '*unless and until*' certain steps have been taken. He must:

i) refer the case to the Parole Board for its advice. The Board may not make a recommendation unless requested to do so. (In passing it would appear that there is nothing in the Act which would prevent the Board 'keeping an eye' on such cases, and indeed keeping a file for future reference);

ii) consult the Lord Justice General, or failing that, his deputy, the Lord Justice Clerk, and, if available, the trial judge.

If granted parole, the prisoner will be released under a single licence. In other words the release relates to the person and not to the number of sentences being served.

There are certain important distinctions to be drawn. One is that to qualify for the status of 'designated life prisoner' (DLP) the offender has to be made the subject of an order by the sentencing court. This order relates to the period decided by the court as 'the designated part', taking into account the seriousness of the offence, any related offences and the previous convictions of the prisoner. This 'designated part' is the point in the sentence term at which he *may* be paroled. The issue may be referred to the Designated Lifer Tribunal (DLT) by the Secretary of State, or it may result in an application by the prisoner. A DLT is a tribunal of three Parole Board members appointed by the chair of the Board to hear the case. The DLT must be chaired by a serving or former High Court Judge or sheriff and operates under tribunal procedures. DLTs have the power to order the Secretary of State to release the prisoner immediately, if it is satisfied that he no longer need be kept in custody to protect the public, or it can make recommendations to the Secretary of

State about his future location, the timing of the his next review, and the steps needed to deal with his offending.

There is a qualification to the prisoner's application. He may not apply where:

- he is serving a term of imprisonment (other than the life sentence), before he has served one half of that sentence.
- less than two years has elapsed since the disposal (read dismissal—otherwise he would not now be in prison) of any, or the more recent if more than one, referral of his case to the DLT.

The conditions for licensing DLPs are stringent. Where the court *does not make a DLP order* it is required to state its reasons, and any such order or decision shall feature in any appeal or review of the sentence (s.2(3)). Any **breach of the licence conditions** are dealt with in exactly the same way as indicated below. These licences are for the term of the sentence—life—unless revoked by the Secretary of State.

Young offenders

Section 6 of the 1993 Act simplifies the matter of young offenders sentenced to detention in a Young Offender's Institution (YOI) on or after October 1st 1993. It provides for licensing arrangements on exactly *the same footing as applies to adult offenders.* It should be noted that in the case of young people between 18 and 21, convicted of murder, they 'shall not be sentenced to imprisonment for life but to be detained in a young offender's institution and shall be liable to be detained for life' (section 205(3) of the CP Act, 1995). The phasing out of statutory supervision for young offenders sentenced to less than four years, does not indicate that this vulnerable group requires less social work assistance. It is, however, likely that many will not seek it on a voluntary basis. The points raised above on voluntary assistance with regard to short-term prisoners apply here with even greater force.

Mental health detainees

The 1993 Act deals with certain issues relating to people detained under *Mental Health (Scotland) Act,* 1984 (section 4). These are matters unlikely to feature on a day-to-day basis, and because of their complexity are dealt with in Chapter 12.

Child detainees

Where a child is convicted on indictment (solemn procedure), the court may order the child to be detained under section 208 of the *Criminal Procedure (Scotland) Act,* 1995, subject to the provisions of section 7 of the 1993 Act, as amended by Schedule 4 para. 86(4) of the *Criminal Procedure (Consequential Provisions)(Scotland) Act,* 1995. Where a child is sentenced for a period of less than four years, he shall be released as soon as half the specified sentence period has been served. Where the child is sentenced to more than four years (excluding life and 'detained without limit of time' sentences), the child shall be released at the expiry of two thirds of the sentence. Children, in effect, are covered by the same provisions for 'short-term' and 'long-term' prisoners. A child detained under section 208 of the CP Act, 1995, irrespective of sentence length, **may be released on licence** at any time by the Secretary of State, following a recommendation by the Parole Board.

Exactly the same considerations apply in respect of further offending and the provision for court action in returning the child to detention (section 7(3) of the 1993 Act) as in relation to adults under licence discussed above. In those very rare cases of murder where a person under 18 is not 'sentenced to imprisonment for life but to be detained without limit of time' (section 205(2) of the CP Act, 1995), for all practical purposes this should be read as a life sentence and treated accordingly.

The provision for children detained under summary procedure (section 8 of the 1993 Act) are included in section 44 of the *Criminal Procedure (Scotland) Act,* 1995, which relates to the detention of a child in residential accommodation, provided under Part II of the *Children (Scotland) Act,* 1995

- The detained child shall be released at the point where half of the detention period has elapsed, and until the entire period of the detention has elapsed, 'may be required by the local authority to submit to supervision in accordance with such conditions as they consider appropriate' (s.44(6(a) of the CP Act, 1995)).
- The local authority may review the case and 'in consequence of such review and after having regard to the best interests of the child and the need to protect members of the public, release the child 'for such a period and on such conditions as the local authority consider appropriate; or unconditionally'(s.44 (6(b)).

The wording here is important and it should be noted that the best interests of the child are weighed against public protection considerations in coming to any decision. The **conditions** and **period** imply considerable flexibility in this provision. The emphasis should be on structured programmes rather than on random provision. Section 44 refers only to the sheriff courts; the district court has no jurisdiction over children. It should be noted that 'the words "conviction" and "sentence" shall not be used in relation to children dealt with summarily' (s.165 of the CP Act, 1995); instead they should be replaced by 'a finding of guilt' and an 'order made upon such a finding' (Nicholson 1992:74).

Where a child is subject to a supervision requirement by a children's hearing, the order resumes operation on release (s.44(7) of the CP Act, 1995)). Further offending during any release period is subject to recall on the same terms as an adult; namely for a period, in whole or in part, equal in length to the period between the date of the commission of the new offence to the date on which the sentence is due to terminate.

Circular HHD 26/1993 requires that supervision of licences under section 208 be informed by the principles and practice set out in NOS.

Fine defaulters

Section 5 of the 1993 Act makes it clear that any one imprisoned (or detained in a Young Offenders' Institute) for fine default shall be unconditionally released on

completion of one half of the sentence i.e. shall have the status of a short-term prisoner. The calculations in Chapter 7 for time in prison against monies outstanding,
holds good. The payment of the outstanding fine should result in immediate release.

Compassionate release

There is provision in section 3 of the 1993 Act for the Secretary of State to release
on licence (i.e. the licence appropriate to the sentence term) any prisoner on compassionate grounds. A request can be made by any party acting on behalf of the
prisoner. Section 3(2) provides for the Secretary of State to consult with the Parole
Board 'unless the circumstances are such as to render consultation impracticable'.
In most instances the governor will be responsible for the initial notification to the
Parole and Lifer Review Division of SOHD.

NOS indicate that the 'most likely circumstances in which compassionate release will be granted are where the life expectancy of the prisoner is short'. This is
a serious matter and only in exceptional circumstances is this likely to be granted.
A Home Circumstances Report will be requested to establish any health-care plan,
and the willingness of family and services to provide adequate support. The social
work unit in the prison and the local authority will be notified so that a supervising
officer can be appointed, with the expectation of liaison, in preparation for the
release. Section 3(3) expressly excludes compassionate release as 'constituting
release for the purpose of a supervised release order'; in short, the SRO, as public
protection measure, remains.

Licence terms and conditions

Parole and non-parole licences under the 1993 Act last until the sentence expiry
date, but under section 17(6) a licence, other than a life licence, may be revoked
early by the Secretary of State. A life licence lasts for the whole of the person's
natural life.

Section 12 of the 1993 Act deals with licence conditions. Standard conditions
and any specific conditions of a licence are a matter for the Secretary of State in
consultation with the Parole Board. In the case of designated life prisoners, the
Secretary of State is bound by the recommendations of the Board with regard to
the licence conditions.

There is a general provision at section 12(2) for standard conditions within a
licence requiring that

a) he be under the supervision of a relevant officer of the local authority; or if
   resident in, or moves to England or Wales, under the supervision of a probation
   officer;
b) he comply with such requirements as that officer may specify, for the purposes of supervision.

Conditions may be subsequently added, varied or cancelled by the Secretary of
State after consultation with the Board. Similarly, early termination of conditions

is possible by the same process. Section 17(6) of the 1993 Act allows the Secretary of State to revoke a licence by cancelling all the conditions in it. The person is then treated as having been released unconditionally.

Distinctions between the licence's **conditions** and the supervisor's **requirements** are important; the latter as a means for setting out clearly what is expected of the licensee by the supervisor is to ensure that the licence is complied with rigorously. It is important that requirements are coherent and appropriate to the individual's situation and that the licensee understands the basic rules governing supervision and the consequences of failure to comply, particularly the risk of recall.

Section 17 of the 1993 Act deals with '**revocation of licences**'. The Secretary of State has the power to revoke the licence of any long-term or life prisoner if 'recommended to do so by the Parole Board'; **or** 'if revocation and recall are, in the opinion of the Secretary of State, expedient in the public interest and it is not practicable to await such recommendations' (s.17(1)). The power of the Secretary of State to act without a Parole Board recommendation should only be invoked in cases where the circumstances demand swift action. Nonetheless recall may or may not be as a result of the commission of a further offence or breach of licence conditions. Where the Secretary of State acts without a Parole Board recommendation or the prisoner makes written representation, the case must be referred to the Parole Board for review.

Further offences by licensees

Section 16 of the 1993 Act is concerned with the commission of further offences by short or long-term licensees, and with offences dealt with on either side of the border.

If during the supervised period a further offence 'punishable with imprisonment' is committed, the court may order the licensee to be returned to prison '**for the whole or any part of the period**' calculated from '**the date of the order for his return**' (i.e. any period spent on remand awaiting the court hearing does not count), equal in length to the period between the date on which the new offence was committed and the date on which he would (but for his release on licence) have served his sentence in full. This is in addition to any disposal the court may make for the new offence. It is unlikely that the court will impose a short sentence for an offence if the recall order runs for a period of years. However, the decision lies with the court. Where the court is inferior to the court of origin then the matter must be referred to the superior court. Where the second court is in England or Wales it may, in addition to, or instead of making an order, remit the matter to the court of origin for action.

The licence, on recall, does not expire and is not revoked; section 11(3)(b) indicates it continues in force. The licence will run until either the term of any sentence imposed by the second court expires, or the period ordered for his return to prison has expired, or the original term of the licence has been completed, whichever is the longer period. For practical purposes a **short sentence** licence is dealt with as a non-parole licence.

SOCIAL WORK IN PRISON AND RESETTLEMENT

The role and significance of prison-based social work as a central part in an integrated approach to throughcare on both sides of the prison wall has remained underdeveloped. Paterson and Tombs (1998) note in a recent evaluation that no arrangements were found to be in place for liaison between community and prison-based social workers across local authorities, resulting in limited communication about the preparation and content of reports and about responsibility for developing release plans.

Social work in prison

A Shared Enterprise (SWSG, 1979) examined the respective roles of prison-based social workers and other prison staff, especially the main grade discipline officers. The title promised more than it delivered. There was little reference to any shared enterprise between social workers in the prison and community-based social workers, which reflected accurately practice at the time. An opportunity was missed to emphasise this, and if anything, the paper tended to underline its separateness from community-based social work.

Parsloe's review of the social work system in prisons (1985) concluded that a national framework should be established and recommended that

> such a framework should establish the overall purpose of prison social work; set policies for organisation and staffing; work to be undertaken; social work methods; premises; security; record keeping; support staff and the relationship between the role of the prison officer and that of the social worker; provide a means by which priorities are set for the different kinds of work undertaken (para. 1.1.3).

Continuity through Co-operation, A National Framework of Policy and Practice Guidance for Social Work in Scottish Penal Establishments (SWSG, 1990) was a major improvement and provided a valuable framework. The focus of the policy was largely on social work *within* prison establishments and did not, in itself, provide a model of integrated provision required for an effective throughcare strategy, but it does stress the importance of developing continuity of provision between prison-based and community-based staff. The model of operation focuses heavily on programmes provided by social work and is in need of updating in the context of SPS's emphasis on opportunity and responsibility within the prison system as a whole, in which social work is but one element.

NOS have attempted to produce a more integrated model, setting social work in prison as a pivotal component in throughcare and sentence planning, providing a distinctive service base within the walls, which has a crucial role in assisting prisoners manage prison life and in preparing for resettlement. The service is delivered by local authorities through a service-level agreement with and funded by Scottish Prison Service (SPS) as part of their overall responsibilities for throughcare. The term 'prison social work', rightly, has been replaced by 'social work services in prisons' or 'prison-based social work'; essentially social workers are in prison, they are not of prisons. The greatest challenge facing the service is overcoming the structural and organisational problems which have been prevalent in the relationship with SPS over many years. NOS have attempted to establish benchmarks for social work in prison which SPS are 'required' to fund in order to meet their own responsibilities. It remains to be seen whether this formula is workable, and how much of a priority social work in prison will receive, particularly if private provision is developed within the prison service.

Revised NOS on Throughcare contain explicit commitments required of SPS which represent 'a joint commitment by SPS and the local authority towards common objectives and service outcomes'. Throughcare is to be seen, ideally, as part of a continuum of services geared, on one hand, to reduce the numbers in custody by the provision of credible community-based disposals, and, on the other, to provide effective resettlement programmes for those in custody, aimed at protecting the community and preventing re-admission and re-conviction. The overall aim of the service is to help prisoners reduce their risk of re-offending and to help them resettle and re-integrate within the community.

NOS recognise that the involvement of prison staff in providing practical assistance and information to prisoners is an essential and complementary component to ensure efficient and effective use of social work in prison. All establishments are required to have formal systems to ensure that prison officers deal with problems in relation to

- providing information about prison procedures and routines, visits etc. and including the availability of social work;
- providing information about assistance with welfare benefits e.g.. housing, discharge grants etc.;
- practical assistance involving contact with prisoners' relatives, routine contacts with DSS, landlords, housing agencies lawyers etc.

Some prison staff will be required to undertake more intensive work, in conjunction with social workers and other specialists, to help prisoners tackle their offending behaviour and related problems as part of the Sentence Planning Scheme. The intention is partnership in provision. However an additional sentence found its way into the NOS at final publication that had not been present in the final draft available to local authorities for consultation: '**SPS will determine the balance of programme-related work between prison staff, social workers and other professional and agencies according to regime requirements**'. The Scottish Office have acknowledged publicly the sensitivity between local authorities and SPS which has resulted. The addition leaves little doubt about the power relationship. There is a risk that this statement may signal that SPS want go it alone. With a range of new SPS appointments aimed at improving provision within prisons, it remains to be seen if common service objectives can be achieved that will establish a social work role in preparation for admission, and preparation for discharge linked to social work services in the community. The specific objectives for social work in prisons outlined in NOS are

- to offer prisoners access to a range and level of social work services similar to those in the community;
- to contribute to public safety by making available a range of individual and group work programmes to address offending behaviour;
- to provide support and assistance to help prisoners resettle and re integrate into society following release.

These services must be delivered by 'fully qualified social workers as an integral part of local authorities' social work services' taking into account their statutory responsibilities before and after the release in respect of many prisoners. They must focus on offending behaviour; seek also to address those problems arising from imprisonment and problems which are likely to confront prisoners on release; assist maintenance of family and community ties as appropriate; and be delivered without discrimination. The core activities of social work in prisons are identified as

Assessment	risk and #dangerousness, personal and social need and re-offending; action plans resulting from assessment
Programme Provision	individual and group work to address particular offending behaviour or associated problems, such as alcohol or drug problems and to prepare prisoners for release;
Programme Co-ordination	programmes from other agencies aimed at assisting resettlement;
Monitoring and Evaluation	social work programmes;
Consultancy	for prison staff and management;
Sentence Planning	social work activity integrated with SPS activity;
Family work	to assist re-integration.

The organisational and resource implications for achieving such objectives are dealt with through a joint planning process involving SPS, SWSG and COSLA. Priorities for services provision are for chief social work officers and governors to establish with regard to the needs of the population and function of each institution.

McAra (1998) stressed that good quality effective prison-based social work depends on good inter-agency links and concluded that the quality of provision had improved since the implementation of *Continuity Through Co-operation*, with social workers undertaking more offence-focused work. However the evaluation also suggested that there was a lack of consistency across prison units in the range and quality of provision. Limitations were attributed to poor strategic planning on the part of some local authorities and under-resourcing.

There is a specific responsibility on social work to initiate early contact with prisoners who will be subject to statutory supervision on release or who fall within the remit of Schedule 1 of the CP Act, 1995. The guidance identifies the twin concerns of '**vulnerability**' and '**risk**' as the guiding principles for priority setting and outlines a 'menu' of priority groups that need to be given attention, where applicable, including the identified 'vulnerable': those at risk of self-injury; mentally disturbed/handicappedn people; HIV/AIDS sufferers; those on compassionate release supervision; those with alcohol or drug-related problems; children and young offenders up to age 18; Schedule 1 offenders; those subject to SROs on release; first-timers in custody; and those seeking voluntary assistance on release.

In addition, the guidance recognises that many **remand prisoners** will have pressing problems, often of a practical nature, arising from or exacerbated by the crisis of custody. While work must always reflect the presumed innocence of unconvicted prisoners the quality of early contact may well influence their subsequent attitudes to social work involvement in the event of conviction. The promotion of social work assistance through contributions to prisoner induction programmes and by providing service description leaflets is also encouraged. The identification of the most vulnerable requires the collaboration of prison staff in alerting social work. and ultimately requires the co-operation of the prisoners themselves. Governors have the responsibility of ensuring that 'effective systems to identify such prisoners' are in place.

The aspirations and principles outlined in guidance are laudable. However there are no working or empirical definitions of 'vulnerable' or 'at risk', nor, as yet, evaluated models of effective practice with these groupings. The priority 'menu' is all-embracing and it remains to be seen whether such needs can be addressed effectively and met within existing resources. What is emphasised is that social work, in principle, is available to all convicted prisoners, while social workers in prison are charged with specific responsibilities to certain categories of prisoners, in so far as resources allow.

All prisoners subject to mandatory supervision on release must be interviewed:

- SRO prisoners within 21 days of reception;
- long-term prisoners during the induction or preliminary sentence-planning process;
- short sentence licensees prior to release;
- compassionate release licensees prior to release.

The objective is to outline and encourage their use of social work during the prison sentence; give information on the release systems, or in the latter two, to explain the nature and obligations of the licence. Reports must be provided for early and conditional release:

- parole/life licence;
- non-parole licence.

Reports from the social worker in the prison are in addition and complementary to Home Circumstances Reports provided by community-based social workers. Liaison is essential to ensure the accuracy and consistency of information and advice offered to the Secretary of State. Such reports should normally be based on at least two interviews and address:

personal circumstances; attitude to offence; attitude to present sentence; attitude to and plans for release; response to imprisonment; family and other significant relationships; employment; alcohol/drug problems etc.; attitude to supervision; risk of further offending.

The report should provide an action plan indicating work undertaken prior to release and proposals for future provision.

Pre-release work: parole and statutory supervision

The task of the social worker in any initial contact is to try and engage the prisoner in developing realistic and achievable release plans. When notice of the **'notification of release'** date is given, this should trigger more detailed planning. This work must be undertaken in liaison with the appointed supervising officer. While the overall focus is particularly on issues to be addressed in the community, the focus in the prison will be the immediate needs of the prisoner. A joint meeting between prisoner, supervising officer and social worker in prison should take place at least a month before the release date and a written note of agreement should be taken by the social worker in the prison. McIvor and Barry (1998) found that only about a third of prisoners interviewed remembered any joint meetings.

Pre-release work: non-parole

The work should be similar to that for parole. The guidance seeks to forge a division between 'welfare tasks', which it sees as becoming much more prominent in the work of prison officers, and 'social work'. Moreover, the management of priority groups within prison, (prisoners at risk of self-injury; mentally disturbed prisoners; prisoners convicted of child abuse; and prisoners with, or at risk of, HIV/ AIDS) places the prison officer in the front line daily, and any involvement with these prisoners on the part of a social worker is likely to be secondary in comparison, certainly in terms of knowledge gained of the people. While the guidance is very positive in its emphasis on collaborative working, there are dangers of advancing unduly inflated claims for the role and influence of prison officer and social worker that cannot be delivered.

The strategy outlined above, equally, requires elementary services to help families survive and function in the prisoner's absence or any work toward resettlement with the prisoner is likely to be undermined before it has even been begun. Programmes in a penal establishment in which wives and family members can participate are to be encouraged, but may prove unrealistic given the catchment areas of most institutions.

The main issues likely to arise, in practical terms, are that non-parole licencees may be unwilling to co-operate in any pre-release planning; they are likely to decide very late where they are going to go; and, even when they do, social work may be notified very late in the day. All of these factors make it difficult for social work to contribute constructively to planning, particularly to finding suitable accommodation. More data is needed on the nature of the populations from which requests for social work help is likely to come, and on groups who do not 'come forward' but do have significant needs and may present risks to the community on their return.

RELEASE ON LICENCE

Administrative arrangements and procedures

Basically there are two aspects of the administrative arrangements and procedures under the present system. One concerns 'voluntary assistance', the other concerns licences. There is considerable scope for action by social work at the point of sentence and at every stage during sentence, both in liaison with the institutions and with families, and latterly at pre-discharge and on liberation. In every case of voluntary assistance the task is to record information on identified issues where help may be offered, identifying what might be possible in the short term and what may require significantly longer input. If the prisoner's confidence in the relationship is not well established at the initial stage, the prospects for meaningful work on return are likely to be limited. The second strand concerns the licensee. Here the situation is very different.

Preparations for release on parole or life licence

Once a prisoner is due for consideration for discretionary release on parole or life licence, a dossier of information to assist the decision making process is compiled, including reports from prison staff and other professionals with a knowledge of the prisoner and his circumstances, and, for those sentenced after October 1st 1993, a report from the trial judge. The supervisor will be expected to be fully involved in the pre-release planning. NOS require that the local authority is given at least four weeks notice of the 'notification of release' date for parole or statutory licence prisoners, and a supervising officer must be nominated within seven days of its receipt. This is intended to trigger detailed planning for release outlined in the guidance. If earlier notification of release is given of life licences or prisoners serving very long sentences, the local authority must, similarly, advise the Parole Board of the nominated supervising officer within seven days.

The supervisor must write to the prisoner within 14 days of being nominated, make contact with the social work unit in the prison and begin the joint process of pre-release planning. At least a month before release, a **pre-release meeting** should take place involving the prisoner, supervisor and social worker in the prison and any other relevant parties. This meeting is intended to finalise the release plan based on earlier proposals contained in reports to the Parole Board; to identify respective responsibilities for tasks to be undertaken; and to set provisional objectives for the initial phase of supervision.

The plan 'must provide an overall assessment of (the prisoner's) needs, and must address any outstanding issues surrounding accommodation, finance, relations and personal or behavioural problems' (NOS). The social worker in the prison has responsibility for circulating a written note of agreement to all participants.

A benchmark for good pre-release planning is clearly established. Possibly recognising the gulf between the intention and current practice, the guidance also notes that where time scales do not allow for such a meeting, '*wherever possible* (emphasis added), such a meeting should be convened prior to release'. It remains to be seen whether the benchmark will become the norm or simply good practice when it can be managed.

The social work authority in the area in which the prisoner intends to reside on release is required to provide a Home Circumstances Report in a number of circumstances.

Home leave

In the case of short-term prisoners, there is no expectation that a community-based social worker from the will make any contact during home leave. However, in the case of those subject to an SRO on release, temporary leave provides a useful opportunity for early contact. NOS suggest that contact should be made with these prisoners during home leave 'at least once prior to the prisoner's final release'. These considerations apply more so in relation to long-term prisoners, all of whom will be released subject to supervision. Again the implication is that they should be contacted at least once in the community prior to release.

Home circumstances reports

This old term provides rather an inadequate description of what is required. In the past, many were precisely that, more like an estate agent's circular than a social work assessment of need and risk. The report writer is required to provide information and assess a range of factors which may influence the resettlement prospects of the prisoner on his release. The social work unit in the prison is required to provide a separate report from that provided by the community-based social worker. NOS on Throughcare outline the objectives of the report, firstly, to provide a description and assessment of

- the social and family context to which the prisoner intends to return on release;
- the extent to which this is likely to be supportive or otherwise, in assisting the prisoner's successful resettlement;

and secondly to provide an indication (prediction) of

- the likely level and nature of supervision and support that will be provided to the prisoner and family;
- any special programmes, facilities or resources which might be offered to assist successful reintegration into the community and reduce the risk of re-offending.

The report writer is required to visit the proposed release accommodation, interview those living there, where appropriate, on at least one occasion, and to contact and liaise with the relevant social worker in the prison to ensure accuracy and consistency of the information supplied.

The issue of 'rights' is stressed and the writer is required to ensure that those interviewed understand that any information supplied is likely to be made known to the prisoner in accordance with the *Parole Board (Scotland) Rules* (see disclosure below) except within the limited provision for withholding damaging information.

The report writer must also explain to those interviewed

- the nature of discretionary release;
- the need for a positive recommendation from the Parole Board;
- the nature and duration of statutory supervision following release; and
- offer to re-visit, if requested, to explain the outcome of the parole review.

NOS emphasise the importance of indicating the source of any information and differentiating throughout between fact, opinion or surmise. In addition, a detailed structure for the report is outlined, which could be used almost directly as headings for the report:

Basis of Report	extent and details of visits and contacts; previous knowledge of family and prisoner;
Family Circumstances	social relationships and functioning; accommodation, finance;
Family Attitudes	to the prisoner, to the impact of his return, to criminality in general and the prisoner's in particular;
Environment	employment prospects, peer contacts and other significant relationships and their likely influence; anticipated resentment in the local community to the prisoner's return.
Specialist Resources	programmes or facilities;
Overall Assessment	risk factors re re-offending; social or personal needs; level of support available from family and network;
Provisional Release Plan	level and nature of supervision to be provided.

It is interesting to note that the requirement to consider community attitudes reinforces the role of social work as working on behalf of victims and in public protection and is consistent with public concern about sex offenders.

McAra (1998:20) found that reports tended to be descriptive rather than analytic and on average included four of the required types of information outlined by NOS, with only 10% including all the required types. Consequently reports to the Parole Board were judged to have minimal impact, partly because of the patchy information on the risk of re-offending. The less well covered areas tended to be specialist resources available on release, and family attitude towards social work supervision. Most of the reports provided an assessment on housing and domestic arrangements and overall level of support, with less than half including assessment in other areas. Some social workers did not see risk assessment or need assessment as part of the task. Most recognised it was difficult to do, since few had access to information about the offence and previous offences on which to base their judgement, and most had very limited knowledge, if any, of the prisoner.

Special cases

In the case of **mandatory life prisoners**, the provisional release date will normally be set to follow a pre-release programme which is likely to involve at least a further year in custody. Home Circumstances Reports (HCR) need to be updated from time to time and routinely about every four months before the release date is due. The report should be prepared by the proposed supervisor in consultation with a manager, and

- address any changes in the home circumstances and their effect on his resettlement prospects;
- where home leave has been taken, assess how successful it has been;
- assess the outcome of any counselling undertaken in the home area in preparation for release;
- confirm any arrangements for ongoing counselling, support etc.;
- comment of the prisoner's employment prospects or plans;
- consider any special factors such as the release of a co-accused into the same area. (para. 152)

In preparing an HCR on a **designated life prisoner**, the report writer may be called to give oral evidence to the designated lifer tribunal of the Parole Board. These hearings will normally be held at no less than seven weeks after the date of the report. If there is a recommendation for release, then the release plan will have to be put into immediate operation. In cases of **compassionate release** the emphasis of the HCR is likely to be on the care plan available, and the willingness of family members, NHS, and other agencies to provide adequate support.

Where a report has been prepared for parole purposes within three months of a prisoner being considered for **temporary release** or **escorted release**, that report will suffice to inform the governor's decision. If no HCR has been prepared or where the report is older than three months, an HCR will be requested for this purpose. Where the report is specifically prepared for temporary or escorted release, it is likely to be less extensive than one for parole or life licence. Nonetheless it is expected to be based on a visit to the address and to report on the proposed accommodation and on those residing there and their relationship with the prisoner.

In the case of escorted release, the writer is expected to alert the escort, who will be given a copy of the report, to any significant factors which might influence the family's attitude to the prisoner or to the escort, in order to minimise risk to either person or to others. The report writer(s) should indicate, in a cover note, their view as to the appropriateness of disclosing the report to the prisoner.

NOS stress the importance of providing available information on the attitude of victims or the local community, particularly in relation to violent or sexual offenders. These are areas of practice that are largely untested and no indication is given as to how this information should be sought or gained and what, **if any**, soundings should be taken from the victim or the victim's family.

Disclosure

It is a matter of policy that all reports prepared in connection with parole and life prisoners reviews should be disclosed to the prisoner. The detailed requirements, which in effect, establish a **system of open reporting** are set out in Statutory Instruments made under the *Prisons (Scotland) Act,* 1989 and the *Prisoners and Criminal Proceedings (Scotland) Act* 1993. The *Parole Board (Scotland) Rules*

1993 and 1995 (SI 1993 No. 2225 (s.235) and 1995 No 1273 (s.99)) require the Secretary of State to send a copy of the dossier to the prisoner at the same time as it is sent to the Parole Board. There is, however, a limitation to disclosing '**damaging information**'. Rule 6(1) applies where the Secretary of State considers that any written information or document contained in a dossier referred to the Board should not be disclosed to the prisoner because its disclosure would be likely to be damaging in one of a number of ways:

- adversely affecting the health, welfare or safety of the prisoner or another;
- resulting in the commission of an offence;
- facilitating the escape from legal custody or prejudicing the safekeeping of a person in legal custody;
- impeding the prevention or detection of offences or the apprehension or prosecution of suspected offenders;
- otherwise damaging the public interest.

This information is not required to be disclosed but may still be taken into account by the Parole Board. In any event, the Secretary of State is required to inform the prisoner, in writing, that certain information supplied to the Board has not been made available to the prisoner and must indicate the nature of the information withheld 'in so far as is practicable without prejudicing the purposes for which the information is not disclosed'. The prisoner must be advised that he can make representation to the Secretary of State and to the Parole Board about his case, including the non-disclosure of information(Rule 6(2)(c)(iii). There are no powers to withhold 'damaging information' in respect of any case involving a designated life sentence.

Social workers should always make clear to third parties that information given is likely to be made available to the prisoner. If information is received which seems damaging—which is only likely in exceptional circumstances—it may be helpful to contact the Parole Unit of SOHD or the Lifers' Branch to discuss the matter informally. The social worker should then prepare the report for the establishment, as requested, including all the disclosable information, and send it to the Parole Unit/Lifers' Branch accompanied by a note of the non-disclosable information and the completed prescribed form in a sealed envelope marked '*For the attention of the Parole Unit/Lifers' Branch: Not for disclosure to the prisoner*'.

The prisoner may well want to discuss the matter with the social worker concerned. In these circumstances there is little option but to advise that this cannot be done without prejudicing the reason for the non-disclosure. The prisoner should be reminded of his right to make 'representation' to the Secretary of State and the Parole Board. The situation requires sensitive handling but may, however, provide an opportunity for ongoing work with the prisoner or for work with the third party, depending on the circumstances.

Appeals and complaints

Prisoners and licensees should be made aware, through leaflets etc., of the formal complaints system that exists both within SPS and local authorities. The issue of appeals can be divided between

- the general grounds for appeal against conviction and/or sentence; and
- appeal against what may be regarded as restrictive or unnecessary supervisor's requirements inserted into licences of whatever kind.

There is the general right of appeal against conviction and/or sentence. Where this is a possibility, the prisoner should have full access to legal advice and assistance and the governor should be made aware of the matter.

It is important for the licensee to have the opportunity, as necessary, to discuss any objections to licence requirements with a manager. The meeting should be conducted as a formal review as outlined within the guidance. The licensee should be informed of his right to have whatever support he needs at the meeting and, like any other review, a recording of the proceedings will be made and filed. The licensee should receive a copy of any notes taken. In difficult situations it is likely that consultation with SOHD will be important. It is important to remember, as noted earlier, conditions as required by supervisors are not a matter for negotiation. It is important that any conditions are reasonable and achievable and that the licensee is aware of the consequences of non-compliance.

Prison-based social workers have a valuable role as 'honest brokers' in assisting prisoners to use the request and complaints procedures within prisons, outlined in SPS circular 9/1994.

Social workers can assist prisoners, on request, to present information to the Internal Complaints Committee or to the SPS Complaints Commissioner and may be invited to offer witness testimony. Such a role is not without its tensions and will require the sanction of management. Where prisoners or licensees have a complaint about any professional aspect of social work, these are dealt with through the local authorities complaints procedures.

Release arrangements

On release, the person will be given a travel warrant, subsistence money, and a letter of introduction to the Benefits Agency. All licensees released on parole and life licence from prison or detention must be seen within one working day of release by the supervisor or a substitute. Any failure by the prisoner to attend should be investigated by visiting the release address '*within two working days*' and if contact is not established, SOHD should be notified immediately. The intention of the initial meeting is to

- clarify the conditions of the licence for the licensee;
- confirm the licensee's address;
- confirm the pre-release plan and check any changes required;
- discuss and offer assistance with any immediate needs and advise on any tasks requiring attention in the first week;
- confirm the frequency of contact during the first three months;

- arrange time and location of the next meeting.

The core requirements of the licence will have been discussed and clarified in writing as part of the pre-release work. It is at this, or a session immediately following, that clarification of any additional requirements to the licence may best be undertaken. There are risks in attempting to undertake this work before release, on the grounds that

a) the danger of agreement to almost anything before reaching the gate, is ever-present; and

b) the requirements are likely to be situation-specific and require clarification on return to the community.

It is important that the licensee understands the relevance of any added restriction, since it is a statutory provision, sanctioned by law and enforceable with the full weight of legal process should the need arise.

Guidance recognises the stress associated with release from prison and the supervising officer is alerted to the need to be aware of any signs which may suggest the licensee presents a greater risk to the community than was anticipated at the time of release. The minimum expectation is that the supervisor or a substitute will see the parolee weekly for the first month, at least fortnightly for the remainder of the first three months, and monthly for the subsequent three months. At least one home visit is expected per month during the first quarter. The experience of the Leisk case (McManus, 1997) is a reminder, if it should be needed, that whatever professional judgements are made, in good faith, about the nature of supervision contact, the reasons for them and the plan should be recorded and the decision shared with the appropriate manager, and where necessary with the police. **NOS represent minimum benchmarks only**.

Formal reviews are required at the end of the first three months, at the end of the second three months, and thereafter at six-monthly intervals. The purpose of the review is to examine progress since release, identify a continuing or a new focus for supervision, allocate respective responsibilities, and determine the level and intensity of contact until the next review. These reviews should be in addition to normal line management reviews of work in progress and should be chaired by a manager whose presence and agreement to any decisions taken is recorded.

In the case of life licences, regular progress reports to Prisons Division are required; this is important in safeguarding the worker if something goes wrong. SOHD will inform the supervising officer from the outset of the frequency at which progress reports are to be submitted to the Secretary of State. In all cases it is for the supervisor to judge the intensity of supervision required in the context of the benchmarks set. If danger signs become apparent—and in this context familiarity with the person's previous criminality and past responses to situations can be crucial—these should be reported or consultation sought with Prisons Division ahead of the date on which the next report may be due.

Transfer arrangements: within Scotland

Administrative arrangements for transfers are complicated by the distinction between parole and non-parole licences. The former requires liaison between the supervisor, SOHD and the Parole Board; for the latter, the procedures are similar but do not involve decisions of the Parole Board

When a licensee indicates his intention to move, on a long-term or permanent basis, to a different area **within the same local authority** from that served by the supervisor, the supervisor must immediately contact the 'new' social work office. If the licensee has already moved, then the new office should arrange to interview him, confirm his new address and satisfy themselves both that the address is suitable and that the licensee intends this to be a long-term or permanent address. Where the licensee gives early notice of a move, the supervisor must contact the new office to request that the proposed address is investigated to assess its suitability. This investigation must be carried out within five working days.

It is for the new office to advise the supervising officer of the suitability of the address etc. and nominate a new supervisor. If considered **suitable**, the new supervisor must write to the current supervisor and formally accept transfer of the licence; on receipt the new supervisor should be sent a copy of:

- the licence;
- the case notes;
- any other relevant material from the case file.

At the same time, a copy of the existing licence and a written progress report should be sent to SOHD informing them of

- the date of transfer and the reasons;
- the licensee's new address;
- confirmation that the licensee has been seen by the new supervisor, the assessment of the suitability of the new address and the acceptance of the transfer;
- the name, office address and telephone number of the new supervisor.

If the transfer is to **another local authority area within Scotland**, SOHD will issue a replacement licence naming the new authority, or in the case of life licences, a new supervising officer. In cases where the proposed address is considered **unsuitable**, or if there are other reasons to suggest the transfer would pose risks, the supervisor must advise the licensee of their concerns, inform him that these concerns will be reported to SOHD, and that, in the meantime, he should maintain agreed contact with the existing supervisor.

The report to SOHD must set out the licensee's proposed or actual living circumstances and the reasons why they are considered unsatisfactory. In addition it should record

- the level of contact with the licensee to date;
- his response to supervision;

- assessment of adjustment to release and resettlement;
- assessment of risks posed by the licensee;
- a recommendation for action e.g. 'careful monitoring', imposition of a 'residence condition' prohibiting the address in question or 'recall'.

The supervisor then awaits a reply from SOHD, which will set out the Parole Board's recommendations, *when appropriate*. Where a licence contains a formal **residential condition**, the condition may specify a particular address or 'as directed by the supervising officer'. In the latter case, the supervising officer's authority is sufficient. Where a particular address is specified, any change will require a change of condition and may only be effected by SOHD, with the agreement of the Parole Board. This requires a series of steps. The supervising officer should make an assessment as to the necessity for maintaining the condition; if unnecessary, the supervisor should inform the 'new' authority for them to make contact and assess the suitability of the new address. If the report is positive, the supervising officer must, in turn, report to SOHD providing information on

- level of contact to date;
- response to supervision;
- adjustment to release and resettlement;
- risks posed by the licensee;
- influence of the specified address on licensee's progress and why it is no longer necessary;
- proposed new address and transfer date;
- confirmation that the new address has been assessed as suitable and that transfer has been accepted, in principle, by the new office;
- recommendation for action, either deletion of condition or substitution of condition for some other.

It is then for the Parole Board to approve the application. In situations where any of the enquiries indicate that there is no suitable accommodation in the proposed area, the supervisor may still apply to SOHD for deletion of the condition, if they consider it unnecessary. Where the supervisor is of the view that the condition remains necessary, she must advise the licensee and agree to review the situation within three months, informing the licensee of his obligations to comply and the consequences of failure. Similar procedures apply where other special conditions are included in the licence.

Transfer arrangements: cross-border transfers

Licensees subject to supervision on licence may have their supervision transferred from Scotland to England and Wales. The procedures outlined above for transfers within Scotland equally apply (sections 12 and 15 of the 1993 Act). Where an offender is released on licence in Scotland, the Parole Board for Scotland, SOHD and the Scottish courts retain jurisdiction notwithstanding the number of transfers, to or from, different locations.

Under section 33 of the *Criminal Justice Act* 1991, all offenders sentenced in England and Wales to at least 12 months imprisonment are released on licence. Offenders sentenced to between 12 months and 4 years are automatically released at half sentence on Automatic Conditional Release (ACR) licence and the enforcement is carried out by the magistrates' courts. As jurisdiction of these courts does not extend to Scotland, it is not possible to enforce conditions of the licences in Scotland. However, social work authorities may offer to provide advice, guidance and assistance within 12 months of release under section 27(1)(c) of the 1968 Act.

Offenders sentenced to over 4 years are released at between half and two thirds sentence at the discretion of the Parole Board on Discretionary Conditional Release (DCR) licence. It is possible for these licences to be supervised in Scotland and the transfer procedures above apply. It should be noted that the Parole Board for England and Wales and the Home Secretary retain the power to deal with breaches, even if the person has moved to Scotland, and they should be notified directly of any breaches.

Transfers to and from Northern Ireland are not permitted, but voluntary arrangements may be negotiated, if appropriate.

SEX OFFENDERS

Concern about sex offenders has risen greatly in recent years, some would argue almost out of proportion to the size of the problem. *Commitment to Protect* (SWSI, 1997) provides a valuable review of current knowledge, policy, law, and responses to the problem in addressing arrangements for supervision in the community.

Sex offending is difficult to define as well as being complex to deal with. The law relating to sex offences is based on a mixture of common law and statutory provision. These include under common law: rape, clandestine injury to women; abduction of a woman or girl with intent to rape; assault with intent to rape or ravish; indecent assault; lewd, indecent or libidinous behaviour or practices; shameless indecency and sodomy; offences under the *Civic Government (Scotland) Act* 1982 such as taking, selling, distributing, being in possession of indecent images of children; and under the *Criminal Law (Consolidation)(Scotland) Act,* 1995 a series of offences relating to children including incest, intercourse with a child or step-child under 16, indecent behaviour towards a girl between 12 and 16, and procuration of homosexual acts.

These different legislative and common law sources do not form a separately identifiable group for which to provide data. Scottish Office statistics record most under crimes of indecency, which includes four sub-categories: sexual assault; lewd and libidinous practices; other offences; and offences related to prostitution.

The courts have powers to deal with sex offenders in a number of ways. However over half of all those convicted of sexual assault and over a third of all offenders convicted of lewd and libidinous practices against children, are sent to prison.

Recorded sex offences usually involve men and most victims are women and children known to them in some way. The peak period of conviction for sex offences is between the age of 25 and 39. Reconviction rates are low but there is a general concern that this may underestimate the problem as many offences go undetected (Waterhouse et al, 1994). Research on how best to assist positive personal change remains contentious; as a result there is a strong emphasis on administrative approaches to monitoring and supervision. The *Sex Offenders Act,* 1997 (discussed below) introduced new administrative mechanisms for registration and information management.

The Minister of Home Affairs (Henry McLeish) in his published statement on the 1997 Act made it clear that government's priority is public protection. Five 'fundamental areas for priority' are identified: prevention of offences, detection, punishment, treatment and monitoring. 'Society has quite rightly decided that sex offending should not be tolerated.' He acknowledged the importance of not seeking a 'quick fix' to a complicated problem and the difficulty of finding the right balance in the degree of supervision and monitoring of sex offenders necessary to minimise the risk to children and the community.

> There have always been people who have committed sex offences but in recent years we have recognised more fully the extent of sex offending and the devious, sometimes persistent nature of some offenders. However our knowledge in this field is still very limited and we must avoid basing our policies on false assumptions...As yet there are no fail-safe systems available for distinguishing those who are likely to be persistent offenders from those who are not.

The policy stresses the importance of treatment and education programmes alongside the monitoring mechanisms, and acknowledges that 'registration by itself will not reduce the risk of sex offending in the community. The key issue is how information is managed'. It is important to recognise that many of the notification methods adopted in the USA seem to have succeeded only in increasing community anxiety, and further exclusion and demonising of offenders. Finding the balance between registration and information exchange, which identifies individuals in order to safeguard the community, and provision that will allow offenders to re-settle and re-integrate within any communities, will be difficult to find. It remains to be seen whether offenders will register and whether the register can be kept up to date.

The current state of knowledge requires agencies to be clear about their responsibilities and those of others, and for collaborative approaches to monitoring, supervision, treatment and personal change programmes to be established.

Schedule 1 offenders

Detailed and specific responsibilities have been placed on local authorities in respect of the imprisonment and preparation for release of offenders convicted of offences against children detailed in Schedule 1 of the CP Act, 1995 (see chapter 6 for details). These were set out in SWSG circular 11/1994 and came into effect in October 1994. A corresponding circular, the Scottish Prison Service Circular 60/1994 advises governors of actions to be taken by prison staff and managers in regard to these prisoners. NOS on Throughcare incorporate the detail of the circulars within a set of procedures to ensure that local authority social work are notified when prisoners convicted of offences against children are to be released from custody. The guidance is intended to inform local authorities on expectations of them in relation to work undertaken by social work with prisoners convicted of offences against children, during the sentence and in the period leading up to release.

Increasingly responses are being developed within multi-disciplinary community safety strategies and within the context of child protection as part of the Secretary of State's *Action Programme on Child Abuse* (circular SW9/1988) and the circular *Child Protection: The Imprisonment and Preparation for Release of Offenders convicted of offences against Children.* The approach is outlined in the *Strategic Statement on Working with Abusers* issued in 1992. The policy addresses the problems generated by adult or young offenders sentenced to custody, whatever the period, for **any** offence against a child. It seeks to promote an integrated approach to the management and provision of services for offenders and children at risk, particularly between local authorities and SPS:

- ensuring early follow up by social workers in prisons of prisoners identified by court staff as having been convicted of a relevant offence against a child;
- ensuring such prisoners are subject to an assessment of the extent and seriousness of the risk they will constitute to children on release;
- ensuring that such prisoners are offered access to programmes to help them reduce the risk they pose to children;
- assisting prison management in the co-ordination of a range of interventions from specialists and prison staff, designed to modify, contain or control the offender's behaviour;
- ensuring local authorities consider any implications for the protection of children arising from the future release of an offender;
- ensuring information is available to the Parole Board or others involved in considering discretionary release;
- assisting the development of a co-ordinated and collaborative approach to the release by sharing information;
- preparing prisoners for release.

The arrangements apply whether they are to be released unconditionally at the normal date or are being considered for discretionary, conditional or temporary release under any of the following:

- interim liberation e.g. pending appeal;
- a home leave scheme;
- Training for Freedom Scheme;
- parole, non-parole or life licence;
- supervised release order;
- any other form of supervision.

Definitions

A **child** can mean a person of various ages *under the age of 16*, depending on the offence. There are three specific cases where the definition of a child extends beyond 16:

- abduction (or unlawful detention) with intent to have sexual intercourse, of a girl up to the 18 years;
- any offence involving bodily injury to a child under 17 years;
- any offence involving the use of 'lewd, indecent or libidinous practices or behaviours' towards a child under the age of 17 years.

A **prisoner** means a convicted adult age 21 years or over and a convicted offender under 21. Special directions are included for alleged offenders on remand.

A **relevant offence** means any offence set out in Schedule 1 of the *Criminal Procedure (Scotland) Act,* 1995:

- any sexual offences committed against a child;
- any offence under the relevant sections of the *Children and Young Persons (Scotland) Act* 1937, or
- any assault on a person under 17 years of age leading to bodily injury.

The **appropriate local authority** may be one of many depending on the circumstances of the case, including:

- the area in which the prisoner's own children live;
- the area in which the victim(s) are living;
- the area to which the prisoner is to be released and where there are children in the household, hostel or accommodation which he is to join;
- the area to which the prisoner is to be released even when it seems there are no children involved.

Administrative arrangements for Schedule 1 offenders

In principle, procurators fiscal should identify the age of any victim in the complaint or indictment in all relevant offences involving a victim under 16, and draw to the attention of the sheriff clerk all other cases which apply. It is the responsibility of the sheriff clerk to mark the warrant of committal in all such cases which result in a custodial sentence. The social work unit in the prison should be notified of a prison reception within one working day and be supplied with a copy of any SER prepared for the court appearance. Additional information will be forwarded by the sheriff clerk or Clerk of Justiciary within five working days of the sentence, including in every case, a copy of relevant part of the complaint or indictment, and where available, psychiatric or other reports.

Governors are expected to give the social work unit in the prison an indication of the length of time the prisoner is expected to spend in the receiving prison. In practice, all offenders against children will be seen on arrival and will be subject to special attention on leaving, whether temporarily or permanently. The disclosed information must only be shared with others on a 'need-to-know' basis and it is important that discussions take place with the offender on the limits of confidentiality, as well as on his rights and obligations.

Within two days of receiving the information, the social worker in prison must advise the prisoner about possible options, arrangements for his release, and the social work help available to him. Similar arrangements apply when the offender is transferred to another institution. These procedures are intended to allow the social worker in the prison making initial contact to have the fullest information available on the offence and on the offender's circumstances to inform judgements about risk.

The social work unit, in consultation with community-based colleagues, has some discretion in deciding whether to implement the full procedures, except in cases of sexual abuse and for those subject to SROs.

The criteria for exercising judgement should be based on the offender's assessed risk to children in general, or to specific children. However the assessment of such a risk is an imprecise activity. The social worker is guided to examine the following factors: the circumstances and nature of the offence; the prisoner's attitude to the offence; frequency and severity of previous offending (if known), any history of substance misuse; willingness and motivation to address offending behaviour.

In cases involving sexual abuse, more specific factors drawn from research are identified by the guidance to assist the social worker complete the assessment and include:

- the degree of sexual intrusiveness, duration /frequency of abuse;
- use of physical violence or aggressive coercion;
- intra-familial or extra-familial abuse;
- age of victims;
- whether the victim was known; previous convictions for similar offences and other offences;
- the extent of prisoner's denial or minimisation of the offence, extent of prisoner's acceptance of responsibility for his behaviour;
- the prisoner's views on the impact of the offence on the victim, and the prisoner's willingness to participate in programmes to address such offending behaviour.

It is for prison management to give as much advance notice as possible to the social work unit of any prisoner convicted of an offence against a child who is due for release. For prisoners being considered for conditional release on parole, notice should be given four months in advance. On receiving notice, the social work unit must contact the relevant local authority as a matter of urgency to advise of the situation.

In every case involving a determinate or life-sentence prisoner convicted of offences against children, or for such prisoners being considered for open or semi-open conditions, the social work unit in the prison must notify the relevant local authority social work agency using prescribed forms accompanied by:

- details of the offender;
- a report incorporating preliminary assessment of risk;
- a copy of any SER or other reports available;
- a standards form for the local authority response.

The local authority must respond, using the form provided, by the date specified.

Local authorities should be notified if release is not agreed. Where a decision is taken to release the prisoner, the social worker in the prison must notify the relevant local authority, preferably at least a month before the release, using a prescribed form and include:

- a copy of the release notification, including any conditions;
- a supplementary report, where relevant, to update previous reports;
- any comments or observations made by the decision-making body.

Similar procedures apply when the normal release date is in prospect, requiring the use of a standard form and including additional information:

- a report from the social work unit including assessment of risk and details of the release;
- copy of the SER and other information provided to the court;
- details of related previous convictions.

For indeterminate prisoners released subject to parole, non-parole and life licence, SOHD must be informed of any planning meeting to establish the details of the pre and post-release plans, if any special conditions are thought necessary.

Copies of the prescribed forms should be sent to the Principal Reporter to the children's panel. In cases of leave, the social work unit must attempt to ensure that the appropriate local authority has all the relevant information required to take any action it thinks necessary to protect children, by telephone, if the situation is immediate, but preferably in writing, and at least five days before the release in question.

It is important for local authority social workers to note the provisions of section 53 of the *Children (Scotland) Act,* 1995, which requires local authorities to 'cause enquiries' where a child may be in need of compulsory measures of supervision, and to notify the Principal Reporter as appropriate. Should children offended against move to another local authority, all the relevant information needs to be passed on to allow them to make such enquiries as they think fit to ensure the protection of the children. These procedures should be implemented in all cases of intra-familial abuse, and in extra familial abuse, in which there are grounds to believe that the prisoner may try to make contact with the victim.

In all cases which have criminal justice and child protection aspects, it is crucial that planning and management are complementary. This will require child care workers keeping social workers in the prison and their community-based criminal justice colleagues well informed about relevant cases, and vice versa. This coordination and liaison function will not be straightforward, since it will require a high level of information exchange between criminal justice and child care teams within the local authority, as well as with other relevant agencies, such as the police and the reporter.

This growing aspect of the child protection 'industry' will need careful joint management to ensure that it acts in the best interests of the child, while maintaining some human dignity for those who have perpetrated the offence. The risk is that the system of information exchange may take up more resources than the services geared directly to help the children and their families, or to help the perpetrators.

Registration of sex offenders

The *Sex Offenders Act* 1997, (Parts 1 and 2) was implemented in September 1997. Part 1 of the Act requires persons convicted of specified sexual offences, mainly sex offences against children and other serious sex offence, to register with the police, providing their names(s), home address and date of birth, and any subsequent changes to these details. To assist with identification the offender is required to provide his name and address at the time of his conviction. Any offender failing to do so could face up to six months in prison or a fine of £5,000.

Those who are required to register are identified in section 1 of the Act as a person (on, after, or before as appropriate):

(2)(a) ...convicted of a sexual offence to which this Part applies but has not been dealt with in respect of the offence; or

  (b) who has been found not guilty of such an offence by reason of insanity or to be under a disability and to have done the act charged against him or her in respect of such an offence but has not been dealt with in respect of the finding;

(3)(a) who is serving a sentence of imprisonment or a term of service detention or is subject to a community order, in respect of sexual offences to which this Part applies;

  (b) who is subject to supervision, having been released from prison after serving the whole or part of a sentence of imprisonment in respect of such an offence;

  (c) who is detained in a hospital or is subject to a guardianship order, having been convicted of such an offence; or

  (d) who is detained in a hospital, having been found not guilty of such an offence by reason of insanity, or to be under a disability and to have done the act charged against him in respect of such an offence.

Sexual offences under Scots law are specified in Schedule 1, para. 2 of the Act (discussed above). A person may be subject to the requirements of the Act by virtue of conviction in other parts of the UK. The provisions (section 8) extend to UK citizens committing certain sexual offences outside the UK.

There are many (unintentional) exemptions within the legislation which will require amendment. At present a number of offences, including abduction with intent to rape, assault with intent to ravish, some categories of indecent assault, and offences dealt with under the *Mental Health (Scotland) Act*, 1984 do not seem to require registration.

The notification period begins from the date of disposal. From 1 September onwards the relevant court will notify the police that the offender is subject to a notification requirement, and will allow the police to update information held on computer. In practice, this presumes much of court administration.

Section 4 of the Act identifies the notification periods as

• Life Imprisonment or imprisonment of 30 months of more	indefinite
• Admission to hospital subject to a restriction order	indefinite
• Imprisonment for less than 30 months but more than 6 months	10 years
• Imprisonment for 6 months or less	7 years
• Admission to hospital but not subject to a restriction order	7 years
• Others	5 years

The notification periods involving 10, 7 and 5 years are halved for those 'under the relevant age', which in Scotland is 16 (s.3(3)). Most children who fall into this category in Scotland are dealt with by children's hearings and will not be subject to registration. However those prosecuted and convicted in the courts will be subject to the arrangements. Special measures will be required to safeguard other children in the authority's care, whether the children are subject to registration or not.

Where local authorities have statutory responsibilities for supervising offenders subject to community disposals, supervision on release, or where they have a duty of voluntary assistance etc., the guidance indicates that criminal justice services should identify, as far as practicable, all sex offenders who have responsibility to register, and inform the offenders 'verbally and in writing', using a prescribed form, of their duty of notification and copy the form to the police. Prison-based social work units are expected to notify the relevant local authority at least four months before the release of an offender.

On receipt of information, the local authority is expected to try to identify the likely level of risk which the offender may present to previous or potential victims. It is for the local authority as a whole under the *Children (Scotland) Act,* 1995 (see Chapter 6) and under section 12 of the *Social Work (Scotland) Act* 1968 Act, to decide what inquiries or action may be necessary to safeguard children or the welfare of members of the community. Local authorities are expected to agree arrangements with their local police about the use and exchange of information that may be held, given the sensitive and confidential nature of information, and it is suggested that a local inter-agency forum should be formed to allow expertise to be shared. The guidance stresses that information should not, normally, be disclosed 'unless they believe serious harm might result from not sharing information about the risk the offender poses'. Similarly police, in deciding when and if to share information, in addition to social work services, are expected to take into account

- the nature and pattern of the offender's previous offending;
- his compliance with previous sentences or court orders;
- any predatory behaviour which may indicate a likelihood that he will re-offend;
- the probability that a further offence will be committed;
- the likely harm such behaviour would cause;
- the extent to which potential victims, such as children, are vulnerable;
- the potential consequences of disclosure to the offender and their family; and
- the potential consequences of the disclosure for other aspects of law and order.

The issue of disclosure has raised many legal and practical problems. Any disclosure by police to a local authority, or vice versa, is a 'full disclosure' and subject to civil liability. If social work shares information within its authority, this is only 'partial disclosure' and does not carry the same legal liability. For information to be shared appropriately, systems will have to be very accurate and defensible decision making will require to be transparent.

Political expectations are unrealistically high about this system of registration and what it can achieve. In law the police have no powers of arrest against those who do not register. For those who do, the requirement is for that alone. At present it is unclear what 'monitoring' the police are entitled to carry out. Some police forces have interpreted their duties 'loosely' and carry out verification visits to ensure the registration details are accurate. In law they have no right of access to a registered person. The resource implication of monitoring and the standard required for high, medium and low 'risk' has not been established.

Community protection

The implications of registration are far-reaching. Current guidance encourages liaison, collaboration and joint assessment between police and local authorities. Agreed criteria to allow joint assessement, to which both police and social work will be committed, is a long way away. Who has the skills and should take the lead role in risk assessment? Risk assessment in work with sex offenders is complex and uncertain. *Commitment to Protect* (SWSI, 1997:18) emphasises the importance of co-ordinated approaches and suggests that four main elements need to be considered:

- how likely is it that the offender will re-offend?;
- if he or she does re-offend how serious a crime is it likely to be?;
- are there changes in the offender (e.g. mental state) which modify the initial assessment?;
- are there changes in the offender's circumstances (e.g. accommodation) which modify the initial assessment?

No-one has the skills of accurate risk prediction expected by the guidance and a range of tools and aids which make explicit the basis of assessment will be required both to assist those making assessments and as a safeguard to the offender. Nonetheless it is to be hoped that this child and victim-centred inter-agency approach will minimise the risk to potential victims, providing it is complemented with appropriate support and help, including personal change programmes, employment training and suitable accommodation for those offenders who may find themselves further isolated, excluded and harassed on their return to the community; factors which themselves may increase the risk of re-offending.

In addition to those convicted of sex offences, politicians are eager to make provision to deal with those offenders who cause concern. Provision has been made in the *Crime and Disorder Act,* 1998 for the introduction of **Sex Offender Orders**, the Scottish version of Community Protection Orders, which will allow certain categories of people with a previous conviction for sex offences to be subject to monitoring and restriction within the community (see Chapter 7). This civil order is primarily aimed at people who have served a prison sentence for a sex offence (no matter when the offence) and who are likely to be unsupervised within the community and judged by the police to represent a potential risk of criminal behaviour. The order will require an application to a sheriff by the police, in consultation with local authorities and other relevant agencies, to allow for monitoring and the control of activity. The person subject to the order will be required to notify changes of address etc. as required under the *Sex Offenders Act*, 1997. The order is likely to be used to plug a gap in the legislation by applying these conditions to offenders who completed their sentence before the Act was implemented. As a civil order, the standard of proof is a balance of probabilities. Equally because it is neither a conviction or a sentence, no conditions of treatment or supervision will be possible.

Scottish provisions in the *Crime and Disorder Act*, 1998 will also allow for **extended post-release supervision** in **indictment** cases for violent offenders sentenced to four or more years in custody, and to sex offenders receiving a custodial sentence. The extended period is the aggregate of the 'custodial term' plus an 'extension period', which is the additional period of supervision considered necessary to protect the public from serious harm once the offender is either released unconditionally (in the case of short-term prisoners), or when he would otherwise have ceased to be on licence (in the case of long-term prisoners). The extension period will be a period on licence and, therefore, subject to the licence provisions of the 1993 Act. The maximum length of post-release supervision is intended to be five years for a violent offender and ten years for a sex offender.

The system at the time of writing for post-release arrangements on indictment cases includes

Length of sentence	Sex Offence	Violent Offence	Other
under 12 months	None	None	None
12 months to 4 years	SRO	SRO	SRO
4 years or over	Automatic licence	Automatic licence	Automatic licence
Life sentences	Life licence	Life licence	Life licence

The arrangements following the *Crime and Disorder Act*, 1998 if introduced will include

under 12 months	Extended sentence	SRO	SRO
12 months to 4 years	Extended sentence	SRO	SRO
4 years or over	Extended sentence	Extended sentence	Automatic licence
Life sentence	Life licence	Life licence	Life licence

SUPERVISION IN THE COMMUNITY

The result of legislative and policy changes in recent years is that supervision in the community is much more complex than anything ever experienced by Scottish social work in the past. As the foregoing discussion on the *Prisoners and Criminal Proceedings (Scotland) Act*, 1993 demonstrates, it is, by its very nature complex and demanding both on the supervisor and on the offender. Each carries a weighty burden of responsibility. In no previous criminal justice legislation has the control element been so strongly stated, nor has the intention to follow through on any failure been so explicit. The social work principle of 'starting where the client is' requires the offender to be clear about his responsibilities to the licensing authority, and of the legal framework within which all social work planning and help is provided.

The majority of releases are likely to be men, many of them under 21 years of age, classified as short-term prisoners (s.1 of the 1993 Act) released unconditionally, some of whom, previously would have been subject to parole supervision. In 1994, for example, an estimated 95% of adults received into Scottish prisons were sentenced to less than four years, the same applied to 96% of young offenders detained (Scottish Office, 1995). Many of these will, in effect, be long-term prisoners, in that many are subject to numerous short periods of imprisonment, often separated by even shorter interludes in the community. The group imprisoned or detained for two to four years is probably the most crime-prone element in the criminal justice system. Contact with this group of offenders will, generally, be on a voluntary basis only. If they are to be assisted and diverted from further custody, and it is in the public's interest that they are, their co-operation will depend on the relevance of the services available to them, services of a practical and material nature.

Local authority social work has rather been abandoned to decide on its own priorities. Any preventive strategy would require conscious targeting of this group for 'voluntary assistance' by prison and community-based social work while they are in prison and a range of relevant provision, probably delivered by agencies in the voluntary sector, easily accessible on their return to the community. In practice since this is not a priority area for policy makers it is unlikely to be one for social work.

NOS on Throughcare indicate that to be effective, supervision must be well focused, consistent and adapted to both the characteristics of the offender and the type of offending and must be based on co-ordinated and collaborative provision. Primary and secondary objectives for statutory supervision are identified. The primary objectives are focused on reducing the risk of re-offending and are in particular:

- to facilitate the discretionary early release of prisoners through the provision of accurate information and the formulation of realistic action plans;
- to seek to ensure that offenders released on statutory supervision adhere to the condition of that supervision;

- to assist former prisoners to re-integrate successfully into the community;
- to provide a range of services to former prisoners and in particular services to build on offence-related programmes begun in prison;
- to work with other agencies where necessary in the provision of specialised services for particular needs such as counselling, supported accommodation or medical treatment.

Secondary objectives seek to support prisoners as members of families and communities, in particular

- to seek to limit and redress the damaging consequences of imprisonment for prisoners and their families, including the dislocation of family and community ties, the loss of personal choice, and the resultant stigma;
- to assist the families of prisoners to cope and to deal with the practical and emotional consequences of a member's offending and imprisonment;
- to help prisoners and their families to develop their ability to tackle their own problems;
- to assist the families of former prisoners to adjust to the changed circumstances arising from the prisoner's return;
- to provide particular support to former prisoners, such as sex offenders, who may have lost their family base through their offending and imprisonment.

Risk assessment is a major challenge to practitioners responsible for supervision in the community. In recent years the growing concern about dangerous offenders being released into the community from prisons has emphasised the importance of the role of social work in community safety and public protection. Circular SWSG 11/94 outlines responsibilities for risk assessment in respect of those released from custody who have been convicted of offences against children. The guidance in respect of the *Sex Offenders Act* 1997 (Circular 11/97) places specific responsibility on social work to identify the risk a sex offender poses and to work with the police on reducing the risk. The SWSI report *Commitment to Protect* indicates that supervision should be based an assessment of risk which includes the 'likelihood of re-offending, the potential seriousness of any future offending and an assessment of what factors in the offender's social and personal circumstances need to be addressed to reduce the risk'. The supplement to NOS, *A Framework of Risk Assessment* (1998), provides useful guidance in this area. It is important to stress that while the task of risk assessment is unavoidable for social work, whatever tools used, it remains a very imprecise process, placing both offender and professional at some risk if too much predictive weight is placed upon the process.

A Commitment to Protect (SWSI, 1998:28) gives a clue as to future directions by identifying a number of steps, not in general use, but which it considers may be appropriate in some very serious cases. These include

- requiring the offender to maintain a daily diary with checks to verify the accuracy of diary entries;
- a frequent schedule of home visits;

- electronic monitoring to check veracity of reports;
- working with police in surveillance activities of the offender's movements;
- checking houses and cars for warning signs, such as pictures of unrelated children;
- regularly telephoning offenders to check their whereabouts;
- unannounced 'report veracity checks';
- organised spot checks on offenders outside of office hours;
- more 'interrogative' supervision.

There should be little debate that adequate surveillance and monitoring is an important part of the social work role on behalf of the community. The Leisk case (McManus, 1997) highlighted many of the shortfalls in current supervisory practice, particularly when an offender is in employment. It is equally important not to allow the pendulum to swing to the other extreme. The best surveillance techniques may not have stopped Leisk murdering again. And certainly an over-emphasis on surveillance techniques without constructive resources to assist personal life changes and ensure adequate and safe accommodation and employment opportunities, will simply lead to the kinds of errors made in the USA in the last 20 years, where surveillance techniques replaced rather than complemented help in many cases, with associated negative outcomes (see Petersilia and Turner, 1993). Practical help and offence-focused supervision need to be part of the same formula if they are to be effective. The proposal to develop four accredited hostels in Scotland will be an important development in the supervision of very serious offenders.

The initial evaluation of community-based throughcare (McIvor and Barry, 1998) suggests that whilst offending behaviour was identified most often as of significance to social workers, ex-prisoners were seen to attach more importance to the practical issues of accommodation and employment. Not surprisingly therefore ex-prisoners viewed community-based throughcare as less helpful than it might be and was acknowledged by social work managers to be the least well developed of the 100% funded services. Over two third of prisoners had received one or more visit from a community-based social worker in prison and about a third recalled having a three-way meeting with the community-based and the prison-based social worker. Most prisoners had been seen within 24 hours of release by their supervising social worker and those who sought voluntary assistance, though small in number, were seen, on average, six weeks after being released. Most work was undertaken on a one-to-one basis by the supervising social worker.

While there was little evidence of non-compliance and most ex-prisoners were seen to respond positively to throughcare, this may simply reflect the limited nature of the contact and demand or provision made for ex-prisoners. Lack of resources was seen as the main issue by social work staff.

Most disappointing was the lack of evidence of multi-disciplinary (joint and collaborative) programmed provision and there seems little sign of the much-promoted continuity of work undertaken with individuals throughout all phases, both during and after a sentence. The extent to which social work-oriented approaches can be integrated, particularly with non-consensual supervision, remains an open question. The report concluded that a number of issues need to be addressed to improve the quality and effectiveness of throughcare including:

- greater clarity about the objectives of throughcare practice, including the distinction between managing risk to the public and addressing offending behaviour;
- a level of resourcing which accurately reflects the requirements of an effective and comprehensive throughcare service;
- a clearer distinction between the role of prison-based and community-based social work staff in the period prior to release;
- improved communication and co-ordination between prison-based and community-based social workers;
- a longer time lapse between prisoners' notification of parole being granted and their release date;
- a more consistent emphasis upon the practical needs of prisoners on release (page x).

Enforcement and non-compliance

A key task for the supervising social worker is to ensure a licensee's compliance to the licence conditions. A distinction has to be drawn between actions to be taken when the licensee is charged with a further offence and actions to be taken when he fails to comply with other requirements. Where a supervisor becomes aware that a licensee has been charged by the police with any further offence which has occurred during the period of licence, they must notify SOHD of the charge by telephone and confirm this subsequently in writing and provide a brief progress report. The progress report should contain:

- date of release from prison, the type of licence and the period of the licence;
- nature of the failure;
- level of contact with the licensee;
- level of response;
- assessment of licensee's adjustment to release;
- relevant personal/family factors;
- any recommendation for action.

If a further court appearance is involved, a copy of the report should be sent to the court, where possible. The powers of the court in such circumstances are dealt with above.

It is a matter for the supervisor's professional judgement to decide when to report to SOHD any failure to comply with other conditions of a licence. The supervisor's responsibility is to act on behalf of the Secretary of State to help protect the community and to ensure that unacceptable and/or repeated failure to comply with the conditions are not condoned. Any apparent failure must be investigated and an explanation sought from the licensee before determining what action to take. The guidance suggests that important issues to consider are

- the seriousness of the failure;
- previous indicators of non-compliance;
- the progress to date with implementing the action plan;
- the extent of compliance and co-operation to date.

In less serious cases of failure the supervisor must exercise professional authority and re-emphasise the conditions and the consequences for non-compliance. Where the failure continues, a written warning should be issued, in person or by recorded delivery, and noted on the case file. The guidance allows for a second and final written warning. Thereafter, following consultation with management, SOHD should be contacted. Where contact with the licensee has been lost, SOHD should be informed in writing within a month of failure to keep an appointment. In more serious cases SOHD should be contacted without delay, and in emergencies by telephone, forwarding written details as soon as possible thereafter. The notification must be accompanied by a brief progress report detailing the issues above.

Supervision and supervised release orders

The supervised release order (SRO) allows sentencers to combine a custodial sentence (of between 12 months and 4 years) with a period of supervision in the community, where the court considers this necessary to protect the public from the risk of serious harm when the offender is released. The legislation does not specify particular offences for which an SRO can be used. However the 1998 Act will limit the use of SROs to convictions on indictment and will exclude sex offences. SROs are available for young offenders sentenced under s.207 of the CP Act, 1995 and for children detained on indictment under section 208. The aim of the legislation is to 'protect the public from certain offenders, particularly those convicted of violent offences or offences against children who may, because of the nature of their offence, be regarded as constituting a more serious risk to the community on release'. An **SRO does not require the consent of the offender**. However the court must 'consider a report' before imposing the order.

Preparation for return to the community should be part of throughcare planning, particularly the establishment of any 'requirements as that officer may reasonably specify' (s.209(3)(b) of the CP Act, 1995). Section 209(3)(a) and (b) of the CP Act, 1995 requires the released prisoner to comply with 'such requirements as may be imposed by the court in the order', and 'such requirements as that (the supervising) officer may reasonably specify...for the purposes of securing...good conduct...or preventing...or lessening the possibility of his committing a further offence'. NOS note that 'this is a more specific purpose than that intended for a probation order where the requirements need only be 'conducive' to the prevention of re-offending'.

In practice the prison governor carries responsibility for establishing the designated local authority prior to release. If the person cannot return to their authority, as in the Leisk case (McManus, 1997), the governor has little choice but to persuade a local authority, based on the prisoners decision on where they want to live. Some of this needs to be anticipated at the time of the SRO, so that the designated authority is known. Where this is impossible, conditions within the order should allow for direction to ensure the offender is accommodated appropriately by a suitable and prepared local authority.

Standard requirements involve reporting to the supervising officer at specified intervals and notifying changes of address. More specific requirements should be reasonable and enforceable. It is the responsibility of the court to 'explain to him (the offender), in as straightforward a way as is practicable, the effects of the order and the possible consequence for him of any breach of it' (section 209(5)). An important provision, introduced by the CP Act, 1995, requires the court to obtain a social enquiry report before making an SRO (209(2). Before April 1996 this was optional. While this is a sensible provision, it raises many dilemmas in assessment for the reporting social worker. Section 209(7) and (9) deals with the 'relevant periods' of the order, namely:

- 'a period not exceeding 12 months after...release' and
- 'no part of which is later than the date by which the entire term of imprisonment specified in the sentence has elapsed'.

Note the reference here is to the *sentence term* and not to the period actually served. The legislation does not set a minimum period for the duration of an SRO but simply that it must not exceed 12 months after the date of the person's release, or half of the sentence, whichever is shorter (s.14(2) of the 1993 Act). An SRO cannot extend beyond the expiry date of the sentence, irrespective of the date of release. If the prisoner is sentenced to a further period of imprisonment, either concurrently or consecutively, the SRO begins on his release and if there is more than one SRO, the order runs for whichever is longer (s.209 (7A)).

It is for the court to notify and supply orders, both to the prisoner and to social work. NOS require the Clerk of Court to send a copy of the order to the Secretary of State '*immediately*' and, within seven days of making an order, to send 'such documents and information relating to the case...as are likely to be of assistance to the supervising officer'. A copy of the order should be issued to the social work unit in the prison within five working days. The information is issued to the 'social work unit to assist the throughcare task'.

Within 14 days of the order being made the Governor must 'serve' the order, explain the requirements of the SRO, check that the prisoner understands them, request his signature and dating of the document and countersign the order. If the prisoner refuses to sign, the Governor notes this on the back of the form. It is for the Secretary of State (Prisons Group) to notify the local authority and the court in the area in which the supervisee proposes to live (s.14(5)), and to designate the supervising authority, no later than 30 days before the prisoner's date of release.

In practice it will be the duty of the Governor to establish the prisoner's proposed release address not less than four months prior to the earliest date of liberation and make arrangements with the relevant local authority (or probation service) for supervision.

Section 15 of the 1993 Act allows for *variation of orders* by the court which imposed the SRO, including cancellation or insertion of requirements. Application can be made by the offender or the supervising officer. Changes of location or circumstances can be accommodated in the normal way. While the order can also be extended, it cannot be made to last longer than the maximum period provided for in section 209(7) of the CP Act, 1995, namely 12 months from the release date or, if shorter, until the date by which the entire term of imprisonment has elapsed. The court must explain any amendments 'in as straightforward a way as is practicable'. The offender's consent is not sought.

Those released subject to an SRO are also subject to the provision of section 16 of the 1993 Act. Under these provisions, if convicted of an imprisonable offence which was committed during the 'unexpired' portion of a determinate sentence, a court may order that they are returned to prison, regardless of any disposal which it makes in respect of the new offence.

Provisions under section 4 of the *Crime and Punishment (Scotland) Act,* 1997, which proposed radical extension to the use of SROs are to be repealed in the *Crime and Disorder Act,* 1998 in favour of extended post-release supervision.

Powers of the court in SRO breach proceedings

Section 18 of the 1993 Act deals with breaches of SRO. There is no longer a requirement that information on the breach be sworn to by the supervising officer. The evidence of **one witness** will be sufficient evidence to establish the breach. The important point to bear in mind here is that the action is *before the court which made the order.* Allegations of breach cannot be dealt with by a court in England or Wales or by a different court in Scotland. Where the court of origin is the High Court then exactly the same procedures noted in respect of probation are to be followed.

The court may, if appropriate, issue a warrant or a citation for the offender's appearance before the court to answer the charge (section 18 (1)). Where the breach is established, the court has options. It may:

- do anything…that might have been done on application under section 15(4) i.e. it may amend, vary or cancel any requirement in the order, **or**
- insert any requirement that might have been inserted earlier on application (section 18 (2)(b)).

Subject to the gravity of the situation, e.g. response or the absence of it, failure to comply etc., the court is empowered to order the offender to be returned to prison. Equally the court could decided to do nothing. The offender can be imprisoned for the whole or any part of the period which begins with the date of the order for his return and is equal in length to the first proven failure (lodged in the complaint of the supervisor), and the date on which supervision under the order would have ceased (section 18 (a)(i) and (ii) of the 1993 Act). The 'formula' is complex and it is important for supervisors to communicate the possible effects of any breach to supervisees.

Example: McCann goes a.w.o.l. on 1 July. This constitutes the 'first proven failure' (good recording systems, will be important). He is apprehended and it is established that supervision would normally terminate on 1 May of the following year. The period of imprisonment to be considered by the court is that covered by 1 July—1 May, a period of ten months. This is not to say that the actual term imposed has to be ten months; simply that this is the 'period of decision'.

It is important to note that any return to prison, if ordered, is not a 'sentence', or 'part of a sentence' (section 18(5)). This has importance in, for example, any calculation of the rehabilitation period under the *Rehabilitation of Offenders Act* 1974 as amended (see Chapter 13) or for an SER; it is a 'return to prison on breach proceedings for N months'.

It should be noted that under section 18(5) of the 1993 Act anyone returned to prison for breach of an SRO will not then be subject to the early release arrangements set out in Part 1 of the Act and will serve the full period ordered by the court. Section 19 makes provision for appeals.

Tagging

A controversial proposal put forward by the Home Secretary in England and Wales is to extend the electronic tagging schemes to release 3,000 prisoners who are serving longer sentences two months before they become eligible for parole. The prisoners will have already been assessed by the Parole Board as presenting no threat to the public before being released on a tagging scheme. Whatever the controversy of tagging itself, the proposal marks a further departure from the previous Home Secretary's 'Prison Works' approach. More pragmatically it is an economic response to the ever-growing problem of prison overcrowding. It remains to be seen if the proposal will be introduced and whether it finds its way north of the border. Pilot schemes for restriction of liberty orders began in Scotland in 1998 in Hamilton, Aberdeen and Peterhead (see Chapter 7).

Resettlement programmes

A major challenge to social work, if throughcare is to be effective, will be to devise meaningful ways of protecting previous and potential victims, while maintaining a helpful relationship with the offender. This will require a range of intervention programmes which help the offender address his offending behaviour and, at the same time, provide opportunities to address other important issues relevant to re-settlement and re-integration.

Social work units in prison will have a key role, in co-operation with SPS, in developing and delivering intervention programmes designed to address particular forms of offending behaviour, such as programmes for perpetrators of sexual abuse and programmes focusing on violence and anger management. The timing of these programmes for an individual must take account of the sentence length, if the programme is to have the maximum effect on the offender following release. Governors are 'required' to develop appropriate regimes within the institutions to facilitate this.

This responsibility requires staff to build on the best models of practice available and will require the expertise of a range of professionals and specialists to help staff develop and carry out these programmes. Monitoring and evaluation of the performance and outcomes of services is complex, but will be an essential prerequisite to establishing effective work in this field. In practice, in the foreseeable future, unless a massive injection of resources is forthcoming, there may be a need to settle for a 'lower level' of throughcare than that set by NOS for some groups in order to develop and test effective models with others.

Wootton's comment (1959) that 'social work is at its best when it serves as the "handmaiden" of the social sciences' remains true today and social workers have a responsibility to contribute to our current sociological understanding of the nature of prisons as institutions and to an understanding of their inmates. Social workers in prisons should constitute an important resource of information on an institution's population and characteristics in terms of personal need and offending patterns. Services which bridge between prison and community, and which provide follow-up data, are equally important.

If after-care began with the voluntary sector, throughcare should not ignore the potential role of the volunteer, (mentor, 'buddy' etc.) and the important and growing role of voluntary sector provision, particularly in providing services to families and voluntary assistance. The issue of access and transport for families, as well as support and participation in pre-release programmes and regular letters to the prisoner throughout sentence providing local information, all present challenges to be tackled.

It was a persistent theme in recent evaluations (SWSG, 1997) that communication between prison-based and community-based social work needs improving. The importance of linking community-based social workers into programme work with the prospect of some continuity across the boundary of institution and community is important if re-integration, rather than simply surveillance, is to be the outcome of throughcare.

At the point nearest release, the prisoner is often located in a prison that is far away from his home area, or the area to which he will be released; this hardly militates in favour of a close involvement of the community-based social worker, or the rebuilding of links with family and wider community resources. If this issue is left to each local authority to resolve, it is likely that workers will be authorised only to carry out the minimum of visits because of the costs involved. If the guidance is serious in the joint nature of the commitment from local authorities, SWSG and SPS to throughcare, then SPS must take steps to make the most effective use of resources by locating prisoners as near their release base as possible. There may, equally, be a case to be made for specialist throughcare social workers.

The Scottish situation has, to date, been characterised by splintered and compartmentalised provision. NOS on Throughcare provide sound benchmarks for developing a more integrated approach to practice. We applaud the section in the guidance on training which recognises the need for a significant investment in the staff, both prison and social work, who carry such demanding responsibilities on behalf of society. We are equally encouraged that the guidance requires the social work responsibilities to be carried out by a qualified social worker. We would like to see some further direction in the nature of training for all workers who carry out these duties and, in particular, the need for specialist training for those who carry special responsibility for providing throughcare services.

Chapter 12

Mental Health and Criminal Justice

Legislation; inquiries into mental condition; insanity; community-based disposals; hospital and guardianship orders; restriction orders; appropriate adults

PREAMBLE

The criminal law normally operates on the basis of assuming that people are sane and rational, and can be held to be responsible for their behaviour. It assumes that behaviour which transgresses the criminal law is intentionally done. It takes what it calls an *actus reus* (wrongful act or omission) and *mens rea* (a wrongful state of mind) for granted, unless it is called into question, except in some statutory offences (see McCall Smith and Sheldon, 1992, Ch. 2). It is a fundamental assumption of the judicial system that people are responsible individuals.

Any exception to this fundamental assumption has to be defined with care and caution by the legal and criminal justice systems. There are special ways of dealing with people who are defined as falling outside these assumptions and normal approaches to behaviour, or whose criminal behaviour is attributed to some condition which is regarded as invalidating the use of normal criminal procedures. The law's provisions accept the existence of **mental disorder**, as defined in mental health legislation; and of the concept of **insanity**. Special provisions are made for dealing with, or particular disposals are used for, people categorised as suffering from mental disorder .

Criminal justice social workers will come across people who suffer from one or other of the conditions which qualify for the law's designation as mentally disordered or insane. In some instances, they will have direct responsibilities for the care and supervision of people who have been subject to such measures. In most cases, however, the term **mental or psychological disturbance** will be more relevant as a description of the problems facing the criminal justice system and of 'the need to distinguish between psychiatric disturbance in the broad sense and mental disorder in terms of the mental health legislation'. (SACRO, 1990:1; Cooke, 1994). The term is intended to incorporate the many individuals who come to attention within the system whose disturbance, or degree of mental disorder or illness, is not sufficient to have them categorised in ways that bring the special provisions of legislation into play but nonetheless may need special consideration. While criminal justice social workers may be less involved in the treatment of those formally designated by the system as **mentally disordered**, they are regularly involved with people whose behaviour and/or condition can better be understood as

mental or psychological disturbance. The distinction is important in discerning the nature, level, and form of disturbance, particularly in the completion of SERs and in planning intervention.

One indication of this need is the finding, in relation to social enquiry reports, that 'over the whole sample there was no reference to the current emotional and psychological functioning of the subject in 71% of all cases...[where it does occur,] the mentioning of psychological or emotional functioning has to a large extent to do with the seeking of explanations for criminal behaviour, and a style of presentation and interpretation of social facts, rather than an awareness that the mental health of an offender is an integral part of the report' (Williams and Creamer, 1989:45-46).

The expectation of National Objectives and Standards (NOS) is that criminal justice social workers have an integral part to play in alerting both courts and penal establishments to any concerns about 'mental fitness', and in assisting with the sentencing and management of such people. Williams and Creamer (1989) also found that only 50% of specialist workers reported familiarity with the findings of the Chiswick Report (1985) on suicide prevention in prison, and that 87% of generalist workers had no familiarity with it. McNeill (1988) summarises crucial sections of that report thus:

> The regime consisted 'essentially of the inmate sitting in his room', the room being furnished with a toughened cardboard desk and chair, a plastic chamber pot, a copy of a paperback book (or comics) and of the Bible. There was no work other than basic cleaning, no education and almost no association with other inmates or staff. They commented that it was 'customary for inmates to wear protective clothing' This comprised 'a canvas gown—a short-sleeved, knee-length garment shaped in similar style to a pinafore dress. Neither underpants nor any other clothing is worn. Slippers are worn on the feet'. Inmates were scrupulously observed at 15-minute intervals—through a peephole in the door—the light being left on all night to facilitate this.
>
> The committee recommended the complete abolition of this approach to suicide prevention which they described as 'inhumane and unacceptable'. Instead, inmates at risk should be treated as they might be in a hospital outside. They should either be given extra attention while remaining in their own unit or transferred to the hospital wing where they might be closely monitored. However, this monitoring should involve interaction with the patient, normal prison clothing should be worn and educational activities offered. On no account should the prisoner be isolated from human contact. Numerous other recommendations about the **general** regime were made.

While new protocols and better management of vulnerable prisoners has been introduced, suicide attempts particularly among young men and women remain all too common and the levels of mental and psychological disturbance in this group is high (see Scottish Office review, 1998a).

The range and prevalence of the conditions likely to be encountered is wide. Studies of the prevalence of mental illness and disturbance amongst those referred for social enquiry reports or put on probation in Scotland are limited, but the extent of the problems emerging within the custodial population is well documented. Over the years Scottish studies have reported fairly consistent findings:

- Bluglass (1966) found the same 40% to be 'psychiatrically distressed';
- Carlen (1983) contended that up to 66% of women admitted had a history of mental illness;
- Baldwin (1988) estimated that 51.6% of women's admissions to Cornton Vale were 'psychiatric cases';
- Cooke (1994) found virtually no evidence of schizophrenia or psychosis within the Scottish prison population. However he found that the rate of depression was twice as high and the rate of anxiety five times as high as the general population with over 50% men and over 60% women found to be experiencing 'psychological disturbance', much of which existed prior to their admission to custody.

There are many unanswered questions in this area of practice: what is the relationship between mental disorder and criminal behaviour? Do mentally disordered people commit offences at a different rate to non-mentally disordered people? In the early 1980s the evidence leaned towards the view that any association between mental disorder and crime was an artefact produced by social processes (Hollins, 1993). Monaghan and Steadman (1983:152) observed that the 'relationship between...crime and mental disorder can be accounted for largely by demographic and historical characteristics that the two groups share. When appropriate statistical controls are applied for factors such as age, gender, race, social class, and previous institutionalisation, whatever relations between crime and mental disorder are reported tend to disappear'. More recently data suggests that such a conclusion was premature and could be wrong. Current data finds a consistent, but modest, relationship between violent and illegal behaviour and the presence of mental disorder (Hollins, 1993:3). This relationship is strongest among people with psychotic symptoms. There is a danger in such conclusions that mental illness may be seen as 'the cause' of offending. It must be stressed that most people with severe mental disorder are not involved in crime.

The nature of the 'disturbance' can range from anxiety and depression to severe 'personality disorder' (see McNeill, 1988; Baldwin, 1988; Cooke, 1994). Anxiety takes many forms and manifestations; it will be normal practice for the social worker to be aware of, for example, nail biting, alcohol or tobacco dependency, general deficiency in self presentation, and so on. The particular problem in the criminal justice context is to distinguish between those manifestations that can be attributed, quite naturally, to the person's very involvement with the system, from any indicators of more fundamental or deep-seated abnormal anxieties that might have influenced involvement in the system in the first place. Similarly any absence of normally anticipated anxiety may range from bravado, through normal sub-cultural or peer group behaviour, to more personalised psychological problems.

Similar points can be made about depression. Two aspects need to be disentangled; first, the degree or level of depression the person may have been suffering before involvement in offending and being caught up in the system, and whether it is of a severity to occasion special attention by the system; and second, the degree to which the very involvement with the system compounds and adds to the experience to an extent that extra measures may be required. In terms of suicide risk, Backett (1988) showed that the time of initial imprisonment was the period of greatest risk in terms of suicide risk. Similarly, Judge Tumin, HM Chief Inspector of Prisons in England and Wales, called attention to the very real impact that the harshness of prison life can have: 'it should not be surprising that some inmates, already unstable or near the edge, should decide to commit suicide' (see SACRO, 1990).

Social workers, particularly when compiling an SER or visiting prisons can play an important role in drawing attention to these conditions, providing an initial assessment and taking initiative either by involving a Mental Health Officer, making referrals to health service professionals, or drawing the matter to the attention of the court, if this seems to be indicated. The Notes on the 1984 Act suggest that in the absence of any precise definition of the two types of 'mental disorder' identified within the Act, 'mental illness' or 'mental handicap', they should be 'understood in their generally accepted sense' (SHHD 1984:15).

Addiction to and abuse of drugs and/or alcohol (or indeed any other mood-altering substances) frequently features in the lives of those who come to the attention of criminal justice agencies. Carr (1983) estimated that alcohol was implicated in 50% of Scottish prosecutions for breach of the peace, 33% of prosecutions for assault, 25% of those for causing death by reckless driving, and 17% for culpable homicide. Within the prison population in 1988/89, the number of inmates treated for alcoholism on a 'first time' basis was 812, whilst the number for drug abuse problems stood at 1659.

The *Mental Health (Scotland) Act*, 1984, section 1(3) makes it clear that, however severe the observed condition of an addicted person may be, the addiction of itself cannot constitute evidence of mental disorder. However, some medical practitioners are prepared to offer treatment in hospitals or clinics to addicted people, and may be prepared to accept that treatment should be a requirement in a probation order.

Terminology in this field is varied. Terms may reflect particular theories about addictive/abusive behaviour in relation to alcohol and/or drugs or other chemical substances, and may, in turn, be related to particular approaches adopted. The word 'alcoholism' tends to suggest a view of the problem as an 'illness' and is suggestive of a 'treatment or rehabilitative' approach. Other terms, such as 'alcohol abuse' or 'problem drinking' are more suggestive of behavioural approaches, and attract different forms of response. Any purely medical ingredient of treatment (for example, detoxification) will be but one strand in the response required. Counselling and social work services are among other elements that are needed for an effective response.

The danger of slipping into moralising is ever-present. Social workers have been seen as seeking to 'excuse' criminal behaviour in their reference to addiction or abuse; whilst some judges have tended to see use of drugs or alcohol as increasing the element of blame and criminal responsibility.

Many community-based facilities and services, particularly for drug users, have been established in recent years and are utilised by social workers. Social workers need to balance, carefully, their care and control role in their response to people with addictive/abusive behaviour in relation to alcohol and/or drugs. The individual's addiction/abuse problem may affect the level of risk to others that his offending behaviour presents, or increase the risk of further offending if the addiction is not addressed.

Research has suggested that an approach to probation supervision in these cases which provides control elements (regular reporting, not taking drugs) without the provision of meaningful help, may result in failure for some offenders, whose addiction-influenced life style makes regularity of any kind unusual; and whose progress is, by the nature of the condition, going to be marked by regular relapses. A range of community-based disposals (see Chapters 7 and 8) are available to assist courts to show a degree of tolerance in the management of these cases, rather than to have recourse to imprisonment, except where the risk to the community is overwhelming.

Criminal justice social workers cannot expect to be experts in this field, but their training and experience will allow them to make an initial assessment with a view to assisting the courts determine possible risk to the community and the need for any specialised provision and the avoidance of prison. While it is not known, and maybe cannot be known, whether the existence of an illness or disturbed condition may, in some way, lend itself to a greater risk of apprehension, prosecution, and subsequent incarceration, nonetheless, there is very compelling evidence that prisons include a substantial proportion of people suffering a degree of disturbance that society feels unsafe in coping with in any other way (Cooke, 1994).

Prisons are not suitable places for many who are mentally or psychologically disturbed, but sentencers may see themselves having little options in the absence of other suitable measures. In some instances, criminal justice social workers have a role in providing credible options involving supervision and help.

Learning disability includes those whose intellectual development results in their personal and social competence falling short of that expected for their age. Mental impairment and severe mental impairment are defined under the 1984 Act as 'a significant impairment (or a severe impairment) of intelligence and social functioning associated with abnormally aggressive or seriously irresponsible conduct' (s.1(2)). Most people with learning disabilities are not involved in criminal activity.

Research suggests, however, that people with learning disabilities are typically over-represented in Western criminal justice systems. They are vulnerable during police questioning and may not comprehend their right to silence, and may confess or acquiesce to the police version of events (Hayes, 1996). They may need assistance with interviews and court procedures (see 'Appropriate Adults Schemes', below).

While offending patterns for this group are mainly persistent and minor, they are over-represented in cases involving assault, serious assault, and sexual assault. (Hayes, 1993). One study found that men with a learning disability were three times more likely to offend than non-disabled men, and five times more likely to commit a violent offence; women were four times more likely to offend and 25 time more likely to commit a violent offence (Hodgins, 1992). The study implies that aspects of lifestyle, characteristics and environment of the person (like many offenders), may increase the likelihood that they will be involved in offending and this needs to be taken into account in assessments. Their behaviour has probably been present for some time and it is vital to address challenging behaviour early. It needs to be stressed that people with a learning disability will **often respond well** to supervision, providing it is consistent, meaningful and well structured.

The health service provides facilities for specialised assessment and treatment of offenders, which may be provided in the community by multi-disciplinary community teams, at a day hospital, in local in-patient facilities, or within secure facilities in the State Hospital. Social Work should provide a range of services in their lead responsibility for care in the community and through criminal justice social work. The consultation paper (Scottish Office, 1998) recommends that there should be joint assessment of need by Health Boards and local authorities to cater for the majority of offenders with a learning disability who require a comprehensive range of health, education, and social work services to meet their needs (para. 8.7).

The presence of **serious mental illness** such as schizophrenia in social work caseloads arising from work in the criminal justice sector is likely to be very rare. On occasions social workers will encounter the issue and need to be alive to the degree of risk and danger presented. Supervision without the support of a psychiatrist or specialist help is likely to be inappropriate, and carries an unacceptable element of risk..

The *Mental Health (Scotland) Act*, 1984 does not attempt to define the psychopathic personality, as does the English equivalent legislation, or specifically include it within the definition of mental disorder; simply stating that the conditions which apply must be treatable. The Notes on the 1984 Act, however, point out 'there is...virtually no difference in effect between the Scottish provisions and those for England and Wales so far as their application is concerned' (SHHD 1984:15-16). Given the confusion which surrounds the term, and its derivative 'sociopath', work in this whole area is made more difficult by the confusion of terms, by their imprecision, and by the inherently difficult task of quantifying, understanding, and defining 'abnormal' behaviour.

Commentators in recent years (SACRO, 1990; Gunn, 1991; McManus, 1992; Cooke, 1994) have adopted a much broader approach to what is a genuine and widespread problem of dealing within the criminal justice system with people whose offending, and indeed, more general behaviour, does not fit easily into that system's usual approach of seeing people as sane, rational and fully responsible human beings. There is at least the beginnings of a more integrated strategy for dealing with them.

Towards a strategic approach

The long-awaited Scottish equivalent to the Reed report (1994) in England and Wales, *Health, Social Work and Related Services for Mentally Disordered Offenders in Scotland* (Scottish Office, 1998) is available for consultation at the time of writing. The review examines the provision of mental health and social work services for mentally disordered offenders in care of the police, prisons, courts, social work, the State Hospital and other psychiatric services in hospitals and in the community, and makes proposals for the organisation and development of services throughout Scotland.

Policy is based on the same guiding principles as the Reed report, that mentally disordered offenders should be cared for

- with regard to quality of care and proper attention to the needs of individuals;
- as far as possible in the community rather than in institutional settings;
- under condition of no greater security than is justified by the degree of danger they present to themselves or to others;
- in such a way as to maximise rehabilitation and their chances of sustaining an independent life;
- as near as possible to their own homes and families if they have them.(p.2)

The report acknowledges that it is often the combination of medical and social factors which leads to offending in this group of people.

When a person suspected of being mentally disordered comes to the attention of the police, in whatever circumstances, a medical opinion should be sought. Any such person found in a public place, who is not suspected of an offence but is in immediate need of care and control, may removed to a place of safety, normally a hospital (s.118), *Mental Health (Scotland) Act,* 1984. Good local co-ordination and inter-agency protocols should ensure the person receives appropriate care and support.

Where a person is taken to a police station due to the seriousness of a suspected offence, they are often seen by the police surgeon who will make an assessment of their fitness for detention by the police. The police surgeon should be in contact with the person's GP, if possible, before concluding the assessment. Where the police surgeon has little experience in dealing with mental disorder, they should attempt to involve a psychiatrist. Police guidance recommends that when interviewing either a witness or an accused who is thought to be mentally disordered, an 'appropriate adult' should also be present (see below).

There is an expectation in the review that Health Boards and social work should develop services for mentally disordered people who come into contact with the criminal justice system through joint planning procedures as an integral part of the community care process. It recommends that Health Boards and local authorities should enter service-level agreements with criminal justice agencies to provide effective and flexible local arrangements for the initial assessment and treatment of people in their charge who appear to be mentally disordered covering

- the use of s.118 of the 1984 Act (removal to a place of safety);

- the availability to the criminal justice agencies of 'duty psychiatrists' and 'appropriate adult' services;
- the facilities and services that can be used for mentally disordered people diverted from the criminal justice system;
- the provision of specialised accommodation for mentally disordered accused persons who might otherwise have to be remanded unnecessarily in custody; and
- the specification should also address the three levels of service to be provided
  1) emergencies within 24 hours;
  2) urgent cases to be covered within one week; and
  3) routine cases to be completed within three weeks.

Health services should operate a Care Programme Approach (SOHHD DGM 1992/9 and SWI 1992/1 Community Care guidance) to co-ordinate services including

- general practitioners operating in their role in Care in the Community;
- local general and forensic psychiatry services;
- Out-patient and Community services, including psychiatric nurses;
- in-patient care;
- Intensive Psychiatric Units (IPCUs);
- secure provision;
- the State Hospital (paras 5.1-5.8).

The specification should also cover the training needs of those who will be required to operate these services on a day-to-day basis (para. 2.13).

The 1968 Act, the 1984 Act and the *National Health Service and Community Care Act*, 1990, place a variety of duties on local authorities to provide social care services for people with mental illness, including services under the specific grant for the development of mental illness services (1990 Act). These services should include

- mental health social work;
- mental health officers;
- specialist criminal justice social workers;
- bail services, information, advice and supervision;
- reports to the courts;
- court-based services;
- community-based social work disposals;
- social work in prison; and
- post-prison supervision (paras 5.9 -5.5.25)

A national approach to high-security care

Successive governments in Scotland have chosen not to establish mediumsecurity facilities but to concentrate investment on the State Hospital, Carstairs, which has become the centre of expertise in forensic psychiatry. This creates a number of limitations:

- limited treatment options for patients who need a decreasing level of security as they recover;
- local forensic services are under-developed;
- the State Hospital is under pressure to take referrals for which there seems no alternative;
- difficulties and delays in transferring patients to local services.

The consultation paper (Scottish Office, 1998) recommends, that while the role of the State Hospital should be maintained, Health Boards should investigate the need for structured development of local facilities to provide for mentally disordered offenders from courts, prisons and returning from the State Hospital, who require treatment in conditions of lesser security than the State Hospital (para. 6.15).

THE LEGISLATION

The criminal law applies certain special considerations, and in some instances particular disposals, to offenders who may be suffering from mental disorder. There are special orders that criminal courts can make in relation to people whose offending is linked with a serious mental disorder. There are explicit arrangements for detention and treatment, particularly in instances where the mental disorder may contribute to the person being a risk to the wider community. There are powers to transfer people from prison to hospital, if it transpires during sentence that they have a mental disorder, or if they become mentally disordered during sentence. There are powers and provisions for release, for appeal against detention, and for supervision on return to the community.

In the mental health field, generally, the governing Act is the *Mental Health (Scotland) Act,* 1984 , as amended by the *Mental Health (Detention) (Scotland) Act*, 1991, the *Criminal Justice (Scotland) Act*, 1995 and the *Crime and Punishment (Scotland) Act* 1997. Legal provisions relevant to criminal justice matters are consolidated in the *Criminal Procedure (Scotland) Act*, 1995. The 1984 Act revised and updated the previous Act, the *Mental Health (Scotland) Act*, 1960. The latter had in turn replaced the older *Lunacy Acts*, and was the initial attempt to bring modern concepts of mental health into the sphere of the operation of the criminal law.

Special provisions exist for those offenders who may be or become mentally disordered, which may require criminal justice social workers to participate in assessment, supervision, and in release planning, as part of their duties.

Part VI of the *Mental Health (Scotland) Act*, 1984 deals with provision for compulsory detention in criminal proceedings, adapting the provisions of Part V of the Act for use by courts and criminal justice agencies. Part V sets out the conditions which must be met in respect of people suffering from mental disorder who require hospitalisation.

Section 17(1)) of the 1984 Act defines those 'who may be admitted to a hospital and there detained'. Section 17(1)(a) and (b) contains four elements that must be present: that the person is mentally disordered as defined by the Act, **and** that the disorder can be alleviated by treatment **and** this requires hospitalisation, **and** it is necessary 'for the health **or** safety of that person **or** for the protection of other persons'. Section 37 outlines the procedure for reception into guardianship.

Section 36 (a) and (b) contains two elements that must be present: that the person liable to be received into guardianship must be suffering from mental disorder as defined by the Act **and** that 'it is necessary in the *interests of the welfare* of the patient' (36(b). It important to note the distinctive criteria of detention and guardianship. The former is a health and public protection order, the latter a welfare order.

The powers of the criminal courts are set out in Part VI of the *Criminal Procedure (Scotland) Act,* 1995 as amended by the *Crime and Punishment (Scotland) Act,* 1997.

Mental disorder in section 1 of the 1984 Act means:

i) *mental illness or mental handicap*, however caused or manifested;
ii) *mental impairment*: arrested or incomplete development of the mind associated with abnormally aggressive or seriously irresponsible conduct;
iii) *severe mental impairment*, which includes severe impairment of intelligence or social functioning, and is associated with abnormally aggressive or seriously irresponsible conduct on the part of the person concerned.

Importantly, section 1(3) stipulates that 'no person shall be treated under this Act as suffering from mental illness by reason **only** of promiscuity, or other immoral conduct, sexual deviancy, or dependence on alcohol or drugs' (emphasis added).

The Scottish legislation avoids the use of terms such as 'psychopath' and 'psychopathy' and with them the controversy as to whether such 'conditions' can be alleviated by treatment, which is a requirement of the Act. The management of people with personality disorders can present many problems, since they are not a homogeneous group for whom social, penal medical provision has proved successful. Most of those who offend are dealt with by the mainstream criminal justice system. Where a treatable mental disorder is suspected they can be dealt with by the provisions outlined.

The consultation paper (Scottish Office, 1998) recommends that because of the difficulties in responding to the needs of these people in ways which adequately secures relevant provision and public safety, a national working group be established to consider experience in Scotland and elsewhere with a view to making proposals for disposal and future management and treatment (para. 6.22).

INQUIRIES INTO MENTAL CONDITION

Criminal courts require assistance in a number of areas:

- in assessing the fitness of an accused to plead;
- in assessing the state of mind of an accused person at the time of the offence;
- the disposal of a case where an Examination of the Facts (EOF) makes a finding

that the person did the act or made the omission constituting the offence; and
* the disposal of a case if a person has been found guilty of an offence.

The consultation paper (Scottish Office, 1998) emphasises the importance of providing the court with properly co-ordinated multi-disciplinary assessment to identify the range of options available for mentally disordered offenders. To ensure a single-entry system arrangements for assessment of this kind should be the responsibility of criminal justice social work.

The *Criminal Procedure (Scotland) Act*, 1995 places a general duty on prosecutors in respect of persons who may be suffering from mental disorder: 'Where it appears to the prosecutor in any court before which a person is charged with any offence that the person may be suffering from mental disorder, it shall be the duty of the prosecutor to bring before the court such evidence as may be available of the mental condition of that person' (sections 52(1)). The outcome of a medical examination of a person charged by the police may be a decision not to proceed at all in the courts. Any contribution from a social worker to the prosecutor's evidence would need to be bound by the usual considerations for pre-trial reports, that is, that the person consents and that the information can aid the court's exploration of disposal options.

'Where a court remands or commits for trial anyone who appears to be suffering from a mental disorder', where a hospital is available, 'the court may, instead of remanding in custody, commit him to a hospital' for assessment (s.52(2)). The person cannot be held for longer than the normal periods. An indictment must be served within 80 days and the trial commence within 110 days; on summary procedure he can be held for 40 days in all (further examination and committal awaiting trial) from the time of the complaint. There is no right of appeal to the sheriff against being remanded to hospital, but there is a right of review if circumstances change. The person will not be held in hospital after the initial period of assessment unless the responsible medical officer (RMO) considers that the disorder justifies detention under civil proceedings in Part V of the 1984 Act. The court will also review the situation. If the person is reported to the court as not suffering from a mental disorder, the court then can deal with him in the normal way.

The CP Act, 1995 also gives courts specific powers to order medical reports, over and above the general power to make inquiries (see Chapter 5). Section 200 of the Act empower courts, either by adjourning or remand, on bail or in custody, to make inquiries into the physical or mental condition of an offender before determining the method of dealing with him, provided:

a) the court finds that he has committed an offence punishable with imprisonment; and
b) it appears to the court that before the method of dealing with him is determined an inquiry ought to be made into his physical or mental condition (s.200(1)).

In the case of inquiry into mental condition (s.200(2)(b)), the court requires the written or oral evidence of **one medical practitioner only** (not an approved doctor or psychiatrist) that 'the person appears to be suffering from a mental disorder' and that a hospital place is available.

Mentally disordered people have the same rights as others to be considered for bail. However the police or the court may be inhibited from releasing the accused on an undertaking or on bail. Good bail information or supervision, at the moment provided on a pilot basis, can assist in these decisions. Requirements of the *Bail (Scotland) Act,* 1980 (see Chapter 3) may include requirements of residence in or attendance at a specified institution (such as a hospital or clinic). The consultation paper (1998) acknowledges that supervised accommodation will not be sufficient to meet the needs of people with a range of mental disorders, and that the appropriate range of accommodation needs to be available through community care service level agreements between health and local authority social work.

Conditions of bail can be appealed against but must be exercised within 24 hours. Where the person is remanded on bail to hospital to give time for medical enquiries, they are classified as an **informal patient** and are **not required to accept treatment**. Hospital staff cannot prevent them from leaving unless they feel they meet the criteria for detention under Part V of the 1984 Act (emergency detention procedures). If the person does not remain in hospital, he will be reported to the fiscal or the court and may be subject to further criminal procedures for breach of bail.

Where the person is committed to hospital (s.200(2)(b)) for medical enquiry, the period of detention shall not exceed three weeks, but is renewable for further periods of up to three weeks. The order can be appealed against but must be exercised within 24 hours.

The law also requires that a court gives to any institution or place in which or at which the offender may be required to reside or attend a statement of its reason for thinking such an inquiry necessary, and any information (such as a social enquiry report) already before it about his physical and mental condition (s.200(7)).

In practice, medical and social enquiry reports are likely to be ordered simultaneously, providing opportunities for liaison and co-operation. The social enquiry report writer should:

i)   share information already known, or as it is gathered, with the medical authorities;
ii) liaise with those authorities, particularly if some form of treatment (whether hospital order, a treatment and supervision order or treatment as a requirement of probation) is under consideration;
iii) support the person and his family through the additional complexities of medical reports as he would support them through the court case.

A remand, or committal for trial, of any person 'who appears to the court to be suffering from mental disorder' may be to a hospital, instead of to a prison establishment, provided a bed is available for his admission, and that the hospital is suitable for his detention. The hospital has to be named on the warrant, and the responsible medical officer has to be satisfied that such a course is reasonable in the circumstances of the case.

A person who comes to trial may be detained on an **interim hospital order** (s.53) for a period of assessment on the evidence of two medical practitioners, at least one of whom must be employed at the hospital specified in the order, normally the State Hospital at Carstairs. A place must be available within 7 days (s.53(3) as amended by the 1997 Act). The maximum period of detention is 12 weeks but it may be renewed for periods of 28 days, up to a maximum of 12 months, and the court must approve each time (s.53(6) as amended by s.11 of the 1997 Act). The order may only be renewed without the offender being brought to court if he is represented by counsel or a solicitor, who must be heard (s.53(7)).

INSANITY

The *Criminal Procedure (Scotland) Act,* 1995, s.54, as amended by the *Crime and Punishment (Scotland) Act,* 1997, makes provision for dealing with people who are insane at the time of their trial, or who were insane at the time of the commission of the act or omission constituting the offence. The concept of insanity is a complex one, and the various issues connected with it fall outwith the scope of this text. It is unlikely that social workers will be involved in the determination of such an issue. However, any information held by a social worker may usefully be shared with the prosecutor and/or medical authorities to assist their consideration of the matter.

A person who is found to be insane, either at the time of the trial, or of the offence, is not convicted and sentenced in the ordinary way. A finding of insanity may be made, either before a trial actually gets under way (so that it cannot, in fact, then proceed), or during the course of a trial. The person is then formally *'acquitted by reason of insanity'*. The court must give the reasons for its decision and a 'temporary hospital order' is made 'until the conclusion of the examination of the facts' under section 55 of the CP Act, 1995, if the case is one on solemn procedure. A person, sane at the time of the offence, may become insane before being brought to trial, in which event, an order under section 54 could be made as described. Conversely, if someone who is insane at the time of the offence regains his sanity before coming to trial, the trial can go ahead in the ordinary way.

Section 57 of the CP Act, 1995 makes provision for a wider range of disposals than was available under previous legislation. When dealing with an accused who is unfit to plead and is *'acquitted on the ground of his insanity'* at the time of the offence, or found at the examination of the facts, to 'have done the act or made the omission' constituting the offence, the court 'as it thinks fit' can make an order 'which shall have the same effect as' a hospital order, with or without an order restricting discharge without limit of time. (In murder cases the court **must** make a hospital order and a restriction order.) The order will specify that the person will be detained either in the State Hospital, Carstairs, or at such other hospital as the court may, for special reasons, specify. **Alternatively** the court may make an order 'which shall have the same effect as' a guardianship order, **or** make a supervision and treatment order (see above) or make no order.

COMMUNITY-BASED DISPOSALS

Supervision and treatment orders

The *Criminal Justice (Scotland) Act,* 1995 introduced a new provision, a **supervision and treatment order**, now dealt with by section 57(5) and Schedule 4 of the

Criminal Procedure (Scotland) Act, 1995. Where an accused is found unfit to plead or stand trial under section 54(6) ('insanity in bar of trial'), or at the 'examination of the facts' (s.55) is found to have done the act with which he was charged, the court may make a supervision and treatment order as one of a range of disposals open to the court. The only restriction on the court is in the case of murder where the court must impose a hospital order and/or restriction order without limit of time (s.57(3)).

The order is defined as one which requires the 'supervised person' to be under the supervision of a social worker of the local authority in which he resides, while subject to treatment, for such period, not being more than three years, as is specified in the order.

The order has three conditions:

a) to be supervised, keep in touch with the officer and notify her of any change of address;
b) to comply, during the period, with instructions given by the supervising officer regarding that supervision; and
c) to submit, during the period, to treatment by or under the direction of a medical practitioner with a *view to the improvement of his mental condition.*

The court can only make such an order if it is satisfied:

a) that the order is the most suitable means of dealing with the accused;
b) on the evidence of two or more 'approved' medical practitioners that the mental condition
   i) requires and is susceptible to treatment; but
   ii) does not warrant a hospital order or restriction order (s.57);
c) that the supervising officer is willing to undertake the supervision; and
d) that arrangements have been made for the treatment intended to be specified in the order.

The order must specify the local authority area in which he resides or will reside and the court is required to explain to him 'in ordinary language', the effect of the order including its requirements. The court has the power to review the order at his request or at the request of the supervising officer.

The order must contain a treatment plan by or under the direction of a medical practitioner, to which he must submit, normally, as a non-resident patient at an institution or place specified in the order. The precise nature of the treatment is not specified in the order and both the treatment and the location of treatment can be varied with the agreement of the patient and the medical practitioner. In such circumstances the medical practitioner must give notice, in writing, to the supervising officer. There is provision in the Act for the order to contain an optional requirement as to residence but **not** in a hospital. If the order requires him to reside in an institution it must specify the period. Before making such a condition, the court must consider his 'home surroundings'.

The court, having regard to the circumstances which have arisen since the order was made, may revoke the order on his application or on the application of the supervising officer, if it considers 'it would be in the interests of the health or welfare of the supervised person'. There is provision for the court to transfer orders to other local authority social workers as the result of a change of residence. and to amend or change requirements providing the order is not extended beyond three years. The medical practitioner is required to notify the supervision officer in writing if he considers:

a) the treatment should be continued beyond the specified period in the order;
b) the treatment needs to be changed;
c) the supervised person is not susceptible to treatment;
d) the supervised person does not require further treatment; or
e) he is unwilling or unable to continue with the treatment.

The supervising officer must then apply to the relevant court for cancellation or variation of the order.

The procedures are set out in Schedule 4 of the CP Act, 1995. After making an order the court must send the relevant sheriff court a copy of the order and any documentation that may be of assistance. It must also give a copy of the order to:

a) the supervised person;
b) the supervising officer; and
c) the person in charge of the institution where he is to reside.

Similarly if the order is revoked or amended, the sheriff clerk must give the supervising officer a copy of the revoking or amending order. It is the duty of the supervising officer to give a copy of the new order to the supervised person and to the person in charge of any institution in which he is or was required to reside. In the case of amendments, it is for the sheriff clerk to notify any new relevant sheriff court and supply them with a copy of the order and any documentation that may be of assistance.

It is the duty of the supervising officer to notify the Mental Welfare Commission for Scotland of the making, revoking or amendment of a treatment and supervision order.

Diversion

In Scotland the procurator fiscal has long had the authority to divert an alleged offender from prosecution, for a variety of reasons including treatment for mental disorder. When the Stewart committee (Cmnd 8958, 1983) considered diversion as a whole it expressed concern at how seldom this authority was used for people with mental health problems and recommended that there should be 'formal recognition of procedures which would enable offenders to agree to seek or continue with medical treatment in lieu of prosecution' (para. 3.28).

As a result a psychiatric diversion scheme was established in Glasgow in 1984 diverting people with psychological and psychiatric difficulties to an NHS clinic as opposed to prosecution. Subsequently diversion schemes were set up in Inverness and in Dundee. Duff and Burman (1994) found, however that few cases were actually diverted. Their respondents thought that fiscals were reluctant to attempt diversion unless they knew the suspect had a psychiatric problem and rarely did they have the relevant information; few people who appeared were considered to have a treatable disorder; and finally the public interest concerns of fiscals dominated for any other than very minor offences. More practically fiscals indicated that diversion processes actually consumed more of their time and effort than would prosecution.

Of those cases that were diverted, Duff and Burman suggest that 'it cannot be assumed that every case falling within a psychiatric diversion scheme would previously have been prosecuted'. The existence of a formal psychiatric diversion scheme served mainly to formalise a decision the fiscal would have probably reached in any event, enabling fiscals 'to change the category of disposal under which the case could be entered in their office's return to the Crown Office; it could be entered under "diversion" rather than "no pro" or warning letter'. Diversion will be funded under the 100% arrangements from 1998. It remains to be seen if this will increase the likelihood of this group being constructively diverted from prosecution in the future.

There are likely to be cases where symptoms of a mental disorder are not recognised until an individual appears in court or is remanded to prison. The consultation paper (Scottish Office, 1998 para. 3.21) recommends that psychiatric services provided by each Health Board should specify that the courts and procurators fiscal in their area require a promptly delivered psychiatric service to assist any accused person to hospital, if required. The service should involve a duty psychiatrist with access to community or hospital resources, supported by social work, nursing and housing services.

Deferred sentence

There are basically two main ways in which the court's power to defer sentence may be used to deal with offenders with identified mental health problems. If the offender is receiving treatment, a deferred sentence provides a means for the court to allow the treatment to continue and to check its progress. A deferred sentence could also be used to motivate the offender to face up to the need for treatment. Voluntary support could be provided by social work and/or other social care agency to assist him to do this (Scottish Office, 1998, para. 3.12).

Probation

Section 230 of the CP Act, 1995, makes special provision for requirements for treatment for a 'mental condition' as part of a probation order, either out patient or in-patient treatment. Before a requirement can be made the offender must give informed consent and must be suffering from a mental condition which requires treatment, and is susceptible to treatment but does not require admission to hospital under the 1984 Act. The evidence for mental disorder is provided by one doctor. This then places the person under the supervision of a social worker and under the direction of a medical practitioner or a chartered psychologist. Any recommendation to the court should include a plan setting out clearly the contribution of health, social work and any other relevant agency.

The primary responsibility for enforcing the order lies with criminal justice social work. However, the person in charge of treatment can make changes to the type of treatment without returning to court providing the treatment was one which the court could have ordered and the probationer and the social work supervisor agree. Orders of this kind require close co-operation between health and social work and, in particular, between the social work supervisor and the person responsible for treatment. The social work supervisory responsibility includes checking that the required treatment takes place. Where they disagree on any changes, the person responsible for treatment can apply to the appropriate court (in this case the one holding the order) for an amendment under Schedule 6 of the CP Act, 1995. NOS require regular reviews, as for any probation order. These reviews, where possible, should involve the participation of all agencies contributing to the action plan.

The requirement for consent means that any in-patient treatment is provided on an informal basis and the person has all the rights of an informal patient, in particular the right to refuse treatment and to discharge himself from hospital, although this is likely to constitute a breach of the probation order. The probation order can last up to three years but the requirement cannot last longer than a year. Amendments and variation are subject to the normal procedures for probation with requirements (see Chapter 8).

HOSPITAL AND GUARDIANSHIP ORDERS

The purpose of a **hospital order** is to enable an offender to be admitted and compulsorily detained in hospital for as long as hospital treatment is necessary. The purpose of a *guardianship order* is similarly for the person to be under guardianship. Part V of the *Mental Health (Scotland) Act,* 1984, is normally the basis on which any person (not being an offender) can be compulsorily detained in hospital or received into guardianship. The availability of hospital and guardianship orders to the criminal courts allows for mentally disordered offenders to receive the resources of the health and social work services, if appropriate, subject to the conditions and arrangements outlined below. In the instance of a guardianship order, the offender is not admitted to hospital, but is under the care of a guardian. A guardian may be:

i)   the local authority (the social work authority);
ii) a person chosen by that authority;
iii) any other person who has been accepted as a suitable person to act in that capacity by the local health authority. Guardianship could thus involve the patient's residence in an institution or establishment run by social work or another appropriate organisation.

In respect of hospital or guardianship orders made by a court:

i)   the nearest relative has no power to order the patient's discharge
ii) the normal limitations of part V of the Act on the continued detention or

guardianship of people do not apply to such orders made by a criminal court.

Before making a hospital or guardianship order, a court must satisfy itself that:

i)   the medical evidence of two doctors, one of whom must be approved, justifies such a course, and in the case of guardianship, that there is 'a recommendation by a mental health officer';
ii) the penalty for the offence is not fixed by law;
iii) the court is of the opinion, having regard to all the circumstances, including the nature of the offence, and the character and antecedents of the offender, and to other available methods of dealing with him, that the most suitable method of disposing of the case is by means of such an order (section 58 of the CP Act, 1995);
iv) a hospital bed is available for him within seven days (as amended by Sch 1, para. 21(6) of the 1997 Act) of the making of a hospital order; or
v)   the local authority, or other 'suitable' person involved, is willing to receive the offender into guardianship (guardianship order).

The court can make a hospital order (without restrictions) or guardianship order (as the case may be) in terms of section 58 of the CP Act, 1995. An order is normally made *only* where a mentally disordered person is convicted of an offence punishable by imprisonment. Offences not punishable by imprisonment are excluded because it is considered more appropriate to use Part V of the 1984 Act alone. Any summary court other than a sheriff court, in other words a district court or Stipendiary magistrate's court, which considers that an accused may be suffering from mental disorder, must remit to the sheriff court. A hospital order can also be made where a person is acquitted on the ground of insanity at the time of the act or omission, charged either by a court or at the 'examination of facts', where the 'examination of facts' makes a finding that the person did act or made the omission constituting the offence.

Where the sheriff court sits as a summary court it may make such orders without proceeding to conviction, providing it is satisfied that the accused did the act or made the omission charged (see SHHD notes, para 289). In addition, the CP Act, 1995 makes provision for committal instead of remand (s.52), for interim orders (s.53), and for medical examination on remand (s.200). The order must specify the form of mental disorder from which the offender is found to be suffering.

A hospital order can include directions for conveying the patient to and retaining him in a place of safety pending the hospital bed becoming available during the seven-day (as amended by Sch. 1, para. 21(6) of the 1997 Act) period. However, no directions for conveying a patient to a residential establishment provided by the local authority under Part IV of the *Social Work (Scotland) Act*, 1968 can be made unless the court is satisfied that the local authority is willing to receive him.

A hospital order shall *not* specify the State Hospital (at Carstairs) as the place of detention unless the court is satisfied on the medical evidence that:

i)   the offender requires treatment under conditions of special security because of his dangerous, violent, or criminal propensities; and

ii) he cannot suitably be cared for in a hospital other than the State Hospital.

A hospital or guardianship order is not intended to run for any specified period, but the patient may be made subject to special restrictions (see below). The order will be reviewed by the responsible medical officer (RMO) every four weeks. Thereafter there will be periodic reviews which may lead to release from liability to detention at any time. The order must be reviewed after six months and the RMO, after consulting with others involved in treatment, then has to decide whether or not detention should continue. If detention is renewed, if is for a further period of six months and thereafter annually.

Renewal does not involve the courts, but on each occasion a fresh medical examination is made and a report submitted to the managers of the hospital or to the guardian. If restrictions have not been imposed, a hospital order can be discharged at any time by the responsible medical officer, the Mental Welfare Commission or the hospital managers. A guardianship order can be discharged by the responsible medical officer, the Mental Welfare Commission or local authority. Where the person has just arrived in hospital after sentence, he may appeal against the sentence within two weeks (solemn procedure) or within one week (summary procedure). Thereafter he can appeal to the sheriff every time detention is renewed.

RESTRICTION ORDERS

Once a hospital order has been made (**not a guardianship order**) the patient falls into one of two main categories:

a) patients not subject to special restrictions, 'ordinary patients' under Part VI of the CP Act, 1995, or

b) a court may make a further order directing that he be subject to special restrictions.

A restriction order is made in terms of section 59 of the *Criminal Procedure (Scotland) Act,* 1995. The following **additional** requirements apply before a restriction order can be made:

i) the approved doctor, of the two doctors providing evidence, must give evidence orally before the court;

ii) it appears to the court, having regard to the nature of the offence, the antecedents of the person, and the risk that as a result of his mental disorder, he would commit offences if set at large, that it is necessary for the protection of the public from serious harm to make such an order .

The order may direct that the person be subject to special restrictions for a specified period, but more usually (as the course of the illness can rarely be predicted accurately) it is made 'without limit of time'.

The effect of a restriction order is that a patient may not be granted leave of absence or transferred to another hospital, except with the consent of the Secretary of State. The patient continues to be liable to be detained until he is discharged. Only the Secretary of State, on a recommendation from the RMO that the person no longer requires to be kept in hospital, or the Sheriff, on appeal, may discharge the patient from the hospital. While a restriction order is in force, patients are reported on as regularly to the hospital managers as those not subject to restriction. The Mental Welfare Commission is notified and its duties to visit under section 3(2)(b) apply. There is no requirement to notify the local authority. However it is assumed that social work involvement is assured. The responsible medical officer (RMO) must report progress annually to the Secretary of State, and the patient will be subject to annual review by an advisor to the Secretary of State. This may result in discharge from the restriction order or from liability to detention.

The discharge of patients subject to restriction orders is controlled by the Secretary of State. The legal and social work considerations parallel in many respects the discharge of an offender on parole from a penal institution (see Chapter 11), and the responsibility of the social worker supervising such a patient carries similar responsibilities for the protection of the public as a high-profile aspect of the task.

There are two forms of discharging a patient subject to a restriction:

i) *Conditional discharge*. The conditions involved in any discharge will always include residence at an approved address and specific arrangements for supervision. These will include the appointment of **two** supervisors—one will be a doctor, and the other will often be a social worker.

ii) *Absolute discharge*. A conditional discharge **lapses** either if a fixed period of restriction expires; or if it is **converted** by the Secretary of State into an absolute discharge. Rarely is the person discharged absolutely from the hospital in the first instance. The absolute discharge, especially where there is no time limit on the restriction order, depends on the patient's progress. The absolute discharge, in the context of 'Secretary of State's patients' is something quite markedly different from the absolute discharge as a disposal announced by a court (see Chapter 7).

The Secretary of State may direct that a patient shall cease to be subject to special restrictions, or the period specified in the order may come to an end. In such cases, the patient remains liable to be detained under the order, as if it were an 'ordinary' order without restrictions on discharge.

Appeals against sentence must be made within two weeks (solemn procedure), or within one week (summary procedure), and again in the period between six and twelve months after sentence, and thereafter every twelve months.

It should also be noted that some people serving sentences of imprisonment may be transferred to hospital, and be subject to detention, if they become, or are diagnosed as, mentally disordered during sentence. It may well be that the disorder responds to treatment in the hospital, and that all concerned with the mental health aspects decide that discharge from the hospital is appropriate. In this instance, however, discharge will be back to the prison, and release therefrom will be determined by the usual criminal justice considerations (see below).

Under section 53 of the CP Act, 1995 (as amended by section 11 of the 1997 Act) the court may in certain circumstances make interim hospital orders authorising an offender's admission to hospital for short periods not exceeding 12 months in total, before deciding whether to make a full hospital order or sentence the offender in some other way.

Hospital direction

The Crime and Punishment (Scotland) Act 1997 (section 6) inserted a new section 59A into the CP Act, 1995 and provided for a new court disposal, a 'hospital direction'. Where a person is convicted on indictment in the High Court or of an offence punishable by imprisonment in the sheriff court, the court may, in addition to any sentence of imprisonment, direct that the person be admitted and detained in hospital. This is likely to cover situations where it appears that the offender is in need of treatment for a mental condition, but where the statutory tests for making a hospital order are not met.

The court must be satisfied that the ground under s.17(1) of the 1984 Act applies (see above) and that the hospital can admit the person 'within 7 days of the direction being made'. The oral or written evidence of two medical practitioners, defined in s.61 of the CP Act, 1995, is required and the form of mental disorder must be specified. The State Hospital is specifically excluded from 'directions' unless the person,

a) on account of his dangerous, violent, or criminal propensities requires treatment under conditions of special security; and

b) cannot suitably be cared for in a hospital other than a State hospital.

Additional direction can be given to admit the person to 'a place of safety', pending admission to hospital, such as a residential establishment if the court is 'satisfied that the managers of that establishment are willing to receive him'.

Section 6(3) of the 1997 Acts amends section 204(2) of the CP Act, 1995 and requires the court to take into account

a) such information as it has been able to obtain *from an officer of a local authority, or otherwise* about his circumstances;

b) any information before it concerning his character and mental and physical condition;

c) its power to make a hospital direction in addition to imposing a sentence of imprisonment.

A hospital direction (s.62A of the 1984 Act inserted by s.7 of the 1997 Act) provides authority for a constable, and a mental health officer, among others, to convey the person to the hospital within seven days. A number of provisions allow for emergency contingencies. The direction can last until the offender is remitted to custody or is discharged under s.74(8B) of the 1984 Act.

REQUIREMENTS OF MEDICAL EVIDENCE

Section 61 specifies the requirements of medical evidence. The purpose of the section is to ensure that at least one of the medical practitioners providing evidence for orders under sections 53(1)(interim hospital orders), 54(1)(insanity in bar of trial) and 58(1) hospital or guardianship orders) must be approved for the purpose under section 20 or 39 of the *Mental Health (Scotland)*, 1984.

Written or oral evidence in section 58(1) orders must include a statement as to whether the person giving evidence is related to the accused or has any pecuniary interest in the person's hospital admission or reception into guardianship.

CHILD OFFENDERS

Children who appear before the courts can be made the subject of orders of detention under section 208 of the *Criminal Procedure (Scotland) Act,* 1995 that normally result in detention in a penal institution, or orders under section 44 of the CP Act, 1995 which may result in their detention in a residential establishment provided by a local authority. If any child so sentenced becomes mentally disordered, then the above arrangements for transfer orders can be applied (and return to the former system if treatment is successful and no longer needed).

Children who appear before the children's hearings, or who are subject to an enquiry in respect of an appearance thereat, are treated under the 'civil' part of the *Mental Health (Scotland) Act,* 1984—that is, Part V of the Act—and not under Part VI, which is the part that gives criminal courts the powers discussed in this chapter.

The *Social Work (Scotland)* Act, 1968, section 46(1), authorised a children's hearing 'after considering the case of a child, if it considers that an application for admission to hospital or guardianship under Part V of the Mental Health (Scotland) Act should be made to the Sheriff, to make a report to that effect to the Mental Health Officer concerned'. Section 46(2) also made it clear that 'nothing in the foregoing . . . shall affect the making of voluntary arrangements for the treatment of mental disorder contained in section 17(2) of the *Mental Health (Scotland)* Act, 1984'. No equivalent provision exists in the *Children (Scotland) Act, 1995.* However it is to be presumed that the same action is open to children's hearings.

APPROPRIATE ADULTS SCHEMES

It is the Scottish Office intention that appropriate adults schemes will be available throughout Scotland by March 1999 to assist and safeguard mentally disordered people in the course of police interview. Draft guidance was issued in February 1998 entitled *Interviewing People who are Mentally Disordered: Appropriate Adult Schemes* (SOHD, 1998b). While the rights at statute and common law equally apply to people experiencing mental disorder, special care is required in dealing with them. The term mental disorder for this purpose includes people who are mentally ill, people with a learning disability, those with acquired brain damage and people suffering from dementia.

In most instances such people are capable of providing reliable evidence but they may have problems in communication which could result in misleading statements or be subject to inappropriate reactions because of impaired understanding. Where there is any doubt about an interviewee's mental state or capacity, police officers should make full use of any local arrangements established to enable psychiatrists (or if impossible, the police surgeon or the person's GP) to visit the place of interview to assist by undertaking a mental state assessment. Where mental disorder is confirmed arrangements should then be made for an appropriate adult to be present.

The guidance advises that where a person is excessively apprehensive and this is accompanied by

- excessive anxiety;
- unusual mood level;
- incoherence (not drug or alcohol induced);
- inability to understand or answer questions;
- unusual behaviour traits; or
- agitation leading to physical activity not in keeping with the situation;

or other signs of mental disorder, the investigating officer should arrange for a medical examination.

Appropriate adult schemes are intended to operate on an inter-agency basis, ideally as an integral part of the joint commissioning arrangements described in the *Framework for Mental Health Services in Scotland* (SOHD, 1997). In practice the expectation is that social work will initiate the process by arranging the links between chief officers in relevant statutory and voluntary agencies.

An appropriate adult should be someone who is completely independent of the police and the interviewee and has a sound understanding, experience and training in dealing with mentally disordered people. In practice many are likely to be professionally qualified such as mental health officers or psychiatric nurses. **They cannot be police officers or employees of the police force**. Where professionals are appointed, they are not engaged to act in their professional role but to apply their professional knowledge and skills to assist and support as appropriate adults. Having a friend or relative available is likely to be helpful to explain the idea of the appropriate adult to the person concerned. Guidance indicates that the role of the appropriate adult is to

- be on hand to provide support and reassurance to the person being interviewed;
- to ensure that the interviewee understands why he or she is being interviewed;
- to ensure that the interviewee understanding the questions being put to him or her and the implications of his or her answers;
- to facilitate communication where possible between the interviewee and the police officer conducting the interview;
- to ensure that proper interview procedures are followed. (para 2.5)

The appropriate adult should be present throughout the interview, ensuring the person understands their rights and entitlements, particularly as regards legal representation, and should have access to any document or statement intended for signature.

TRANSFER FROM PENAL INSTITUTIONS OF MENTALLY DISORDERED OFFENDERS

Section 70 of the *Mental Health (Scotland)* Act, 1984, makes provision for a prisoner committed to custody, whether before trial or sentence, to be transferred from prison to hospital (not a private hospital) on an order by a sheriff, if they are found to be suffering from a mental disorder. This procedure is specific to situations where the condition only becomes apparent **after** the committal to custody. It places the person in the same position as someone committed under section 52 **except** the transfer requires the approval of **two doctors**, at least one of whom must be approved. The transfer is at the request of the Secretary of State, which means that the person cannot be transferred from hospital to another place, or granted leave of absence from hospital, without the permission of the Secretary of State. Any transfer order has to be effected within 14 days, otherwise it lapses, and, if transfer is still necessary, a new order has to be sought. If the proceedings against the person are dropped, or if they are found not guilty, detention under section 70 ceases to have effect, but the person may still be detained under civil proceedings in Part V of the 1984 Act.

Section 71 of the 1984 Act makes provision for a person serving a custodial sentence to be transferred to hospital without restriction (**a transfer direction without special restriction**). Custodial sentence, in this context, includes young offenders, children sentenced to detention and children undergoing residential training under section 44 of the *Criminal Procedure (Scotland) Act,* 1995. Subject to the approval of two doctors, at least one of whom must be approved, the person now becomes a patient, in terms of Part V of the *Mental Health (Scotland) Act*, 1984 and ceases to be a prisoner in terms of the criminal justice legislation. His release will be reviewed in accordance with the civil procedures under Part V of the 1984 Act. He must be released from liability to detention as soon as his disorder is no longer considered, by the RMO, as being such as to justify detention. While not required to return to prison, he may have to remain in hospital after sentence expiry, if further treatment is required. Detention will continue at the end of six months, in other words as an ordinary formal patient, unless the RMO considers this unnecessary. A transfer direction is subject to appeal to the sheriff within one month of transfer. If the appeal is successful the person will be returned to prison. Section 71A (inserted by Schedule 1 para. 5 of the 1997 Act) makes further provision, where the person is no longer mentally disordered, as defined, or detention is no longer necessary for health, or safety, or the protection of others, and it is not appropriate for him to remain in hospital, the Secretary of State can direct that the person be remitted to 'any prison or other institution or place' in which he might have been detained had he not been removed to hospital.

If the person is transferred under section 72 (**a restriction direction**) the effect is the same as a restriction order under section 59. Even although in hospital, he will not be excluded from any early release provisions which would have applied in prison, nor have the right to be considered for parole. If, before the end of the prison sentence, the Secretary of State is satisfied that he no longer requires hospital treatment or protection, he must be sent back to prison. The restriction direction can be appealed to the sheriff within one month. In any representation to the Mental Welfare Commission, commissioners can do no more than recommend to the Secretary of State that he is returned to prison.

Broadly, the considerations indicated above as to medical evidence and the advisability of transfer apply.

However, if the disorder responds to treatment, and the medical authorities advise the Secretary of State that his detention in hospital is no longer appropriate, then the Secretary of State can order his return to the prison system (or, if a young offender or child, to an appropriate non-medical institution) if some part of the original sentence would have remained unserved. Equally the Secretary of State may order release from that prison or penal institution under the terms of a parole or other licence if such would have applied to the original penal sentence.

THE SOCIAL WORK CONTRIBUTION TO PATIENT CARE

It will be seen that the care of the mentally disordered is a specialised field, largely the province of medical practitioners with special qualifications, or those social workers specifically approved in this field. However, there may be a number of contributions that social work can make to the treatment for which the doctors are responsible:

a) There are a number of points at which background information and social data may be of assistance to the doctor's assessment of the person;

b) There is a whole series of practical 'welfare' issues emanating from such orders with which social workers can assist—securing premises, informing landlords, protecting goods and property and so on, of the kind commonly met in the through care and resettlement of those sentenced to penal custody (see Chapter 11);

c) Social workers may in some cases be nominated as guardians, in terms of a guardianship order, although this provision is very seldom used. Guardianship involves acting for and with the patient, and for and with the medical authorities in any treatment or supporting role (see Whyte and Hunter, 1992; Connor et. al 1993). The introduction of the treatment and supervision order would indicate that it is important that a number of specialist criminal justice social workers should also seek training and accreditation as designated 'mental health officers'. Section 9 of the Mental Health (Scotland) Act, 1984 sets out the position, and section 41 defines the powers of the guardian, which include 'powers relating to residence, attendance for treatment, occupation, training and education, and power to require access to the patient';

d) The supervision of the Secretary of State's 'patients' on release may also involve social workers. The field may be complex, and the behaviour difficult, but social workers can make a contribution to the care of mentally disordered offenders, and to avoiding the inappropriate use of penal measures when treatment is more what is needed. The strategy outlined in the SACRO report (1990) gives even further indications of the need for dealing with mental disturbance outwith the penal system.

Chapter 13

The Rehabilitation of Offenders Act, 1974

Effects of rehabilitation; further offences; disclosure; limitations of rehabilitation

'Some sentences release their poison only after years'—E. Canetti.

This short Act of eleven sections was sought to bring UK legislation into line with that of, among others, Commonwealth countries, notably New Zealand and Canada. The brainchild of Lord Chancellor Gardiner, it can be seen as a product of its time when ideas of rehabilitation, as a mechanism for halting the growth of crime and repeat offending, were in favour. It is an Act of considerable complexity. In essence it intends to enable offenders to put their past behind them, by erasing their criminal records after a suitable crime-free period. The Act, which has been amended extensively since 1974, expresses its aims as:

> to rehabilitate offenders who have not been convicted of any serious offence for periods of years; to penalise the unauthorised disclosure of their previous convictions; to amend the law of defamation and for the purposes therewith.

The provisions of the Act apply equally to Scotland, England and Wales, except Section 3, which is specific to disposals made by the children's hearings under the *Children (Scotland) Act*, 1995.

The provisions of the Act are qualified by Statutory Instruments, which provide a range of important 'exceptions and interpretations'. Not all of these are of concern to social workers.

The important principles of the Act are:

- some sentences are outwith its provisions and may never be erased;
- the periods of rehabilitation vary according to the sentences;
- a further conviction during the rehabilitation period may render null and void the rehabilitation consideration for the original sentence;
- disclosure of convictions of persons with whom they have dealings can be part of the official duties of officials in social work, police, etc., but only in very specific situations;
- entry to certain professions may necessitate disclosure of all (if any) convictions of the applicant; this includes candidates for social work training.

The Act takes into account offences committed before and after its enactment, 31 July, 1974. Throughout the Act, the word **'spent'** is used to describe convictions which have been lived down, and which, therefore, may not be disclosed without specific authority.

THE EFFECT OF REHABILITATION

The Act says that, **with some exceptions**, a rehabilitated person 'shall be treated for all purposes in law as a person who has not committed, or been charged with, or prosecuted for, or convicted of, or sentenced for, the offence or offences which were the subject of that conviction'. This means that a rehabilitated person can regard himself as a person of good character with no criminal convictions to disclose. The right of non-disclosure applies not only to the fact of a conviction, but also to a range of matters detailed in section 4.

Guidance on the Act provided some examples of situations in which the rehabilitated person need **not** disclose his spend convictions:

- filling in forms (for example, for a job, to join a union) or at interviews;
- refusal of or dismissal from employment because of a spent conviction, except in relation to excluded professions;
- making an agreement for hire purchase or insurance;
- giving evidence in civil proceedings.

An important point to stress is that, even including the examples given, there are numerous **exceptions** to these general rehabilitative provisions; including, for example, matters relating to 'judicial authority' (s.4)6)) (below). Convictions never become spent where the person is applying for certain types of jobs such as medical practitioner, solicitor and social worker working with children or older people. The exceptions are listed in the Statutory Instrument (*Rehabilitation of Offenders Act, 1974 (Exceptions) Order* 1975 (S.I. 1975 No. 1023).

A further important exception is that when the person appears in **further criminal proceedings**, whether as a witness, or as an accused person, the Act does not apply. He is not free to deny any convictions, whether 'spent' or not, as in other circumstances. However, in relation to accused people, procurators fiscal can take account of the intention of the Act, and provide only a selection of previous convictions, depending on the kind of case under consideration.

Section 1(4) makes it clear that:

> references to a conviction, however expressed, include references to: a conviction by or before a court outside Great Britain: and to any findings (other than a finding linked to a finding of insanity) in any criminal proceedings that the person has committed an offence or done the act, or made the omission charged.

Exempted sentences

Some convictions can never be wiped clean (section 5). Some major penalties remain on the record, and never become spent; for all practical purposes they should be considered as outwith the scope of the Act.

The following can never be spent:

- a sentence of life imprisonment;
- a sentences of detention without limit of time, formerly 'detention during Her

Majesty's Pleasure' (imposed on young offenders convicted of murder);
- a sentence of imprisonment or detention for a term in excess of 30 months. This includes such a term served, in whole or in part in Youth Custody (England and Wales), or detention in a Young Offender's Institution;
- a sentence of detention in excess of 30 months passed on a child by a court;
- other sentences, corrective training and preventive detention, now unlikely to come to attention.

Section 1, as amended, stipulates that where a person:

a) ...did not have imposed upon him in respect of that conviction a sentence which is excluded from rehabilitation under the Act; and
b) he has not had imposed upon him in respect of a subsequent conviction during the rehabilitation period applicable to the first mentioned conviction in accordance with section 6 below, a sentence which is excluded from rehabilitation under this Act...then...that individual shall...be treated as a rehabilitated person in respect of the first mentioned conviction and that conviction shall for these purposes be deemed as spent.

Section 1(2) makes it clear that 'a failure to pay a fine or other sum adjudged to be paid, or imposed, shall not prevent a person from becoming a rehabilitated person'. It needs to be said in this context that a 'failure to pay' will undoubtedly have resulted in some further sanction by the court, and it is this latter sentence/ order which is likely to be relevant. Section 1(3) emphasises that 'sentence' includes most orders of the court. However it specifically excludes 'any order made in default of payment of any fine'.

As we have noted a broad definition of conviction and sentence operates within the legislation. Conviction includes the acceptance of an offence ground at a children's hearing and sentence includes any disposal by a children's hearing based on an offence ground. However it should be noted that a period of imprisonment resulting from fine default is not counted as a sentence for the purpose of calculating the period of rehabilitation.

Section 5 is of particular importance. It lists the sentences which are excluded from rehabilitation. These are sentences of:

- life imprisonment;
- terms in excess of 30 months;
- detention without limit of time/during Her Majesty's Pleasure;
- 30 months under section 53 of the Children and Young Person Act 1933;
- a corresponding court martial punishment

Any other sentence is subject to rehabilitation under the Act.

Section 6 (2) states that 'where more than one sentence is imposed...the rehabilitation period applicable...shall be the longer or the longest' and section 6(3) provides the authority for saying that a breach of order/sentence shall constitute the rehabilitation period to its end, providing this extends beyond the term of the original order/sentence.

Rehabilitation periods

With the above exceptions, any other conviction is subject to the terms of the Act. The Act's complexities further continue with the calculations necessary to work out the rehabilitation period for the various sentences, together with the age of the person at the time of the conviction. It is important to note that special considerations apply to young offenders, and to some of the specific sentences relating to them.

Section 5 (2) of the Act sets out the rehabilitation period. These include:

Table A: Standard Sentences

Table A refers to a standard list of convictions, none of which is a sentence exceeding 30 months in duration. **The rehabilitation period shown should be halved if the person was under 18 at the time of the conviction.** (*Criminal Justice Act*, 1991, s.68 and Schedule 8 para.5 amends section 5(2)of the 1974 Act.)

Sentence	*Rehabilitation Period*
Sentence of imprisonment for a term exceeding 6 months, but not exceeding 30 months.	10 years
Sentence of imprisonment, or, if a young offender, a sentence of detention (YOI), for a term not exceeding 6 months.	7 years
A fine, supervised attendance order, compensation, admonition	5 years

In respect of Supervised Release Orders (SRO) (see Chapter 11) i.e. a consideration of any sentence between 12 months and four years, thus spanning this rehabilitation period of 10 years and the sentences outwith the 'spent' consideration, the SRO has to be seen as part of the sentence per se, irrespective of what portion is 'served' in the community.

Any fine imposed, irrespective of amount, or of such matters as fine supervision, of the substitution of a supervised attendance order, or imprisonment in default, is, for the purposes of this Act, deemed to be a 'spent' conviction after five years. Remember that if the person was under 18 at the time of the conviction, these periods are halved.

Examples

A, aged 25, is given a sentence of 12 months imprisonment for an offence of theft on 3 January, 1995. Provided he commits no further offence, he would be rehabilitated, and the conviction 'spent', on 2 January, 2005;

B, jointly charged with A, but who is aged 16, is sentenced to five months detention in a Young Offenders Institution. Provided he commits no further offence, he would be rehabilitated and his conviction be 'spent' on 3 July, 1998.

Table B: Other court orders and requirements

This table includes a range of orders made both by courts (including Youth Courts in England and Wales) and by children's hearings in Scotland. It is important to note that decisions taken by the Reporter **alone** are NOT convictions. There is **NO difference in**

the rehabilitation periods according to the age of the person at the time of the conviction. The important point about this table is that there are alternative rehabilitation periods depending on the length and nature of the orders concerned. The period is calculated from the date of the conviction, or finding of guilt (s.5).

Nature of Order	*Rehabilitation Period*		
	I	OR	II
Absolute Discharge	6 months		(not applicable)
Discharge of Referral by Children's Hearing where the grounds had been agreed by the child	6 months		(not applicable)
Conditional Discharge; Bound Over to Keep the Peace, or to be of Good Behaviour; Caution;	1 year		OR to the end of the order, whichever is the longer period
Supervision Order (*Children and Young Persons Act*, 1969, England and Wales)	1 year		OR to the end of the order, whichever is the longer period
Supervision Order under section 70 *Children (Scotland) Act* 1995	1 year		OR to the end of the order, whichever is the longer period
Probation	5 years		see below
Community Service Order	5 years		see below
Supervised Attendance Order	5 years		see below

Probation Orders The rehabilitation period for a Probation Order, irrespective of any special requirements that may be inserted, is five years from the date of conviction (section 5(4A)(a)). For a person under 18 years the period is two and a half years from the date of conviction OR a period beginning with the date of conviction and ending when the Probation Order ceases OR ceased to have effect, which ever is longer (section 5(4A)(b)). This provision, inserted by the *Criminal Justice and Public Order Act,* 1994 s.168(1) and Schedule 9, para 11, applies to orders after February 3 1995.

Examples:

Z was put on probation for two years on 1 May 1995; the order is completed on April 30th 1997 but the rehabilitation period is not completed until 30 April 30 2000, at which point the conviction is 'expunged', subject to the exceptions in the situations noted hereunder.

Z's co-accused Q was also put on probation for the same offence, for the same period. He successfully applies for an early discharge of the order after 18 months; but, importantly, the rehabilitation period remains the same as that for Z, namely 2000.

A third co-accused X was similarly dealt with, but breached the order within five months, and the court dealt with the original offence by the imposition of a prison sentence of 12 months; as shown the period is one of ten years *from the date of conviction*, effectively outweighing any consideration of the rehabilitation of the probation conviction. If however the court had decided to take no action on the breach and allowed the order to continue, then for all practical purposes the rehabilitation period remains at five years from the date of the original conviction.

Community Service and Supervised Attendance Orders

Curiously, even in its most up dated version, the Act makes no direct mention of CSOs or of SAOs. The position is that section 5(2)(a) and Table A which follows, stipulates a five-year rehabilitation period for 'any other sentence'. It is to be assumed that CSOs are included in this catch-all phrase. As with the illustrations given in respect of probation, the same considerations apply. It should, however, be noted that where, for example, a Community Service Order is made in respect of a probation breach, then it follows that the rehabilitation period under consideration must be five years from the *date of conviction on the breach*.

SAOs made as an alternative to fine carry five years in their own right; when made in default of fine payment, s.1(3)(a) applies and the relevant period relates to the date of conviction on which the fine was imposed.

Table D: Orders under the Mental Health Acts, as amended

This table is concerned with hospital orders made by criminal courts under the Mental Health Acts of both Scotland and England/Wales as a result of the person being convicted of an offence. Section 5, subsection 7 of the Act provides:

Nature of Order	*Rehabilitation Period*	
	I	II
Order under Part VI of the *Mental Health (Scotland) Act*, 1984, with or without a restriction order (Section 58 of the *Criminal Procedure (Scotland) Act*, 1995)	5 years	OR until 2 years after the order ceases to have effect, whichever is the longer period

Examples:

i) A is made the subject of a Hospital Order on 14 June, 1995; no restrictions are imposed. Hospital Orders are not specified by the Court as being for a fixed period. If no restrictions are imposed by the court, they lapse after 12 months, unless reviewed and renewed by the medical authorities. Assuming A's order actually lapses before five years, his conviction, whatever the period of his actual detention, will be spent on 13 June, 2000.

ii) B is made the subject of a Hospital Order on the same day, but a restriction on discharge is imposed without limit of time. His actual discharge is determined by the medical authorities, but the discharge of his order may not follow for some time after his release (see Chapter 11). His conviction becomes spent two years after the order ceases to have effect—i.e. after he is discharged from the order, not from when he may be physically discharged from hospital.

Table E: Miscellaneous provisions

Nature of Order	*Rehabilitation Period*
Any sentence, not otherwise covered in the above provisions, which is open to rehabilitation. For example, community service orders are not mentioned in the Act, so would be covered by this five-year rule; including unpaid work as a requirement of probation which would be incorporated within the rules affecting probation as amended by the *Criminal Justice (Scotland)Act* 1995;	5 years
Any order disqualifying, prohibiting, or imposing any other penalty; a driving disqualification could thus extend the rehabilitation period that would otherwise have applied—for example, a 16-year-old fined, but disqualified for three years could not regard his conviction as spent at the two and a half year point, but would have to wait a further six months;	To the end of the order
Supervised attendance order (fine default); this is part of the provisions relating to fines, and thus comes under the rule for fines in Table A, including the halving if under 18 at the time;	5 years
Deferred sentence—this is NOT a disposal in its own right; the decision made at the end of the period of deferment will be the governing consideration;	
Consecutive and concurrent sentences of imprisonment: a) in the case of consecutive sentences, it is the overall length that counts—i.e. two consecutive six-month sentences have the effect of a twelve-month sentence;	10 years
b) but two concurrent sentences of six months would only count as one six-month sentence;	7 years

Offenders abroad

i)   The Act does not apply to Northern Ireland. However, certain orders made under

British legislation but having an effect in Northern Ireland are within the scope of the Act. For example, under section 72(2) of the *Social Work (Scotland) Act,* 1968, children made subject to a supervision requirement by a Children's Hearing (section 70 of the *Children (Scotland) Act* 1995), who subsequently move to Northern Ireland, can become the subject of a probation order there, and rehabilitation considerations applicable to the section 70 order would have force. Again the reference is to the original order made and not to its subsequent 'career'.

ii) Convictions recorded in foreign courts are regarded as coming within the scope of the Act, providing that the foreign convictions would have been a crime or offence here; this includes convictions in Northern Ireland.

iii) The Act is not valid outside Great Britain and spent convictions here are not necessarily so regarded anywhere else.

Convictions in the services

The Act also applies to those convictions in the services which were either for offences against the ordinary criminal law or for service offences which carry some serious moral blame. However, if the offence was a purely service one of a kind which most people would not consider criminal, the Act only applies if the sentence was for three months' detention or more. Home Office guidance to the *Rehabilitation of Offenders Act*, 1974, gives the following example:

> On 30 March, 1971, a sailor was convicted by a Naval Court Martial of indecency with another sailor and sentenced to one month's detention. Being an ordinary crime in civilian law, the usual rehabilitation considerations apply (i.e. it becomes spent on 30.3.76. On 9.4.72 he receives seven days' detention from his C.O. for swearing: this is too trivial either to attract the attention of the Act, or to extend the period in relation to the first offence.

The rehabilitation periods are:

Sentence of cashiering, discharge with ignominy, or dismissal with disgrace	10 years
Sentence of dismissal	7 years
Any sentence of detention	5 years

FURTHER OFFENCES DURING THE REHABILITATION PERIOD

In general terms, when a further offence takes place during the rehabilitation period, the period applicable to the earlier offence is considered to be extended for the duration of the later one. A person would need to quote both if obliged to disclose his convictions, even if the rehabilitation period for the first one would otherwise have expired.

If the rehabilitation period for the later offence is shorter than for the earlier offence, it, nonetheless, continues in effect until the expiry of the period applicable to the earlier offence. There are some minor offences which do not carry imprisonment as a possible penalty (for example, plain drunkenness, various bye-law offences and other matters typically tried by District Courts) which represent **exceptions** to the above considerations. Similarly convictions in foreign courts are also subject to the same exceptions.

It should be noted that diversion from prosecution does not represent any formal conviction, even if the person admits to some offence (see Chapter 7). These matters, therefore, fall outwith the scope of the *Rehabilitation of Offenders Act.*

DISCLOSURE OF SPENT CONVICTIONS

A further important aim of the *Rehabilitation of Offenders Act,* 1974 is to 'penalise the unauthorised disclosure' of previous convictions (s.9(2)). To underline the importance of this, the Act creates a new statutory offence, for which the maximum penalty is a fine of level 5 on the Standard Scale. The Act stipulates that it shall be a defence to show that

a) the disclosure was made to the rehabilitated person; or
b) a person whom he reasonably believed to be the rehabilitated person; or
c) another person at the express request of the rehabilitated person; or
d) to one whom he reasonably believed to be such a person.

The Act also creates an offence of obtaining specified information from official records by means of fraud, dishonesty, or bribe, which not only carries a maximum fine on level 5 of the Standard Scale, but also one of a maximum of six months' imprisonment (s.9(3)).

Social workers in possession or receipt of information concerning a person's previous convictions, and particularly perhaps clerical staff handling such information, should be very aware of the provisions and intentions of this Act. The Act refers to this information as 'specified information', and defines it in section 9 (1) as:

> information imputing that a named or otherwise identifiable rehabilitated living person has committed, or been charged with, or prosecuted for, or convicted of, or sentenced for, any offence which is the subject of a spent conviction.

The wide scope of this definition should be noted. It embraces not simply lists of actual convictions, but also suggestions or imputations of crime. In practical terms this covers outcomes such as verdicts of not guilty or not proven; references to No Action and like decisions of reporters; and indeed anything which did not result in a formal disposal by a court or by a children's hearing.

Disclosure of previous convictions is NOT an offence if it is part of a person's official duties. The meaning of this phrase is not defined in the Act.

Circular 26/1975 offered useful guidance on this topic:

i) 'The term has a wide meaning, and is not, for example, confined only to duties imposed by statute...the purpose is to prevent deliberate disclosure to a person who has no right to the specified information and would have no lawful use for it.' The circular can be taken as endorsing some aspects of practice in social enquiry report writing that we discussed in detail in chapter 4;

ii) Disclosure in the following circumstances should not be regarded as contravening section 9 of the Act:

   a) disclosure in accordance with a statutory duty;

   b) disclosure to persons or authorities, who by virtue of the exceptions provided for by Order of the Secretary of State, have a lawful use for information about spent convictions;

   c) disclosure to persons or authorities who, though not exempted, will continue to have a proper use for such information (for example, local authorities assessing the suitability of a person to have the care of children);

   d) disclosure for official purposes between officers of the same organisation (for example, different departments of a local authority), or officers of related organisations (for example, social workers and the police).

iii) Special care should be exercised in disclosing information about previous convictions to those who require the information to assess a person's suitability for employment. We noted above the effect of the Statutory Instrument in allowing that social work is an exempted profession under the Act.

There are other more general circumstances in which disclosure of spent convictions can lawfully be made:

1. Disclosure can be made to the rehabilitated person. It would not be an offence to draw the attention of the person, where official duties require, to any or all of his previous convictions (including any spent ones). A social worker would be within his rights to make reference to past criminality in pursuance of his official duties as part of supervision—for example, if discharge of probation were to be applied for by the probationer, or more generally helping the probationer face reality, or to assist in preventing a further relapse into crime;

2. Spent convictions may be disclosed to any other person at the expressed wish of the rehabilitated person. Situations may arise where the person positively wants it known that he has been crime free for a period of years—for example, a person previously on probation wishing to enter a particular kind of job, or the armed forces. It is important that the official concerned is absolutely sure that he acts on the express, and not the implicit, wish of the rehabilitated person, and written confirmation may be advisable.

Specific social work considerations

As noted above, nothing in the Act limits social workers using previous convictions, where these serve a purpose, as distinct from providing a list denied to the court by the prosecution. Entry to the social work profession requires that there be a full disclosure of previous convictions. This does not mean that anyone with a past history of crime and sentence(s) would automatically be debarred from professional employment. It means simply that *there has to be a full disclosure* at the point of application/interview.

In an appeal court case (IRL R264, 1996) it was decided that the words in section 12 of the 1975 Order 'in connections with social services' denote a wider range of employees than social workers and extend to employees carrying out administrative duties. This is an important authority for managers to consider and requires administrative staff to be briefed on their responsibilities and their accountability under the law. This provision (s.4(5)) extends to social work training, and previous high profile cases involving child abuse in residential establishments simply underline the importance of Selection Boards being aware of their responsibilities in this area. This is not to say that candidates with previous convictions, whether spent or not, should be denied access to training, but that there should be openness about the issues and that, for example, placements should be made appropriately.

Schedule 1 of the Act provides that 'any employment by a local authority or by any other body, in connection with the provision of social services, being employment which is of a kind to enable the holder to have access to any of the following classes of person in the course of his normal duties, falls within the scope of the considerations above; persons:

- over the age of 65 years;
- suffering from serious illness or mental disorder of any description;
- addicted to alcohol or drugs;
- who are blind, dumb or deaf;
- who are substantially handicapped;
- who are under the age of 18; and
- in any employment which is concerned with the administration of , or is normally carried out wholly or partly within the precincts of penal institutions.

Children's hearings

We have noted the considerations governing the under-18 age group in section 5. Added to this is the provision of section 3, which deals with children and young people under section 52(2)(i) of the *Children (Scotland) Act*, 1995 (offence grounds). The acceptance or finding of the offence grounds in a referral shall for the purposes of the Act be deemed to be a conviction (but not otherwise) and any disposal of the case thereafter by a children's hearing shall be treated for those purposes as a sentence.

LIMITATIONS ON REHABILITATION

There are certain limitations imposed by the Act (at section 7) which qualify the guiding principles set out in the introduction. For certain purposes, spent convictions are still regarded as 'live'. Nothing in the Act shall affect:

i) the Royal Prerogative to grant free pardons, to quash convictions, or to commute sentences;

ii) the enforcement of any process to enforce fines or any other sum to be paid under a court order; for example, even if a conviction in respect of which a fine has been ordered becomes spent before payments of the fine are completed, the penalties and sanctions for non-payment can be pursued and applied;

iii) the issue of process in respect of breach of any condition or requirement of a court order; for example, a breach of requirement of probation can still be pursued, even if the order terminates before the matter has finished its progress through the court;

iv) any prohibition, disqualification, disabling or other penalty which extends beyond the rehabilitation period of the associated conviction.

The exceptions include proceedings for fine enforcement or breach of probation proceedings and proceedings relating to parental responsibilities and rights. Possibly the most significant exceptions are detailed in section 7(3). This section gives **judicial authorities** (defined in s.4(6)) discretion to consider spent convictions where it is satisfied that justice cannot be done without reference to them. It has been suggested that in court proceedings evidence of spent convictions may be relevant and necessary for the purposes of assessing a person's propensity to act in particular ways (e.g. risk assessment) or in assessing their credibility as witnesses. The former has major significance for SER authors and suggests that any conviction can be raised in an SER, no matter how old. The current emphasis on risk assessment, particularly in relation to sex offenders, strengthens this position.

Examples:
A is sentenced to imprisonment for possessing firearms, but banned from possessing firearms for life; even if his conviction becomes spent, the prohibition still applies. Section 7 also provides certain safeguards to protect the public welfare, and that of individuals who might be placed in 'jeopardy' by the operation of the rehabilitation clauses. In certain circumstances spent convictions can be referred to without penalty, and in some situations people can be required to admit them. The following situations can include such reference:

i) any criminal proceedings, including any appeal;
ii) any service disciplinary proceedings, or appeal therefrom;
iii) any proceedings relating to adoption, guardianship, wardship, marriage, custody, care or control, or access to any minor (i.e. child under 18), or the provision of care, schooling, or accommodation for minors;
iv) any care proceedings, or appeal therefrom, under section 1 of the *Children and Young Persons Act* (England and Wales),1969; or in any proceedings relating to the variation or discharge of an order made under that section;
v) any proceedings before a Children Hearing, or any appeal therefrom. The intention of the Act is that, notwithstanding its primary purpose, there should be no obstacle to justice being seen to be done, especially in such situations where the public interest, or the rights of an individual, are at stake.

If the rehabilitated person is a party or witness in such proceedings, he can consent to the revelation of any spent conviction(s); but equally a judicial authority has power to order disclosure if it is considered necessary to the justice of the proceedings—the emphasis is on 'has power', not on any automatic ordering of disclosure. *Finally*, subsection 5 states 'no order made by a Court otherwise than on conviction shall be included in any list of convictions given or made to any court which is considering how to deal with him in respect of any offence'.

Legislative changes

An important point to note is that the fundamental changes which the *Criminal Justice (Scotland) Act*, 1995 and the *Prisoners and Criminal Proceedings (Scotland) Act*, 1993 introduced to Scottish sentencing do not alter the core elements of the *Rehabilitation of Offenders Act*, 1974 as amended. The length of sentence imposed remains the key consideration.

Chapter 14

Records

Records, data protection and access to personal files

Section 27(3) of the *Social Work (Scotland) Act,* 1968, requires that each local authority has a probation scheme, approved by the Secretary of State, which has regard to the following matters:

d) arrangements for the keeping of adequate records and statistics regarding the performance of functions under this section...

The need and demand for adequate management of the information and recording system in criminal justice social work is ever increasing. The value and use of information technology is underdeveloped in social work compared with many other professions. Most local authorities have developed their own separate information gathering systems and practitioners are constantly completing standardised forms as part of their daily routine. Few authorities, however, have yet created systems which integrate individual case recording with management information systems to provide information that can be used both to enhance the individual supervisor's professional performance and provide adequate data for strategic and policy planning purposes. Equally good data management systems are required as part of systems established for monitoring effectiveness and risk, for example, sex offenders and those who present a high risk to the community. The Leisk case in Aberdeen (McManus, 1998) highlighted the importance of good communication systems and the requirement for good data recording. Without integration, which demonstrates the direct value of data gathered to practitioners themselves, as well as the organisation, data sets will often remain incomplete and the quality of the data variable.

Some systems are under development and a few good examples exist which illustrate the power of information. Some systems provide supervisors with regular reports on the actual outcomes of their SER assessments against their predicted or recommended disposal, for example; some allow examination, at a glance, of the pattern of attendance of particular types of offenders. Aggregated data is now regularly used to monitor the operation of court decision making against social work assessment, important in liaison discussions with sheriffs, and used to identify key characteristics of groups of offenders, including type of offending, drug and alcohol usage and other problem indicators. Despite their limitations, prediction scores, such as Dunscore and the Level of Service Inventory—revised (LSI-R)(Bonta, 1995), are now more widely available as additional aids to practitioners and managers in monitoring individual and agency provision and performance. While the nature of forecasting and adequate costing of local service demand against projected resources is in its early stages, some authorities are making progress in this direction. Modern technology offers the means to extract information from individual records, or records from programmes, for use in this more corporate way.

While it is important for agencies to generate data independently of government as a means of identifying service demand, service provision and, most importantly, attempts at some qualitative measure of effectiveness, a major gap in available data is the lack of a national database against which performance trends can be established. Attempts to develop a National Core Data System were made by Scottish Office in the mid-1990s and most local authorities gathered statistical data for this purpose. Unfortunately the system has still to get off the ground. A further gap in nationally available data is the fact that SCRO information on convictions is not readily available to social work to allow follow-up evaluation. This data should be readily available to local authorities and it is essential that offenders are followed up, at least over a 12 -24 month period following the completion of social work supervision.

The potential of having a consistent and well structured system of social work recording, combined with workload management tools as a means of generating information that will serve the purposes of the individual supervisor, individual professional planning, and management's requirements, has still to be realised. The introduction of National Objectives and Standards (NOS) and the 100% central funding arrangements has introduced practices and systems that lend themselves to more systematic recording both within and between authorities. Equally accurate file recording on individual offenders is crucial.

The former Scottish probation service recognised the value of systematic and standardised data recording and had a regulated recording system which included gathering general information and information on assessment and planning. Current expectations would require recording of certain standardised assessment measures, outcome measures, review and follow up data, particularly data on subsequent convictions, in ways that can be used for individual working plans and aggregated to produce meaningful organisational data.

Confidentiality

A code guidance under section 5 of the 1968 Act on *Confidentiality of Social Work Records* was produced by SWSG in 1989. The guidance relates to the confidentiality of identifiable personal information held in records retained by local authority social work, irrespective of how the information is held and the circumstances in which it may be disclosed to third parties. The guidance is confined to local authority responsibilities to 'donors' of information. Some general principles were identified:

• all information should be regarded as confidential and donors should be provided with guidance on the circumstances in which relevant personal information may be shared within social work and with other agencies;

- information supplied by donors for one purpose should not be used for another purpose; the purpose should be clear from the outset;
- information supplied by donors should not be disclosed without the donor's consent, in other than exceptional circumstances;
- where information has been supplied by another agency, disclosure should be made in accordance with the policy and procedures agreed with that agency (para. 10).

Personal information should normally be available only to staff in social work directly involved with the service user. A limited range of others who may need personal information to carry out their duties includes:

- social work finance staff for assessment purposes;
- legal advisers;
- other agencies, particularly if providing services on behalf of the authority;
- senior staff in their normal supervisory or management roles;
- social work students and practice teachers;
- researchers;
- informal carers;
- officers of the Secretary of State (para 12).

Exceptional disclosure may be required by law or in the public interest, overriding a person's right to have information kept confidential. Professional and legal advice should be sought in each case and information disclosed should be the minimum necessary to meet the requirements of the situation. Particular requirements of this kind may include:

- statutory requirements—where there is a statutory right to information, local authorities are not required to obtain consent, but should notify the donor, where practicable;
- requirement by a court—for example, social enquiry reports; donors should be notified;
- children's hearing requirements; disclosures to appointees—for example, safeguarders are entitled to access to information;
- disclosure to police—to prevent, detect or prosecute serious crime (no legal definition);
- risk to personal and public health—medical advice should be sought as required;
- disclosure of personal information by the media (para.13).

In addition to guidance, legislation on data protection and access to personal information is increasingly under scrutiny from a European perspective. A number of recent European directives have led to the requirement for the UK to overhaul the legislative provision on data protection and access to personal files. New legislation is expected to be in place by 1999. Current legislative provision is dealt with below.

THE DATA PROTECTION ACT, 1984

The *Data Protection Act,* 1984 'is difficult to understand at first'—as even the series of Notes and Guidelines produced by the office of the Data Protection Registrar admits. 'The Act is complicated', continue the Notes—and even by the standards of some of the concepts and arrangements dealt with elsewhere in this text, the *Data Protection Act* is complicated.

Social work authorities involved in computerised record creation and maintenance have to register as 'computer bureaux', and must ensure that users conform to and comply with the provisions of the Act. Fuller and more comprehensive guidance may be obtained on application to the office of the Data Protection Registrar and in Scottish Office circular SWSG8/87.

As it is likely that authorities will steadily increase their use of computerised record systems, these services are designated under the Act as 'Standard purposes'. Each standard purpose is allocated a number, and PO 54 is allocated to 'the provision of social, social work or social welfare services'. In the present context, this includes the supervision and rehabilitation of offenders.

The Act seeks to provide **access rights to persons about whom information is recorded on computer**. However, it may be useful to note that the use of a word processor to produce a script, record, or report is regarded as an exemption from the general rule. The essence of what the Act covers is the storage and retrieval of material in a computerised system. The Act places obligations on '**data users**'— that is, on those who record and use personal data. They (and not simply the authority as the registered bureau) must be 'open about the use…and follow sound and proper practices…' (Guideline 1). The provisions apply only to information which is computerised, processed, and stored. However this Act and the *Access to Personal Files* Act (see below) are two sides of the one coin, as it were. The two are inseparable in concept and in intent.

Statements both of fact and of opinion about the individual are personal data and must be disclosed, if requested. However, an indication of the user's intentions towards the individual is not (Guideline 1:4). This distinction might well serve to assist a clarification in social work practice and recording. If, for example, the form of recording clearly distinguishes between sections on information and events from assessment and planning, and the latter is construed as 'intentions towards the '**data subject**', rather than merely 'opinions about the individual', then there could be grounds under this Act for withholding this information, even if requested to disclose it, and it was on computer. The important distinction created by the Act is between 'opinions about' the person, which have to be disclosed on request; and 'intentions towards', which need not be. This distinction needs much more clarification in record keeping than hitherto has been characteristic in social work.

There are certain **exemptions** from these general principles (*Data Protection (Subject Access Modification) (Social Work) Order*, 1987 no. 1904). These relate to the withholding of data where giving access **would be likely** (emphasis added) to prejudice the practice of social work:

a) where access to information by the data subject would be likely to result in serious harm to the data subject or some other person; or

b) where access to the information might enable the data subject to know or deduce the identity of another person (other than an 'employee') or identify that other person as the source of the information.

This has a direct bearing on issues of confidentiality for donors of information discussed above. It may be important that the record clearly states and distinguishes the basis and understanding on which information was imparted. Another complexity relates to parole dossiers: these are compiled (see Chapter 11) by an Assistant Governor in a penal establishment asking for information and opinion about the prisoner from a number of different prison staff, who may not be aware at the time of giving it that it might subsequently find its way into a system operated by a different agency.

The 1987 Order fails to specify who is to exercise the professional judgement on what might cause 'serious harm' and whether a request for such information is to be met, and on what basis or evidence a decision (about harm arising if access is granted, for example) is to be made. It is envisaged that withholding information on this basis would be most exceptional as would withholding in order to protect the identity of another person. It is important to note that withholding data supplied by an employee in an official capacity is specifically excluded. Any decision may be challenged by an 'aggrieved data subject' by applying to the Data Protection Registrar or to the courts. These decisions will involve managerial sanctions and the advice of the authority's legal officers is likely to be required.

Serious harm could arise where one party is presently suffering from a mental disorder. Cases involving children can create particular difficulties, given that under Scots law parents could, technically, apply for information on behalf of their children. In these cases the terms of section 26(4) of the Act, which overrides existing statutory provision preventing or restricting disclosure of information, will apply to the local authority's duty in section 20 of the 1968 Act.

For those people who are considered vulnerable or in need of protection from damaging revelations about themselves, or which might cause serious harm to others, in considering whether to withhold information, local authorities should give thought to

- providing information along with specially arranged counselling to provide support to the data subject; or
- suggesting to the data subject that it would be in their interest to defer access to a 'specified period not exceeding 12 months'.

The Act also underlines the need for social workers to be clear in distinguishing between evidence, opinion, and assessment, and the need for records to be similarly disaggregated.

The intention of the Act was that consent, or the withholding of it, by a parent or guardian of a child is NOT required if the child, as 'data subject', requests access. This right, for some strange reason was lost, in the *Age of Legal Capacity*

(Scotland) Act, 1991. New legislation will rectify this error. While there are large and complex responsibilities imposed upon 'bureaux' by the Act, there is also a body of sound practice guidance for users. Much is consistent with good social work practice. The principles set out in Guideline 4 are summarised below. Fuller reference to the source is advisable:

- **Information shall be obtained and processed fairly and lawfully.** It would be interesting to see what action the Registrar might take if a complaint were made in respect, for example, of some aspects of social enquiry report practice. The Registrar would only be involved if the report were to be kept in a compu-terised form (as part of a case record, for example), but not if all that was in-volved was typing it on a word processor. For example, is any opinion as to disposal 'complete and accurate'? Again the guideline speaks of ensuring that 'no-one is misled as to who the information is for, why it is required, or why it will be used or disclosed'.
- **Personal data shall be held only for one or more specified and lawful purpose(s).** This principle is consistent with the *Social Work Statement of Values* (ADSW, 1991) which emphasises minimum intrusiveness and calls for a clear understanding of the background and offence-relevant information required.
- **Personal data held shall not be used or disclosed in any manner incompat-ible with that purpose.** In registering as a bureau, an authority has to define what arrangements exist in respect of the transmission of information across boundaries and other agencies. Users need to be safeguarded from data gath-ered for one purpose being used for another. Equally social workers need to be mindful that, within large social work authorities, information gathered for court and penal purposes is not used subsequently for purposes quite unrelated to the **primary purpose** for which it was acquired and, importantly, **provided** by those that gave it.
- **Personal data shall be adequate, relevant, and not excessive.** Hearsay mate-rial should have no place in any social work record.
- **Data should be accurate and kept up to date.**
- **Personal data should not be kept for longer than is necessary.** Much informa-tion gathered by social work. e.g. child care records, has to be kept indefinitely for adoption counselling purposes. The same would not be true for most criminal justice records except for very serious offenders, such as sex offenders.
- **There is a right for the subject to be informed of the data of which he is the subject; to access to any such data; where appropriate, to have any such data corrected or erased.**
- **Appropriate security measures shall be taken against unauthorised access to, disclosure or destruction of, personal data and against accidental loss or destruction of personal data.** The main responsibilities here lie with the designated 'bureau', and a number of very technical matters in relation to com-puters may be involved (passwords, backup systems, etc.).

The Act, whatever the technical issues in relation to the computers themselves, nonetheless serves to profile some aspects of professional practice, and encourages the development of good practice and the principles of case recording in social work.

ACCESS TO PERSONAL FILES ACT, 1987

This Act follows the *Data Protection Act* 1984 just discussed, and **brings within the open access system all manually maintained records kept by social work and housing**. It enables those persons concerned to see, and to have corrected, any misleading or incorrect information contained in the record which relates to themselves.

The Act is not retrospective, and does not extend to any material placed on record before 1 April, 1987, when the Act was passed, except 'to the extent that access to it is required to make intelligible information recorded on or after that date (1 April, 1987)' (section 2(4)). The provisions of the Act are qualified by the *Access to Personal Files (Social Work) (Scotland) Regulations* 1989 (S.I. 1989 No. 251) which outline in detail exceptions to the requirements to disclose information.

The regulations require local authorities on receipt of a written application to inform an individual, whether a user of its social work services or not, of any personal information about him held in any manual record maintained for the purposes of their social work function,. Access to information is not restricted to that held on a personal file in the name of the individual making the request; it covers all personal information about the individual, however or wherever held. It does not apply to

- automatically processed records defined by the *Data Protection Act*, 1984;
- records of voluntary organisations or other bodies, even where they are directly involved with a local authority in provision of a social work service;
- records maintained by reporters to children's panels;
- records of persons in prison or in the State Hospital, where local authorities act on behalf of the Secretary of State.

The Act places no positive duty on the authority or on an individual worker to initiate access, and the intention of the Act is that the initiative will rest with the person named in the record (regulation 3(1)). Initially the individual has to apply in writing to secure access. There is power to ask for a small search fee (not exceeding £10), but the service can be provided free of charge. The required file or files must be made available within 40 days of the application (regulation 6), and **any jargon, abbreviations, or technicalities employed must be explained in ordinary language** (emphasis added).

Information from the file can be withheld under certain circumstances. Where third party consent to disclosure is necessary, regulation 5 requires the local authority to seek the consent of that person within 14 days. Information from **health professionals** can be withheld if the appropriate person informs the social work authority in writing that the information would be likely to 'cause serious harm to the physical or mental health of the individual who is the subject of the information, or any other person' or if it would disclose the identity of another person (regulation 8(4)). Similarly information provided to the authority by **reporters** in pursuit of statutory duties is exempted from disclosure (regulation 9). The social work authority must notify the reporter in writing within 14 days of receiving a request which might relate to such information.

More generally the social work authority can withhold information if disclosure would prejudice the social work function by reason of serious harm to the physical or mental health, or emotional condition of the individual subject of information or any other person, or where it might identify another individual who has not consented to disclosure (regulation 10). The local authority is under no obligation to explain why information is withheld but may (and should) do so.

The local authority cannot withhold or restrict access to information where the person providing the information

- is or was an employee of the authority in pursuance of its social work functions; or
- is in performance of, or has performed for reward, direct from the local authority, a service the same as or similar to a social work function of the local authority itself.

This latter group would include paid carers. No special provision is made in the regulations about request for access in respect of people with mental disorders. Many will be very capable of seeking access in their own right; others may need assistance or application may be made on their behalf by a person appointed, e.g. curator bonis or simply a friend or relative.

The Act creates a need for every department to nominate an officer of senior rank to vet all material intended for client scrutiny. It will be essential that any and every file and record held, within the terms of the Act, is of a quality which lends itself to an access request. Management and the Inspectorate will have a responsibility to see that records conform to this standard.

The role of the scrutineer would be particularly concerned with examining those parts of the record contributed by people *other than* the subject of the record and that person's supervisor/social worker. It is under this heading that reports and/or information, opinion, and comment provided by other agencies and professionals (teachers, doctors, prison officers, etc.) as well as by people known to the subject in other roles (employer, landlord, etc.) need to be considered carefully.

It is here that special care is needed to establish the basis and understanding on which information, opinion, and intention was given. It may well be that the scrutineer will need to contact people, in the light of a challenge from the person who is the subject of the record, and clarify and agree any matters in contention.

Once the person has seen or received the information, he can ask the authority to remove inaccuracies or to correct them (regulation 11). The term 'inaccurate' relates only to facts. An opinion which does not purport to be a statement of fact may not be challenged on the grounds of inaccuracy. However where a social work authority agrees that information is inaccurate it must rectify the inaccuracies or erase any opinion based on inaccurate information, or, where it is not satisfied that the information is inaccurate, make a written note within the file that the subject considers the information inaccurate (regulation 11(5)).

Refusal, or the concealing of information, or where the individual is 'aggrieved by any decision' entitles the client to a review by a local authority committee of three members within 28 days of being notified of the decision (regulation 12). Representation can be made in writing or orally to the committee. Such a review is, for all practical purposes, the end of the matter.

Whilst the Act leaves the initiative for requesting access with the person who is the subject of the record, rather than on a worker or a department, there could be advantage in social workers taking a more proactive stance. Records which have been shared between practitioner and client are less likely to become problematic at a later date. In probation practice, for example, regular reviews will be made more meaningful if the probationer feels involved in the process.

Table of Statutes

Access to Personal Files Act, 1987
Bail Etc. (Scotland) Act, 1980
Age of Legal Capacity Act, 1991
Children Act, 1975
Children Act, 1989
Children and Young Persons Act, 1937
Children and Young Persons Act, 1969
Children (Scotland) Act, 1995 (CS Act, 1995)
Civic Government (Scotland) Act, 1982
Community Service by Offenders (Scotland) Act, 1978
Crime and Disorder Act, 1998
Crime and Punishment (Scotland) Act, 1997
Crime and Sentencing Act, 1997
Criminal Evidence Act, 1898
Criminal Justice Act, 1982
Criminal Justice Act, 1991
Criminal Justice (Scotland) Act, 1949
Criminal Justice (Scotland) Act, 1963
Criminal Justice (Scotland) Act, 1980
Criminal Justice (Scotland) Act, 1987
Criminal Justice (Scotland) Act, 1995
Criminal Justice and Public Order Act, 1994
Criminal Law (Consolidation) (Scotland) Act, 1995
Criminal Procedure (Scotland) Act, 1887
Criminal Procedure (Scotland) Act, 1975
Criminal Procedure (Scotland) Act, 1995 (CP Act, 1995)
Criminal Procedure and Investigations Act, 1996
Criminal Procedure (Intermediate Diets) (Scotland) Act, 1998
Data Protection Act, 1984
District Courts (Scotland) Act, 1975
Health and Social Security Adjudications Act, 1983
Law Reform (Miscellaneous Provisions) (Scotland) Act, 1990
Legal Aid (Scotland) Act, 1986.
Local Government (Scotland) Act, 1975
Local Government (Scotland) Act, 1994
Mental Health (Scotland) Act, 1984
Mental Health (Detention) (Scotland) Act, 1991
Misuse of Drugs Act, 1971
National Health Service and Community Care Act, 1990

Police and Criminal Evidence Act, 1984
Police and Magistrates' Courts Act, 1994
Police (Scotland) Act, 1967
Prison (Scotland) Act, 1989
Prisoners and Criminal Proceedings (Scotland) Act, 1993
Probation of First Offenders Act, 1887
Probation of Offenders Act, 1907
Protection from Harassment Act, 1997
Rehabilitation of Offenders Act, 1974
Sex Offenders Act, 1997
Social Work (Scotland) Act, 1968
Solvent Abuse (Scotland) Act, 1983

Parliamentary Reports

Children and Young Persons (1960) (Ingleby), London, HMSO
Report of the Interdepartmental Committee on the Business of the Higher Criminal Courts (1961) (Cmnd 1289) (Streatfeild), London, HMSO
Report of the Interdepartmental Committee on the Probation Service (1962) (Cmnd 1650) (Morison), London, HMSO
Children and Young Persons, Scotland (1964) (Cmnd 2306) (Kilbrandon), Edinburgh, SHHD/SED
Report of the Committee on the Sheriff Court (1967) (Cmnd 3248) (Grant) Edinburgh, HMSO
Report of the Advisory Council on the Penal System: Non-Custodial and Semi-Custodial Penalties (Wootton) (1970), London, HMSO
Report of the Committee on Mentally Abnormal Offenders, Home Office and Department of Health (1975) (Butler Committee) (Cmnd 6244), London, HMSO
Report of the Committee on Criminal Procedure (1975) (Thomson), Edinburgh HMSO
Report of the Committee on Reparation by Offenders (1976) (Dunpark), Edinburgh, HMSO
Report of the Inquiry into the United Kingdom Prison Service (1979) (Cmnd 7673) (May) London, HMSO
Report of the Committee on Keeping Offenders Out of Court: Further Alternatives to Prosecution (1983) (Stewart) (Cmnd 8958), Edinburgh, HMSO
Report of the Committee on Parole and Related Issues in Scotland (1988) (Cmd 598) (Kincraig), Edinburgh, HMSO
Report of the Inquiry into the Removal of Children from Orkney in February (1991) (Clyde) H.C. Papers 1992-1993, No 95, Edinburgh, HMSO
Report of the Inquiry into Child Care Policies in Fife (1992) (Kearney), H.C. Papers 1992-1993, no. 191, Edinburgh, HMSO

Bibliography

ACOP (1989a) *Surviving Poverty: Probation Work and Benefits Policy,* London, Association of Chief Officers of Probation

ACOP (1989b) *Response to the White Paper, 'Crime, Justice and Protecting the Public',* London, Association of Chief Officers of Probation

ADSW (1987) *Fines and Fine Default,* Glasgow, Association of Directors of Social Work

ADSW (1996) *Towards a Safer Community,* Glasgow, Association of Directors of Social Work

ADSW (1996) 'Policy on Victims of Crime', in *Towards a Safer Scotland,* Glasgow, Association of Directors of Social Work

Andrews, D.A. *et al* (1990) 'Does correctional treatment work? A clinically relevant and psychologically informed meta-analysis', *Criminology,* vol. 28 no. 3, pp. 369-404

Andrews, D.A. and Bonta, J. (1995) *The Psychology of Criminal Conduct,* Cincinnati, Anderson Publishing

Anthony, W. and Berryman, D. (1998) *A Magistrate's Guide,* London, Butterworth

Audit Commission (1990) *The Probation Service: Providing Value for Money,* London, HMSO

Audit Commission (1996) *Misspent Youth: Young People and Crime,* London, Audit Commission

Backett, S., McNeill, J. and Yellowlees, M. (eds) *Imprisonment Today: Issues in the Prison Debate,* London, Macmillan

Baird, G. and Neuenfeldt, D. (1990) *Improving Correctional Performance through Better Classification,* San Francisco, National Council on Crime and Delinquency

Baldwin, P. (1988) 'Women in Prison', in *Imprisonment Today: Issues in the Prison Debate,* Backett, S., McNeill, J. and Yellowlees, M. (eds) London, Macmillan

Baumer, T. and Mendelsohn, R. (1992) 'Electronically Monitored Home Confinement: Does it Work?' in *Smart Sentencing,* Byrne, J. *et al,* Newbury Park, SAGE

Bluglass, R. (1966) *A Psychiatric Study of Scottish Prisoners,* St Andrews, University of St Andrews

Bochel, D. (1976) *Probation and After-care,* Edinburgh, Scottish Academic Press

Bonta, J. (1996) 'Risk-Needs Assessment and Treatment' in Harland, A. (ed) *Choosing Correctional Options that Work: Defining the Demand and Evaluating the Supply,* Thousand Oaks, California, Sage

Bottoms, A.E. (1974) 'The De-criminalization of Juvenile Justice' in Hood, R. (ed.) *Crime, Criminology and Public Policy,* London, Heinemann Education

Brown, A. (1994) *Scottish Law Gazette* vol. 62, no. 4 pp. 135-136

Brown, A. (1997) 'The Protection from Harassment Act, 1997', in *Criminal Law* issue 27 June pp. 2-3

Brown, L., Levy, L. and McIvor, G. (1998) 'The National and Local Context', *Social Work and Criminal Justice* vol. 3, Edinburgh, the Stationery Office

Brown, L. and Levy, L. (1998) 'Sentencer Decision Making': *Social Work and Criminal Justice* vol. 4, Edinburgh, the Stationery Office

Bruce, N. and Spencer, J. (1976) *Face to Face with Families,* Edinburgh, MacDonald

Bucholz, E., Hartmann, R., Lerschas, J. and Stiller, G., (1974) *Socialist Criminology,* Saxon House

Carlen, P. (1983) *Women's Imprisonment: a Study in Social Control,* London, Routledge, Kegan and Paul

Carr, A. (1983) 'Problems and Issues in the Study and Treatment of Alcoholic Offenders' in Lishman, J. (ed) *Social Work with Adult Offenders, Research Highlights,* Aberdeen, Aberdeen University Press

CCETSW (1997) *Assuring Quality for Post-Qualifying Education and Training— Requirements for the Post-Qualifying and Advanced Awards in Social Work,* London, Central Council for Education and Training in Social Work

Christie, N. (1982) *Limits to Pain,* Oxford, Martin Robertson

Cleland, A. (1995) *Guide to the Children (Scotland) Act 1995,* Glasgow, Scottish Child Law Centre

Clemmer, D. (1958) *The Prison Community,* New York, Rinehart

Cohen, S. (1983) *Social Control and the State: Historical and Comparative Essays,* Oxford, Robertson

Cohen, S. and Taylor, L. (1972) *Prison Secrets,* London, National Council for Civil Liberties

Collins, S. (1997) 'Anti-social Behaviour Order', *SCOLAG Journal,* Nov/Dec. 1997 pp. 184-189

Cook, D.J. (1994) *Psychological Disturbance in the Scottish Prison System: Prevalence, Precipitants and Policy,* Edinburgh, Scottish Prison Service occasional paper no. 3

Cowperthwaite, D. (1992) *The Emergence of the Scottish Children's Hearings System,* Southampton, Institute of Criminal Justice, University of Southampton

Coyle, A. (1991) *Inside: Rethinking Scotland's Prisons,* Edinburgh, Scottish Child

Creamer, A. and Williams, B. (1989) *Social Enquiry within a Changing Sentencing Context,* Edinburgh, Scottish Office Research Unit

Cressey, D.R. (1961) (ed.) *The Prison: Studies in Institutional Organisation and Change,* New York, Holt, Rinehart and Winston,

Curran, J. and Chambers, G. (1982) *Social Enquiry Reports in Scotland,* Edinburgh, HMSO, Scottish Office Research Unit

Denham, S. (1984) *The Use of Unruly Certificates,* Edinburgh, Scottish Office CRU

Dews, V. and Watts, J. (1994) *The Review of Probation Officer Recruitment and Qualifying Training,* London, Home Office

Dhaliwal, G., Porporino, F., and Ross, F. (1994) 'Assessment of Criminogenic Factors, Program Assignment and Recidivism', *Criminal Justice and Behaviour* vol. 21 no. 4 Dec. pp. 434-467

Duff, P. and Burman, M. (1994) *Diversion from Prosecution to Psychiatric Care*, Edinburgh, Scottish Office CRU

Ewing, K.D. and Finnie, W. (1988) *Civil Liberties in Scotland*, Edinburgh, W. Green

Farrington, D. (1996) *Understanding and Preventing Youth Crime*, York, Joseph Rowntree Foundation

Ford, J. *et al* (1992) *Probation in Scotland*, Edinburgh, Scottish Office CRU

Fox, L. (1952) *The English Prison and Borstal System*, London, Routledge, Kegan and Paul

Fraser, P. (1993) *Young Offenders and the White Paper 'Scotland's Children'*, Edinburgh, Kenneth Younger Memorial Lecture

Fraser, P. (1994) *Social Work Criminal Justice Services: Partnerships for the Future*, Coylumbridge, keynote speech at ADSW Conference

Garland, D. (1985) *Punishment and Welfare*, Aldershot, Gower

Gemmell, M. (1995) 'An Evaluation of Sentencing Planning', *Scottish Prison Service Research Bulletin*, vol. 2, pp. 23-26

Gendreau, P. and Ross, R. (1987) 'Revivification or Rehabilitation: Evidence from the 1980s', *Justice Quarterly, 4*

Gendreau, P., Cullen, F.T., and Bonta, J. (1994) 'Intensive Rehabilitation Supervision: the Next Generation in Community Corrections?' *Federal Probation*, March p73-78

Graham, J. and Bowling, B. (1995) 'Young People and Crime', *Research Findings* no. 24, London, Home Office

Greenawald, D.K. (1974) 'Perspectives on the Right of Silence', in Hood, R. (ed.) *Crime,Criminology and Public Policy*, London, Heinemann Education

Griffiths, R. (1988) *Community Care: Agenda for Action*, London, HMSO

Gross, H. (1979) *A Theory of Criminal Justice*, Oxford, Open University Press

Gunn, J. (1991) *Mentally Disordered Prisoners*, London, Institute of Psychiatry

Hallet, C *et al* (1997) *Decision Making in the Scottish Children's Hearings System*, Stirling, University of Stirling

Haxby, D. (1976) *Probation, a Changing Service*, London, Constable

Hayes, S. (1993) *People with an Intellectual Disability and the Criminal Justice System*, Research Report no. 4, Sydney, NSW Law Reform Commission

Hayes, S. (1996) 'Recent Research on Offenders with Learning Disabilities', *Learning Disability*, vol. 1 issue 3, pp. 7-15

Hodgins, S. (1992) 'Mental disorder, intellectual deficiency and crime', *Archives of General Psychiatry* 49 (6) 476-83

Hollin, C. (1993) 'The Mentally Disordered Offender: a Clinical Approach' in Howells, K. and Hollin, C., *Clinical Approaches to the Mentally Disordered Offender*, Chichester, John Wiley

Home Office (1968) *Report of Inter-Departmental Committee on Local Authority and Allied Personal Social Services* (Seebohm) Cmnd 3703, London, HMSO

Home Office (1989) *Supervision and Punishment in the Community,* Cmd 966, London, HMSO

Home Office (1990) *Crime, Justice and Protecting the Public,* (Cmd 965), London, HMSO

Howard League (1997) *Lost Inside—the Imprisonment of Teenage Girls,* London, Howard League for Penal Reform

Hudson, B. (1987) *Justice through Punishment : a Critique of the 'Justice' Model of Corrections,* New York, St Martin's Press

Johnstone, H. (1995) *Interface of the Children's Hearing System and the Criminal Justice System,* Edinburgh, University of Edinburgh, unpublished MSc. thesis

Keamey, B. (1991) *Children's Hearings and the Sheriff Court* (second edition), London, Butterworths

Kennedy, R. and McIvor, G. (1992) *Young Offenders in the Children's Hearing System and the Criminal Justice Systems: a Comparative Analysis,* Dundee, Tayside Regional Council/Social Work Research Centre, University of Stirling

King, J. (1969) *The Probation Service,* London, Butterworths

Lister, B. (1995) *Children's Hearings, Lawyers, the Courts and the Children (Scotland) Act 1995,* Glasgow, seminar paper, Legal Services Agency, October

McAllister, D., Bottomley, D. and Liebling, A. (1992) *From Custody to Community: Throughcare for Young Offenders,* Aldershot, Avebury

McAra, L. (1998) 'Early Arrangements', *Social Work and Criminal Justice* vol. 2: Edinburgh, the Stationery Office

McAra L. (1998) 'Parole Board Decision Making', *Social Work and Criminal Justice* vol. 5, Edinburgh, the Stationery Office

McDonald, S. *et al, (1994) Is Misuse An Issue?: Drug and Alcohol Assessments in Social Enquiry Reports,* Aberdeen, Grampian Regional Council/SWSG

McCall Smith, A. and Sheldon, D. (1992) *Scots Criminal Law,* Edinburgh, Butterworths

McGuire, J. (ed.) (1995) *What Works: Research and Practice on the Reduction of Re-offending,* Chichester, John Wiley and Sons

McIvor, G. (1992) *Sentenced to Serve: the Operation and Impact of Community Service by Offenders,* Aldershot, Avebury

McIvor, G. and Barry, M. (1998) 'Community-based Throughcare', *Social Work and Criminal Justice* vol. 1, Edinburgh, the Stationery Office

McIvor, G. and Barry, M. (1998) 'Probation', *Social Work and Criminal Justice vol. 1,* Edinburgh, the Stationery Office

MacKay, R. (1988) *Reparation in Criminal Justice,* SACRO, Edinburgh

McMahon, M. (1990) 'Net-widening, Vagaries in the Use of a Concept', *British Journal of Criminology,* 30, 2, pp. 121-146

McManus, J. (1995) *Prisons, Prisoners and the Law,* Edinburgh, W.Green/Sweet and Maxwell

McManus, J. (1997) *Report on Investigation into Aberdeen City Council's Social Work Department's handling of the case of Mr Steven Leisk,* Aberdeen City Council

McNeill, J. (1988) 'Mentally Disturbed Prisoners: Imprisonment is No Answer' in Drucker, N. (ed) *Creating Community Health Services in Scotland,* Edinburgh, Scottish Association for Mental Health

Macguire, M. and Raynor, P. (1997) 'The Revival of Throughcare', *British Journal of Criminology,* Vol. 37, No. 1, pp. 1-14

Marshall, F. (1994) in Martin, C. (ed) *Resolving Crime in the Community: Mediation in Criminal Justice,* London, ISTD

Marshall, F. (1992) 'Restorative Justice on Trial in Britain', in Messmer, H. and Otto, H. U. (eds) *Restorative Justice on Trial,* Dordrecht, Kluwer Academic Publishers

Martin, F. *et al* (1981) *Children Out of Court,* Edinburgh, Scottish Academic Press

Mental Health Foundation (1996) *Too Many for the Road,* London, MHF

Merton, R.K. (1957) *Social Theory and Social Structure,* New York, Free Press

Monaghan, J. and Steadman, H. (1983) *Mentally Disordered Offenders,* New York, Plenum

Moody, S.R. (1983) *Diversion from the Criminal Justice Process: Report on the Diversion Scheme at Ayr,* Edinburgh, Scottish Office Central Research Unit

Moody, S.R. and Tombs, J. (1982) *Prosecution in the Public Interest,* Edinburgh, Scottish Academic Press

Moody, S.R. and Mackay, R. (eds) (1995) *Alternative Dispute Resolution in Scotland,* Edinburgh, W. Green/Sweet and Maxwell

Moore, G. (1984) *The Practice of Social Inquiry,* Aberdeen, Aberdeen University Press

Moore, G. (1989) *Guide to the Children's Hearings,* Edinburgh, W. Green

Morris, A. and McIsaac, M. (1978) *Juvenile Justice,* London, Heinemann

Mortimer, E. and Mair, G. (1996) *Curfew Orders with Electronic Monitoring: an Evaluation of the First Twelve Months of the Trials in Greater Manchester,* London, Home Office Study no. 163

Mulholland, F. (1996) 'Criminal Procedure and Investigations Act, 1996' in *Criminal Law* issue 24, December pp. 3-4

Nicholson, C.G.B. (1992) *The Law and Practice of Sentencing in Scotland,* Edinburgh, W.Green/Sweet and Maxwell

Nicholson, L. and Miller, A. (1989) *An Evaluation of the Fines Officer Scheme,* Edinburgh, Scottish Office Research Unit

Norrie, K. (1996) *Green's Annotated Act: Children (Scotland) Act 1995,* Edinburgh, W.Green/Sweet and Maxwell

Norrie, K. (1997) *Children's Hearings in Scotland,* Edinburgh, W.Green/Sweet and Maxwell

Parole Board for Scotland (1986) *Annual Report,* Edinburgh, HMSO

Parsloe, P. (1986) *Social Work Units in Scottish Prisons,* Report for Her Majesty's Chief Inspector of Prisons for Scotland, Edinburgh, SHHD

Paterson, A. (193*2) Principles of the Borstal System,* London, Prison Commission, Home Office

Paterson, F. and Whittaker, C. (1994) *Operating Bail,* Edinburgh, HMSO, Scottish Research Unit

Paterson, F. and Tombs, J. (1998) 'The Impact of Policy', *Social Work and Criminal Justice* vol. 1, Edinburgh, the Stationery Office

Pease, K. (1980) 'The Future of Community Treatment of Offenders in Britain', in Bottoms, A.E. and Preston, R.H. (1990) (eds) *The Coming Penal Crisis,* Edinburgh, Scottish Academic Press

Petersilia, J. and Turner, S. (1993) 'Intensive probation and parole', in Tonry, M. and Morris, N. (eds) *Crime and Justice: an Annual Review of the Research* (vol. 17), Chicago, University of Chicago Press

Prison Reform Trust (1997) *The Prison Population in Britain, Europe and the Rest of the World,* London

Raynor, P., Smith, D. and Vanstone, M. (1994) *Effective Probation Practice,* Basingstoke, Macmillan

Reed, J. (1994) *Report of the Department of Health and Home Office Working Group on Psychopathic Disorder,* London, Home Office

Rifkind, M. (1989) 'Penal Policy: The Way Ahead', *The Howard Journal,* vol. 28 no. 2, May pp. 81-90

Robert, J. (1993) *Implementing Psychosocial Interventions Linked to Community Sanctions,* Twentieth Criminological Research Conference, Strasbourg

Robertson, A. *et al* (1983) 'Discharged Prisoners' Problems and Some Professional Concerns' in Lishman, J. (ed.) *Social Work with Adult Offenders,* Aberdeen, Research Highlights no. 5, Aberdeen University Press

Russell, M.N. (1990) *Clinical Social Work,* Newbury Park, Sage Publications

SACRO (1990) *Mentally Disturbed Offenders: Report of a Working Party,* Edinburgh, Scottish Association for the Resettlement of Offenders

Scottish Office (1998) *Health, Social Work and Related Services for Mentally Disordered Offenders in Scotland,* Edinburgh

Scottish Office (1992) *Reporters to Children's Panels: Their Role, Function and Accountability* (Finlayson) Edinburgh, HMSO

Scottish Office (1998a) *Women Offenders—a Safer Way,* Edinburgh, Social Work Services and Prisons Inspectorates for Scotland

Scottish Office (1998b) *Interviewing People who are Mentally Disordered: Appropriate Adult Schemes,* Edinburgh

SCRA (1997) *Just in Time: Report on Time Intervals in Children's Hearings Cases,* Stirling, Scottish Children's Reporters Administration

Sheldon, B. (1994) 'Social Work Effectiveness Research: Implications for Probation and Juvenile Justice Services', *The Howard Journal,* vol. 33 no. 3, August

SHHD (1984) *Mental Health (Scotland) Act 1984: Notes on the Act,* Edinburgh

SHHD (1985) *Report of the Review of Suicide Precautions at H.M. Detention Centre and Young Offenders Institution Glenochil* (Chiswick), Edinburgh, Scottish Home and Health Department

Shiels, R. and Bradley, I. (1996) *Green's Annotated Act: Criminal Procedure (Scotland) Act 1995,* Edinburgh, W. Green/Sweet and Maxwell

Sinclair, S. (1998) 'The Protection from Harassment Act, 1997', *SCOLAG Journal,* January pp. 5-8

Siporin, M. (1975) *Introduction to Social Work Practice,* New York, Macmillan

SOED (1964) *Report on Children and Young Persons (Scotland)* (Cmnd 2306), (Kilbrandon), Edinburgh, HMSO

SOHD (1995) *Making the Punishment Fit the Crime,* Edinburgh, HMSO

SOHD (1996) *Crime and Punishment,* (Cm 3302), Edinburgh, HMSO

SOHD (1997) *Framework for Mental Health Services in Scotland,* Edinburgh, Scottish Office

SOHD (1998) *Interviewing People who are Mentally Disordered: Appropriate Adult Schemes,* Edinburgh, Scottish Office

SPS (1985) *Report of the Review of Suicide Precautions at H.M. Institution Glenochil* (Chiswick), Edinburgh, Scottish Prison Service

SPS (1990) *Opportunity and Responsibility: Developing New Approaches to the Management of the Long-Term Prison System in Scotland,* Edinburgh, Scottish Prison Service

Statham, R. (1990) *The Probation Service in a Market-Driven World,* Cleveland, Probation Service

Statistical Bulletin *Social Work Statistics and Criminal Justice Series* Edinburgh, Scottish Office

Stevenson, O. *et al* (1978) *Social Service Teams: the Practitioner's View,* London, HMSO

Stewart, G. and Tutt, N. (1987) *Children in Custody,* Aldershot, Avebury

SWSG (1979) *A Shared Enterprise,* Edinburgh, Social Work Services Group

SWSG/SHHD (1989) *Continuity through Co-operation: a National Framework of Policy and Practice Guidance of Social Work in Penal Establishments,* Edinburgh, Social Work Services Group and Scottish Home and Health Department

SWSG (1992) *Another Kind of Home: A Review of Residential Child Care* (Skinner), Edinburgh, HMSO

SWSG (1997) *Scotland's Children, The Children (Scotland) Act 1995 Regulations and Guidance,* vol. 1, 'Support and Protection for Children and their Families', Edinburgh, the Scottish Office

SWSG (1997) *The Children (Scotland) Act 1995 Regulations and Guidance,* vol. 2, 'Children Looked After by Local Authorities', Edinburgh, the Scottish Office

SWSG (1997) *Review of Criminal Justice Social Work Services,* Edinburgh, the Scottish Office

SWSI (1996) *Realistic and Rigorous: the Report of an Inspection of Discipline and Enforcement of Community Service Orders in Two Local Authority Areas,* Edinburgh, Social Work Services Inspectorate for Scotland

SWSI (1996) *A Secure Remedy,* Edinburgh, Social Work Services Services Inspectorate for Scotland

SWSI (1996) *Helping the Court Decide,* Edinburgh, Social Work Services Inspectorate for Scotland

SWSI (1997) *Commitment to Protect,* Edinburgh, Social Work Inspectorate for Scotland

Tayside Regional Council (1994) *Supervised Attendance Order Pilot Scheme,* Dundee

United Nations (1989) *United Nations Convention on the Rights of the Child,* 28 International Legal Materials, 1448

Walker, N. (1995) 'Police and Government in Scotland', *Scots Law Times,* 22, 23/ 6/95 pp. 199-204

Warner, S. (1992) *Making Amends: Justice for Victims and Offenders,* Aldershot, Avebury

Waterhouse, L., Dobash, R. and Carnie, J. (1994) *Child Sexual Abusers,* Edinburgh, Scottish Office Central Research Unit

Whyte, B. and Hunter, S. (1992) 'Guardianship of the Person in Scotland', *British Journal of Social Work,* no. 22, pp. 167-186

Whyte, B. *et al* (1995) *Social Work in the Criminal Justice System,* Edinburgh, the Scottish Office

Whyte, B. *et al* (1998) *Children's Hearings: Outcomes in Children Care Decision Making—Jointly Reported Young People,* (unpublished report for Scottish Office) Edinburgh, University of Edinburgh

Whyte, B. (1998) 'Rediscovering Juvenile Delinquency' in Lockyer, A. and Stone, F., *Juvenile Justice in Scotland,* Edinburgh, T&T Clark

Wilkins, S. (1998) *Albyn House: Designated Place and Support Hostel,* Stirling, University of Stirling, unpublished MSc thesis

William, B. (1991) *Work with Prisoners,* Birmingham, BASW Venture Press

Williams, B. (1992) *Bail Information,* Horton Publishing, West Yorkshire

Wood, C. (1976) *The Social Worker's Guide to Reports for Criminal Courts,* Edinburgh, Lothian Regional Social Work Department

Wood, C. (1991) *The End of Punishment,* Edinburgh, Saint Andrew Press

Wootton, B. (1959) *Social Science and Social Pathology,* London, Allen and Unwin

Wilson, J. and Hernstein, R. (1985) *Crime and Human Nature,* New York, Simon and Schuster

Young, J. (1994) 'Recent Paradigms in Criminology', in Maguire, M., Morgan, R. and Reiner, R. (eds.) *The Oxford Handbook of Criminology,* Oxford, Clarendon Press

Zamble, E. and Porporino, F. (1990) 'Coping with Imprisonment and Rehabilitation: some Data and their Implications', *Criminal Justice and Behaviour,* vol. 17, no. 1, March

Index